D1103854

ENTERPRISE DENIED

Enterprise Denied

Origins of the Decline of
American Railroads, 1897-1917

ALBRO MARTIN

Columbia University Press
New York & London   1971

This book received the Columbia University Prize in American
Economic History in Honor of Allan Nevins

Acknowledgment is made to the Macmillan Company for permission to
reprint the following from *Collected Poems* by Vachel Lindsay: 4 lines
from "The Chinese Nightingale" (copyright 1916 by the Macmillan Company, renewed 1945 by Elizabeth C. Lindsay); and 3 lines from "Bryan,
Bryan, Bryan, Bryan" (copyright 1920 by the Macmillan Company, renewed 1948 by Elizabeth C. Lindsay).

In Memory of

MY FATHER,

who is part of the story

FOREWORD

It is a pity Allan Nevins did not live to see this book. Winner of the first Columbia University Prize in American Economic History in Honor of Allan Nevins, *Enterprise Denied* exemplifies many of the values Nevins held dear, especially his convictions that history should be written for everyman and that scholarship can be wedded to literary grace. Surely, too, he would have applauded Albro Martin's decision to change course in mid-career, to turn from the world of business to that of scholarship. Like so many of Nevins' books, *Enterprise Denied* is a work for the general public as well as for the professional historian, one that attempts to re-create the "sights, sounds, and smells" of the period of its concern. Explicitly rejecting what he calls the "vague, gray mass" of social science, Albro Martin takes his stand on the ground that all historical events are unique.

And surely they are. But were this the end of the matter, historians might appeal to the senses of their readers without addressing their sense. For all their uniqueness, facts do not come to us from the sources in prearranged patterns of meaning; it is the arranging historian who supplies them. Whether or not the threads are visible, he strings his beads of fact on hypotheses. And it is an important function of history as social science to provide a laboratory in which colorful facts may be tested to see if they wash well.

Fortunately, Professor Martin's narrative is rich in hypothesis. Political as well as economic historians will debate his caustic characterization of the Mann-Elkins Act as an example not of reformist legislation but rather of "archaic Progressivism." The concept is of course a value judgment, and whether or not one shares it will depend in part on one's view of the "railroad problem" of the Progressive Era. Some may define the problem in terms of a social need to so regulate the railroads as to prevent a repetition of the abuses of the Gilded Age—rebating, long-haul–short-haul discrimination, poor and unsafe service, stock watering, and other "devil-dare financial gymnastics." Others will agree with Professor Martin that the essential problem was economic in nature, that following the extensive reorganizations of the nineties and the emergence of communities of interest among the major systems, the fundamental need was for investment capital to enable the lines to rebuild and modernize. Still others may agree with Martin while holding that it was railroad history that made it difficult for the Interstate Commerce Commission to respond to the economic needs of the new era.

The key argument of the book is the suggestion that the unwillingness of the ICC to grant general rate increases during a period of policy uncertainty commencing with the enactment of the Hepburn Act in 1906 prevented the flow of investment funds from keeping pace with the demands upon the system and paved the way for a collapse in the profitability of railroad operations after 1911. Martin's measure of "demands on the system" is railroad transportation output, and he maintains that the relationship between the trendlines of output and net annual new investment was "rational" between 1898 and 1906 and "irrational" thereafter. "It is relatively easy to demonstrate statistically," he holds, "that some other, higher trendline of investment in the railroad facilities of the United States would have ruled if an enlightened, rather than a repressive, policy of rate regulation had been followed." The long-term effect of capital undernourishment, he believes, was a loss of the spirit of enterprise in the railroad sector.

In an Appendix in which he explains the bases on which his statistical calculations are made Professor Martin makes it clear that it is not his intention to argue that if the railroads had gotten the rate increases they sought investment would in fact have attained the precise levels he projects as plausible. For one thing, he suggests, the "requested increases were probably smaller than the rise in the price level alone would justify, and were decided upon by the railroad leaders merely because they thought the increases were the most they could get." For another, he does not believe the historian should conduct argumentation in the counterfactual mood. The relationship between all factors in a historical situation, he rightly maintains, is "one of total interdependence." Surely it would be dangerous to specify the precise factual consequence of altering one of them. But I see no difficulty in using the counterfactual so long as the time period is a short one—as it is in this case—and so long as we are aware that the object of its use is not to create figments to replace facts but rather to test our explanations of the facts. What Professor Martin suggests in this work of reinterpretation is that the failure of the ICC to grant general increases in rates is the most important explanation of the eventual collapse of the system of private management of the railroads, that patterns of investment and enterprise might well have been different from those of recorded history had men acted differently from the ways in which they did. Facts are indeed the building blocks of history, but to explain why men did what they did and failed to do what they might have done, together with providing defensible estimates of the consequences of both, is the essence of the problem of historical reconstruction. The importance of this book lies in its being no mere narrative of events but instead a vigorously argued work of reconstruction.

STUART BRUCHEY

Columbia University

PREFACE

To a person reaching adolescence in the 1930s, the nature of the "American Railroad Problem" was all too clear. In a time when it was almost unpatriotic not to be on the brink of starvation, the plight of the railroads seemed hardly different from that of everybody else. Like the "rich folks on the hill," the railroads' past left them rather less well prepared than most of us for hard times, but the Problem was no more complex than that—or so I thought.

But I soon learned that there had always been a Railroad Problem, and that it had been just as acute during the years of vigorous maturity of the trains: before World War I, before the depression, before cars, trucks, and airplanes—before all of the great events which transformed American life after 1914. But why? There has never been an Air Transport Problem, a Truck Problem, or an Automobile Problem, at least as far as their vitality is concerned. (If there is a problem in these industries, it is in their excessive vitality.) Bankers, I was told, ruined the railroads, especially during the happy, prosperous years between the Gay Nineties and the war.[1] Although outstanding statesmen of this period, like Theodore Roosevelt and Woodrow Wilson, brought

---

[1] The leading monograph on the reorganization of American railroads during the depression of the nineties contains the following epilogue: "Altogether the assumption of control over the country's railroads by banking interests who welded together huge monopolies failed to bring with it the benefits which had been promised. . . . After the turn of the century visible progress stopped; relieved of the pressure of competition, the roads did not make very serious efforts to improve their service and it is significant that no important new inventions were introduced in railroading until the age of electrification and motor bus competition began. The size of locomotives and cars was increased and half-hearted attempts to install block-signalling systems were made, but there were no great technical advances until competition forced the roads to act." Edward G. Campbell, *The Reorganization of the American Railroad System, 1893–1900* (New York, 1938), 341.

forth wise laws to control the railroads and the other bloated trusts and to regulate their activities in the public interest, still by World War I the "interests" had so debauched the railroads that only the intervention of the government saved the country from complete transportation collapse.

And there my understanding of the problem remained for twenty years. Still, I could never understand why men with a stake in the railroads, whether they were bankers or operating executives, should have been so peculiarly incompetent, insensitive, corrupt, and generally blind to their own long-run interests. It was a behavior pattern unique among the giants of American business. Perhaps there was more to it.

Textbooks on American history in the Progressive era never fail to mention two great legislative milestones in the government regulation of economic activity, the Hepburn Act of 1906 and the Mann-Elkins Act of 1910. The textbooks invariably include these statutes among the outstanding achievements of the age of reform, and then pass on quickly to the story of the Insurgent-Progressive movement of 1910–12. Seldom is there even a hint that the execution of these laws posed any particular problems, or that the results achieved were anything less than a full vindication of the men who labored so hard and so long to get them on the books.[2]

This volume is the result of an effort to unravel the inconsistencies in the story as it has been taught to me and to millions of others. What I have to relate is a story of the most intense frustration of the human spirit; of the brutal substitution of petty consistency for a sensible pragmatism; of the unconscionable elevation, by the government of a republic, of one set of interests over another and over the general welfare; and of a self-serving and all but cowardly refusal to face public duty. For me, the story demolishes once and for all the traditional concept of the just and wise commissioner, that paragon of public service who, for a salary of $10,000 a year, was to have adjudicated the nation's great economic problems under the New Nationalism

---

[2] Three recent standard textbooks all follow the usual treatment of this subject. Richard B. Morris and William Greenleaf, *U.S.A.: The History of a Nation* (2 vols., Chicago, 1969), II, 508; Oscar Handlin, *The History of the United States* (2 vols., New York, 1968), II, 288; Samuel E. Morison, Henry S. Commager, and William E. Leuchtenburg, *The Growth of the American Republic* (2 vols., New York, 1969), II, 325.

of Theodore Roosevelt and Herbert Croly. It casts even more doubt on our present-day faith in the commission management of economic affairs.

I have attempted to solve the problem of describing the physical and financial transformation of American railroads in the Progressive era by concentrating on three leading systems—the Pennsylvania, the Illinois Central, and the Santa Fe—which represent the eastern trunk lines, the Middle West and South, and the Southwest and West. The story could be extended almost without limit. While it is true that there was much that was bad about the way the railroads reacted to the demands of the new century, it must not be forgotten that most of the tonnage and passengers, if not the total route mileage, was accounted for by strong, soundly managed roads like these three which so little deserved to be included under the stereotype Americans drew of their railroads in those years.

A further word is in order concerning my efforts at what historians call, not always as a compliment, "color." Mine is a subject which, however prosaic it may seem today, was in its time full of drama and *color*. There seems to be a great deal of pointless controversy nowadays over just what history is. I had thought that history (i.e., written history) was an attempt to re-create the past. I have been told, "Oh, *that* is impossible." Nevertheless, I believe that it is the historian's particular curse that he must make the effort. He may fail—certainly total success is unlikely—but if he does not try, the alternative is for history to dissolve into some vague, gray mass called "social science." I believe that there is no higher purpose to which the historian can strive than the discovery of universal truths in his researches, but at the same time I am convinced that all historical events are unique. They have their own sights, sounds, and smells. Strip these away (or, worse still, pretend that they never existed) and some kind of skeleton will still remain, but it will not be history. I shall be very pleased if others find something useful in this book, but I am proud to say that I have not sought primarily to write an essay in economics, or political science, or sociology, but a *history*.

My deep appreciation for his help and encouragement goes to Professor Stuart Bruchey, Allan Nevins Professor of American Economic History at Columbia University. I am grateful also to Eric L.

McKitrick, Donald J. Dewey, Jerome Sternstein, and Alfred S. Eichner, who read the manuscript and offered many valuable suggestions, and to Bernard Gronert and William Bernhardt, of the Columbia University Press, who helped turn it into a book. I am indebted to James H. McKendrick for bringing to my attention some acute but little-known present-day problems that will certainly affect the future of the American transportation system. To the many others whose comments and encouragement cannot be recorded in detail, I also extend my thanks. It goes almost without saying, of course, that the choice of what I retained and what I rejected out of the many suggestions offered was my own, and mine the sole responsibility for the result.

My thanks, and my admiration for their cheerfulness under conditions which are not getting any better, go to the staff of that jewel which still shines brightly in the tarnished setting of Morningside Heights, the Butler Library. The New York Public Library, as always, was a sturdy staff to lean upon. I owe an especial debt of thanks to Dr. Thomas Sinclair, Special Assistant to the Vice-President, and Mr. Harry L. Eddy, librarian, of the Association of American Railroads, who are carrying on the traditions founded by the old Bureau of Railway Economics. The Secretary of the Interstate Commerce Commission and his staff graciously opened the official archives of that body to me. I regret that I am unable personally to acknowledge, in this life, the kindness of Dr. I. L. Sharfman, who so generously granted me a lengthy interview in the spring of his last year.

ALBRO MARTIN

Bethel, Conn.
December, 1970

CONTENTS

ENTERPRISE DENIED

Businessmen . . . are much milder than politicians, at the same time allured and terrified by the glare of publicity . . . only too anxious to take a cheerful view, vain perhaps but very unsure of themselves, pathetically responsive to a kind word. . . . It is a mistake to think that they are more immoral *than politicians. If you work them into the surly, obstinate, terrified mood, of which domestic animals, wrongly handled, are so capable, the nation's burdens will not get carried to market; and in the end public opinion will veer their way.*—JOHN MAYNARD KEYNES *to* FRANKLIN D. ROOSEVELT, *Feb. 1, 1938*

It seems to me . . . that what we call the interest of the public is little more than a phrase. . . . Once accept the postulate that political power is the handmaiden of economic power . . . and I think it follows that the state which manipulates that power is also a capitalist institution.—MR. JUSTICE HOLMES *to* HAROLD J. LASKI, *1917*

CHAPTER I

BRAVE NEW CENTURY

The desert shall rejoice, and blossom as the rose.—ISAIAH 35:1. *Inscribed on
the façade of the Washington Union Station, 1906*

". . . One thing I remember:
Spring came on forever,
Spring came on forever,"
Said the Chinese nightingale.—VACHEL LINDSAY

I

Bicycling was still a sport for dignified adults in 1901, and one
of the most enthusiastic wheelmen in New York City was the very
dignified president of the First National Bank, James Stillman. Pedaling
up Park Avenue (then still Fourth Avenue) one fine day in that early
year of the new century, Stillman looked about him with a new vision
at the dowdy, familiar buildings which lined the street. His thoughts
were on something which a friend had told him at dinner a few days
before. Next day he sent out a call for a business associate to drop in
to see him at his office at the earliest opportunity. To Henry Morgenthau,
Sr., a rising star in the banking and real estate world of New York, this
meant immediately. Stillman was Morgenthau's most important financial
supporter in the younger man's real estate operations, and he had recently
agreed to go along with Morgenthau's insistence that they should acquire
a construction company. "Mr. Morgenthau," said the banker, "as I was
bicycling up the Avenue yesterday I was constantly thinking . . . that
New York had to be rebuilt, and the more I looked around the more
convinced I became. . . . We ought to secure a substantial share of the
work." Morgenthau, therefore, was not to let out any more shares of the
newly acquired construction company. New York City and the George A.

Fuller Company had a great future, and the smart thing for those who knew it was to keep as much as possible for themselves.[1]

The Fuller firm was making architectural and engineering headlines at that very moment, for it was the contractor on the new Flatiron Building going up on a dubious piece of land at Twenty-third Street and Fifth Avenue. The northward sweep of Gotham soon passed this oddity by, but its existence settled the future of the city once and for all. The process of suburban expansion, already well under way by 1900, continued, but the intensive development of the critical core of the metropolis now began in earnest. A person who last stood at Forty-second Street and Fifth Avenue in 1930 would quickly realize where he was if he were suddenly set down on that spot today. But one who had last stood on that spot in 1900 would have found himself in another world if he had gone back there in 1930. What had been at the turn of the century a city of low, gray tenements and squat, awning-laden commercial buildings, relieved here and there by examples of the artisan's cast-iron work, had become the sleek, vertical home of a self-satisfied, hard-driving society on the eve of the Great Depression. And most of the transformation had taken place in those golden decades which ended with World War I: America's version of La Belle Epoque.[2]

What was happening to New York and other cities in these decades was repeated in almost every walk of American life. "The decade from 1896 to 1906," emphasized Morgenthau, "was the period of the most gigantic expansion of business in all . . . history. In that decade the slowly fertilized economic resources of the United States suddenly yielded a bewildering crop of industries. Vast railroad systems . . . steel . . . Standard Oil Company spread . . . to the ends of the earth. . . . The cry everywhere was for money—more money—and yet more money." [3] The flowering of this great growth era was based, as Morgenthau saw so clearly, on four decades of painful preparation which had given the nation the transportation network and the iron and steel in-

[1] Henry Morgenthau, *All in a Lifetime* (Garden City, N.Y., 1922), 72.

[2] The urban transformation, of course, was nationwide, but the hemmed-in nature of New York dramatizes the fact that it was as much a rebuilding as a building phenomenon. The accomplishment is recorded in two excellent architectural and social histories: John A. Kouwenhoven, *The Columbia Historical Portrait of New York* (New York, 1953), and Grace M. Mayer, *Once Upon a City* (New York, 1958).

[3] Morgenthau, *All in a Lifetime*, 73.

dustry which made the expansion possible. The response to the unique growth climate which settled on the nation once the cruel, Darwinian depression of the nineties was over manifested itself in a rise in population, a heightened rate of innovation, and a monumental struggle for the scarce resources of economic growth which left some older forms of endeavor behind and propelled others to the level of predominance which they enjoy today. The effort of American political institutions to grapple with the accelerating transformation from an agrarian to an industrial society, and with the problems which the new society brought, produced a reform movement which has etched itself into history as the Progressive era. Many were its successes, and many and far-reaching in their effects were its failures.

II

Sometime between 1910 and the outbreak of World War I, the United States became a nation of 100 million souls. It had taken over three hundred years for the uprooted Europeans to people the vast, rich, yet terrifying spaces with so many of their kind. As recently as 1880 there had been only fifty million people in the land, and in the uncertain twenty years which followed the population had grown to only seventy-six million. Then, from 1900 to 1910 sixteen million people were added to the total, the largest increase in any decade up to then. Trends in the make-up of the population which are thoroughly familiar today had already begun to be revealed. The median age rose consistently, from twenty-one in 1880 to twenty-five in 1920, a development which reflected not only the modest increase in the standard of living which was achieved but also the fact that the wave of immigrants included relatively few children. The number of people living in cities nearly doubled, while persons living on farms grew by only about one-eighth. In 1900 there had been only thirty-eight cities in the entire country with more than 100,000 residents; by 1920 there were sixty-eight, and sixteen out of every hundred persons lived in a city of over half a million.[4]

But it was not merely a flight from the drudgery and loneliness of

[4] U.S. Bureau of the Census, *Historical Statistics of the United States: Colonial Times to 1957* (Washington, 1960), 7–14.

the farm which was behind these movements. People pull up their roots not only because of the unattractiveness of the old but also because of the promise of the new. Perhaps no other single factor so influenced the geographical distribution and the sources of growth of American society as the opening of new opportunities for employment in the expanding industrial complex. This factor is most obvious in its impact on immigration. Writing with a frankness which would almost surely be criticized as prejudice today, analysts of the mass of data and testimony assembled by the Immigration Commission in the first decade of the century complained that the motive behind the new immigration was primarily "economic." Perhaps it always had been, in a sense, but what these commentators were trying to say was that there was an enormous difference—one with profound implications for American social institutions—between a family which came to America's shores to carve out a farm and a new life for themselves; and a young bachelor whose aim was to trade his brawn and stamina for the wherewithal to return to his native land for a life of ease. Whatever the motive, and however many of the immigrants attained their goal, a fundamental change had overtaken the stream of Europeans entering the country. Before 1883, 95 per cent had come from northern Europe, and nearly half of them were women. Suddenly 81 per cent were from southern and eastern Europe, and there were three men for every woman.[5]

Whatever the concern which labor organizations may have felt about the new tide, industry welcomed the newcomers enthusiastically, and put them to work at jobs which had always been difficult to fill with native Americans. They came in a "necessitous condition," and they were willing—eager, in fact—to live modestly and work cruelly long hours so that they could save as much of their wages as possible. "Immigration is a dynamic factor in industry," said the experts. Indeed it was. A native American who had only his back and hands to offer found the going rough, for the eager Slovaks, Poles, and Italians made it easy to preserve for another two decades the punishing working conditions of the steel mills and mines. But the immigrant, whose tractability was accompanied by language and educational deficiencies, called for a new class of supervisory workers. The growth of labor unions was

[5] Jeremiah W. Jenks and W. Jett Lauck, *The Immigration Problem* (New York, 1911; rev. ed., 1926), 11, 25, 27, 29.

stunted, but the revolution in the industrial work force made possible greater economic mobility for the native American.[6]

Workers came from the decadent empires of Europe, but in greater numbers still they came from the farms and the small towns of America. Public officials in states like Kansas, Nebraska, and Iowa, from justice of the peace to United States Senator, watched in chagrin as a disturbing development of the nineties showed little or no sign of righting itself after 1900. Seven states of the western north central area had in total only two million more people in 1920 than in 1900. More people in their productive years, in fact, were leaving than were coming into many of these states. Iowa, which had not fared nearly so badly in the dark days of the last century which produced the Populist movement, lost almost a quarter of a million more residents than it gained between 1900 and 1910; this was the highest intercensal loss of any state between 1890 and 1920. And those leaving were not all going to California. Illinois and Ohio, industrializing rapidly, each gained as many people as Iowa lost; Michigan gained half as many, while Pennsylvania checked in a half-million, and New York over a million. In the next decade, with the movement intensified by the war, the industrialized states of the Midwest gained twice as many more. What did people have against Iowa, Kansas, Nebraska, and Wisconsin? The relative unattractiveness of farm life had endured. The germ which had caused the paranoia of Populism was far from eradicated.[7]

III

Railroads, mines, and the "dark satanic mills," in their classic nineteenth-century intimate relationship, still constituted "industry" at

[6] *Ibid.*, 195–210.

[7] *Historical Statistics*, 41, 44; William S. Rossiter, *Increase of Population in the United States, 1910–20* (Washington, 1922), 180–83; C. Warren Thornthwaite and Helen I. Slentz, *Internal Migration in the United States* (Philadelphia, 1934). Internal migration in the period 1899–1919 helped to broaden established industrial centers into suburban and peripheral areas, while industrial jobs in the sparsely settled areas became scarcer than ever; Daniel Creamer, *Is Industry Decentralizing?* (Philadelphia, 1935), 13–15. These trends are confirmed in Simon S. Kuznets *et al.*, *Population Redistribution and Economic Growth, United States, 1870–1950* (3 vols., Philadelphia, 1957–60), II, 78, 105–10, 269–71.

the turn of the century. True, the volume and variety of manufactured goods was growing. Daring businessmen even attempted to anticipate the consumer goods revolution of the 1920s (a practical home washing-machine seemed their most common obsession). But the large, widely owned, multimillion-dollar manufacturing establishment was still a rar-ity outside of ferrous metals and supporting industries. This concentra-tion of industrial muscle contributed to the abruptness and the severity of the nineties depression. During one summer twelve of the largest ore steamers on the Great Lakes never left their home port, while the pools which had brought some stability to the confused steel industry fell like flies. The recovery, when it came in 1899, was just as abrupt. Suddenly everybody wanted steel. Behind much of the demand was the giant ex-pansion program which the railroads were undertaking. The Pressed Steel Car Company broke all precedents by committing itself to take 30,000 tons of plates a month from Carnegie Steel for a period of ten years.[8]

The mercurial nature of the steel industry, however, was not tamed by the giant amalgamation which produced the United States Steel Corporation in 1901. While that coup by Morgan and his asso-ciates clearly staved off a disastrous war between producers of basic steel and the products made from it, and avoided the installation of ex-cess capacity which could have depressed the industry for years, ups and downs were marked throughout the decades before the war. A re-cession occurred in 1904 as big steel fought to make the amalgamation stick. The panic of 1907 cut the company to three-quarters of capacity in spite of deep price cuts. But by 1909 the mills were laboring to fill a six months' backlog. In 1912 an abnormal expansion of plant, largely to take advantage of the relatively new open-hearth process, and a collapse of demand from the belt-tightening railroads, led the country into the severe recession of 1913–14. The year 1914 was "the worst in the his-tory of the steel industry." Recovery, fed by Allied war orders and later by the preparedness program of the United States, was beyond all ex-pectations.[9]

[8] Victor Clark, *History of Manufactures* (3 vols., New York, 1929), II, 99, 101. Clark lays heavy stress on the railroads' "embarrassing" lack of facilities to carry this traffic, so much of which was destined for their expansion program. The epi-sode illustrates the highly interdependent nature of factors in economic growth, and the folly of speaking too glibly about "backward and forward linkages."

[9] *Ibid.*, 99–106.

The industry was propelled forward, not only by the perfection of the open-hearth process, which encouraged the start-up of smaller mills than were practical with the Bessemer process, but also by the development of the fabulous ore deposits of the Lake Superior region. Myriad technical problems, as well as quite a few financial relationships, had to be unsnarled before this development could be felt, but by 1910 steel-making in the United States almost invariably meant the combining of ore from that region with bituminous coal from the Alleghenies. In 1890 it had taken a week to discharge 2,000 tons of ore from a lake ship into the puny railroad gondolas which awaited it. By 1910 a 10,000-ton cargo was discharged in less than two hours. Capacity had grown to the point where solid trains of ore were coming down the Duluth, Missabe, and Iron Range Railroad at forty-five-minute intervals. And tying everything together was the most impressive railroad system in the world. Which was father and which was son is a pointless discussion: neither the railroads nor the steel industry would have been possible (nor would they be possible today) without each other.[10]

As might be expected, old industries such as textiles and food processing grew less rapidly than newer fields after 1899. Whereas their output almost doubled by 1914, industries such as iron and steel, chemicals, machinery, and railroad equipment, not to mention industries that hardly existed in 1899, increased by two and one-half to three times. But the output of bituminous coal in 1915 stood at *four times* the level attained just before the nineties depression. Anthracite coal, used almost exclusivly for domestic heating, merely doubled, and fuel oil was in its infancy. Where did all of this additional soft coal go? Most of the new tonnage was being consumed by the railroads themselves. The startling growth in locomotives and the gross weight of the trains they hauled sent coal usage by the carriers, who continued to be the largest single users of coal until the diesels came in after World War II, to new records. But increasingly coal was being demanded in an entirely new industry. This industry, which was to change American life more than any other innovation except the automobile, and which would have a considerable impact on the railroads themselves, was electricity.[11]

[10] *Ibid.,* 17–22, 41, 65–70.

[11] *Historical Statistics,* 414; Harold Barger and Sam H. Schurr, *The Mining Industries, 1899–1939: A Study of Output, Employment and Productivity* (New York, 1944), cited in *Historical Statistics,* 354.

It is impossible to do more than suggest here the interaction between the development of electric light and power and the railroads. The most spectacular early achievements in the new industry were in the generation of huge quantities of power at Niagara Falls and its successful transmission to distant points of consumption. This happened in the nineties.[12] But within ten to fifteen years virtually every community had its power station, almost invariably fueled by coal hauled to it by rail, and 94 per cent of all street railways were electrified. At the very end of the nineteenth century the new industry gave birth to a number of industrial titans of the twentieth. American technology, driven forward by an amazing collection of scientist-inventors, was far out in front by 1897 when a group of American manufacturers received the contract for the cars, locomotives, and machinery for the London Central Underground Railway. In 1896 General Electric and Westinghouse had agreed to pool their patents, and by 1900 they were about to change the old definition of "industry" forever. Westinghouse, in fact, was already integrated backward as far as the handling of raw steel ingots. And the more industry centralized and integrated, the more transportation was required to assemble the materials and distribute the finished products.[13] But with all these spectacular achievements in electricity, a development was taking place all but unnoticed which provided a tremendous boost to industrial activity. The change from steam power (with its forests of dangerous, cumbersome, and expensive belting) to electric motors in the operation of machinery revolutionized manufacturing. By 1919, 45 to 50 per cent of industry was electrified. Truly, "numerous changes of a minor sort, in some industries, outweigh in importance the more spectacular innovations." [14]

If a thumbnail sketch of the electrical industry is unlikely to do it justice, such a treatment of the automobile industry is almost unthinkable. Only a few observations on its early impact on the railroads can be attempted. In our day the culmination of the automobile as a primary means of transportation has seemed so logical and inevitable that it is

[12] Harold I. Sharlin, "Electrical Generation and Transmission," in Melvin Kranzberg and Carroll W. Pursell, Jr., *Technology in Western Civilization* (2 vols., New York, 1967), I, 582–85.

[13] Clark, *Manufactures,* II, 165–70.

[14] Harry Jerome, *Mechanization in Industry* (New York, 1934), 20.

hard to understand that for over three decades after the first horseless
carriage was exhibited at the Chicago fair of 1893, the role of the automobile in American economic life was still evolving. By 1910, to be
sure, automobile manufacturing was a prominent industry. Railroads
were hauling thousands of the machines, no longer a rich man's toy, to
all parts of the nation, more and more frequently in railroad cars especially designed for the purpose. No category of finished manufactured
goods added more to the railroads' traffic burden in these years. Until
after World War I the railroads looked upon the automobile as an almost pure blessing. Since the dawn of the railroad age, the lack of a
practical road vehicle to bridge the gap between farm and depot had
been one of the major irritants of American life, and when one became
available farmers turned out to be the first mass market for cars. Henry
Ford transformed the problem from one of vehicles to one of roads.
After 1910 the chorus of complaints grew rapidly into the good roads
movement, of which the railroads were a highly vocal sponsor. Rails
and motors had, if anything, a symbiotic relationship before about
1916. Present-day notions of their antagonistic relationship are not applicable to their history before World War I.[15]

Throughout the Progressive era, the increased tempo of industrial
activity continued to be matched by the expanding diversity and com-
plexity of economic life. At every grade crossing in America the casual
train-watcher, sitting in his buggy or shiny new Model T, was conscious
of a change in the "consist" of the freight trains which rumbled by.
More and more tanks cars were in evidence, and the variety of mark-
ings testified to the changes which were taking place in the chemical
and petroleum industries. Still based almost entirely on the production
of inorganic chemicals for industrial use, the American chemical industry nevertheless was revolutionized by the introduction of the Solvay
process for production of alkalis and by the exploitation of vast deposits
of sulphur in Louisiana. And in one of the most fortuitous combinations of circumstances in all of economic history, the decline of the illu-

[15] Clark, *Manufactures,* II, 157–63; Edward E. Kennedy, *The Automobile Industry* (New York, 1941), 42–73; Charles L. Dearing, *American Highway Policy*
(Washington, 1942), 46–54, 225–26, 228. Compare these observations with Fogel's speculation that the existence of the railroad delayed the invention of the
automobile; Robert W. Fogel, *Railroads and American Economic Growth* (Baltimore, 1964), 14–15.

mination market for petroleum (as a result, first, of the switch to gas and then the advent of electricity) was being more than counterbalanced by the emergence of the automobile, which had a voracious appetite for a fuel that for decades had been merely a troublesome by-product of the kerosene industry. As if this happy coincidence were not enough, at the very threshold of a new era of demand for petroleum products man's geological inquisitiveness broke the Standard Oil monopoly where the puny antitrust laws had substantially failed. The discovery of great new oilfields in the Southwest added thousands of tank cars, with strange-sounding new names, to the American freight train.[16]

There was another kind of railroad car of which the observer was seeing more than ever before by 1910. The refrigerator car was not new. Its introduction by the great Chicago meat packers in the last third of the previous century had revolutionized that important branch of the food industry. But the changes wrought by the "reefer" car in the diet of Americans were accelerated in the new century. Agriculture, so long one of the most disaffected sectors of society, had its own golden age in these years. Almost every index of prosperity—farm population, the number of farms, the value of land and improvements, prices, and the value of production per farm—was in the ascendant. The value of farm implements in use tripled and use of commercial fertilizers doubled. All was not perfect, by any means. Farm tenancy showed a disturbing upward trend, while the post–Civil War problems of race and poverty, white and black, continued to plague the South. But those who possessed some capital and know-how and the willingness to take a chance found agriculture a rewarding pursuit in these years, especially those who flocked to the Southwest and the Pacific slope. For that is where so many of the new refrigerator cars were coming from, as the nation's consumption of vegetables and fruits—especially the exotic citrus fruits which for centuries had been unknown except at Christmas—on a year-round basis increased. Life on the average American farm still meant long hours of hard, lonely work, but by the time the war brought agriculture to its peak of prosperity, most of the nation's food and fiber

[16] Clark, *Manufactures,* II, 283–87; Harold F. Williamson *et al., The American Petroleum Industry:* Vol. II, *The Age of Energy, 1899–1959* (Evanston, 1963), 3–4, 6, 195.

growers felt closer to the mainstream of American life than they had for decades.[17]

The observer who was intrigued by the changes in freight trains found more to think about on the shelves of the grocery store and in his own home. The changes there turned out to be only the early stages of a trend which is in full cry today, but after 1900 more and more food preparation was taking place in factories and less and less in the home kitchen. Nowhere was the accelerated concentration of the food industry more apparent than in the meat and dairy products industry, which clustered around the enormous investments that some five companies had made in processing and cold storage facilities in the big cities. Distribution of consumer goods reflected the same nationalizing impulse. Mail-order companies had grown rapidly after the advent of rural free delivery in 1896, but substitution of low-cost parcel-post service for express in 1913 accelerated the decline of the distinction between Fifth Avenue and Main Street. It was all a part of the geographic rationalization of production which the doctrine of comparative advantage dictated. The breathtaking scale and dramatic rate of development were the result of a meeting of two conditions that made America unique: the largest hospitable area of the earth's surface free of artificial trade barriers; and a railroad system which by 1900 had tied the most isolated spots tightly into the most highly interdependent society in the world.[18]

IV

The panic of 1907, occurring so conveniently in the exact center of the two decades with which this study is concerned, revealed the inadequacy of America's economic institutions and of its understanding of the forces that were at work. These inadequacies, it turned out, were not removed by the far-reaching changes which the first years of the

[17] *Historical Statistics,* 278–85; Harold Barger and Hans Landsberg, *American Agriculture, 1899–1939* (New York, 1942), 21–23, 151, 204, 251.

[18] Clark, *Manufactures,* II, 263–68. The advent of the parcel-post system is discussed in the next chapter.

Wilson administration brought. Economic institutions, and especially economic wisdom, have a way of remolding themselves to the problems and situations of the past, which may or may not be the problems of the present. Americans discovered this in 1907, 1913–14, 1921, and, on a colossal scale, in the 1930s. They may well rediscover it again in the 1970s. Powerful new economic forces were clearly at work in the two decades before World War I, but it can hardly be said that anyone really understood them at the time. The inflation which was the outstanding feature of the era is, in its causes and its significance, nearly as much a subject of controversy among economists today as it was at the time. We must take a stand on the issue, however, if we are to make economic sense out of what happened to American railroads in the Progressive era. Let us begin by reviewing briefly what happened to the American economy.

The great expansion of human activity, first of all, was marked by a near-doubling of the real gross national product in these decades. All of the major branches of economic life contributed about equally to this growth, relatively speaking; manufacturing, somewhat more, and service industries quite a bit more. Despite this increase in the stream of created wealth, the relative amount plowed back to increase future production (i.e., net capital formation) remained remarkably stable as a percentage of the total. This is hardly a surprising discovery in view of the numerous capital-devouring developments just recounted. Production grew at an average annual rate of 3.1 per cent, while the population among whom it had ultimately to be divided increased at a rate of only 2 per cent. Productivity (the volume of production per worker) increased by some 50 per cent. Real wages of labor, however, remained virtually stable throughout the period, revealing that working men, whatever their achievements in formally organizing themselves in these years, failed to cut themselves a larger slice of the American pie. And yet prices rose consistently throughout the period.[19] After making some

[19] *Historical Statistics,* 91, 115, 139, 140, 599; Solomon Fabricant, *The Output of Manufacturing Industries* (New York, 1940), 302, 315; Frederick C. Mills, *Economic Tendencies in the United States* (New York, 1932), 21, 43, 46, 290–97; John W. Kendrick, *Productivity Trends in the United States* (New York, 1956), *passim;* Don D. Lescohier and Elizabeth Brandeis, *History of Labor in the United States, 1896–1932* (New York, 1935), 51, 56–57, 62–63; 66; Lewis L. Lorwin and John M. Blair, *Technology in Our Economy,* TNEC Monograph No.

allowance for the fact that there were assuredly setbacks to this price trend, notably in 1908 and 1914, and that some prices rose more than others while a few rose not at all or even declined, there was little doubt then, as there is little now, that the dollar was shrinking in purchasing power. It was a strange sensation, after three decades of consistent appreciation of the dollar (an even rarer phenomenon in human history than the inflation being described), to discover that a wage earner or a businessman who had the same number of dollars—or even more—at his disposal was less and less able to bid for the consumption and capital resources of the nation. Was this phenomenon a mere coincidence, fully explainable by certain changes in the supply-demand relationship of gold? Or was the inflation a mechanism, independent of any such fortuitous circumstance and bound to occur without it, which brought about a fundamental reordering of economic relationships? The question is a fundamental one in our study of what happened to the place of the American railroad system in the economy.

It was long thought sufficient as an explanation of the steady rise of prices in the Western world from 1896 to the eve of World War I to point to the rapid increase in gold stocks which resulted from new dis-

---

22 (Washington, 1941), 36; Wilford I. King, *The National Income and Its Purchasing Power* (New York, 1930), 91. The rapidly rising cost of living was widely attested to in the popular press and in official government reports in these years. Using techniques developed by the U.S. Bureau of Labor, the *Report of the Commission on the Cost of Living,* Commonwealth of Mass., House Doc. No. 1750, May 1910, p. 72, concluded that the cost of living had risen 20.5 per cent from 1901 to 1910, implying a considerably higher rise since the last depression year of 1896. These views, which were amply supported by the obvious, rapid rise in the wholesale price index, were borne out in Paul H. Douglas, *Real Wages in the United States, 1890–1926* (Boston, 1930), *passim,* whose conclusion that real wages did not rise in the two decades before World War I was the accepted view for over thirty years. Albert Rees, *Real Wages in Manufacturing* (Princeton, 1961), 116–19, 120, 126, seeks to reverse this conclusion, on the basis of his finding that the cost of living rose only 20 per cent from 1897 to 1914. But Rees's indexes of rent and the cost of clothing and home furnishings, based as they are on advertised prices (real estate advertising and mail-order catalogs), may well be subject to much more downward bias than he grants, inasmuch as they bear little resemblance to the steep upward trend in the wholesale price index. Considering the enormous philosophical and statistical problems involved in producing a current consumer price index, it is hardly likely that historians will ever agree on such a series constructed *ex post facto.* But assuming that the cost of living paralleled the wholesale price index as closely from 1897 to 1917 as it did from 1945 to 1963 (a roughly comparable period in length and the absence of a major war), which was very closely indeed, then the American cost of living doubled in the Progressive era.

coveries and reductions in the cost of refining gold. Such an explanation
has much merit, especially since the world was still closely tied to gold
as the basis for currency expansion. In recent years there has been a re-
crudescence of the quantity theory of money, as inflation once again
strikes at the established relationships between the multitudinous classes
and interest groups in American society. The leading proponent of the
theory, in its modern, post–Keynesian dress, asserts that the "proximate
cause" of the pre–World War I inflation was indeed the expansion of
gold stocks, on which all other forms of money were based.[20] While not
so simplistic as its opponents have charged (its authors are put to considerable ingenuity to squeeze their hypothetical foot into the uncompromising shoe of history), the quantity theory satisfies few people
today, and least of all the economic historians who have delved deep
into the musty details of industrial innovation and its impact on Western societies.[21] Economists, whose propensity to reason deductively
from a few general propositions involves the danger of taking leave of
reality, past or present, owe more attention to economic historians,
whose inductive method brings into view the wide range of human activities which—by whatever "equation" combined—have produced the
phenomena we seek to explain. Every theory can probably contribute
something, and it is proper that the rich debate should continue. I believe, however, that the following conclusions of a student of European
economic history in this period add powerfully to our understanding of
the economic trends in the Progressive era, and of the epoch—so very
different—which preceded it:

> The explanation for the aberration of the nineteenth century [the long-
> term decline in prices] seems to lie precisely in the productivity gains that
> stimulated and made possible . . . economic growth. Over the century, real
> costs dropped steadily, at first mainly in manufacturing, and then—after a
> revolution in transport that opened vast new lands to cultivation—in food
> production as well. (It is the harvest of advances in both sectors that ac-
> counts for the particularly sharp drop of the years 1873–96.) . . .

[20] Milton Friedman and Anna J. Schwartz, *A Monetary History of the United
States, 1867–1960* (Princeton, 1963), 137–38.

[21] For a compelling argument that institutional developments in this "great day
for commercial banking" produced changes in the velocity of money which were
at least as important as changes in money stocks, see the Federal Reserve Bank
of New York monograph, George Garvy and Martin R. Blyn, *The Velocity of
Money* (New York, 1969), especially 80–81.

Not until a series of major advances opened new areas of investment around the turn of the century was this deceleration [in productivity gains] reversed. These years [1896–1914] saw the lusty childhood . . . of a cluster of innovations that have earned the name of the Second Industrial Revolution. . . . The initial boost to prices imparted by bullion inflows . . . was relayed and reinforced by a pattern of investment that yielded slow returns in consumable goods and services.[22]

What happened in the Progressive era, then, was not only a continuation of the eager demand for capital investment which had marked the last third of the nineteenth century, but also a shift away from quick-payoff commitments to more complex, more sophisticated, and generally slow-payoff investments. Not that this implies an abrupt shift from old to new industries: there was at the same time a shift from extensive to intensive development of old industries (or, as I prefer to think of them, "priority" industries). The point is that these priority industries—iron, steel, and railroads—which made all that followed possible, produced in their primitive nineteenth-century form near-term cost reductions which neutralized the potentially inflationary effects of their demands on savings. But in the first two decades of the twentieth century their demands for intensive development were as inflationary in the deferred character of their returns as any of the new technologies.[23]

The Progressive era, in short, was a scramble—a scramble between those who wished to continue to build up the nation's production capacity and those who wished to continue at least the very modest gains in real consumer incomes which were registered in the nineteenth century. More significantly, it was also a scramble between competing forms of capital investment. The crucial role of the price mechanism in such periods of realignment of classes and the imperfect manner in which it operates in the real world have been lucidly expressed by one

[22] David S. Landes, *The Unbound Prometheus: Technological Change and Industrial Development in Western Europe from 1750 to the Present* (Cambridge, 1969), 234–35.

[23] It is interesting to note that Landes does not address himself to transportation technology, except tangentially. This may be rationalized (although not entirely) in the case of the European experience by the twin facts that European railroads were built for an existing traffic and therefore required relatively little rebuilding; and that the economic isolation which was the product of nationalism reduced the relative importance of transportation after the short era of free trade was over. Neither rationalization, of course, applies to the United States.

whose intimate involvement with the evolution of United States financial institutions is well known:

Inflation is essentially a process of wealth transference or the regrouping of economic classes. . . . There is no necessary connection between the mechanism of money and banking and the forces of inflation, although it is usually true that the mechanism of money and banking is employed in effecting or making operative an inflation movement. . . . There usually occurs a distortion of wealth forms which may result in the overincrease of certain classes of goods or in the undue expansion and enlargement of capital forms.[24]

The frustration of constantly rising prices, which seemed continually to withhold the fruits of apparent prosperity, contributed greatly to that sense of lost leadership which has been so persuasively advanced as the central motivating force of the "age of reform." The situation demanded a scapegoat, and many looked for one in the giant corporations which had grown to such disturbing proportions. Mr. Dooley noted that in the world of 1905 the omnipotent J. P. Morgan would impatiently wave an idealist like Horace Greeley along to his assistant, George Perkins. William Allen White, much changed since the inanities of Populism were ashes in his mouth, said simplistically that as far as public policy was concerned, "all of these fish will go on one string: the restriction of capital." Walter Lippmann, full of the youthful illusion of one who believes that he has been born at the beginning of the millennium, trumpeted that "those who are young today are born into a world in which the foundations of the older order survive only as habits or by default." [25]

What significance has all of this for a history of American railroads in the Progressive era? Did they fare any differently from other forms of big business as the nation passed, by stages, from Roosevelt's showy but insubstantial trust-busting, to Taft's legalistic support of the Sherman Act, to Wilson's lukewarm efforts to legislate the New Free-

[24] H. Parker Willis and John M. Chapman, *The Economics of Inflation* (New York, 1935), 59. The quotation is from Chapter Four, "Inflation and Industry," by Willis.

[25] Richard Hofstadter, *The Age of Reform* (New York, 1955); Robert Hutchinson, *Mr. Dooley on Ivrything and Ivrybody by Finley Peter Dunne* (New York, 1963), 197–98; William Allen White, *The Old Order Changeth: A View of American Democracy* (New York, 1910), 67; Walter Lippmann, *Drift and Mastery: An Attempt to Diagnose the Current Unrest* (New York, 1914), xvii–xviii.

dom, into the consuming fire of the war? Walt W. Rostow seems to think not. "The progressive objectives," he writes, "had . . . fifteen years of relative dominance over domestic policy; and they left their mark. . . . But the progressive period was more a matter of mood and the direction of policy than of drastic reallocation of resources." [26] Concentration on the flamboyant events of the trust-busting area, such as the Standard Oil and American Tobacco dissolutions of 1911, can lead to such a conclusion. Certain it was that these two behemoths, standing on the threshold of drastically altered demand situations for their industries, felt this invocation of the Sherman Act about as much as an elephant feels a pinprick. The key fact is that insofar as the businessman retained a voice in the price which he charged for his goods or services, and in the price which he would pay for the labor and materials which went into them, reform movements had little impact on his position in the race. But during the Progressive era the greatest of all American industries lost such a voice in its affairs, with what consequences we shall now explore.

V

No understanding of the history of American railroads from 1896 to World War I is possible for him who perceives them as they were before the nineties depression: overbuilt, financially undernourished, divided into hundreds of poorly integrated corporate entities, and ridden by rate wars which reduced the profits of the best-situated roads drastically and drove the weaker ones to the wall of bankruptcy. That was the "railroad problem" in the nineteenth century, but the depression of the 1890s changed all that. Not that the great "shake-out" which brought strength out of weakness via financial reorganization and consolidation was the spontaneous result of the panic of 1893. It had been gathering momentum for at least a decade, but it accelerated sharply after massive defaulting on bonds removed old managements from one railroad after another. The trustees of these bonds, which were usually secured by first mortgages on the physical assets of the railroads, were banks. The heads

[26] Walt W. Rostow, *The Stages of Economic Growth* (Cambridge, 1960), 75.

of these institutions thus found themselves more and more involved in railroad affairs, and it was perhaps inevitable that after 1893 they would never be far from the day-to-day management of many of the lines. Thus there grew up the legend that sensible management policies, based on what was good for the roads and the territories which they served, were replaced by "banker control," which was ignorant, incompetent, and interested only in "speculative" gain. If a banker had come up not through the relatively respectable ranks of commercial banking, but instead had started life on Wall Street as a "broker's boy," so much the worse for the railroad which found itself in his clutches, according to the reform-era school of thought. That the "bankers" (a catch-all term for anyone who had made a fortune in financial dealings) were in the great majority of cases competent judges of railroad properties and their problems, frequently combining in one person the equally indispensable skills of financial analyst and operating expert, has been little appreciated. But the character of railroad management in the Progressive era is a subject for the next chapter.[27]

The most significant features of the railroads in the decades after 1890 were the "communities of interest" which had seemed to emerge so suddenly in the troubled years that followed, and which achieved a high degree of stability where the nineteenth-century pools had failed. The origins of these arrangements in the East go back at least as far as the mid-eighties.[28] By 1906, when the Interstate Commerce Commission drew attention to them, they accounted for the greater part of the nation's railroad mileage and an even greater share of traffic. In the most simplified and compressed form, they consisted of:

1. The eastern trunk lines (New York Central and Pennsylvania), which had reduced their rate competition with each other to a minimum and, by ownership of large blocks of stock, controlled the policies of the

---

[27] For a classic statement of the attitudes of men of the "age of reform" toward this new breed of railroad leader, see Harold U. Faulkner, *The Decline of Laissez Faire* (New York, 1951), 198–202, 218. Despite his "robber-baron" approach, however, Faulkner provides a very useful summary of railroad affairs in this period. The basic treatment of the railroad reorganizations of the 1890s is still Edward G. Campbell, *The Reorganization of the American Railroad System, 1893–1900* (New York, 1938).

[28] Albro Martin, "Crisis of Rugged Individualism: The West Shore–South Pennsylvania Railroad Affair, 1880–1885," *Pennsylvania Magazine of History and Biography*, XCIII (April, 1969), 218–43.

Baltimore & Ohio, Erie, Chesapeake & Ohio, Norfolk & Western, and certain important anthracite-carrying roads. The management of these roads, backed up by highly profitable operating results, shaped their destinies with no more than a nod toward the "bankers."

2. The southeastern system of "Morgan roads." Morgan did not take over a system and financially rehabilitate it; there *was* no system before his men brought one forth from the wreckage of the numerous southern railroads after 1893.

3. The "Hill roads," dominating the northwestern United States under the firm guidance of James J. Hill, who shone brightly in all departments of railroading.

4. The "Harriman roads," consisting of the properties which Edward H. Harriman had been ministering to beginning with the Illinois Central in the eighties, and including the Union Pacific, which he rebuilt, and, more recently, the Southern Pacific. In 1906 it was widely assumed that Harriman would ultimately control all of the routes in the west central and southwestern United States, and that he would succeed in merging such holdings with one or more of the eastern trunk lines.

5. The New Haven system, which was reaching out for every form of transportation in sight, including the Boston & Maine, under the nominal leadership of Charles S. Mellen, who was desperately trying to guess what it was that the aging J. P. Morgan wanted him to do. It was shaping up as the railroad debacle of all time.

6. The "Gould lines," Jay's legacy to his son George, consisting primarily of the Wabash in the Midwest and the Missouri Pacific and the Texas & Pacific in the Southwest, an aggregation of only moderately prosperous lines which would go under when the going got rough after 1910.

7. The "Moore-Reid" lines, named for the most flamboyant wheeler-dealers of the era, who took two of the weakest sisters in the Mid- and Southwest (the Rock Island and the Frisco), debauched them, and tarred the entire industry with their brush.[29]

Harriman's accomplishments in integrating the American railroad systems under his care were on such a scale and, on the whole, so suc-

[29] ICC, *Intercorporate Relationships of Railways in the United States as of June 30, 1906* (Washington, 1908), *passim;* Campbell, *Reorganization of the American Railroad System*, 40, 329, 331; Faulkner, *Decline of Laissez Faire*, 192–98.

cessful that he has generally been credited with thinking up the idea of the community of interests. Early in 1907 Frank B. Kellogg, one of Theodore Roosevelt's young troubleshooters, was in hot pursuit of Harriman, whose friendship with T.R. had been a casualty of the railroad regulation controversies of the previous two years. As the railroad magnate was being grilled at public hearings in connection with the ICC's investigation of his business methods, the following exchange took place:

Mr. Harriman: It [a conversation with Morawetz and Ripley of the Santa Fe] was in substance that we ought to try to establish a better relationship between all the railroads . . . deal more frankly with each other . . . and not operate our lines for the purpose of destroying each other, and . . . I would be willing to even put him [Morawetz] on the executive committee of the Southern Pacific, so that he might know what our intentions were. . . .

Mr. Kellogg: Well, this establishing of closer relations and friendly interests is what is commonly known as community of interest?

Mr. Harriman: I never invented that; I don't like the term.

Mr. Kellogg: I thought you invented it. . . . I would like to find the inventor.

Mr. Harriman: That was somebody else. I call it a common interest.[30]

The "inventor" of the arrangement, if not the name, as of so many other epochal railroad developments, was the Pennsylvania Railroad. In one of his last annual reports as president of the line, George B. Roberts, who had cooperated with J. P. Morgan in bringing about harmony between the New York Central and the Pennsylvania in the eighties, reflected the gloom which encircled the year 1894. Rate competition, he noted, had never been more rampant, and since 1887 not even pooling arrangements (which had never been much good anyway) held out any hope, for the reason that they were illegal. But by 1899 things were looking up, and the new president, Alexander J. Cassatt, determined to sew up the rebate hole in the bottom of the sack once and for all. "The only alternative [to indefinite cost reduction] is to arrest the reduction in revenue, which has been largely brought about by apparently uncon-

---

[30] ICC, *Testimony of E. H. Harriman before the ICC in the Matter of the Consolidation and Combination of Carriers, Relations between Such Carriers, and Community of Interests Therein, Their Rates, Facilities and Practices* (New York, 1907), 141–42.

trollable conflicts between the railroad companies. . . . To establish
closer relations between the managers of the trunk lines, it seemed wise
to your Board to acquire an interest in some of the railways reaching
the seaboard and to unite with the other shareholders who control these
properties in supporting a conservative policy." By 1902 Cassatt could
report that the company owned $52 million of B. & O. common stock,
$26 million of Norfolk & Western, and $10 million of Chesapeake &
Ohio; and that the community of interests was working well. Other
prosperous roads, notably the Central, had followed suit. After 1902
neither government nor shippers could count on disunity and interne-
cine warfare among the major railroads to maintain "competition." [31]

[31] P.R.R. Co., *Annual Reports*, 1894–1902.

CHAPTER II

THE CHALLENGE OFFERED

For its true history was always the history of transportation, in which the names of railroad presidents are more significant than those of Presidents of the United States. Those names emerged—Gould, Vanderbilt, Hill, Huntington, and Harriman.—PHILIP GUEDALLA, *1936*

If Germany, like the rest of the civilized nations of the Old World, has grown stronger and gained new life through the construction of railroads, the United States . . . have been actually created by the building of railroads.—SUPERIOR PRIVY COUNCILOR W. HOFF *and* PRIVY COUNCILOR F. SCHWABACH, *1906*

I

The superintendent of the New York Central's Adirondack Division had never been so busy. Although it had been a lively summer for his division and for the many resorts in upstate New York in that prosperous year of 1910, he had generally found that ten passenger cars were sufficient for his best train, the *Adirondack Express.* But on Sunday, September 4, he had got wind that traffic would be somewhat heavier than usual. The increase was to be expected. All vacationers, then as now, try to go home at the same time. He made a few inquiries at the bigger hotels, and what he heard caused him to blanch. In less than twenty-four hours, he had to round up 150 parlor cars and coaches. They were barely enough, for by the next afternoon the *Express* had grown into sixteen sections—sixteen separate trains which, at five-minute intervals (the last section arrived an hour and twenty minutes late), poured 12,500 people through the chaos of Grand Central Station, then still under construction. In all, the Central operated 253 extra cars into the terminal on that memorable Tuesday. Over at the nearly completed Pennsylvania Station the story was much the same. The *Seashore,* from

Atlantic City, arrived in nine sections, many consisting of eight to eleven of the new all-steel coaches that held eighty-eight passengers each. Despairing at the mountain of trunks which had begun to flow into wayside depots the day before, the line consolidated the entire load into two solid baggage trains. The day set a record for long-distance passenger travel into Gotham, with over 200,000 arrivals.[1]

The two decades before World War I were the golden age of the railroad passenger train in America, for those years were the last period of great prosperity before the automobile and the airplane. Except for a relatively small volume of lake and coastal travel by boat, the railroads had it all, from the traveling salesman who was making his way through his territory in ten- and twenty-mile hops, to the well-to-do family setting out in Pullman drawing-room comfort for a tour of the great American West. These years are unique in the history of railroad travel, not just in the rate of growth (although that was spectacular, nearly tripling between 1896 and 1916), but also in the relationship between freight and passenger business. Almost since the beginning of the railroad age, passenger traffic had been falling relative to freight, although there had been a time in the 1880s when freight rate wars made passenger business somewhat more profitable. Passenger miles per 100 freight ton-miles were at their lowest point in history in 1900 (11.33), but by 1908 this ratio had risen to 13.32. Only after 1911 did freight traffic regain its steeper trend. Pullman journeys, reflecting the good times, shot upward in an unbroken line, from 5 million in 1900 to 26 million in 1914.[2]

II

What was the source of this great increase in travel in the prewar decades? Who was doing all of the traveling? Where did they go, and why? And what were the consequences for America's railroads? We do not have many solid statistics for the travel industry for these years, but through the mists we can discern some facts consistent with what we

[1] New York *Times* (hereinafter referred to as *NYT*), Sept. 7, 1910, 1.

[2] Thor Hultgren, "Railroad Travel and the State of Business," *National Bureau of Economic Research Occasional Paper No. 13* (New York, 1943), 11–12, 34, 39.

know about the travel business today. First, let us dispel one of the notions which Americans entertain most fondly about themselves—that they are a travel-addicted people. As recently as 1965 the economic consultant to the Travel Research Association was complaining about "the great bulk of the population that just doesn't travel at all." Travel is today, as it was in the Progressive era, highly concentrated among a small percentage of the population whose businesses or ideas of pleasure make them frequent travelers. In 1911 it was estimated that some 5 per cent of the population accounted for most of the traveling that was done. Still, it is likely that relatively more people traveled by rail in those years than travel by all forms of public conveyance today, since there was as yet no private mode.[3]

Business travel, then as now, appears to have accounted for the greater part of passenger travel, although we do not know this for certain. Even if we ignore commuter travel, however, it is rather obvious that the great expansion in business activity, combined with the rapid conversion from a regional to a national economy, brought forth a great increase in business travel. The enthusiasm with which the railroads catered to this premium class of business and the hotels and theaters which were erected in every city for the businessman's comfort and entertainment testify to it.[4] More significant in explaining the travel boom, since the business travel would have existed in any case, is the railroads' success in promoting pleasure travel.

Fortunes have been made throughout the civilized world in helping the middle-class man "on the make" feel that he is living a life like that of the tastemakers. Today the pacesetters are the "jet set," who make up in visibility for what they lack in style, and the good bourgeois works hard at emulating them. In the Edwardian era it was the resort crowd, whose antics at Newport, Bar Harbor, Palm Beach, and lesser watering places were the subject of rotogravure sections throughout the land. And as America's pioneer past dwindled in the distance, the ap-

[3] Paul Cherington, Address to the Travel Research Association, in *Proceedings of Third Annual Travel Conference* (Boston, 1965), 29; Logan G. McPherson, *Four Railroad Speeches* (Washington, 1911), 21.

[4] The first transient hotel, as distinguished from the "family hotel" of the nineteenth century, was opened in 1908 in Buffalo, New York, by Ellsworth M. Statler. Jefferson Williamson, *The American Hotel: An Anecdotal History* (New York, 1930), 161–62.

peal of faraway, romantic places grew in the imaginations of a people
who had money to spend on travel. Out there, beyond the puny hills of
Pennsylvania, there was the great American West, and now it beckoned
enticingly. It would be difficult to prove that the comforts of Pullman
travel "made" our National Parks; the reverse is probably just as
true. But by 1900 they were ready for each other. The oldest park, Hot
Springs, Arkansas, had already developed a reputation for its healing
waters, and to bring the hordes of prosperous people who came there to
bathe and, incidentally, to gamble and see the races, not one but two
railroads were built from Little Rock. The significant growth, however,
was in travel to more exotic places like Yellowstone (whose Old Faithful geyser found its way into every child's geography textbook), Yosem-
ite, and Mount Rainier, parks which by 1915 were growing in attendance by 50 per cent a year.[5] Goading them on were magazines like the
National Geographic, greatly expanded since Gilbert Grosvenor's arrival as editor in 1903, which seldom let an issue go by without an article about the West. Meanwhile, to the despair of do-gooders everywhere, an uncounted but growing number of Americans availed
themselves of the free travel opportunities offered by the empty boxcar
and the lenient brakeman.[6]

III

Because passenger service is a high-fixed-cost operation in which
"one more" passenger can almost always be carried at nearly clear
profit, the railroads promoted service with all of the arts of advertising

[5] Cleveland Amory, *The Last Resorts* (New York, 1952), 212–28, 263, 335, 337,
353; Jenks Cameron, *The National Park Service: Its History, Activities, and Organization* (New York, 1922); Francis J. Scully, *Hot Springs, Arkansas and Hot
Springs National Park* (Little Rock, 1966), 164–66, 171; "Our National Parks,
Playgrounds for the People Unsurpassed in the World," *Scientific American Supplement,* LXXXII (Nov. 11, 1916), 312–13.

[6] Vol. VII (1897) of the *Geographic* contained 373 pages and extolled the En-
chanted Mesa, Crater Lake, and the forests and deserts of Arizona. Vol. XVII
(1906) had grown to 718 pages, and Vol. XXII (1912), had 1,284 pages, circula-
tion of 140,000, and many full-page advertisements by western railroads. Josiah
Flynt, "The Tramp and the Railroad," *Century,* LVIII (n.s. XXXVI) (June,
1899), 258–66.

and salesmanship available to them. By the turn of the century they were aggressively seeking new and more effective ways to build traffic. At the 1899 meeting of the Association of General Passenger and Ticket Agents, the Burlington's top passenger traffic executive reviewed the work of a committee which had been critically studying the excursion business. That this was, indeed, the golden age of the excursion and the convention can be seen from his report. Small conventions, to which a minimum party of 100 were given a round-trip ticket for one and one-third of the one-way fare, were not very promising, he concluded, since most of the passengers would have gone to the event even if standard fares had been charged. Real conventions, of which there were over 200 in the Burlington's territory in 1898, were more fruitful, but there were tough problems involved in policing the highly attractive privileges, which often extended to offering a round trip for a one-way fare. Most troublesome of all, however, was the mammoth convention, like the Christian Endeavor get-together which had just been held in Los Angeles, or the G.A.R. reunion in Philadelphia, or the Dewey reception in New York. The net gains to the railroads were doubtful, and the congestion a hindrance to regular passenger service and freight movement. As for local excursions, the traffic man complained that the railroad usually had to supply the attraction, and often ended up with no profit after deducting the cost of free transportation of brass bands, baseball teams, and watermelons.[7] Railroad passenger traffic policies would become much more hard-boiled during the Progressive era, and there would be many who would not like the change.

Travel promotion in the decades before World War I was the province of the traveling passenger agent and the ticket broker. The former was a highly gregarious type, directly employed by the railroad to travel almost constantly throughout the country, calling on ticket agents who wielded the enormous power of selecting the connecting routes on which their own customers would travel. The opportunities for graft are obvious, and the traits which made a good traveling agent are revealing. "Personality" and "ability to hold your liquor" were believed to be of the greatest importance in the serious business of persuading a local ticket agent to punch the box opposite the name of one's own railroad,

[7] *Proceedings of the Association of General Passenger and Ticket Agents, Boston, Massachusetts, Oct. 17–18, 1899* (New York, 1899), 404–7.

on the yard-long tickets with which long-distance travelers often had to contend. Presumably the results lasted only until the next personable, bibulous traveling agent hauled himself and his Gladstone off the flyer. In 1902 these colorful men (and, surprisingly, some women) were confident of their future, inasmuch as they had heard rumors that the "great railways are about to wipe out commissions" to local ticket agents, who would then need more personal attention than ever. And so they went on holding their mammoth annual conventions, from which they were treated to lavish excursions ("Did anyone ever hear of a successful businessman who undertook to sell his wares without having seen them?"), until the species, although certainly not the genus, perished during the great war.[8]

The ticket broker was another breed. It is interesting to note that the travel agency business evolved in much the same way as the advertising agency business. Both, in these prewar years, worked for the supplier of the services rather than the user. (Inasmuch as both agencies are still compensated by commissions from the carriers and the media involved, today's travelers and advertisers may sometimes wonder if the change has been very great, after all.) Ticket brokers, whose offices were scattered through the streets in the vicinity of the railroad stations in all cities of any size, provided the convenient service which American travelers demanded, and which was eventually taken over by offices run by the railroads themselves. It was not a highly ethical business, judging from the frequent complaints by travelers and the railroads themselves of scalping of tickets (which the brokers acquired through illegitimate channels) at varying discounts from the published rates. But it was a vital service in a country where people disliked to stand docilely in line. "This ticket brokerage business is of almost as great importance as it is a feature of rather unpleasant aspect," reported two executives of the Prussian State Railways whose government had sent them, in 1906, to study American railroad practices. The American's demand for quick service, his desire to make travel arrangements in advance, and the rate wars of the previous decade—all accounted for the brokers and for the brisk business in railroad tickets which even the hotel porters carried

[8] *Proceedings of the American Association of Traveling Passenger Agents, 1902–1916*, especially 1902, 1913, and 1916.

on.[9] The gullibility of the American away from home, and the existence of a large floating volume of unused special-rate tickets, return portions of excursion tickets, and the like, complicated the situation. Scalping, a simple manifestation of weak price control and poor sales management, threatened to become a national issue until the sheer volume of travel and the cementing of the communities of interest made the custom obsolete.

Phoebe Snow lives on in the annals of transportation and advertising. A mythical young lady smartly turned out in the Gibson Girl styles of the period, she tells us more than volumes can about the triumphs of travel advertising in these years. Budgets were tiny by modern standards, but the successes of the railroads in giving their routes and their trains distinctive personalities ("images," they would be called today) would excite the envy of airline executives who are fighting a losing battle to do the same with multimillion-dollar budgets. The truth is that the product almost sold itself, for Americans identified closely with their railroads and the trains that ran on them. Phoebe became such an effective symbol for the relatively clean trains of the anthracite-burning Lackawanna ("My dress stays white though I ride all night, when I take the road of anthracite") that a train was named after her. She has long since been interred beside the sleepy little boy who sold Fisk tires, but it is hard to resist even at this late date just one example of the skill with which the writer capitalized on the events of the day. At the height of the Republican state convention in Saratoga, New York, in 1910, which presaged the split in the party, Phoebe counseled the traveler from the comfort of her smoke-free observation platform:

> My policies
> Are bound to please
> No matter who
> Your nominees.
>
> With platform right
> Let all unite
> And vote for Road
> of Anthracite.[10]

[9] W. Hoff and F. Schwabach, *North American Railroads: Their Administration and Economic Policy* ["Special expert private translation"] (New York, 1906), 245–50.

[10] *NYT*, Sept. 28, 1910, 3.

IV

And what did the railroads have to sell in those years? Foreign travelers reported that American railroads were unmatched for convenience, comfort, speed, and dependability. (The safety of the trains was more debatable, but see Chapter III.) The German railway executives mentioned above were appalled at the exaggerations of the timetables (they suspected that the train crews had a different schedule from the one given to passengers), and as officials of a nationalized system they had nothing but contempt for the *Official Railway Guide*. This long-lived monthly, which has been published continuously since 1868, was and is a highly individualistic collection of the various railroads' timetables, and the maps which the roads supplied in 1906 invariably insisted that each line was the only railroad between the points that it served. But the Germans noted enviously that the traveler's baggage would be picked up at his hotel or his home, and that he need never see it again until it was delivered by the local expressman at his destination. Americans paid something extra for this convenience, but to the European traveler in 1906 the arrangement seemed well worth the cost.[11]

A few years earlier an English railroad expert had also looked at American passenger service and found it excellent. Strong competition, he noted, ensured punctuality, as did the much heavier locomotives used to pull passenger trains "that weigh nearly as much as an English freight train." Not once, he marveled, had he seen a locomotive slipping its wheels in a struggle to get out of a terminal, a familiar sight in his homeland.[12]

Only the briefest sketch of the gains in the quality of American railroad passenger service during the Progressive era can be attempted here. (The next chapter, which deals with the physical transformation of the railroads, touches on the subject.) We may note only a few of the outstanding examples of the more luxurious accommodations and the shortened travel times which were introduced. A feature which Europe-

[11] Hoff and Schwabach, *North American Railroads,* 252, 264–65.

[12] William M. Acworth, "American and English Railways Compared" [reprinted from the London *Times*] (Chicago, 1898), 8–10.

ans repeatedly noted with envy was the universality of the Pullman car. With the greater distances involved in the United States, such facilities obviously were a necessity, but at the same time it was noted that the absence of any kind of class system on American railroads encouraged their more general use. Before World War I, in fact, there was only one basic railroad fare, which, without further charge, was good in chair cars. Pullman sleeping car or parlor car luxury was available for a small additional space charge. With rates even more rigidly regulated than freight charges, passenger travel became a greater bargain with each passing year of the Progressive era.

The first all-Pullman train had been placed in service between Chicago and New York in 1881. The pride of the Pennsylvania Railroad, it was the first train anywhere to attempt the same variety of conveniences as a hotel. In 1902 the age of luxury rail travel was ushered in with the inauguration of nonstop, all-Pullman trains on a twenty-hour schedule between New York and Chicago by the two arch-rivals, the Pennsylvania and the New York Central. The *Twentieth Century Limited* and the *Pennsylvania* (later the *Broadway*) *Limited* thus began a competition which in its intensity and the publicity it attracted during the next half-century was equaled only by what was happening in transatlantic steamship travel at the same time. By 1910 all-Pullman limited trains were in operation between Chicago and Los Angeles on the Santa Fe, and so popular did they become that at times there were as many as forty-five sections strung out over the line at one stage or another of their sixty-three-hour trip. The Harvey Girls who ministered to the dusty, tired travelers at hostels along the way had given up the ghost. By 1900 the symbol of luxury travel was the Negro dining car waiter or Pullman porter, whose genial smile and even temper, considering the poverty from which he had generally escaped, were probably genuine.[13]

There seems to be no way of assessing the over-all trend in the quality and quantity of railroad passenger service in these years. There is no doubt that where the service was poor, it was very bad indeed. As

[13] M. A. Whiting, "Fifty Years of Pullman Travel," *Stone and Webster Journal* (Dec., 1931), 835–41; Russell Doubleday, "New York to Chicago—20 Hours," *World's Work,* IV (Aug., 1902), 2455–62; Henry M. McClure, "Shortening Time Across the Continent: The Twentieth Century Train," *National Geographic,* XIII (Aug., 1902), 319–21; James Marshall, *Santa Fe: The Railroad That Built an Empire* (New York, 1945), 290, 302.

early as 1900 some branch lines were heading for oblivion, and on those lines, as well as on many another road, service probably never advanced much beyond late nineteenth-century standards. The rails, almost literally, went everywhere, but not with the same kind of service. Many passenger lines had never been profitable, and by World War I the obligation to haul people was already threatening to become an incubus for all of the railroads. After 1907, abandonments, notably in New England, where the New Haven had consolidated numerous formerly competitive short lines, became more and more common. The automobile had begun to make inroads by 1916, while the electric interurban systems had gobbled up large chunks of the steady, highly profitable local traffic by that year.[14]

The Pullman car, without which much travel in America would have been unthinkable, was also becoming a burden by 1917. The Pullman Company itself prospered mightily as the number of its cars in operation climbed from an estimated 2,500 in 1900 to 7,580 by 1917.[15] Contracts between the railroads and the Pullman Company were negotiated individually, but in general they provided that the railroads would haul the cars and maintain their running gear without charge to or by Pullman, while the sleeping car company would see that the interior of the cars measured up to the first-class hotel which had been George Pullman's standard. The railroad pocketed the railroad fare; Pullman, the space charge. The advantages to the railroads were that they could offer their patrons sleeping car accommodations without the bother of actually operating such a service (which they had never been very successful at), and they did not have to provide a coach for the passengers

[14] These lines, which proliferated outside of the regulatory powers of the national government, must rank as one of the most meteoric industries in history. Technologically impossible until the last decade of the nineteenth century, they flourished virtually everywhere in a burst of speculative construction until, in the third decade of the twentieth, they quickly succumbed to the automobile. They have been exhaustively treated in George W. Hilton and John F. Due, *The Electric Interurban Railways in America* (Stanford, 1960), and more informally in John A. Miller, *Fares, Please!* (New York, 1941). That they were not confined to densely populated areas is clearly revealed in Allison Chandler, *Trolley Through the Countryside* (Denver, 1963), which chronicles the interurban in Oklahoma, Kansas, and southwestern Missouri. The New York subway system, which was extended to the edges of the city in these years, similarly deprived the area's railroads of a highly profitable short-haul business.

[15] The Pullman Co., *Annual Statements,* 1899–1900 to 1916–17.

to ride in. In high-density service the railroads could generally bargain for a share of the gross above a certain minimum, while on some poorly traveled routes they had to pay something for the use of the cars. By 1917 Congress had become sufficiently disturbed by the unprofitability of passenger service to listen intently as Julius Kruttschnitt, head of the Southern Pacific, explained to the Newlands Committee why sleeping car service was a growing problem. The cars were much heavier than ordinary equipment, he noted, while the number of passengers carried was much smaller. (A standard Pullman consisting of twelve open sections and a private "drawing room" could comfortably accommodate only about twenty-seven passengers.) "There is not much in it for the railroads . . . there is no money in it," Mr. Kruttschnitt declared bluntly, but he quickly added, "it is our duty to provide the public with sleeping cars." [16] Fifty years later the problem would still be unsolved.

V

Up ahead of the Pullmans and the coaches, however, were some of the most frustrating aspects of railroading. In the early days of the railroads their mail and express services, which were a first giant step toward unification of the nation, had been their most glorious achievement. By 1913 government policy in respect to these services had reached the peak of insanity, while railroad officials wrung their hands in despair. The Hepburn Act of 1906 had brought express companies under regulation by the ICC, which effectively froze rates until the war. These independent companies collected high-class package freight at shippers' establishments, brought it to the passenger terminals, and loaded it aboard cars provided by the railroad. At the destination they performed the service in reverse. Wayside stations might have only one factotum who performed all of these duties and many more. The most common arrangement was an even split of the revenues between railroad and express company. Despite their inability to raise rates, however, the railroads and the leading express companies earned money on what was an increasingly indispensable service, not only to individuals

[16] *Hearings before the Joint Committee on Interstate and Foreign Commerce,* 64th Cong., 1st and 2d Sess. (Washington, 1917), 1043–46.

but especially to department stores and specialized mail-order houses.

Meanwhile the railroads were worried about the mail situation. The long-standing arrangement between government and railroads was that the carriers would receive a flat rate, based on the average weight of mail being carried on a specific route. The catch was that the tedious job of weighing was to be performed only once every four years, and in 1913 another weighing was not due for two years. Meanwhile it was common knowledge that the total volume of mail was growing mightily, but the Postmaster General clung to his technical advantage with all of the tenacity of a private businessman who has just bested another in a deal.

On January 1, 1913, the new parcel-post service was inaugurated by the postmaster in Washington, who mailed a silver loving cup to his counterpart in New York. To historians the new service is one of the golden achievements of the Progressive era. To the railroads and express companies it was a disaster. The parcel post, of course, was to be carried by the railroads as part of the regular mail. Whether a spiteful Congress wished to exact a service without paying for it, or whether Congress naïvely underestimated the initial volume of parcels, we do not know. But we do know that mails tonnage shot up some 25 per cent almost immediately, while express volume plummeted accordingly. Of course, the parcel-post act had provided for *some* additional volume. The Postmaster General, at his discretion, was authorized to increase mails payments by not more than 5 per cent. Even if this relief had been granted, which it was not, it would have amounted to only two million dollars. Meanwhile the loss in revenue to the railroads and the express companies was estimated at fifty million dollars. Congress had taken the parcels out of the express cars, where the railroads were paid for carrying them, and placed them in the U.S. mail cars, where they were not. It was as simple as that. And the legislative atrocity would not be rectified until the war had begun to sweep away the excesses of archaic Progressivism. The fine old Adams Express Company, which had served the Northeast's express needs for over a generation, watched helplessly as profits of $1.2 million in 1912 were converted to a deficit of $800,000 by 1914. American Express saw its handsome profit of $2.4 million in 1912 almost wiped out. The United States Express Company, after a parting observation that parcel post, so far from being

a great boon for the general public, was in reality a public subsidy to
the department stores, went into liquidation. Next year the ICC reduced
rates by 20 per cent on what express business was left.[17]

But archaic Progressivism was not yet through with its reorganization of the express business. Early in 1914 Congress extended parcel-
post service to cover butter, eggs, fruit, vegetables, and poultry in the
first and second zones, and specified that farmers need not pack their
produce any more elaborately than they had for the express companies.
Then someone in the Post Office Department had a bright idea. Why
not remove the middleman between consumer and farmer altogether?
Why not display in each post office a list of farmers who were interested in mailing eggs, milk, cream, and butter once or twice a week to
"subscribers" in the city? This system was actually tried in ten test cities, but with what malodorous results is not known.[18]

There appears to have been only one constructive aspect of public
policy in these departments of railroad service. In 1913 the roads peti-
tioned the ICC for permission to put volume as well as weight limits on
baggage, of which up to 150 pounds was carried free on a full-rate
ticket. Commissioner Edgar E. Clark, reporting favorably, noted that
"with the development of what may be termed 'commercial travel' " the
privilege had become a burden to the railroads. Indeed it had. One Chicago dry goods house had salesmen constantly on the road, with a total
of 2,000 sample trunks. Trains were being delayed at way stations while
crew members pitched in to help the lone baggageman wrestle with the
growing mountain of baggage. The last straw, entered in evidence before the Commission in a hilarious photograph, showed a millinery
salesman insisting on checking as baggage his samples of the mammoth
hats then in vogue. Piled up on the baggage truck beside him were
twenty-three hatboxes.[19]

[17] *Commercial and Financial Chronicle* (hereinafter referred to as *CFC*), XCVI
(Jan. 4, 1913), 40; March 15, 1913, 761; XCVII (Aug. 16, 1913), 419; Nov. 22,
1913, 1501; Oct. 4, 1913, 959; XCIX (Dec. 5, 1914), 1670; Nov. 14, 1914, 1448.
An executive of the United States Express Company charged that no sooner had
the express companies complied with the antirebating law than John Wanamaker
Company, formerly one of their largest customers, began to lobby for a parcel-
post act. Notwithstanding the fact that the express companies were deprived of
the "cream" of their business, the railroads still had to provide a service for items
which could not conveniently or safely be handled in the mails.

[18] *CFC*, XCVIII (March 21, 1914), 883; March 28, 1914, 971.

[19] 26 ICC 292, 297–98.

VI

Superior Privy Councilor Hoff and his traveling companion, in their study of American railroads, could not contain their enthusiasm at the freight operations they observed. What they saw reflected the fact that, whereas by 1906 Europe was retreating at top speed from free trade and the advantages of regional specialization of which Adam Smith had spoken so persuasively, the United States, "a young giant destined to do great things in this world," was involved in no such economic retrogression. Freight transportation in the United States, they marveled, was ten times as important per capita as it was in Germany, a nation whose rapid and impressively successful industrialization in the late nineteenth century otherwise paralleled so closely that of the United States. That American railroads had many problems, most notably the rebuilding of a railroad system which to the Germans' practiced eyes was manifestly inadequate to the demands the new century was making upon it, Hoff and Schwabach emphasized freely. That the Americans were equal to the challenge they seemed to have no doubt.[20]

This peculiar dependence upon an efficient freight transportation system in the United States is less well appreciated today than in 1906. It seems to have escaped general notice that the United States has the largest continental land mass in the world with the human and natural resources necessary for intensive economic development, within which commerce is free from the restrictions that characterize peoples living under divided sovereignties.[21] Perhaps it is this insensitivity to the American situation that prompts incredulity at the rate of growth of freight traffic in the twenty years before World War I. Whereas the gross national product roughly doubled (in dollars of constant purchasing power) in the period, railroad ton-miles virtually doubled in *each* of

---

[20] Hoff and Schwabach, *North American Railroads*, 413–14.

[21] The economic geographers are perhaps most aware of this unique situation; see, for example, Harold H. McCarty, *The Geographic Basis of American Economic Life* (New York, 1940), 31–32. I do not mean to suggest that the states and, indeed, even smaller political divisions have been unable to erect trade barriers from time to time, but it seems clear that the sum total of these activities is inconsequential.

the two decades.[22] Such an impressive growth from a well-established base (the railroads were, after all, seventy years old in 1900) is unique in American economic history.

VII

Things had not always been so good for the railroads. Traffic grew consistently throughout the nineteenth century, it is true, but railroad mileage grew even faster. The competitive situation had changed almost daily in the hectic decades between the two great depressions of 1873 and 1893. When the Baltimore & Ohio laid its own tracks into Chicago, William H. Vanderbilt had moaned that now there were four trunk line railroads between New York and Chicago, with traffic enough for only two. Pools, or cartels, as they are perhaps more accurately called, were almost invariably ineffectual in stabilizing rates, and railroad men were wont to remark ruefully that it was a wise man who could guess what tomorrow's rate would be.[23]

Why were the bare-fisted railroad executives of the nineteenth century, to whom historians have been so eager to attribute the most cloven-hoofed talent for conspiracy, unable to keep their pools in being? The answer seems to lie in the undeveloped state of the management structure of the industry. The fact is that the loose organization of the traffic solicitation system almost guaranteed that rates would be cut, unfair rebates offered, and all manner of favors granted to get business.

[22] ICC, *Annual Statistical Reports*. This view is totally at variance with that advanced by Robert W. Fogel, *Railroads and American Economic Growth* (Baltimore, 1964), 223 and *passim*. The basic methodological approach of Fogel has been seriously questioned in Peter D. McClelland, "Railroads, American Growth, and the New Economic History: A Critique," *Journal of Economic History*, XXVIII (March, 1968), 102–23. But even if Fogel's estimate of the "social saving" of the railroads (5 per cent of gross national product in 1890) is accepted, it would be wrong to suppose that such a saving was small. It was, in fact, equal to one-half of net investment. If this growth factor had indeed been only one-half of its actual value, the result, compounded over the twenty-year period of Fogel's analysis (much less back to 1850, by which time railroads were already of critical importance), would be a gross national product in 1890 far below the actual figure.

[23] Paul W. MacAvoy, *The Economic Effects of Regulation: The Trunk-line Railroad Cartels and the Interstate Commerce Commission before 1900* (Cambridge, Mass., 1965), is a study of the forces that caused pools to fall apart.

The modern railroad traffic department, with its strict surveillance and post-audit features extending right down to the local freight agent, is a product of the Progressive era, when the railroads were choking on a volume of traffic which they could barely handle at the published rates, and when the federal government was finally moving to enforce the anti-discrimination provisions of legislation that had been on the books since 1887. But a man who could bring in the business when others failed could expect special treatment in the cold world of the late nineteenth century. Indeed, he remains in great demand. Ribald jokes about the independence of the demon salesman from rules that apply to ordinary folk still abound. Give a man the agency in a town or city which originates a substantial freight volume, and which is served by two or more railroads; put him exclusively on a generous commission; and inform him that the tonnage he brings to the road will be the basis for continuing the arrangement; and you have the perfect recipe for discrimination between shippers. It was a climate in which even the principled man would be quickly corrupted. Charles Francis Adams had seen the problem clearly:

The whole complicated system under which through or competitive railroad business is done is curiously vicious and extravagant, and must be radically reformed as a preliminary to any final settlement. [There is at present] a vast army of subordinates whose very existence depends on that not being done, which those controlling the lines which feed them are continually trying to do. . . . Walk down the leading business streets [and] see that a great number of expensive offices bear the signs of railroads and of car and dispatch companies [whose cost] comes out of the railroad corps. . . . The interests of the retainers and the corps are exactly antagonistic—the first are always working to bring about railroad wars . . . while the last are always trying to effect combinations. . . . His day [the "fighting superintendent"] is over.[24]

Chauncey Depew, after twenty-five years with the New York Central during this anarchic era, was equally sure in 1892 that such days were over. "Freight agents, clothed with unlimited discretion, exercised their favoritism or their animosities upon individuals and communities; but such officers are now as extinct as the Mastodon," he insisted.[25] But

[24] Charles Francis Adams, Jr., *Railroads: Their Origins and Problems* (rev. ed., New York, 1893), 117, 192, 194, 196.

[25] Chauncey M. Depew, "A Retrospect of Twenty-five Years with the New York Central Railroad and Its Allied Lines, 1866–1891" (New York, 1892).

they were far from extinct. The onset of the depression the very next year brought back all of the old pressures from big shippers, and all of the abuses by which their business was sought, as strong as ever. In 1903 Congress passed the Elkins Act, which made rebating a crime on the part of both the seeker and the granter of the unfair rate. Three years later, in 1906, the railroads would still be dissatisfied with the ICC's record of enforcement, but by then the perfection of the community-of-interests technique, and the advent of a volume of freight which threatened to overburden the railroads, had already gone a long way toward solving the problem. By 1910 the patent ability of the railroads to agree among themselves on a uniformly higher tariff and put it into effect, rather than their inability to collect the published rate, would be viewed as the nation's number-one domestic problem.

VIII

Railroad rate-making systems have always been a mystery to the great majority of people, and it is probably safe, and not unfair, to say that the level of understanding has not been high among historians. Just as it is said that there is no taxicab driver who knows all of Brooklyn, so there is probably no rate expert who understands the entire edifice of freight rates. It was virtually impossible to get agreement in the Progressive era on whether rates were too high or too low, or whether, indeed, they were in the process of going up or down. The fact is that the rate structure was a living organism, with continuous internal change giving the outward impression of relative stability. Some of the leading authorities in the country were convinced that rates were on the upswing around 1905. But the economist and statistician of the ICC, Henry Carter Adams, concluded that such was not the case. During the monumental political backing and filling between 1904 and 1906 which eventually produced the Hepburn Act, the Senate had held hearings on the question of bestowing on the ICC the power to fix maximum rates. Faced with five volumes of testimony on the eve of adjournment in July, 1905, Chairman Stephen B. Elkins of the Senate Committee on Interstate Commerce wrote in desperation to Adams, asking him and his assistant, H. T. Newcomb, to prepare a digest of the material, and, while they were at it, to prepare for the Congress a study of the entire rate-making problem. The result was a penetrating analysis of the system which reveals how thoroughly the lawmakers, shippers, and railroad men failed to anticipate the conditions and events of 1910–17.[26] Adams wrote:

It was generally conceded by all witnesses that the general level of rates is not higher than can be justified, and even those who argue that there are instances of rates which may be called excessive in themselves with few exceptions agree that differences in charges for different services constitute the greatest source of complaint. . . .

There was also a good deal of controversy concerning recent changes in rates, as to whether the general movement has been downward or upward since January 1, 1900, when certain changes in classification were made. . . . The testimony includes numerous illustrations of specific rates which have been advanced and at least equally numerous examples of those which have been reduced. . . . With very few exceptions the witnesses before the Commission declared that "rebates" have either wholly ceased or are much less frequent than formerly.[27]

Adams gave his statistician's approval to the use of the ton-mile average as a trustworthy indicator of what was happening to rates over the long run. While changes in the make-up of freight traffic may very well produce changes in average ton-mile rates that have nothing to do with actual rate changes, he noted, the bias, if any, was upward, because traffic was growing fastest in areas with higher proportions of high-rate traffic. The change since 1900, Adams concluded, was no more (and probably less) than the 7.73 per cent increase in the average ton-mile. And, he pointed out significantly, when the greater increase in the general level of prices was considered, there had really been a decrease in freight rates. Dr. Adams, unfortunately, was shouting into the wind.[28]

[26] *Regulation of Railway Rates. Hearings before the Committee on Interstate Commerce, Senate of the United States, December 16, 1904, to May 23, 1905, on Bills to Amend the Interstate Commerce Act*, Senate Document 243, 59th Cong., 1st Sess. (5 vols., Washington, 1905), hereinafter referred to as "1905 Senate Hearings"; and Henry Carter Adams, *Digest of Hearings on Railway Rates. Testimony before Senate Committee on Interstate Commerce, 1904*, Senate Document 244 [Vol. 21], 59th Cong., 1st Sess. (Washington, 1905), hereinafter referred to as Adams, *Digest*.

[27] Adams, *Digest*, 76–77.

[28] *Ibid.*, 77–78. At the height of the Senate battle over the Mann-Elkins Act in 1910, Senator Robert M. La Follette could slip entirely the surly bonds of fact:

As "indeterminate" as rates might appear to be in theory, however, in practice they were established. The tariffs were published and more and more rigidly adhered to as the tempo of economic activity mounted in these years, and somehow the great majority of shippers and consignees were kept satisfied. How did the system work? Adams' excellent study revealed what an art rate-making was, and what the Commission would be getting into if it should seek to tell the railroads what a reasonable rate was in a particular instance, and especially if it should insist that that rate be maintained inflexibly over a long period of time. Rate-making, in fact, had been a matter for joint discussion between various interested parties ever since the days of the pools. Although the Act of 1887 made pools illegal, it was clear that the only people with the technical knowledge necessary to comply with the requirement that tariffs be published were the rate clerks and traffic men who had struggled to keep the pools together. Their work, therefore, became the cornerstone on which the complex and highly eclectic rate structure has rested ever since.

There were two kinds of rates. Commodity rates, which were quoted individually for a specific commodity, accounted for most of the ton-miles of freight carried. Class rates were a more sophisticated system in which an attempt was made to categorize the myriad articles that make up the commerce of a great nation into relatively few classes, on the basis of value of the article (the origin of the "what the traffic will bear" principle), bulk in relation to weight, fragility, perishability, special handling requirements, and a host of other factors. Many of these rates were quoted for "LCL" (less than a carload) and in full carload shipments, the latter rate constituting a substantial discount.

The country was divided, for rate-making purposes, into three great areas (Official Classification Territory, east of the Mississippi and north of the Ohio and Potomac rivers; Western Territory; and Southern

---

"The average family pays today," he ranted at one point, "a total freight charge amounting to over 38% more than the average family paid in 1900. The rates are going higher every day, and men on this floor, supposed to represent the public interest, doggedly resist an amendment to halt this advance." *Congressional Record* (hereinafter referred to as *CR*), 61st Cong., 2d Sess. (May 26, 1910), 6908. The average ton-mile rate in 1900 was 0.729 cents (about seven and a quarter mills); in 1910, after a long-term rise in prices, rates averaged 0.753 cents.

Territory), but within each of these there were a number of freight bureaus or traffic associations which were occupied in gathering the information necessary to the making of intelligent rates, an amazing process
which involved nearly every trade association, chamber of commerce,
and influential businessman at frequent intervals. In the highly organized Official Classification Territory there were almost 10,000 articles
arranged into only six classes; in the Western Territory, 8,000 articles
fell into ten classes; and in the Southern Territory, there were 14 classes
for only 3,700 items.

Early in the history of railroads, rates had been scaled quite rigidly
to mileage, but it had soon become apparent that gross disparities in
rates, not related to either the cost or the value of the service, resulted
from such a procedure. Ultimately the rates charged by the trunk lines
(Pennsylvania, New York Central, and B. & O.) became the standard
for the Northeast, and a rate between two points (e.g., Cleveland and
New York) would be fixed as a percentage (in this case 71 per cent) of
the Chicago–New York rate, which, for first class, was 75 cents a hundredweight. In the case of traffic confined entirely to the local stations
of a given railroad, the rate was entirely up to that carrier and its customers, and thereby hung the long, wearying tale of long- and short-
haul discrimination. In addition, there were East Coast port differentials: on shipments from Chicago, for example, Philadelphia was six
cents lower than New York and Baltimore was eight cents lower, reflecting the crushing superiority of the port of New York. Analogous to
these were route differentials whereby the 75-cent New York–Chicago
rate on the three trunk lines became 70 cents on the Erie, Lehigh Valley, West Shore, and Lackawanna, 67 cents on the Ontario and Western, and 65 cents on the Chesapeake & Ohio, reflecting the disadvantages of shipping by these longer, slower routes. The two most
significant features of this structure (the complexities of which have
only been suggested) are, first, that it was the outcome of thousands of
on-the-spot compromises among a bewildering variety of interests, that
is, shippers, railroads, and localities; and second, that by 1900 the system had come to represent to most businessmen the best arrangement
they were going to get. It was, in short, the product of enlightened flexibility of bargaining combined with a respect for the historical validity

of existing arrangements. Woe unto him who would attempt to eliminate the former while retaining the latter! [29]

Almost no one thought in terms of entire rate schedules in the
pre-Hepburn days. Controversies were matters of individual rates, and
more particularly of classification, because a first-class rate, for example, might be "reasonable" for one article, but not another. Adams told
the Senators, in effect, to forget about the possibility that conferring the
power to fix maximum rates would tempt the ICC to invalidate entire
schedules. "While it is clear that these [complaints to the ICC under
the Act of 1887] might . . . challenge the reasonableness of an entire
schedule of rates," he wrote, "it is a fact that during the history of the
act no such proceeding has been brought." [30]

IX

So it was a matter of thousands—theoretically millions—of individual bargains struck between railroads and shippers. But was it a fair
fight? Did the railroads not have all the power? They certainly had a
great deal. As veteran Commissioner Martin A. Knapp told the Senate
in 1905:

Do you realize what an enormous power that is putting into the hands of
the railroads? That is the power of tearing down and building up. That is
the power that might very well control the distribution of industries, and I
. . . think on the whole it is remarkable that the power has been so slightly
abused. . . . Undoubtedly . . . they [the railroad men] try as honestly and
as conscientiously as men can to make fair adjustments of their charges. But
suppose they do not. Is there not to be any redress for those who suffer?
That is really the problem.[31]

His statement was an eloquent appeal for an "ombudsman" form of rate
regulation, which seemed to be almost exactly what was needed.

It is a crude analysis of the situation, however, which concludes
that the power was all on one side. Consider the actual rate-making
process, as described to the Senate in 1905 by Edward P. Vining, recently retired after a lifelong career as traffic manager for several railroads:

[29] Adams, *Digest*, 57–75.   [30] *Ibid.*, 25.   [31] 1905 Senate Hearings, 3298.

There are several thousand of these general [traffic] officers, and each of them has under him a large force of station agents and other employees to report to him and assist him in the proper performance of his work. These men are scattered throughout the country . . . and there is no place of importance whatever that has not at least a station agent who is interested in the prosperity of his town. . . . He is . . . prepared to listen to any representation that [local shippers] may make as to disadvantages which limit their business and [how] it could be increased.

These are reported to the railroad headquarters, and it is the business of the head of the traffic department to give them prompt and careful consideration. Woe be to him if he does not! His position is naturally dependent upon his success in assisting the development of the natural resources of his road. If the business does not increase, the railroad directors naturally look about for another man who knows how to bring about an increase, and the incompetent traffic man thus loses his place.[32]

We are almost as far, however, from answering the question of how rates were actually set as we were. That is not surprising, inasmuch as the ICC ultimately concluded that there was no objective method of judging a rate "reasonable." In his valedictory to the ICC, Chairman Thomas M. Cooley had warned that the cost incurred by the railroad in providing a service was no guide. On this point he seems to have been on firm ground. Professor Frank W. Taussig of Harvard had pointed out in 1891 that most of a railroad's costs are *joint* costs; that is, they are incurred in the providing of a number of different services, and assigning each piece of business its "proper" share of fixed costs would always be an arbitrary procedure, as, indeed, it remains today.[33] Discussions such as this always come around sooner or later to the threadbare old principle, "what the traffic will bear." Oversimplified, this means simply charging a man whatever it is worth to him to have his goods in one place rather than in another. The principle is beautifully logical. What businessman does not seek to charge for his product the value which his customers place on it? Why should the railroads be any different? Of course, one must take the long view. It would not do to charge a farmer, for example, all but a few cents of the market price for his grain at destination (even though it is worthless to him at the farm) because he would not stay in the wheat-growing business at that rate.

[32] Adams, *Digest*, 13.

[33] Joseph Dorfman, *The Economic Mind in American Civilization* (5 vols., New York, 1946–59), III, 258.

Furthermore, wrote a contemporary commentator, competition greatly softened the principle in practice. "It is a case of charging what the traffic will bear without being diverted; not what it will bear without being destroyed," he said. But even where there was no competition, railroad executives emphasized that a rate which did not permit the shipper to make a profit, stay in business, and grow was not a reasonable rate from the viewpoint of either the shipper or the railroad.[34]

Under the regulatory system which the nation established in 1906, the ICC was to perform the role of ombudsman. It was not to usurp the actual rate-making function, but to confine itself to relieving individuals from the indifference, incompetence, and malice which in the real world frequently impede the smooth workings of economic theory. What problem remained, then, to cause such dissatisfaction among the railroads' customers? The problem was the soggy cake of custom which in the end seems to determine men's destinies more than theories or laws. There were, after all, many shippers and only a few railroads, and the "general public" was a potential ally of the shippers whenever it should become worth their while to woo that public. Shippers with favorable rates—favorable, that is, relative to rates paid by competitors in other cities, or in relation to the price which they received for their goods in the market, which for most businessmen had increased steadily during these years—were dead set against any increases. The ICC would insist time and again upon the desirability of maintaining the rate relationships to which business had adjusted itself in the twenty-five or thirty years since they had been established. At the same time, shippers who were in a relatively unfavorable situation were determined to redress their position, even though they were, for the most part, better off than they had been in years. That is why the old long-haul–short-haul discrimination problem, simmering for a decade since the Supreme Court had emasculated the provision of the Act of 1887 which dealt with it, boiled over in these years.[35]

No practice, not even rebating, looked so wrong on its face as the practice of charging more (relatively, and frequently absolutely) for a short haul confined to the lines of the railroad company than for a long

[34] Harry Gunnison Brown, *Transportation Rates and Their Regulation* (New York, 1916), 180; Adams, *Digest,* 12–13.

[35] 169 U.S. 144, The Alabama Midland case.

haul which the shipper was free to send over a competing line; and yet
no rate-making practice was more firmly rooted in the economic realities of railroad competition. The controversy would hinge, ultimately,
on whether the Commission should be directed to abolish such practices
absolutely, without regard to whether the long- and the short-haul business dealings took place under substantially similar conditions of competition. In the end, however, the problem for the railroads was simply
how to raise a general schedule of rates which their customers had enjoyed without a change for thirty years, a problem the railroads would
fail to solve. Meanwhile, shippers aggressively pursued their own interests in rate-reduction cases brought before the rejuvenated post-Hepburn Commission, many of which were successful. And thousands more
continued to practice on a wide front all of the arts of subterfuge (mis-
labeling, fraudulent billing, blind packaging, et cetera) which, more
likely than not, they had been taught by an ambitious freight agent in
the bad old days.[36]

X

As the pressures on railroad men to raise rates became more intense after the panic of 1907, the leader in the industry's efforts to
swing public sentiment to its side was William C. Brown, senior vice-
president and heir-apparent to the presidency of the New York Central.
Under his auspices a booklet entitled "Freight Rate Primer" was widely
circulated. It sought to show that the cost of a 10 per cent raise in rates
to consumers would be so small as to be barely noticeable. "Lesson
One" showed eleven men in different walks of life who lived in the
Mississippi Valley. Their clothes, from the mason's coveralls to the
businessman's somber, tightly cut suit, although they were made in New
England, would cost an average of only one cent more per man if rates
were raised. Out in western Iowa a farmer operated a $130 harvester

[36] Ralph L. Dewey, *The Long and Short Haul Principle of Rate Regulation* (Columbus, 1935), 14–15 and *passim,* clarifies many aspects of this knotty problem.
Isaac Beverly Lake, *Discrimination by Railroads and Other Public Utilities* (Raleigh, 1947), reveals that there is no substitute for a knowledge of the grass-roots
practices which gave birth to discrimination. For some examples of fraudulent
practices of shippers, see *CFC,* XCV (July 27, 1912), 197.

which had been shipped 300 miles from the factory to his town at a total cost to the farmer of $1.76. The higher rate would have increased the cost of the harvester seventeen and one-half cents. The pamphlet failed to say what had happened to the price of the harvester f.o.b. Chicago since 1897. Perhaps Brown realized that the farmer was quite aware that harvesters were costing more all the time, and would reason that if the freight was the *only* element in the delivered price that he could do anything about, then he would be all the more justified in trying to keep the railroads from raising their rates. It was indeed a very weak position in which the carriers found themselves, but just how weak they did not yet realize.

Other examples of the impact of a 10 per cent increase in rates showed that a $60 cooking range would cost twenty-five cents more; a $30 icebox, seven and one-half cents; a man's $10 to $35 suit, one-third cent; an eight-pound roast (large enough for the big families of the era), worth $1.92, one-half cent more. Working with U.S. government figures, the writer asserted, he had found that the average yearly expenditures of a family of five for freightable expenses was $446, and the freight costs thereon, $9.90, or about 1.4 per cent of their total annual consumption expenditures. The rate increase, in short, would cost the family one dollar a year more.[37]

Brown, however, had missed the point. No one, except possibly someone as unhampered by the facts as Senator La Follette, doubted that the increased cost to consumers would be small if carried forward to them. Now, it is true that the opponents of rate increases would talk out of both sides of their mouths on the question of who would pay the higher freight charges, but it seems that shippers were convinced that they would have to absorb them. James T. Hoile, secretary of the Manufacturers Association of New York, had written to New York Central president W. H. Newman to remind him that, despite "panics and business booms," rates had remained unchanged for thirty years, and therefore the panic of 1907 could not logically be made the basis for an increase. Besides, an increase would hurt business. Brown, to whom

[37] Warren J. Lynch, "Freight Rate Primer" (Chicago, 1908), pages not numbered. The ICC never made a study of the potential impact of rate increases. No such information, indeed, would have been of any use to the Commission in its interpretation of the regulatory laws adopted in the Progressive era.

Newman had referred the letter, wrote, "The whole fabric of freight rates, from the first shipment of raw material, is simply a transfer or carrying forward of freight charges, until it reaches the final purchaser or consumer, and he pays the freight." To Charles T. Page, chairman of the executive committee of the Leather Belting Manufacturers Association, Brown wrote that whereas freight rates had remained at their 1899 levels, wages paid by the railroads had increased by one-third to one-half, and materials anywhere from 20 per cent to 95 per cent. The Central, he could not refrain from remarking significantly, bought $75,000 worth of leather belting a year, at prices 25 per cent higher than in 1899. Brown's argument was a strong one, but Page's trade-association hide was thick. Twitting Brown for making their correspondence public, he said, "Your conclusion that the 'customer will pay the freight,' at least so far as the leather belting industry is concerned, is fanciful and inaccurate." In his industry, he asserted with an appealing lack of sophistication, the manufacturer paid the incoming freight, and "delivers the goods." Besides, he argued defensively, belting prices had dropped 20 per cent since the panic. B. D. Rising, who operated a paper mill in Housatonic, Massachusetts, introduced a new angle into the argument. Freight rate increases could not be passed along to the customer for the very reason that they were *too small,* he argued. What he meant was that a luxury product like the high-quality writing paper which he made had to be sold at a good, round, dignified figure. His argument illustrated the fact that the smooth demand and supply curves which economists delight in have little application to the real world. But perhaps Rising had a point of sorts, after all. As a distinguished public relations man would tell the railroad executives in a few years, the public is not interested in logical arguments if they lead to an increase in prices.[38]

Who was right? Everybody and nobody. The blind men were fumbling at different parts of the elephant, and each earnestly described the very different beast which he "saw." The fact is that to generalize about the incidence of an increase in rates was and is futile. The concept of a general level of rates is a product of the analytical mind, useful for generalizations, but describing something which has no actual existence.

[38] These exchanges are printed in William C. Brown, *Freight Rates and Railway Conditions: Addresses and Correspondence, 1908–1909* (New York, 1909), 30, 41, 52, 68–69, 70–88, 89–90, 110.

Every shipper, every product, every pair of shipping and destination points was and is a separate economic problem—a microcosm. In the "long run" (which is a period long enough for theories to work themselves out), all costs, obviously, must be borne by the consumer, which simply means all of us. In the "short run," however, it seems clear that *whether* a freight rate increase is passed along by adding it to the selling cost, or absorbed by the shipper (i.e., added to production costs), the result is a decline in net revenue to the shipper. In the first case, under the assumption of the familiar negatively-sloped demand curve, a price increase means that the number of units demanded will be smaller. In the second, assuming the classic U-shaped unit cost curve, the curve will be raised equally at all points, all firms will make correspondingly smaller net profits, and the marginal firm will succumb. But, one might have argued, a *general* rate increase would not only have been very small but would have left everyone in the same relative position as before. No practical man of business would have accepted such an argument. The steady inflation with which businessmen had been contending for ten years had left some of them worse off than others. It was possible that a general rate increase would have worked the same way. It is no consolation to be told that the stream in which one is drowning averages only three feet in depth. Another aspect of the problem, not instantly recognizable, is the fact that a shipper who had to transport his goods a greater distance to market than his competitors had enjoyed a constantly improving situation, because the difference between his higher rate and that of his competitors, *as a percentage of the delivered price of his goods,* had constantly declined as prices rose. A general rate increase would have rudely deprived him of that happy state of affairs.

In a larger sense, however, it was equally fatuous for shippers to suppose that the increased costs of doing business on the railroad, unlike all other costs in life, could be avoided. The visiting German admirers of American railroads had warned Americans what to expect if enormous capital resources did not continue to flow into the railroad industry. They had barely recovered from the gastronomic shock which a trip to Germany on the North German Lloyd line entailed when their predictions began to be borne out. The winter of 1906–7 marked the coincidence of the normal seasonal traffic peak and the highest level of economic activity which the United States (and, in fact, the entire Western world) had ever seen. America's railroads stiffened for the blow, stumbled, and almost fell. Impressive as the expansion and improvement program of the previous decade had been, it had not been enough. Delays in transit were bad, but they were not the major problem. Shippers, their factories and warehouses jammed with merchandise with which Americans planned to celebrate what Mr. Dooley called "this pleasant Christmas," could not get cars in which to load their goods. The eastern railroads, after struggling for ten years to bring their fleets up to the strength which their own traffic demanded, watched in helpless indignation as their less provident western brothers calmly held on to the easterners' cars (which they regularly received in interline traffic), refusing to return them promptly as they were required to do under the rules of the American Railway Association. The Pennsylvania and the New York Central were hard hit, especially when midwestern roads (whose financial situation, it would develop, was skidding fastest of all) hung on to scarce coal cars. Tempers flared so badly at emergency meetings of the Association that outsiders had to be barred from the sessions. The per diem rate (the rental which a railroad paid for each day that it held another's car beyond the stipulated unloading time) was supposed to be punitive in its effects, but it had turned out to be an inexpensive means of supplementing many a railroad's inadequate fleet. It was raised, and raised again, to no avail.[39]

Theodore Roosevelt, furious at a situation which threatened the tranquillity of his remarkably felicitous years in the White House, turned Franklin K. Lane loose on the railroads. The ambitious Interstate Commerce Commissioner, looking ahead to the presidential election year of 1908, was happy to oblige the President with a crusading investigation of the railroads' failure to carry the nation's burdens. But what he and his fellow Commissioners heard was not reassuring. Howard Elliott of the Northern Pacific said that the railroads were "attempting to force a three-inch stream through a one-inch nozzle." James J.

[39] *Proceedings of the American Railway Association,* Auditorium Hotel, Chicago, April 24, 1907, 27, 28, 31, 52; *ibid.,* Emergency Session, Waldorf-Astoria Hotel, New York, Oct. 30, 1907, 76; *ibid.,* Special Session, Chicago, Feb. 7, 1908, 270–71. American Association of Local Freight Agents, *Compilation of Convention Topics,* 1888–1908 (n.p., 1909), 254–58, gives the grass-roots view and reveals that the rank and file knew perfectly well that the emergency would recur.

Hill said that the roads were "trying to bore a one-inch hole with a one-half-inch auger," and that money—five billion dollars of it—and not new laws or attacks by the government, was what the railroads needed.[40]

If the panic of 1907 had not happened, it might have had to be invented, so crippling was the lush prosperity which gripped the nation. As for the congestion on the railroads, it was a harbinger of things to come. Certainly it was a warning which no intelligent society could ignore.

[40] 12 ICC 561, 565.

CHAPTER III

THE CHALLENGE ACCEPTED

The development of the country has followed a somewhat impetuous course; the youthful body has grown up too rapidly without, at the same time, maturing harmoniously in all parts. Such growth must leave weakness which must be overcome. . . . No one who has had occasion, as we have had, to cross this great country from ocean to ocean can . . . doubt that here is a youth . . . destined to grow to a giant and to accomplish great things in this world.—SUPERIOR PRIVY COUNCILOR W. HOFF and PRIVY COUNCILOR F. SCHWABACH, *1906*

During the enormous development of the last four years, the railroads have found it very difficult to keep pace with the requirements imposed upon them, and the so-called surplus earnings, as well as additional capital, have been devoted to providing additional facilities. . . . This work . . . must go on [and] during the next decade every single-track railroad in the country will have to be double-tracked, and provide enlarged terminal and other facilities.—EDWARD H. HARRIMAN *to* THEODORE ROOSEVELT, *1904*

I

Engineer John W. Wiskar was an intense young man who had risen rapidly in the echelons of the New York and Harlem Railroad. He did not intend, however, to remain an engineer on a commuter division of the railroad. Promotion had come fast since the discouraging days of the nineties depression had been replaced by the optimism of the new century. Men like Wiskar, who were close to the work they were engaged in, often saw trends while they were still in the making, and not merely after months or years, like some highly placed executives and public officials. They knew that the railroads were going to need all of the help they could get if they were to continue to carry the nation's burdens efficiently and on time. Assignment to one of the fast long-distance trains on the main line was the ambition of nearly every engineer on any railroad, and rumors about a new, limited, all-Pullman train which the New York Central was planning to put into service were seductive indeed to a man like Wiskar. He had one of the best on-time records on the Harlem Division, and he intended to keep it. When the new trains came along, the brass would be looking for men who could bring them in "on the advertised," that is, at the hour proudly claimed in the expensive advertising which already touted the best trains of America's railroads.

His mind fixed on bringing his train in on the advertised, Wiskar swung himself into his seat at the head of No. 118, due in Grand Central at 8:15 on that bitterly cold morning in January, 1902. His train was virtually a duplicate of thousands which at that moment were chuffing across the American landscape. Drawn by an "American type" (4-4-0) locomotive which was identical in design to, and only a little heavier than, the engine which had drawn President Lincoln's train on that last trip to Springfield thirty-seven years before, its consist of seven open-vestibule wooden cars, light as they were, made a full load.[1] Wiskar would need all of his skill, and perhaps some bending of the operating rules, to make the schedule. His irritation mounted as he approached the four-track open-cut "throat" which led from the Bronx down the Fourth Avenue spine of Manhattan and into the grimy old terminal. All of his skill in jockeying the modest horsepower under his command had not availed to keep him on schedule. The closer he got to the bridge across the Harlem River (which meant a clear track into the terminal, give or take a few signal lights in the two short tunnels at 86th Street and 56th Street), the more the traffic congestion on this heavily traveled route got in his way. Start, stop; start, stop; every engineer on the line knew that it was only a question of time before the entire flow of traffic would freeze solid unless something were done. Now, within sight of his goal, he was instructed to fall in behind the New Haven's No. 223, which was due in Grand Central after Wiskar's train, at 8:17. He would have to wait while the New Haven, which crankily insisted on having its own arrival tracks at the extreme eastern edge of the ter-

---

[1] Locomotives are classified by a three- (or more) digit number which expresses the number of pilot wheels, driving wheels, and trailer wheels. The American type, therefore, had a four-wheel pilot truck, which served to lead the four rigidly mounted driving wheels into the curves, and no trailer wheels.

minal, passed its train in front of him. Wiskar's frustration matched the full head of steam which he always insisted that his fireman maintain right up to the very end of a run.

New Haven No. 223 was virtually indistinguishable, from locomotive to tail lantern, from Wiskar's train. It had clanked down from Danbury to Norwalk that morning on a typical branch line whose steep grades, tight curves, and skimpy rails were not much changed since that frosty day in 1852 when the people of Danbury, eager to see the vital link completed to tidewater, had insisted that the rails be laid directly on the frozen ground from the bustling hat-town of Bethel into their city. At New Rochelle, on the main line, the express became a commuter train, as it stopped to allow two more wooden coaches to be coupled at the rear. Passing through the short tunnel at 86th Street in Manhattan, and again in the one at 56th Street just above the Grand Central yards, both engineer and fireman had to squint closely to see the small signal lights down at track level which told them whether to proceed or to hold up. The clouds of coal smoke which regularly made passage through the tunnels so unpleasant were complicated on that cold morning by billows of opaque white steam from the locomotive. The signal in the second tunnel was red, and the engineer stopped, confident in the knowledge that a similar signal light a few hundred feet to his rear would protect his train and its passengers. The signal turned green, and No. 223's locomotive, protesting under the weight of seven coaches, slowly resumed the last few hundred feet of its journey. The signal turned red again behind No. 223. It was now Wiskar's turn to heed it.

Daily train movement at Grand Central had reached a total of 161 inbound and 160 outbound by 1902, nothing compared to what it would be in fifteen years, but far more than the old terminal, which Commodore Vanderbilt himself had laid out in 1870, could properly handle. At 50th Street the four tracks fanned out into yards which, filled day and night with snorting, clanging locomotives belching clouds of smoke, lay like a black scar in the heart of "uptown" Manhattan. Ugly red-brick express-company warehouses lined both the western and eastern edges, confining train movements to the middle section. Everywhere railroad men worked frantically to position the trains, load them, and get them out again. And in the arrival building to the east (added when the original depot had proved inadequate after only thirteen years), the process was being repeated in reverse. In the station itself, which had been handsomely remodeled and enlarged from the cast-iron-quoined, mansard-roofed monstrosity of which the Commodore had been so proud, the usual crowd of travelers, greeters, idlers, and men and women of darker motives jostled each other uncomfortably.

Wiskar, who knew just how to get the best time out of his puny locomotive on the congested route he had to follow, shut off his steam at 72d Street and coasted. By the time he reached the last tunnel, he knew that he would be going only twenty miles an hour. It was a crisp, clear day. Plenty of room to stop if New Haven No. 223 was being timid or temperamental. Down the open cut he came, his full boiler pressure popping off into great mushrooming clouds of steam. The last tunnel was already full of steam, and smoke too, by the time Wiskar reached it. He later said that he could not see the signal. That was too bad, because it was red. Within seconds his high-wheeled locomotive was resting two-thirds of the way into the last coach of No. 223, in a tangle of splintered wood, hissing steam, and parboiled, broken bodies. Fifteen of New Rochelle's citizens, ancestors of today's hardy breed of commuters, lay dead or dying in the wreckage.

A serious collision in a terminal is a frightening thing. Many people see it, and passionate indignation can produce an angry mob. Wiskar and his fireman were hustled away from the scene by the police. The district attorney demanded, and got, Wiskar held for the grand jury without bail. The fireman was let go on $5000 bail. And then the cries of indignation began in earnest. Suddenly it seemed that everybody in public life had been warning against the continued use of steam locomotives in tunnels. In 1882, someone recalled, two people had been killed in a similar collision in the 86th Street tunnel, and in 1891 seven unfortunates had met their end in exactly the same spot and manner. Mayor Seth Low said that the "lesson" to be learned was that electricity must be used in the tunnels. Two days after the accident the New York Central announced that it had just completed engineering plans for a third-rail electric system from the terminal to Mott Haven, in the Bronx. How these modest plans flowered into the modern Grand Central Terminal development is one of the most fascinating chapters in architectural and engineering history.[2]

[2] *NYT,* Jan. 9, 1902, 1–2; Jan. 10, 2; "New Grand Central," *Harper's Weekly,* XLII (Feb. 5, 1898), 130; James Montgomery Bailey, *History of Danbury, Con-*

II

That tragic accident in the old Grand Central Station, barely one year into the twentieth century, was merely the most dramatic of countless reminders to American railroad men that they could not hope to carry the traffic of the brave new century on the existing railroads. Almost every aspect of railroading was inadequate and would have to be improved and enlarged as quickly as possible: motive power, rolling stock, signal systems, terminals, and all the rest. Right down at the track level, in fact, was the biggest job of all. Expansion of railroad *route* mileage would not be spectacular after 1900; extensive development of the country had been an affair of the previous century. But intensive development of the system would involve the laying down of thousands of miles of second, third, fourth (and, in a few cases, fifth and sixth) main line tracks, heavier rails, and an untold amount of regrading, straightening, and rebridging of much if not most of the 200,-000 miles of American railroads. Within fifteen years there would be relatively few passengers and little freight passing over track which was exactly as it had been in 1900.

The process of intensive development of the railroad system had actually begun not long after the original links had been laid, and in the case of the major railroads had been maintained throughout the last third of the nineteenth century. The railroad counterpart of the city street-repair gang, ripping away at the avenues while the heavy traffic flows unabated around it, was a familiar sight to travelers. Nowhere was this truer than on the mighty Pennsylvania. This remarkable organization, which in the 1840s had snatched the city of Philadelphia from the jaws of economic disaster by laying an all-rail route across the Alleghenies to Pittsburgh, had been in the 1870s merely the best-engineered of America's predominantly single-track railroads. Then, in the decade and a half before the depression of the nineties, the Pennsylvania had been transformed into an all-steel, double-track route from New York (more accurately, Jersey City) to Chicago. And hundreds of miles of

necticut, 1684–1896, ed. Susan Benedict Hill (New York, 1896), 273. The congestion at Grand Central had been common knowledge for several years. "Congestion of Traffic at the Grand Central Station, New York," *Scientific American,* LXXXIII (Dec. 1, 1900), 338.

feeder lines, covering central Pennsylvania in a dendritic pattern, had been added. The acquisition of weaker trunk lines transformed the Pennsylvania from a Philadelphia-to-Pittsburgh project into the most highly developed railroad in the world, with western termini at Chicago and St. Louis. These subsidiaries were quickly brought up to Pennsylvania main line standards.

During the closing years of George B. Roberts' presidency, the Pennsylvania was committed to a development program which it prosecuted aggressively in the face of the 1893–96 depression. In the first year of that sad economic entr'acte, the Pennsylvania was busily elevating its tracks in Elizabeth, New Jersey, and North Philadelphia, where grade-level traffic had reached such a point that either the trains would have to stop running or local traffic be prohibited. In the same year one of the most obvious needs of the system, a bridge over the Delaware River to Camden and to the already extremely popular New Jersey seacoast further on, replaced an inconvenient ferry. Roberts told stockholders the next year, when times were really bad, that the railroad was spending two million dollars to reduce grades and curves, in addition to the Camden improvements, and he noted proudly that none of this was being capitalized, but written off as current expense. This policy the Pennsylvania would continue to follow until the new accounting rules of the ICC prohibited the practice. It was a good example of the conservative financing which characterized the best American railroads.

When the leadership passed to Frank Thomson in 1897, there were only a few miles of four-track line on the Pennsylvania, between Altoona and Kittanning Point, and a three-mile stretch at the east end of the Gallitzin tunnel. That was all. Cautious President Thomson reluctantly announced the establishment of an "extraordinary expenditure fund," to which further improvements, no longer deferrable, would be charged. By the end of 1898 there were seventeen miles of four-track line, and in that same year the phenomenal growth of a new American pastime required the building of a passenger-coach yard at Princeton to accommodate the crowds which were coming to watch the football games. Four-tracking went on apace after Alexander J. Cassatt succeeded Thomson to the leadership in 1899. Passenger traffic out of New York had reached the point where two additional tracks had to be laid across the Jersey meadows. By the end of 1900 there was a "broadway of steel" four tracks wide from Jersey City to Harrisburg. Only 129 miles still remained to be four-tracked between the capital and Pittsburgh, and this was being rapidly filled in. In his 1902 annual report, Cassatt described the details of a staggering project to bring the Pennsylvania into Manhattan. As if that were not enough, he laid the incredible demands of the twentieth century right on the line: the increase in traffic had outstripped facilities at virtually every point on the system. The development of industry along the main line was such that the Pennsylvania would have to double its existing facilities. A new four-track freight line was needed to bypass Pittsburgh. Trenton to Newark was being six-tracked. Leaving the Manhattan project aside, the Pennsylvania was committed to spend $67 million within the next two or three years on these projects.

And still they fell behind. Cassatt noted regretfully in his 1903 report that in spite of all the new facilities, congestion had reduced efficiency to the point where freight operations per ton-mile were costing 25 per cent more than just a year before. One could stand at a certain point on the main line between Harrisburg and Pittsburgh and see 28 passenger trains and 140 freight trains, hauling 7,000 cars, pass by in twenty-four hours. There was nothing for it but to think big, and the Pennsylvania did. Let him who thinks that American railroad building stopped with the end of the nineteenth century consider what the Pennsylvania was up to now. Increasingly heavy freight trains had forced the executives to admit, after nearly sixty years, that the original route surveyed for the railroad had not been, after all, the very best possible. The Pennsylvania announced that it would build an entirely new, low-gradient, double-track freight line, 137 miles long, through the most difficult terrain traversed by its original main line. All through freight would go over the new route in the future. Thus, in the middle of the first decade of the new century, the Pennsylvania became the center of the world for railroad construction engineers. The new line provided an opportunity for an expression in the heaviest steel rails of all the elegant track-design mathematics which the profession had devised in the preceding decades. Backed up by a generous purse in the hands of a confident, determined management, the project was the best example of how America's railroads meant to meet the challenge.[3]

[3] P.R.R. Co., *Annual Reports,* 1894–1906; Miles C. Kennedy and George H. Burgess, *Centennial History of the Pennsylvania Railroad, 1846–1946* (Philadelphia, 1949), is the best history of the Pennsylvania so far. Edwin P. Alexander, *The*

If the Pennsylvania had earned a reputation as the "broadway of steel" by 1906, the Illinois Central was well on its way toward the title of "main line of mid-America." The blend of conservatism and far-sightedness which Stuyvesant Fish and Edward H. Harriman had brought to this pioneer land-grant railroad in the eighties and nineties had paid off handsomely. Throughout the last decade of the old century, Fish bragged in an annual report, the railroad had continued to make improvements at the bargain prices of the depression. And, as was the custom among well-run railroads, these expenditures had been charged to expenses. Nowhere did they go to swell the capitalization of the railroad. Even the canny management of the I.C., however, was unprepared for the demands which were being made on it after 1897. The long, north-south system basked in the double-barreled prosperity of the established Midwest and the "new" South, from New Orleans, chief port of entry for the rapidly expanding Southern Hemisphere trade, to Chicago, whose role in the trade of the nation needs no elaboration.

Apart from the monumental task of replacing hundreds of wooden bridges and trestles (one of the biggest single jobs which railroads faced everywhere), which would not bear up under the new locomotives, the job on the I.C. was largely one of double-tracking. In 1897 Fish proudly announced that the system had 31 miles of double track, most of it in the Chicago area. Four years later, in 1901, there were 89 miles, and it was not nearly enough. In that year it was decided to double-track the entire main line from Chicago to New Orleans "at the earliest date." A year later there were 200 miles of second main track and 82 miles of third-track line. By 1904 all but 38 miles of main line was double-tracked. Now the I.C. could begin in earnest to meet the challenge, by completely revolutionizing motive power, rolling stock, and all of the other appurtenances which a modern roadway demands.[4]

Many a great railroad had its main offices in Chicago, and the rising number of executives which helped run the systems counted heavily in the prosperous upper-middle-class society which the Windy City boasted. Few of them can have spent much time in their offices or

---

Pennsylvania Railroad: A Pictorial History (New York, 1947), is worth several thousand words.

[4] I.C.R.R. Co., *Annual Reports,* 1897–1904; Carlton J. Corliss, *Main Line of Mid-America* (New York, 1950), *passim.*

boardrooms in those days of rapid growth, however, for the decisions which had to be made required a firsthand knowledge of properties stretched out over thousands of miles. The most sprawling of all was the Atchison, Topeka & Santa Fe, which in 1896 had taken over the assets of a predecessor company that had been most effectively run through the wringer of receivership. Under the new management, headed by legal and financial expert Victor Morawetz, and operating expert Edward P. Ripley, the history of the Santa Fe in the next decade was a whirlwind of decision-making. Through a highly selective policy of integrating local railroads into the system, the Santa Fe became the most important supplier of transportation services in Kansas, Oklahoma, and northern and western Texas. Great segments of new line were built to make a practical transcontinental line out of two regional railroads (the Santa Fe and the Atlantic and Pacific) which a hopeful management had attempted to paste together in the previous century. No western railroad had anything on the Santa Fe when it came to nineteenth-century jerry-building. In 1897 alone, 382 wooden bridges and trestles had to be replaced with steel structures. It almost seemed as if the men working on a given project might not get the new bridge in place before a member of the new generation of locomotives (which would have gone right through the old bridge) hove into view. In that same year the road proudly announced that the "throat" of the system (six miles between Emporia and Florence, Kansas), over which all through traffic had to pass, had been double-tracked. It was only the beginning. Thousands of tons of heavier steel rails were placed in the main line, the old steel rails going to replace branch line rail, much of which was iron. The results were startling. The Santa Fe leaped back to life from the invalid it had been before the reorganization. In 1900 the annual report noted proudly that the railroad had carried $5.6 million more traffic than the year before, but *total* operating expense had declined by $85,-000. The annals of business contain few examples of such dramatic opportunities to make money by spending money.

But the Santa Fe's work had just begun. Now restored to athletic good health, it would need every bit of muscle it had, for the economic development of the southwestern United States, and especially Texas and southern California after 1900, was marvelous. By 1910 the Santa Fe was double-tracking at the rate of nearly 250 miles a year. In 1906 it had undertaken to build the Abo Pass line, a short cut across the continental divide at an altitude thousands of feet below the old Raton Pass line (over which the scenic passenger trains continued to run). Enormous savings in human and natural resources were expected from this shorter, straighter, and flatter main line.[5]

It would be ironic if the reader should acquire the impression that these great railroad rebuilding projects, impressive as they are, exhaust the possibilities of example. It is almost an insult to the many great railroad men of this era to describe the achievements of the Pennsylvania without mentioning the beautiful machine for transportation which the New York Central made out of its superb route through the Hudson and Mohawk River valleys and along Lake Erie; or the promethean struggle of the Baltimore & Ohio to master the punishing grades west of Harpers Ferry which caused division superintendents to grow old before their time. If the contemporary presidents of chambers of commerce in America's cities could read this account, they would press upon the writer their own proud examples by the hundreds. How about the Lucin cutoff, the man from Salt Lake City would ask indignantly. Straight across the Great Salt Lake the intrepid Harriman ran it, saving the better part of a day for freight trains. How about the San Pedro line, bringing the Union Pacific into Los Angeles, a southern Californian would demand—there's an example of a brand-new railroad in this "non-railroad-building era." Don't forget the Western Pacific, which has just given us another link due west to Salt Lake City, his arch-rival from San Francisco would surely retort, while the man from Seattle would note proudly that the Chicago, Milwaukee, and St. Paul, recently extended across Montana to his city, had just added "and Pacific" to its name. A midwesterner would cite the pioneering triumph which had just been celebrated in Detroit, a tunnel of tubular design under the Detroit River which for the first time brought trains from the East directly into that rapidly growing city. Even Henry M. Flagler would remind us that he had seen his Florida East Coast, "the railroad that went to sea," extended into Key West before he died. There would be no stopping them.

The popular notion that route mileage did not increase after 1900,

[5] A.T. & S.F. R.R. Co., *Annual Reports*, 1896–1910; James Marshall, *Santa Fe: The Railroad That Built an Empire* (New York, 1945).

therefore, is not accurate: the total of "first main track" (route mileage) kept right on rising, from 193,000 to 258,000 by 1915. The total did not increase much after 1910, it is true, for reasons which will be all too clear later on. Second-track mileage increased by two and one-half times, from 12,000 to 29,000—far short of Harriman's impossible dream of universal double-track, but enough to take most of the pressure of overutilization off the nation's most heavily traveled routes. One of the most impressive and most significant developments, reflecting as it does the onrushing industrial development of the country, was the expansion of other trackage (passing tracks, industrial sidings, and freight yards), which doubled from 52,000 miles in 1900 to 100,000. The enlargement of such facilities is a direct index of the increased utilization of the route mileage of the system. Gross trackage of American railways shot upward in these years. By 1915 the railways were reporting to the ICC, along with the mountain of other statistics which the Commission reported annually in the *Statistics of the Railways,* a total of 391,000 miles of track. A decade and a half earlier there had been only 259,000 miles. But it must always be borne in mind that such broad figures obscure the main story, which lies in the physical transformation of heavy-traffic lines, over which the bulk of the burden was carried. Although a relatively small percentage of all railroad route mileage, these aortas of commerce, on which so much toil and treasure was lavished in these years, were the most vital part of the industrial body. It is a story which is difficult to overdo, for it proves that America's railroads were, indeed, built *twice:* once in the nineteenth century, and again in the exhilarating era we call, with so much justification, Progressive.

III

Late at night, when the passenger expresses had cleared the main line in both directions, a railroad was free to do the serious work of hauling freight. This was especially true of a road like the Erie, which had to drag its throbbing freight trains over some of the steepest grades of any of the trunk line railroads. The inferior route which had been laid out for the Erie back in those dim days of the 1830s, when the southern tier of New York counties screamed for relief from the murderous competition of the Erie Canal, had become an acute problem. Heavy rail on well-ballasted roadbed, easing of curves, and even the building of a single-track relief line from Suffern to Port Jervis still left the Erie with the job of bulling its way through the rugged Shawangunk Mountains before it could break out into the valley of the Delaware River to the west, or the Ramapo to the east. Especially troublesome were the long, money-making trains of coal which the Erie lugged eastward over the ridge in a never-ending procession. One night in 1914 the division was abuzz with activity. Top brass were there. And out on the siding, getting up steam and waiting for the eastbound coal train, was the biggest locomotive anybody had ever seen. She was three locomotives in one, if the truth were told. Front to back, she looked like this: a two-wheel pilot truck; then eight powerful driving wheels, free to pivot beneath the boiler behind a pair of mammoth cylinders; another set of eight driving wheels, rigidly mounted beneath the boiler behind a second set of cylinders; and then, strange to relate, yet a third pair of cylinders articulated directly beneath the engineer's cab, and propelling a third set of eight driving wheels mounted beneath the tender which, as usual, carried the coal and water for the monster. She was an engineer's terror, a maintenance man's nightmare, and a fireman's backache. She had only one role to play in life, so highly specialized had locomotive design become: to replace the three conventional locomotives which customarily hauled the heavy coal trains, two at the front and one pushing at the rear. So enthusiastic were the Erie executives at the expected savings in their rapidly rising wage bill that they had ordered three of these behemoths—a new and untried design—from the Baldwin Locomotive Works.

Such a Goliath of a locomotive, it was generally recognized, could not possibly hope to generate steam at a rate equal to that at which her giant cylinders—six of them—would consume it. But, then, she did not have to. All she was expected to do was to exert her incredible tractive effort of 160,000 pounds for a mere eleven miles. Then she could creep to a siding, rebuild her head of steam, and perform the same favor for the next freight bound in the opposite direction. On the night of her maiden trip her performance was closely observed. When she was a little more than two miles short of her goal, the men who were crowded into the cab began to exchange worried looks. The power dropped perceptibly. By the time she reached the end of her short run she was barely moving. All of the tinkering which Baldwin and Erie experts could contrive could not erase the basic problem: not enough steam-making capacity. Within two years all three sisters had been unceremoniously torn down and rebuilt as conventional types. The experiment with the largest steam locomotive ever built in the United States had ended in abysmal failure.[6]

In many respects the steam locomotive passed its peak of development on that Erie division in 1914. As far as efficiency in the use of fuel went, it had passed the point of diminishing return years earlier. But coal was cheap in America, whereas labor was expensive and getting more so each year. And so the steam locomotive continued to grow until it finally re-created in steel and brass the role which the dinosaur had enacted in flesh and blood in another age. It is not for us, however, to discuss here why the railroad industry continued to pin its hopes on the steam locomotive until after World War II, despite the fact that the diesel locomotive was a technological possibility by 1920. In 1897, when our story begins, the steam locomotive was all that railroads anywhere had to work with. Our job is to tell the story of how American railroads, and the great locomotive works, took the *fin-de-siècle* steamer, so little changed from the early post–Civil War model, and turned it into a machine which was equal to the challenge of the Progressive era.

It is dramatic testimony to the inexorable power of live steam and the strength of iron and steel that the steam locomotive was ever a practical vehicle. The demands upon it were almost ludicrous. First of all, it was very heavy (although the traction which resulted thereby was what made the flanged wheel, running on the low-friction metal rail, practical in the first place), and in addition to its own lumbering self, it had to carry all of the makings of its power—coal and water—on its back, so

[6] Alfred W. Bruce, *The Steam Locomotive in America: Its Development in the Twentieth Century* (New York, 1952), 322–23 and Plate 86. This locomotive is designated 2-8-8-8-OT. (Where there are two or more sets of drivers, the fact is indicated by the use of two or more digits between the first and last digits, which always represent pilot and trailer wheels.) Compare this locomotive's pulling power—160,000 tons—with the most powerful conventional Mallet type then built, a 2-10-10-2 of 147,000 pounds of tractive effort, which the Virginian Railroad put in similar heavy-grade service in 1918. (Plate 85 in Bruce, *Steam Locomotive.*)

to speak. Its width was strictly limited by the woefully narrow gauge of four feet eight and one-half inches which George Stephenson had imposed upon the industry, and its length was only somewhat less critical. (Until articulated locomotives came into use, length was rather strictly limited by curvature of the track.) Within the narrow space that was available a firebox had to be provided, the limited size of which necessitated all sorts of compromises with efficiency of fuel consumption, smoke pollution, and employee welfare in order to get the highest possible rate of combustion out of it. These limitations would have been serious in a stationary engine, but the steam locomotive had to perform all of its functions while propelling itself along at speeds of fifty or sixty miles an hour.

The lightweight cars and the short trains of the first five or six decades of the railroad era did not demand much in the way of motive power, and, indeed, the thin iron rails and weak wooden structures of the nineteenth century would not have tolerated any more robust steed. That is why the American-type locomotive quickly became the overwhelming favorite of American railroads for both passenger and freight service. In those days of low wages and high capital costs, it was more practical to double-head locomotives when extra power was needed than to design heavier machines and rebuild the railroad to take them. By 1885, however, the picture was changing. It is at this time, according to a contemporary authority, that the differentiation between freight and passenger types began. In the stages of locomotive growth which followed, the unifying theme is the need to increase the rate of combustion (primarily by enlarging the firebox and improving its design) and traction (primarily by increasing the number of driving wheels).[7]

The search resulted in two new types, which were the forebears of

---

[7] For the early period, see John H. White, Jr., *American Locomotives: An Engineering History, 1830–1880* (Baltimore, 1968). Angus Sinclair, *Development of the Locomotive Engine* (New York, 1907), 647 and *passim,* is excellent because of its contemporary nature and the intimate involvement of the author in the subject. Paul T. Warner, *Locomotives of the Pennsylvania Railroad, 1834–1924* (Chicago, 1959), a reprint of several articles which appeared in 1924 in the house organ of the Baldwin Locomotive Works, reveals that the American type was still being turned out as late as 1902 in a strange-looking combination of nineteenth-century wheel arrangement and twentieth-century boiler and stack design. This type was capable of speeds of over 100 m.p.h., but it lacked both the traction and the pulling power for the new trains.

the most important twentieth-century designs: the ten-wheeler (4-6-0), which was the American type with a third pair of drivers added; and the Consolidation type (2-8-0), which "consolidated" as much of the weight as possible on the driving wheels. At the very end of the century an equally important third type was produced by lengthening the firebox of the American type, deepening it at the rear, and supporting the larger structure on two added trailer wheels. The new locomotive was very fast and, being a direct descendant of the American, virtually "bug-free." Introduced in the famous one-hour service between Philadelphia and the booming seaside resort of Atlantic City in 1897, the "Atlantic type" (4-4-2), as it was named, quickly made a reputation for dependability and punctuality. It was the most widely used locomotive for main line passenger service in the Progressive era.[8]

The steam locomotive was developed not only in the dimension of sheer size but in technology as well. The most significant innovations, insofar as their influence on the extremely rapid diversification of designs after 1900 is concerned, were the compound cylinder, improved firebox design, more sophisticated valve gear, and automatic stokers. The name of Vauclain is inseparably linked to the first two developments. Samuel M. Vauclain, who joined the Baldwin Locomotive Works in 1883, was the prime mover in its growth to a preeminent position in the industry by 1910. After only six years at Philadelphia he produced one of the most important innovations in locomotive engineering, a feature which was ultimately to divide locomotives into the "before" and "after" eras. This was the technique of compounding. After steam has been used to push a piston through its stroke, the pressure has dropped but considerable pressure remains. Compounding involved using the steam twice, once in a small, high-pressure cylinder and again in a larger low-pressure cylinder. The two cylinders were first placed on either side of the locomotive, and ultimately wound up in pairs on each side of the vehicle. Almost immediately thereafter an even more revolutionary technique, the superheating of steam, made lower pressures and a return to the simpler, single-expansion design possible, at great savings. Vauclain and others also made significant contributions within the rather adamantine limits of firebox design. In a more sophisticated field, engineers set their

[8] Fred A. Talbot, *Cassell's Railways of the World* (2 vols., London, n.d.), II, 182–90, 218–30, 288–93.

minds to the complex problem of when, in the piston stroke cycle, to admit steam to the cylinder and when to shut it off. The result was the Walschaerts valve gear, a European development which by 1905 was nearly universal on American locomotives. And, now that locomotives were so quickly outgrowing the physical capacities of the human fireman, real progress was made in the design of a practical automatic stoker. The locomotive was now ready to grow, and grow it did.[9]

Just as the American type was enlarged into the Atlantic type by adding a longer, deeper firebox over a pair of trailer wheels, the ten-wheeler was enlarged into an even more powerful vehicle which was just as fast. The result was the Pacific type (4-6-2), perhaps the most important workhorse of American Railroads right down to the end of steam motive power. By World War I many of the first-class passenger trains in America were being drawn by this new engine. The demand for speed, despite the fact that the new, twelve-wheel all-steel coaches and Pullmans were inordinately heavy, made the Pacific locomotive an absolute necessity. In World War II the rugged old steed, infinitely refined from its early version, hauled thousands of troop trains across the nation, and was still the most important single form of transportation power in the world. One of the few remaining specimens of the Pacific locomotive stands, gleaming in the green livery of the Southern Railway, in the Transportation Hall of the new building of the Smithsonian Institution. Another sits stolidly exposed to the elements on a siding at the Burlington railroad station in Galesburg, Illinois, a permanent exhibit which fewer and fewer people see.

Meanwhile the rapidly growing weight of freight trains called for dramatic innovation in the department of brute force. The Consolidation type was greatly enlarged: the eight drivers became ten and even twelve, while trailer trucks and additional pilot wheels were added. But the most significant break with conventional design was provided by a Swiss inventor, Anatole Mallet, who conceived of literally placing two locomotives beneath a single boiler. The resulting monster was so long that the front section had to be articulated, that is, pivoted under the boiler so that it could lean into the curves along with the pilot wheels. The American Locomotive Company built the first one in the United States.

[9] Bruce, *Steam Locomotive,* 49, 98–99, 160–63, 186–93, 200.

A 0-6-6-0 type, it caused a "sensation" when the company exhibited it at the St. Louis exposition in 1904. "Old Maude," as she was affectionately known on the Baltimore & Ohio, was soon outclassed by a horde of ever-larger Mallets which poured out of American shops. Pilot and trailer wheels were added, and drivers increased, and now that stokers were available locomotives quickly grew longer than entire trains had been in the early days. By 1914, as we have seen, the Mallet had reached the peak of its development as a type, although refinements would continue right down to World War II.[10]

These developments, and many that have not been mentioned, meant much more powerful locomotives. The first Atlantics, with which locomotive growth began in the twentieth century, exerted about 16,000 pounds of tractive effort. The first Pacifics could pull about 26,000 pounds. By World War I the two types could haul about 30,000 pounds and 50,000 pounds, respectively. At the brute force end of the scale, as we have seen, the Erie had the strongest locomotive on the rails. But the reader must not get the impression that the railroads opted for size instead of numbers of locomotives. Traffic grew enormously while train-lengths increased correspondingly, so that more and more units were needed. America's railroads had numbered 36,000 engines in 1898; by 1915 there were 66,000, and while many of the 1898 vintage remained, they were almost never seen on the main lines.[11]

Until the diesel came, the steam locomotive reigned over all but a few hundred miles of American railroads. But in the new tunnels and subterranean stations which were built in the Progressive era, the electric locomotive had made its appearance. This striking innovation in motive power was far simpler in design than the steam vehicle. It contained few of the large, highly-machined moving parts which made the railroads the largest single employer of master mechanics in this era, and it could be used all day, every day, without round-housing for service at the end of each run. It was free from the necessity of hauling its fuel around on its back. But it required a heavy investment in power distribution facilities, and on all but the most heavily used lines the traffic did not justify the outlay. The electric traction device revolution-

---

[10] Talbot, *Cassell's Railways*, II, 440–52.

[11] ICC, *Annual Statistical Report*, 1898, 1915; Bruce, *Steam Locomotive*, plates 1–32.

ized city and suburban transportation in this pre-automobile age, but it relieved little of the iron horse's burden. Nevertheless, it made railroad service possible in locations and under conditions where it would otherwise have been impossible, and must rank with the most outstanding motive power developments of the era.[12]

IV

Two of the most important inventions in the history of transportation were products of the late nineteenth century, although the enormous job of applying them to railroad motive power and rolling stock was not completed until about 1905. In George Westinghouse, the versatile inventor, developer, manufacturer, and promoter of the air brake, the railroad industry had one of the few true geniuses of the second industrial revolution. Before 1880, when his brake became available, each piece of rolling stock in a train, including the locomotive, had to be braked individually. The brakeman who scurried along the top of a moving string of sleet-covered boxcars to twirl the brake wheels at the end of each car, when the signal of "down brakes" was given from the engine, has been so ignored among the histories of American pioneers as to make the whaling captain, the cowboy, and the pony express rider blush with shame. By the turn of the century he was all but extinct. The air brake, operated by the engineer from his cab, goes on simultaneously throughout the entire train. As a result, longer and faster trains of heavier cars became possible, and not only did passengers ride in infinitely greater safety, but as the years rolled by the number of legless and armless men who stared pitifully over the backyard fences on Railroad Avenue slowly declined. The other invention was the gift of a self-effacing group of men who pioneered one of the earliest technical organizations in the United States, the Master Car Builders' Associa-

[12] Frank Sprague, "The Electric Railway," *Century*, LXX (July and August, 1905), 446, 525; Victor Clark, *History of Manufactures* (3 vols., New York, 1929), II, 166; Kent T. Healy, *Electrification in Steam Railroads* (New York, 1929). In 1910 George Westinghouse, whose air brake made the modern railroad train possible, wrote an impassioned plea for adoption of a universal technical standard which, unfortunately for today's merger-minded railroads, was never adopted; *The Electrification of Railways, and the Imperative Need for the Selection of a System for Universal Use* (New York, 1910).

tion. The MCB automatic coupler, an ingenious device whose principle of operation is not unlike a handclasp, made it possible to couple cars without the workman's actually standing between the cars, and its standardization by the Association made it possible for freight cars to be interchanged freely between railroads throughout the land. That the MCB "knuckle" coupler was universally applied, in a few years, to the millions of cars operated by the hundreds of separate railroad companies is one of the most outstanding examples of constructive cooperation in the annals of economic history.[13]

The train brake and the automatic coupler were born of sheer necessity. By 1900 it was apparent to observers that in this land where transportation played such a strategically important role, railroad rolling stock was evolving in a manner far different from that of the puny railroads of England and the Continent. Evolution manifested itself in two revolutions: one in construction design, and another in sheer size. By 1900 the use of steel in railroad passenger cars had only just begun. At first, steel had been used for the very practical purpose of increasing the total weight of the string of cars which it was possible for the big new locomotives to haul. This is a striking example of how innovations are closely linked in an interdependency which often makes their separate study ludicrous. The trend in American railroads from the late nineteenth century on, as we have seen, was to get more out of the existing system while simultaneously increasing its theoretical capacity; and if this could be done with improved service and safety, so much the better. The new, heavy-duty roadbed and the huskier engines were useless so long as the first several cars in a train were likely to pull apart should anyone be so foolhardy as to couple as many behind the new locomotives as they were able to pull. And so the steel underframe was born. Upon this expensive but most effective new frame the designers were quick to erect a steel body, and with the Pullman Company (whose reputation was based on comfort and safety) showing the way, it

[13] Bruce, *Steam Locomotive*, 265–68. By 1909 the "bible" of the Master Car Builders' Association was in its sixth edition, and the chance of any railroad or car manufacturer committing a major sin of nonstandardization had been reduced to a minimum. *The Car Builders' Dictionary*, ed. *The Railway Age Gazette* (New York, 1909). Although uniformity was less of a problem with locomotives, which did not usually circulate from one railroad to another, there was a similar "bible" for them.

was only a matter of a few years before all of the cars coming out of the shops were made entirely of steel. The revolution in size followed as a matter of course. The passenger car, which had grown from forty to fifty feet in length in its all-wood nineteenth-century form, was lengthened to about sixty feet when the steel underframe came in. By 1914 the 76-foot, all-steel coach was standard. Pullman had turned out an 84-foot sleeping-lounge-observation car, the first of many such proud conveyances, in 1908.[14]

The Keystone Bridge Works, one of the earliest units in the Carnegie Steel empire, was understandably proud of its ability to handle large steel plates. In the nineties it hit upon a way of exploiting this know-how which promised to eclipse the mere job of building bridges. Out of its cavernous shops one day rolled two experimental all-steel hopper cars, ideal for hauling sand, gravel, ore, coal, and similar "frangibles" which were the bread and butter of America's railroads. One of these battleships could carry forty tons, nearly twice the capacity of many a railroad car then in operation on American lines, and almost four times the payload of the foolish, four-wheeled carts which the English still insisted on using. The effects of the big new cars was electric. By 1912 simple gondolas (which had no hoppers) could carry fifty tons, while their big brothers were passing the eighty-ton mark. The other basic workhorse of the railroads, the boxcar, almost invariably had a steel frame and underframe by 1914, and by 1909 all-steel boxcars with capacities of fifty tons or even more were coming in. Stock cars, which could hold only twenty-five tons of piteously bawling bovines in 1892, crowded in forty tons of no less uncomfortable beasts by 1917. Flatcars,

---

[14] Walter Arndt Lucas, ed., *One Hundred Years of Railroad Cars* (New York, 1958), 163, 166, and *passim;* August Mencken, *The Railroad Passenger Car* (Baltimore, 1957); *The Car Builders' Dictionary*. The all-steel car almost succeeded too well. By 1913 the hard-pressed railroads were being threatened with legislation that would have required them to replace all wooden cars with steel, although there was disagreement that this was the best of all possible ways to save lives in wrecks; "Steel-Car Efficiency in Wrecks," *Literary Digest,* XLVII (Oct. 4, 1913), 559–60. A host of other innovations transformed the railroad passenger car into its modern form. One that came slowly until the perfection of the storage battery was electric illumination. As late as 1910 the Pintsch gas lamp was still widely used, and the Burlington Railroad was so proud of the introduction of electricity on its best trains that it was taking large advertisements in eastern newspapers to announce the fact; *NYT,* June 23, 1910, 4. The luxurious new Pullman cars, their enormous weight carried on two lavishly over-engineered six-wheel trucks, provided a quiet and comfortable ride which the lightweight, four-wheel-trucked cars that began to replace them after 1930 could never match.

which carried the unwieldy miscellany of an increasingly sophisticated industrial society, weighed in at 100 tons with their load by 1912, an even greater testimonial to roadway and structural improvements than to car-making technology.[15]

As the Progressive era wore on, it became more and more obvious that the striking gains in the size of railroad rolling stock were all of a part with the increased length of trains. What had begun as a frank attempt to handle the staggering burden which the nation was laying on the railroads became more and more an effort to cut costs in a situation of rising wage rates and frozen freight rates. The larger the cars, the more likely they were to be dispatched less than full, however; and the fight for volume, to make up for rates that were not allowed to rise, made for more and more lax policing of customers by the railroads. The big cars took longer to be loaded and unloaded, too, so that demurrage regulations were at first winked at, then disregarded altogether. What had begun as a giant step in productivity, therefore, had become a not unmixed blessing by the end of this period. Nor did these developments satisfy the insatiable hunger of shippers for cars. All forms of rolling stock greatly increased in numbers as well as size in these years. The newer types, such as tank and refigerator cars, were merely the most obvious. The total number of freight cars on America's railroads doubled from 1.2 million in 1898 to 2.4 million in 1915, while passenger cars increased from 34,000 to 56,000. But the most significant development, as we have seen, was not the increase in sheer numbers, impressive as that was, but the greater size of the units and the efficiency with which they were utilized once they were made up into one of the longer, faster freight trains. Despite the depressing influence of competitive practices such as those just described, the net result of these developments was a massive gain in productivity on the nation's railroads, which we have shortly to consider.

V

How many of the millions of travelers who pass through the sleek new terminals of America's great airports stop to look at these edifices? If experience is any guide, few give the matter a thought. And if few

[15] Lucas, *One Hundred Years of Railroad Cars,* 2, 19, 48, 66–67, 101, 105.

passengers take note of them, then they are surely among the most un-
seen buildings man has ever erected. For these buildings, in many ways
so worthy of admiration for their intelligent use of modern materials,
their clever avoidance of the expensive hand of workmen whose wages
exceed the pay of many a professional man, and their studied avoidance
of the past (as hopeless as the efforts of the eclectics of an earlier era to
re-create the past in rows of Doric columns), exist only on the edge of
the life of the great cities they serve. Not so the great railroad terminals
whose construction was perhaps the most prominent feature of the modern cities which grew out of the Victorian banalities of the previous
century. As their designers intended, these monumental structures came
to be identified with the gigantic and ostensibly indestructible railroad
corporations which reared them. From the small-town depot to the great
metropolitan terminal, in fact, the railroad station became the symbol of
civic pride and the "go-getter" spirit which was creating twentieth-century America. The greatest of these symbols now reposes, for the most
part, as rubble in the Jersey meadows, and all are inexorably slipping
into similar oblivion. Their day was short, as time is reckoned: barely
fifty years for Charles Follen McKim's masterpiece, the Pennsylvania
Station; but their cost was large. Were they worth it? Or were they a
strange aberration in the men whom we have portrayed, thus far, as
paragons of capitalistic efficiency?

    It can hardly be debated that the great railroad station projects of
the Progressive era had their origins in sheer necessity. By the time engineer Wiskar's locomotive plowed into the hapless citizens of New Rochelle, the nineteen tracks of the old Grand Central Station had become
dangerously inadequate. The project to electrify the tracks from 42d
Street to Mott Haven, in the Bronx, quickly grew into the heroic job of
placing the entire complex, except for the waiting room itself, below
ground. Sixty-seven tracks, the engineers said, would be required to
serve the traffic which—the way things were going in 1902—would
eventually have to be handled. While the engineers solved the incredibly difficult problem of keeping an already overworked station in operation as they dug out a new one beneath it, the architectural firms of
Reed and Stem and of Warren and Wetmore labored over their drafting
boards, and in a few short weeks brought forth a station building which,
if we are to believe the architectural historians, deserves to live on for-

ever. When these men were finished, New York had a terminal capable of handling three to four times the traffic of the old one.

Even grander in conception was the Pennsylvania Station, for the terminal building, monumental as it was in its unabashedly eclectic duplication of the Baths of Caracalla, was merely the most visible part of the development. Under the Hudson, which earlier generations had despaired ever of crossing except by ferry, the builders bored two tubes to connect with the main line on the New Jersey side. And the tubes didn't stop in the station. On they went, beneath 33d Street, past the subway station at Fourth Avenue (where, to the everlasting inconvenience of Long Island commuters, a projected suburban station was never built); under the East River, where, oddly enough, more trouble was encountered than under the broad Hudson; and into Long Island City. No stopping there, either, for this was the junction point with the Long Island Railroad, which, after seventy years and to the uncontrollable excitement of a horde of real estate agents, finally had a direct entrance to Manhattan. By now, the dream of a direct connection with New England had seduced the Pennsylvania's planners into swinging the tracks northward at Long Island City, in a gentle curve through the borough of Queens, and over the Hell Gate channel on one of the noblest bridges ever reared to a connection in the Bronx with the Harlem branch of the New Haven Railroad. Before Pennsylvania Station and the Hell Gate bridge, the southernmost railroad crossing of the Hudson had been the bridge at Poughkeepsie, and trains had had to go miles out of their way to get from New England to Washington by a through route. Now the East Coast was one magnificent railroad, from Maine to Florida, and it passed through the very heart of the greatest city in the world.[16]

[16] The definitive technical work on twentieth-century railroad terminals is John A. Droege, *Passenger Terminals and Trains* (New York, 1916). The terminals of Gotham, of course, generated tons of editorial comment ranging from highly perceptive to unabashedly maudlin. The best has been refined and placed in the perspective of architectural history in Carroll L. V. Meeks, *The Railroad Station: An Architectural History* (New Haven, 1956), especially 110–12, 124, 133–34. For an appreciation of the modest character of American railroad stations before 1900, see Walter Gilman Berg, *Buildings and Structures of American Railroads* (New York, 1900). The basic study of an entire city's retreat underground is still G. H. Gilbert et al., *Subways and Tunnels of New York* (New York, 1912). Edward Hungerford, "Greatest Railway Terminal in the World" [Grand Central], *Outlook*, CII (Dec. 28, 1912), 900–11, is a good example of the interest with which Americans followed the progress of these inspiring projects. The Pennsyl-

Space precludes further apostrophizing of these achievements in brick and mortar. The story could go on and on. The movement toward "union stations," which brought all of the railroads serving a city into one terminal, can barely be mentioned. A spectacular success in St. Louis' *fin-de-siècle* station, where over twenty different railroads were involved, the union station was the natural solution in the nation's capital. By 1906 a monumental terminal faced the handsome plaza below the Capitol which today is a forbidding maelstrom of automobiles. In this grand structure, proclaiming on its front façade an assortment of optimistic slogans, the spirit and the art of the World's Columbian Exposition of 1893 live on, although, if the forsaken air that pervades the interior is a warning, not forever. Out in Kansas City the town fathers served notice on the railroad magnates that what they had done for the decadent metropolises of the East, they must now do for the up-and-coming cities of the plain. No arch, no colonnade which had once graced a Roman temple, escaped the inevitable process of its transfer, in successive stages, through the studios of the classic revival architect, to the buildings of the great cities and lesser ones, finally to come to rest in a pathetic hint of its former self on a small-town railroad station or bank building.

What a waste, the cynic will say; *did* say, in fact, in the 1930s when the stewardship of the pre-depression business leaders was so seriously in question. But the only critical point that seems germane to a historical essay is whether the railroad leaders were giving the nation what it demanded. The answer seems to be that they were. Except for a few insinuations during the rate-increase hearings after 1910, there is almost no trace of contemporary condemnation of what Meeks has called "the third phase—Megalomania" in railroad station design. Midwesterners who mindlessly condemned the railroads for tying their rates to an inflated capital structure marveled at the great new terminals, and then went home determined to redouble their efforts to make Zenith the greatest little city in the world. When the Pennsylvania opened its new station to the people in New York, the staid *Times* cheered. It was, said

vania project, and the earlier plans which were discarded, are ably described in Alexander, *Pennsylvania Railroad,* Plate 79, and in the company's *Annual Reports, 1902–10.*

the editor, "a gift to the city," from which the railroad probably would never get a direct return. "The new station," he said, "is not only an example to other public service corporations, but it should serve to warn the people against . . . the calumnies of self-appointed guides and teachers who make the villifying of great corporations their business." [17]

In the thirties, attitudes changed. Of the same building, Dean Joseph Hudnut of the Harvard faculty of design said, "Architecture existed at the time for its own sake or at the most as an ornament applied to civilization. . . . So judicious a creature as the Pennsylvania Railroad could heavily increase its corporate debt in order to hide the steel roofs of its station under the vaults of Caracalla." Meeks himself scorned the heroic proportions of the Grand Central concourse as "opulent dimensions [which] are not functionally necessary; the companies could afford magnificence and enjoyed their munificent role, as princes had in predemocratic ages." But he admitted, a few sentences further on, that it was "one of the outstandingly successful stations of history." And he might have pointed out that the "predemocratic princes" almost always had the masses squarely behind them when they builded so magnificently.[18] Dean Hudnut and many others changed their tunes when the profit-oriented professional managers, taking them at their utilitarian words, set out after World War II to smash the monuments. Pennsylvania Station the aesthetes could not save. Grand Central they have probably only managed to embalm for a few years in the sales-promotion squalor which, though it disfigures the handsome interior, has not obstructed its role as the busiest town square in the world.

What I have tried to say here is that the monumental railroad stations, while they have served their original purposes, did indeed have just such a purpose as the one for which the heroic designs were drawn. The people of the Progressive era, like people of all eras, paid their money and they took their choice. The railroads met the demand for grandeur as squarely as they met the challenge of carrying the nation's burden. The skills which produced these monuments, extinct as they are today, were abundant in prewar America. Men carved those noble pedi-

[17] *NYT*, Nov. 27, 1910, 12.   [18] Meeks, *Railroad Station*, 110–11, 124.

ments for wages which would not get concrete poured today. In the end, their efforts created real estate values in the hearts of the great American cities which have surpassed all possible dreams of avarice.[19]

In the midst of all this preoccupation with magnificence, the railroads struggled with a problem which they never really solved. Once they had had the cities and their environs pretty much to themselves. In the nineteenth century Commodore Vanderbilt had turned pretty St. John's Park into a freight terminal and run his trains down the west side of Manhattan to reach it. Slowly, but inevitably, real estate values drove the railroads out of the inner cities. By 1915 the Central yards at 69th Street and the Hudson River were the only freight yards left in Manhattan. Fortunes were spent to relocate marshaling yards, for not only were the old ones uncomfortably located, but trains were making longer and longer runs between stops and many an old yard no longer served any purpose. Most of the developments, capital-devouring though they were, escaped public notice almost entirely. One twentieth-century development there was, however, which in its photogenic qualities found its way into the sixth-grade geography books. This was the development of the ore and coal terminals at the edge of the lakes and oceans, where gargantuan mouths eviscerated steamships of their cargoes, and giant hands picked railroad cars up bodily and emptied them into the holds of other ships. Impressive as the volume of resources sunk in expanded and improved freight-handling facilities was, however, it was never enough. Money and managerial brains seem simply to have given out by the time the challenge reached its sternest form. Most freight terminals, in fact, "just grew," and as the unprecedented trials of World War I approached, more and more of the fine new equipment in which the railroads had invested so heavily would bog down at the ends of the line.[20]

The railroads would never have been able to handle the great and always growing volume of traffic that wound up at their terminals as well as they did, however, without great advances in the art and tech-

[19] *Ibid.,* 133–34. Hungerford, "Greatest Railway Terminal," noted that the Grand Central development transformed a noisome railroad yard into sixteen blocks of the most valuable urban real estate in the world, and made it possible for the streets from 44th to 50th, closed for half a century, to be reopened to traffic.

[20] John A. Droege, *Freight Terminals and Trains* (New York, 1912), 7, 9, 10, 276–85, and *passim.*

nology of signaling. Europeans were frank in their admiration of the way Americans controlled train movements. Conditions, of course, were very different in Europe. The density of train movements, the shortness of runs, the predominance of passenger trains, the large number of crossings to be guarded, and the relative abundance of cheap labor encouraged continuation of the nineteenth-century custom of local control of trains. In America, however, the dispatching of trains from a central office was universal by 1900.[21] American signaling practice, complicated by the constant problem of congestion at terminals, was a challenge to which the engineers responded with vigor. The automatic and remote-control switching and signaling equipment which was installed on American railroads in these years represented a remarkably aggressive exploitation of the electromechanical arts at an early state of their development. These "interlocking" systems, as they are called, involved the use of electrical control circuits and electrical or mechanical energy devices to set, change, and signal the position of the hundreds of switches in yards, at junction points, and along the routes of highly traveled lines. Because the "safe" position of a given switch is frequently determined by the particular position of some other switch or switches in the system, the problem was not as simple as it might seem. It was, in fact, extremely complex, and we should not forget that there was no preexisting art on which the engineers could build. Perhaps it is just as well that there was not. For these men, in their ingenious application of a primitive scientific knowledge to an unprecedented problem, were the true pioneers of the age of automation. By 1907 they were turning their attention to the staggering task of devising and installing automatic block signals on the main lines. (These devices freed the engineer from dependence upon fallible human advice as to whether to proceed or to stop on account of other traffic ahead.) The most heavily used lines, especially the eastern trunk lines, had had prototype systems for years. Now the industry began a drive to make these devices, which greatly increased both the efficiency and the safety of railroad operation, universal. But the program was a major casualty of the shortage of capital which the railroads never solved after the panic of 1907. By 1912 only 20,000 miles (less than 10 per cent, albeit a segment repre-

[21] W. M. Acworth, "American and English Railways Compared" [reprinted from the London *Times*] (Chicago, 1898), 11–12.

senting a much larger share of total traffic) of American railroads were protected by automatic block signals. It was a national tragedy.[22]

The transformation of American railroads in the Progressive era was not accomplished without considerable cost in life and limb as well as in treasure. By 1907 the railroads were operating under a most unfavorable combination of circumstances: at the very time that nearly every mile of heavily used line was undergoing some kind of improvement which resulted in disarrangement of tracks and routines, and required hordes of men to swarm over the right of way, a record volume of traffic was being carried. The bottom of the manpower barrel was scraped. Men were promoted to engineer who had never been especially dependable as firemen. Employees who had been known to break the cardinal rule of railroading—no drinking on duty—stayed on. Young and inexperienced men failed to receive the supervision they should have had. All of these factors, the ICC explained in its *Annual Statistical Report* in 1909, had led to a considerably higher accident rate, both for passengers and for employees. Whereas 359 passengers and 3,929 employees had been killed on the railroads in 1906, the corresponding figures for 1907 were 610 and 4,534. By 1909, however, things were back to "normal," and only a few more human lives were lost in that year than in 1900.

That railroading was a hazardous business is beyond question. In the bloody year of 1907, 87,644 employees and 13,041 passengers, bystanders, or trespassers had been injured on or by trains in the United States. After that year a steady downward trend set in, and as the new equipment and improved rights of way asserted themselves, the heavy

[22] James Brandt Latimer, *Railway Signaling in Theory and Practice* (Chicago, 1909), a contemporary authority, said that no other branch of railroading was receiving more attention, but "signal engineering is still in its infancy"; 345–46, 348, 351. The first interlocking plant was installed by the Pennsylvania at Trenton in 1870. The big new terminals, however, made the perfection of signaling an absolute necessity after 1890; Edward Everett King, *Railway Signaling* (New York, 1921), 1–2, 22–23. Union Switch & Signal Co., *Electro-Pneumatic Interlocking* (Swissvale, Pa., 1914), 5–79 and *passim,* although it promotes the company's own equipment, is illuminating. Ralph Scott, *Automatic Block Signals and Signal Circuits* (New York, 1908), reveals the state of the art in these years. The ICC continuously studied automatic block signals and other devices for promoting efficiency and safety. ICC, *Annual Reports of the Block Signal and Train Control Board* (Washington, 1909–12); Martin A. Knapp, *Report of the ICC on Block-Signal Systems and Appliances for the Automatic Control of Railway Trains,* 59th Cong., 2d Sess., Senate Document 342, *passim.*

toll of the years of transition declined. It is no surprise to discover, however, that the enemies of the railroads used the accident statistics against them. Back in 1897 the ICC, alarmed at the grossly unfair comparisons which were being drawn between American and European railroads, explained that in this country every accident, no matter how minor, had to be reported. In Europe, by contrast, an employee had to be incapacitated for from three to fourteen days to become a statistic. The unfair comparisons continued, however, and in 1909 an angry Congress relieved the railroads of their obligation to report accidents to the Commission. Until the air age and television brought the horror and the thrills of disaster into the living room, however, the train wreck remained a sensational feature of American life.[23]

VI

Edward H. Harriman sat atop the best-run and most thoroughly integrated of the railroad combinations in 1907. What he said, therefore, and especially the way in which he said it, was likely to be viewed by the vast majority of Americans as reflecting both the spirit and the practice of American railroad management. That being the case, it was unfortunate for the railroads' image that Harriman carried over into the twentieth century much of the individualism (and, many people would thus be convinced, the morals as well) of the public-be-damned tycoons of the previous century. His advisers, particularly Robert S. Lovett, constantly beseeched him to modify his public tone. By 1907 it had got him into considerable hot water. No less a person than the President had set the ICC and its most energetic Commissioner, Franklin K. Lane, a "Roosevelt Democrat," to work investigating "the matter of consolidations and combinations of carriers." While the official title of the investigation was couched in the most general terms, few doubted that it was Harriman that the Rough Rider was after. Late in 1906, as government attorney Frank B. Kellogg questioned him, Harriman treated himself to the following dialogue, for which the railroads paid heavily in the coming years:

[23] ICC, *Annual Statistical Report,* 1897, 1906, 1907, 1909.

Kellogg: Supposing that you got the Santa Fe?

Harriman: You would not let us get it.

Kellogg: How could we help it?

Harriman: How could you help it? I think you would bring out your power to enforce the conditions of the Sherman anti-trust act pretty quick. If you will let us, I will go and take the Santa Fe tomorrow. . . .

Kellogg: Then it is only the restriction of the law that keeps you from taking it?

Harriman: I would go on as long as I live.[24]

If a generalization about the character, quality, and motivation of American railroad management in the nineteenth century is not as easy as the simplistic "robber baron" school of history once thought, it is virtually impossible for the Progressive era. All of the old styles— wheeler-dealer, debaucher, and charismatic leader—were still very much in the picture, while the new breed of professional managers were already in charge of a large part of the railroad system. If, as is no doubt true, leadership can only be judged by the fruits of its labors, little is to be gained by attempting to arraign here the good and the bad, the competent and the incompetent, the honest and the criminal. Because of the popular belief during the Progressive era that railroad management was universally greedy, selfish, and corrupt, however (a belief which railroad enemies carefully nurtured, although many of them were growing too sophisticated to go on believing it), we must take a look at railroad leadership, warts and all, to see how justified the national image really was.

What looks to the general public like evil genius often turns out to be stumbling incompetence. A surprising amount of the chicanery in the Progressive era, it seems, was in the final analysis the result of incompetence, stupidity, and even indifference. The most notorious operators of the period were William Henry Moore and Daniel G. Reid, who seized the Rock Island, the Frisco, and several smaller midwest railroads between 1901 and 1904, and then did not seem to know what to do with them. The evidence is overwhelming that their stewardship was, to say the least, not helpful to the roads. Not that anyone ever succeeded in finding out how much the partners made out of the deal. Reid, a robber-baron stylist to his high-top shoes, verbally thumbed his

[24] 12 ICC 277, 281. The report was written by Lane.

nose at the ICC, telling its members that he had no idea what his profits were, because he burned his books each month. Astronomical profits can be imputed to these men's operations, which included the building or acquisition of numerous branch lines of dubious usefulness in Oklahoma and Texas, by assuming that they resold at par the bonds which they received at heavy discounts. Nothing, of course, was less likely. Even without the depredations of these men, however, the Rock Island and the Frisco would have been in deep trouble by 1914. Operating expenses (apart from fixed charges on the funded debt) were rising much more rapidly than revenues. It was a situation common to all of the western roads, especially such unfavorably situated and poorly managed railroads as these. It is a good bet that their railroad operations never yielded Moore and Reid the kind of profits they had expected—the kind, for example, they had made out of the National Biscuit and U.S. Steel mergers.[25]

Much more bizarre is the story of what happened to that most unfortunate of railroad properties, the New York, New Haven, and Hartford Railroad. Few corporate jungles have been so thoroughly beaten down by investigation after investigation, for no other railroad came into daily contact with so many important and highly moral people as the New Haven. No unfeeling tyrant ever built up more resentment among his subjects than the New Haven generated among the people of New England. Its agonies have provided grist for the mills of untold numbers of antirailroad publicists. The story is, indeed, one of the most unedifying chapters in American entrepreneurial history. It has its pathetic side as well, in what it reveals about the decline of the faculties of a great financial leader. For the untidy corporate tangle which went by the name of the New Haven was the child of J. P. Morgan's declining years. Morgan had never thought that the old nineteenth-century New Haven management had made the railroad the center of New England transportation services which he thought it should be. Beginning in the nineties, the company, under Morgan's tutelage, began to gather all of the railroads in southern New England into a consolidated system. If he had stopped there, all might have been well. But Morgan, with the

[25] "William Henry Moore," *DAB*, XIII, 142–45; 36 ICC 43 [investigation of the Chicago, Rock Island & Pacific Railroad]; 29 ICC 139 [investigation of the St. Louis–San Francisco Railroad Co.], 143–44, 160–61.

wholehearted approval of his senior associates, set the company on a course to scoop up steetcar lines, interurban electric railways, steamship companies, warehouses (all at greatly inflated prices which consistently diluted the basic earning power of the railroad proper), and eventually the Boston & Maine Railroad, in northern New England, as well. Morgan's lieutenant in these operations was Charles S. Mellen, a competent and thoroughly experienced railroad man. But there were only two ways to deal with the cross and crusty and frequently absent Morgan of the last years. George Perkins, a smarter man than most, saw the light and got out.[26] Mellen chose to remain and become a "yes-man."

By 1906 Mellen was ready to despair. He no longer knew what was going on. When the word came to buy the New York, Westchester, and Boston Railroad, Mellen knew he had to do something. The Westchester was an electric commuter line which, in its hopeless efforts to build a line from the south Bronx to White Plains, without any access to Manhattan island, was obviously falling flat on its face. But it paralleled the New Haven, and this meant that Mellen had to run out and buy it, no matter what the price. The price and the terms both looked fishy. A few minutes in Morgan's office, however, were enough to humiliate poor Mellen and set him back in his assigned role. Morgan asked him if he knew who had written the report setting forth the acquisition terms. "Yes," said Mellen, "Mr. Stetson [Francis Lynde Stetson, law partner of former President Cleveland and long-time legal counsel to Morgan] wrote it." "Do you think you know more than Stetson?" Morgan growled. Mellen, red-faced, shuffled out of the august presence, but when he got back to his office he bared his soul in a note written on the back of the report: "I have never known the first thing about [these] securities . . . and no one has thought I was entitled to know. Perhaps I am not." [27]

As the decade wore on more and more people began to suspect that the robust façade which the New Haven displayed hid a confused and shaky financial interior. When the New Haven tried to grab the Boston & Maine, opposition coalesced around a skillful Boston lawyer, Louis Dembitz Brandeis, who displayed incredible powers of seeing

[26] John A. Garraty, *Right-Hand Man* (New York, 1960), 234–38.

[27] 31 ICC 32, in re financial transactions of the New York, New Haven, and Hartford Railroad Co., July 11, 1914, 37.

through financial reports which to others were opaque. The B. & M. acquisition fell through. Then, one day in 1913, just two weeks before Christmas, the directors dropped a bombshell which made the front page of the newspapers. The New Haven, which had paid 130 consecutive quarterly dividends since its incorporation, was passing up its 131st. There was only $1.5 million available to apply against the customary $3.6 million Christmas disbursement, and that was needed for working capital. It was just as well that Morgan, who had died in Europe earlier that year, did not live to see what a mess he had made of things. The New Haven publicity was a bitter cup that would not pass. The damage to the railroads' collective reputation was incalculable.[28]

By 1900 the charismatic railroad operator who exercised his leadership through a vivid personality, intense dedication to grand objectives, and direct ownership through a large personal fortune was rapidly becoming extinct in the American railroad picture. James J. Hill, who had molded the railroads of the Northwest into a viable and efficient servant of that rapidly growing region of the country after a previous generation of "money men" had failed, was nearing the end of his colorful career. Jay Gould, whose preeminent position in the robber-baron pantheon has been effectively challenged by the voluminous scholarship of Julius Grodinsky, had passed from the picture nearly ten years earlier.[29] The none too robust railroads in the Southwest which for years had been known as the "Gould lines" had passed to his son, but George's grip never matched that of his father. By 1915 the Goulds would belong to the checkered past of America's railroads.

On the eve of the Progressive experiment in strict government regulation of railroads, the unquestioned leader of the American railroad industry was Edward H. Harriman. He had achieved more than any other man, with the possible exception of J. P. Morgan, in the battle for stability. His standards of personal conduct were high. When it was learned that socialite Stuyvesant Fish, president of the Illinois Central, was practicing favoritism in respect to a certain Chicago bank, and was

[28] 31 ICC 32, 63; *NYT*, Dec. 14, 1913, 1. The New Haven investigations, and especially Brandeis' role, are ably summarized in Alpheus T. Mason, *Brandeis: A Free Man's Life* (New York, 1946), 177–214. Frederick Lewis Allen, *The Great Pierpont Morgan* (New York, 1949), 233–35, describes Morgan's influence on the hapless New Haven.

[29] Julius Grodinsky, *Jay Gould: His Business Career* (Philadelphia, 1955).

in trouble with his fellow directors of the Mutual Life Insurance Company, Harriman saw that Fish was removed.[30] Harriman himself worked long hours at a career in which the rehabilitation and improvement of railroad systems and the making of large sums of money were intimately related. By 1900 the reputation of the slight, walrus-moustached genius had reached that point in the career of the spectacularly successful man at which the masses conclude that he can make no mistakes in his financial dealings, nor do anything ethical in the process. It was perhaps inevitable that neither Harriman nor any other man could wield the power and leadership in American economic affairs which he did, in these intensely political years, without being challenged. Harriman's virtuoso use of radical new financial techniques, which not even his most articulate associates could explain to the less brilliant, combined with a personality that was too bluntly independent for the game of business-cum-politics, ultimately brought his stewardship into grave question. The magnate's activities were severely, even viciously, attacked after 1906, and the railroads' public image undoubtedly suffered accordingly. By 1910 a majority of Americans probably believed that the railroads as a whole were financially mismanaged. Much of their attitude would stem from the sensational investigation of Harriman's reorganization of the Chicago & Alton Railroad. A close look at this episode will tell us much about the archaic economic thinking of the Progressive era.

Harriman and his associates had entered the Alton picture in 1898 at the request of a majority of the stockholders and, over the stubborn opposition of the road's long-time president, had gained control. In the next three or four years the railroad was radically reorganized financially, and extensively rebuilt and reequipped. (In 1904 the Moore-Reid interests, operating through the Rock Island, gained effective control in one of the few outmaneuverings which Harriman ever suffered.) Until late in 1906, the Alton reorganization had attracted no attention outside financial circles. But the condition of the Alton in 1898, its clouded prospects under the old management's policies, and the full details of the intricate financial reorganization had been thoroughly publi-

---

[30] *Commercial and Financial Chronicle, Bank and Quotation Supplement* (hereinafter referred to as *CFC, BQS*), LXXXII (March 3, 1906), 21–22. See also Chapter IV below.

cized at the time, a fact which is of the greatest significance in examining the objectivity of Harriman's Progressive critics.[31]

What awakened intense public interest in the Alton case? The unavoidable answer seems to be that it was the hurt pride and moral indignation of the peppery and politically astute man who occupied the White House. In the fall of 1906 Theodore Roosevelt received a letter from James S. Sherman, Republican party wheelhorse, which made him hopping mad. Harriman, Sherman reported, had flatly refused to contribute to the party campaign fund when Sherman visited him the week before. Apparently anticipating T.R.'s demand to know Harriman's reason, the fund raiser spilled the beans about a much more important meeting which he had had with Harriman during the campaign of 1904, when T.R. was leaving no stone unturned to be elected President in his own right. At that time, Sherman related, Harriman had confided to him that the President had asked him for the enormous sum of $250,-000 and promised in return to appoint Chauncey Depew ambassador to France. But Depew had not been appointed, and to make matters worse Harriman's recommendations on railroad regulation had been rebuffed and the Hepburn Act, which the railroad leader felt was entirely unnecessary, had been passed. On his second visit, Sherman reported, Harriman had indulged his talent for contempt without restraint. He didn't care who was elected, he said, because he could buy whomever he wanted or needed in public life. Roosevelt, perhaps already sensing that a President would find his former closeness to men of great wealth more and more of an incubus in the years ahead, seized the initiative. Mr. Harriman's remark, he said, "shows a cynicism and deep-seated corruption which makes the man uttering such sentiments . . . at least as undesirable a citizen as Debs, or Moyer, or Haywood." [32] The outcome of the clash was an investigation of Harriman's affairs, concentrating on

[31] *CFC,* LXVI (Feb. 26, 1898), 402–3; LXVII (Dec. 17, 1898), 1262; LXVIII (Feb. 11, 1899), 249; LXVIII (various dates), 230, 281, 330, 376, 379, 427, 523, 617, 670, 925, 976, 1022, 1224, 1225; LXIX (various dates), 26, 129, 178, 228, 384, 541, 591, 645, 1061, 1147; LXX (May 19, 1900), 995, is a detailed report on the financial structure of the new company.

[32] The President's statement and his detailed summary of the Depew and regulation matters appear in his letter to Sherman, Oct. 8, 1906, *Letters,* ed. Elting E. Morison (8 vols., Cambridge, Mass., 1951–54, V, 447–52). Whatever the original sources of the friction, the hard words which the two men used do not seem to be in doubt.

the Alton reorganization, an investigation which men like Attorney
General Charles Bonaparte, ICC Commissioner Franklin K. Lane, Sec-
retary of War William Howard Taft, and antitrust attorney Frank B.
Kellogg recommended enthusiastically.

It is true that "prior to 1898 the Chicago & Alton was a conservatively financed and tremendously prosperous railroad." [33] Therein lay
its troubles. The "tremendous prosperity" was the result of a long-continued policy of resisting every opportunity for expansion or moderniza-
tion of the railroad, while ignoring its growing inadequacies. This policy stemmed logically from the other problem, the "conservative"
financial structure of the company. The fact is that except for a relatively small amount of bonds, virtually all of the physical assets of the
company were represented by stock, on which the regular payment of a
generous dividend had practically become a permanent obligation. No
such arrangement had made any sense on American railroads for at
least a quarter of a century. The instability which it might have caused
in the eighties and nineties had been prevented only by the fact that the
Alton's president owned one-third of the total, and very little was free
to circulate in the market. Truly conservative financial policy had long
since called for the funding of the majority of the assets of a railroad in
long-term, fixed-interest bonds, whose holders have a lien on the properties under a mortgage, but otherwise play no part in the affairs of the
company so long as the management performs satisfactorily. To make
matters worse, the Alton's small bond issue would fall due between
1898 and 1903.[34]

But it was not primarily the financial structure of the Alton, despite its backwardness, which had the line's stockholders worried when
they came to Harriman in 1898. The hard fact is that the Alton was
one of the most troublesome "old maids" in the entire family of midwestern railroads. Operating the best routes between Chicago and St.
Louis, and between Chicago and Kansas City, the Alton could also
have had, by a little cooperation with certain other railroads, the best
line between St. Louis and Kansas City. During the last third of the
nineteenth century its strategically fine location had served the Alton

[33] Harold U. Faulkner, *The Decline of Laissez Faire* (New York, 1951), 199.
[34] *Poor's Manual of Railroads, 1894*, 885.

well. It received a rapidly growing volume of freight from southern, southwestern, and western railroads, which it carried north; and from the railroads at Chicago and St. Louis, including the trunk lines which originated staggering amounts of freight, it received a handsome volume of traffic ultimately destined for connecting railroads. But as the century wore on, more and more of these connecting railroads made other arrangements. The Santa Fe built its own line from Kansas City to Chicago. The Rock Island constructed a link from Kansas City to its main Chicago line. The Illinois Central worked out an entry into St. Louis via the Big Four. Other railroads were built to exploit the rich passenger business between St. Louis and Chicago. Throughout these years the Alton steadfastly refused all offers of "marriage" with other railroads, which finally had to make less advantageous arrangements. A link-up with the Gould lines to the southwest would have been one of the most logical of all the consolidations of the nineties, but it seems never to have been considered.

The consequences of such a shortsighted policy for the Alton, which actually went on from year to year proudly announcing that more and more of its business was "local," were becoming painfully clear after 1893. Throughout the first fifty years of the new century the Alton would remain a problem, with first one railroad and then another trying to marry her, until she finally found an enduring engagement with the Gulf, Mobile, and Ohio after World War II. In 1898, it is certain, the opportunity to place the Alton in the hands of a man like Harriman, who had demonstrated such a talent for integrating individual railroads into systems, was extremely seductive to the Alton's worried stockholders.[35]

It was not only Harriman's financial and organizational genius

---

[35] One of the Rock Island promoters' objectives in seizing control of the Alton in 1904 had been to reroute its Kansas City–Chicago business over the better road. This fact, and other examples of the need to integrate the Alton into a larger system, were cited by Harriman in his lengthy testimony during the ICC investigation. It is unfortunate that these lines of investigation were not pursued, but it is clear that they did not produce the kind of information which the ICC and attorney Kellogg were seeking. ICC, *Testimony of E. H. Harriman before the ICC in the Matter of the Consolidation and Combination of Carriers, Relations between Such Carriers, and Community of Interests Therein, Their Rates, Facilities and Practices* (New York, 1907). The narrow vision of the old Alton management is revealed in the company's *Annual Reports.*

which attracted the stockholders of the Alton. His record of outthinking some of the best engineers in the country when the job of rebuilding the rickety Union Pacific fell to him was the brightest jewel in his crown. If there ever was a practical man of affairs who could recognize an opportunity to make money by spending it, Harriman was the man. The road was thoroughly "Harrimanized." In an expansion and improvement program which was as dramatic a break with the past as the financial reorganization, the road's main line was virtually rebuilt. Mile after mile was ripped up and realigned to remove curves. A forty-mile segment between Springfield and Chicago remains to this day the longest and most level straight stretch of railroad track east of the Mississippi. A bridge over the Mississippi on the Kansas City–Chicago route, of which the old management had been inordinately proud as the first all-steel bridge in the world, was unceremoniously replaced by a new one. Tracks in the city of Chicago were elevated. The net amount invested in the railroad by the new owners was approximately $15 million.[36]

The Alton was magnificently transformed (in later years it was much admired for its physical condition), but unfortunately the toughest problem, that of integrating it with other railroads, was never solved. Harriman apparently was spread too thin to take care of his new responsibility in this regard, and the Moore-Reid interests seem never to have descended to such prosaic problems of business. The Alton's financial performance for the two or three years just before Harriman was put on the witness stand, however, revealed clearly for those who wished to see it that the railroad was carrying a volume of traffic and turning a net profit which it could never have attained as it stood in 1898.[37] In no sense was it a "looted" railroad. But the ICC, although in full possession of all this information, chose to publish a formal report which from beginning to end was a condemnation not only of Harriman's policies but of his motives as well. Lane, who wrote the report,

[36] F. H. Spearman, "Rebuilding a Great Railroad," *World's Work*, VIII (Oct., 1904), 5371–77; 12 ICC 277; George Kennan, *The Chicago and Alton Case: A Misunderstood Transaction* (New York, 1916), 15.

[37] In 1898 the Alton had a gross revenue of $7.2 million; in 1906, $11.6 million. In the earlier year, after the traditional dividend on the stock was paid, plus interest charges of $1.1 million, a surplus of $200,000 remained. In 1906, after a smaller dividend but with interest charges of $2.5 million, a $200,000 surplus was also earned.

refused even to suggest that there was any evidence to the contrary, but placed the government body of which he was a member unequivocally on record as convinced that Harriman had made every effort to conceal the syndicate's plans and its operations. The financier was condemned for paying a stock dividend of six million dollars to the new stockholders out of the proceeds of a bond issue, brushing aside the legally unassailable fact that the dividend arose from the recapitalization of twelve million dollars in permanent improvements which the old management had written off in earlier years. The sale of bonds at substantial discounts from par was likewise condemned, despite the fact that this was the time-honored mechanism by which the market discounted the low coupon rate of interest (3 per cent) which the securities bore. Lane omitted to mention that Theodore Roosevelt, as governor of New York, had signed the bill which made bonds with such a low rate of interest a legal investment for insurance companies. Nor did he explain why the astute New York Life Insurance Company would take ten million dollars of the bonds at a price of 96.

The most virulent criticism, however, was aimed at the "forty million dollars" in stock which the syndicate members issued to themselves. In our day no-par-value stock has long since been accepted, but in 1906 it was not the way things were done: investors wanted a dollar sign somewhere on the expensive pieces of paper they bought. It was also against the law in many states to issue no-par stock. As Robert S. Lovett would explain to the Hadley Commission in 1910, if Harriman had issued no-par-value stock in 1899, no one would ever have insisted that he had saddled the railroad with forty million dollars of "debt" for which no value had been received. But the state of Illinois, he noted, did not permit such stock. Apparently only a slight further stretch of the imagination was required for an archaic Progressive like Lane to blandly add this forty million dollars in equity securities, for which the Alton was not obligated to pay anybody anything, to what he called the "capital indebtedness" of the company.[38]

Lane's report contained no words of praise for the physical trans-

[38] Robert S. Lovett, "Statement before the Railroad Securities [Hadley] Commission, December 21, 1910" (New York, 1911), 17–18; 12 ICC 277, 297 and *passim*. The ICC's report must rank as one of the most partisan formal administrative reports ever issued by a government agency at the federal level.

formation of the Alton and revealed no understanding of the fundamental problems which had made its continuance under the old management policies impossible. Near the end of the lengthy document, however, the Commissioner (reluctantly, one must conclude) admitted, "It is true . . . that . . . while the total of bonds and stocks were doubled, there was no such proportionate increase in the fixed charges of the railroad. Under Blackstone [the former president] yearly charges for dividends and interest amounted to $2.8 million whereas [now] fixed charges amount to but $3.5 million." He might have added that for the additional $700,000 in charges the railroad had received about $15 million in fresh capital (at, therefore, an interest cost of about 5 per cent). He might also have noted that in the expenditure of this new capital the railroad had had the services of the most competent railroad man in the world. None of this was said. The overwhelmingly condemnatory tone of Lane's report, clothed as it was in the aura of official objectivity and respectability, virtually ruled out any danger of a libel suit against Harriman's detractors. The affair, in fact, opened the way for a chorus of indignation. The usually calm Professor of Political Economy at Harvard, William Z. Ripley, lost all perspective in the matter. In his chapter on railroad stock practices, which is a broadside against no-par-value stock, his accusations took such leave of reality that George Kennan, alarmed at the Olympian character of their source, was goaded into writing a defense of Harriman, his long-time friend and associate.[39]

In retrospect it seems clear that the Alton investigation never had any other purpose than that of propagandizing against the railroad men's fitness to continue their stewardship without close governmental supervision. None of the charges that stockholders were deprived of essential information about the deal could stand the light of truth. No important new laws pertaining to the issuance of securities by railroads or industrial concerns resulted from the sensational ICC investigation. The underwriting procedures and the financial techniques of the Harriman syndicate were models of prudent business practice which, if anything, were ahead of their time. What did result was a McCarthyite "where-there's-smoke-there's-fire" mentality among men in both private and

[39] William Z. Ripley, *Railroads: Finance and Organization* (New York, 1915), 262–67; Kennan, *The Chicago and Alton Case.*

public life which worked as well then as it does in our time. And when, by 1914, the Alton was in deep financial trouble for reasons that had nothing to do with the Harriman reorganization, the affair would be used as a tragic obfuscation of the real railroad problem. As an influence on public policy, the case happily lasted only until America outgrew the inanities of archaic Progressivism. As myth it is as alive today as ever.[40]

A new breed of railroad manager had long since taken hold by the time the Harriman shield had become so tarnished. Charles S. Mellen's retirement in 1913 awakened many to that fact. But the beginnings of modern railroad management can be traced back to the last quarter of the nineteenth century, when the organizational structure of the Pennsylvania Railroad took shape. An English expert attributed the effectiveness of American railroads to the characteristic arrangement in which those responsible for the operation are free from the constant meddling of stockholders and even of boards of directors. This had led, he noted, not to profligacy of management as a general rule, but instead to a closer identification of the management's interests with those of the railroad system itself. It had produced a great motivation to plow back into the enterprise one-half of net income, and sometimes more, rather than paying it out to the stockholders. No English railway executive, he

[40] By 1914 all of the midwestern railroads were in grave financial trouble, as the ICC would be forced to recognize. Gross revenues were not rising as rapidly as on the trunk lines, while operating expenses, especially wages, were essentially beyond the railroads' control. For the Alton, which was now totally isolated, these factors were especially acute. By 1914, in fact, operating expenses had risen to $12.3 million, not much below gross revenues of $13.7 million. No railroad, regardless of its financial structure, could exist under such conditions. *Poor's Manual of Railroads, 1914*. Harriman considered the Alton affair to be the worst blot on his record, but refused all suggestions by subordinates that he try to rebut the accusations. H. J. Eckenrode and Pocahontas Edmunds, *E. H. Harriman, the Little Giant of Wall Street* (New York, 1933), 190–91. James C. Bonbright, *Railroad Capitalization* (New York, 1920), 184, takes the ICC and Ripley to task for their more egregious distortions, but still complains that the Alton deal was complex and "sure to confuse the ordinary investor." That the myths of par-value stock were not confined to archaic Progressives and other enemies of railroad management can be seen in the fact that long-time railroad publicist Slason Thompson, in his *Short History of American Railways* (Chicago, 1925), 353, concluded a long paean of praise for Harriman with the confused conclusion that the magnate "left the Chicago and Alton an improved and rehabilitated but impoverished common carrier."

said, could ever get away with such a policy. "I question whether the most conservatively managed English railway is as conservative as the best American roads," he concluded.[41]

The management structure which evolved came to be known as the "unit" system. Essentially it is an application of the military system of division between staff and line. The key elements of the system are simply those of any large organization in which there exists the constant danger that some tasks will be duplicated while others are totally neglected. The most important feature is that everybody shall clearly understand what his job is, the criteria on which his performance will be based, and the fact that he is to run his part of the organization without interference from others. How authority is passed, especially in the absence of the chief, was only slightly less important. The most significant feature of the new management, however, was the division of the sprawling organization into well-defined "units" of authority and responsibility. Within his own sphere the chief engineer or the superintendent of motive power, for example, was supreme, as long as he worked at the long-run improvement of the railroad. But the key man in the organization was the division superintendent. Although his authority ended abruptly at the limits of his division, within it no staff man could tell him what modifications should be made in yards, sidings, or right of way, nor what kind of locomotive to use for a specific run, nor even whether the service he was giving a particular shipper was adequate or inadequate. Of course he was held strictly responsible for the outcome of his efforts in these regards, but the significant fact is that the touchstone of his success was not whether he made some other executive happy, but whether the division was turning in a profit for the railroad. Or, to put it in broader social terms, not whether he was "playing the game," but whether the nation's burdens were being carried. It was an arrangement which most men turned into a fierce con-

[41] Acworth, "American and English Railways Compared," 12–13, 14–15. Another and more famous commentator on the American scene had noted this peculiar separation of ownership and management of railroads ten years earlier; James Bryce, *The American Commonwealth* (2 vols., London, 1889), II, 512–16. Alfred D. Chandler, Jr., *The Railroads: The Nation's First Big Business* (New York, 1965), documents the inventiveness with which the railroads faced organizational problems, wherein they were forced to play the role of pioneer as in most other phases of their affairs.

test, and still do.[42] After 1910 most of the railroad executives who had the responsibility of guiding their systems through the crossed-up switches of Progressive era regulation were the products of the unit system. And, while the system never worked in practice so smoothly as it has been idealized in this sketch, it provided the best available climate for enterprise to do its work.

VII

That the railroads met the challenge of an enormous expansion in freight and passenger traffic, generated by the busy, exciting years of the Progressive era, is obvious. The burden was carried, although not always as fast or as well as it should or could have been. That they met the challenge by a program of redevelopment and reequipping their facilities that was so extensive as to justify the name of rebuilding has been the main theme of this chapter. But it is also true that this neverending improvement program involved not merely large infusions of capital to satisfy the demand for more track, more locomotives, more rolling stock—more, in short, of everything—but also a synergistic combination of more resources with better ways of doing things: in short, a process of innovation which brought about not only a straightline growth in American railroads but an increase in productivity as well.

Few close students of the railroads or, for that matter, of any other aspect of the highly dynamic Western capitalistic system in these years ever needed much convincing of the startling strides which were being taken in productivity. For others the fact has not been so obvious. The measurement of productivity, as a technique of economic analysis, has only fairly recently been developed to the point where we can draw

[42] Apart from the Pennsylvania, the leadership in the development of railroad management was most notable on Harriman's Union Pacific and Julius Kruttschnitt's Southern Pacific. The former leader has been rather fatuously referred to as the "Napoleon" of railroading and the latter, emphasizing his general staff approach, as the "Von Moltke of transportation." Charles D. Hine, *Letters from an Old Railway Official to His Son, a Division Superintendent* (Chicago, 1904), 69, 70–72, 101, 108; and Hine, *Modern Organization: An Exposition of the Unit System* (New York, 1912), *passim*.

confident conclusions about a given industry. Before we consider what modern economic thought tells us about productivity in the Progressive era, however, we must consider some of the clues to the achievements of the railroads which were available to their friends and foes at the time, and on which national railroad policy ought to have been based.

It is a simple matter to demonstrate that remarkable strides were made in the production of transportation with relatively less and less labor, a significant contribution in those inflationary years. In 1910 American railroads produced about 125 per cent more transportation "units" (passenger plus freight) than in 1898, with only about 93 per cent more labor. By 1914 the two measures had diverged even more: transportation was 155 per cent above 1898; labor, only 95 per cent. Clearly, the wartime burden could not have been carried in 1916–18, a period of critical labor shortage, without these gains. The impressive gains in intensity of utilization of the basic railroad plant which were made possible by the rebuilding programs are dramatized by the fact that whereas in 1898 an average mile of railroad route produced 618,-000 ton-miles of freight, in 1910 it produced 954,000, and in 1913, 1,245,000. The exhilarating way that the bigger cars and the beefier locomotives paid off is easy to see: in 1900 an average freight train hauled only 271 tons of payload. By 1910 it had been transformed into a longer train of heavier cars, hauling 380 tons; and by 1915 the average tonnage was 474. In 1898 the old-fashioned locomotives of America's railroads had scurried 5.5 billion miles on their appointed freight rounds; by 1910, despite a burden 125 per cent higher, locomotives traveled only 7.2 billion miles. Most amazing of all, however, were the figures for 1914. Although tonnage had continued to climb, the total mileage run by locomotives had actually *decreased* since 1910. All of these data, and many more, the men of the Progressive era had. It would be a resourceful man who would seek to denigrate the railroads' accomplishments.

The foregoing figures, of course, make no provision for increased capital input. While it would be a remarkable situation in which the entrepreneur would knowingly substitute capital for labor where there was no gain in productivity, we must address ourselves nevertheless to the question of the *net* gain in railroad productivity. This work has been done up to the year 1910 by Albert Fishlow, in a study which deserves to be brought down to the present at the earliest possible opportunity. Mr. Fishlow's sophisticated techniques reveal, in summary, a growth of 30 per cent in net productivity from 1890 to 1900, and a further growth of 15 per cent from 1900 to 1910. (His data reveal that the most dynamic input was equipment.) Our approximations of the productivity trends beyond 1910 suggest that Fishlow's findings would also hold for the period between the passage of the Mann-Elkins Act in 1910 and the onset of the war in 1917. All of these data, of course, support the hypothesis that the demand for capital by American railroads, and the opportunities for its productive use, were very considerable in 1910. As we shall see, the rate of capital investment in American railroads rose *in relation to traffic* up to the time that strict government regulation was applied. How this was accomplished, what happened to the trend after 1907, and why are investigated in the following chapters.[43]

[43] ICC, *Annual Statistical Report,* 1897–1917; Albert Fishlow, "Productivity and Technological Change in the Railroad Sector," in *Output, Employment, and Productivity in the United States After 1800,* Vol. 30 of "Studies in Income and Wealth" (New York, 1966). See also the earlier work of Harold Barger, *The Transportation Industries, 1889–1946* (New York, 1951).

CHAPTER IV

THE FINANCIAL RECKONING

*Thrift may be the handmaid and nurse of Enterprise. But equally she may
not. . . . For the engine which drives Enterprise is not Thrift, but Profit.*
—JOHN MAYNARD KEYNES, *1930*

*A man in St. Louis purchased a sheep's kidney for seven-and-a-half dollars.
In his rage at the price he exclaimed: "As a public man I have given twenty
of the best years of my life to bringing about a friendly understanding
between capital and labor. I have succeeded, and may God have mercy on
my meddlesome soul!"*—AMBROSE BIERCE, *1909*

I

Brokers, bankers, and their clerks, emerging from their Wall
Street offices into the late afternoon gloom of January 23, 1899, had
something exciting to talk about. Volume of shares traded that day on
the Stock Exchange had broken all previous records. Following a Saturday which saw the most active short session in history, members had
rushed to the trading posts at the opening bell on Monday and by closing time had exchanged an unprecedented 1,600,000 shares, "with
many thousand shares more, it is believed, unrecorded," as one authority claimed.[1] The immediate reason for the buoyancy of the market was
a rumor on Saturday that the forces which had been laboring to stabi-
lize the nation's railroads following the debacle of the 1893–96 depression were about to link the Vanderbilt and Harriman lines—the New
York Central, the Chicago & Northwestern, the Illinois Central, and the
Union Pacific—into the first ocean-to-ocean system.[2] The rumor was

[1] *Commercial and Financial Chronicle, Quarterly Supplement* (hereinafter referred to as *CFC, QS*), LXVIII (Feb. 4, 1899), 6; *NYT,* Jan. 22, 1899, 22,
and Jan. 24, 8. The Exchange, like virtually all business offices in those days,
was open a half day on Saturdays.

[2] *CFC, QS,* LXVIII (Feb. 4, 1899), 6.

denied immediately, but not before Central common had leaped ten points. The stock of the New York, Ontario & Western, a weak road with possibilities, which seemed sure to be brought into the new system sooner or later, was the most heavily traded on that record-breaking Monday.[3]

The turn-of-the-century securities market, if not exclusively a barometer of investors' opinions of the railroads' financial prospects, was nevertheless dominated by this industry. The relatively small proportion of the nation's wealth which was invested in exchange-listed corporate enterprises was overwhelmingly concentrated in railroads and the industrial enterprises which had grown up to supply the steel and the rapidly growing variety of equipment and mechanical devices which they required. In its monthly summary of stock price movements, the authoritative *Commercial and Financial Chronicle* listed thirty-eight railroad stocks and twenty-two "miscellaneous" stocks. Of the latter group, three were municipal railways and the majority were dependent to a considerable degree on purchases by railroads.[4] The few pages of stock prices, however, were preceded by page after page of bond prices, for debt securities still dominated equities in the nation's financial center. And most of these bonds were railroad issues.

The immense capital sums which had gone to provide the nation with a comprehensive, if rather rickety, transportation network by 1893, and the realization that much more would be required in the years just ahead, set the tone for the entire financial community. Investors, many of whom had been badly burned by the violent reorganizations which followed the epidemic of bankruptcies in the nineties, slowly began to turn their attention from the high-priced issues of such solid roads as the Central and the Pennsylvania to low- and medium-priced issues "of reorganized roads whose real standing had not yet been determined, but whose prospects naturally appeared bright in view of the revival in trade and the great expansion in earnings of the properties affected." An example of a security which a year before had had virtually no credit standing at a price of 54¾ was the reorganized Santa

---

[3] *NYT,* Jan. 24, 1899, 8.

[4] A star performer was New York Air Brake Co., busy with the gigantic task of equipping the nation's trains with automatic air brakes. In March the stock went from 147 to 200. *CFC, QS,* LXVIII (April 1, 1899), 18.

Fe's $100-par adjustment income bond, which had climbed to 79½ by December, 1898, and eventually sold at par. The same road's basic security, its general mortgage 4 per cent bond, from which investors had been demanding a net yield of 4.7 per cent (by bidding it down to 85), was selling at par when the Exchange's big day arrived.[5]

The bears were in total eclipse. The seemingly insatiable demand of the railroads for capital with which to increase the load-carrying capacity of their nineteenth-century lines and (of nearly equal importance) the efficiency with which they carried the ever-growing burden would be met exuberantly by Wall Street and its satellites, and by the great European financial centers to whose tune American investment bankers still paid close attention. The month of Janury, 1898, had seen 9.3 million shares change hands on the Exchange—three times as many as in the still-depressed month of January, 1897. But this was nothing. As the old century began its next-to-last year the first month saw 24.3 million shares traded.[6] Soon there would follow, during the first decade of the new century, a series of capital flotations by the railroads each more breathtaking than the last.

II

Confidence ran high in the financial world in 1899 because there was abundant reason to hope that the railroads would be free to resume the program of stabilization of their business relations which had progressed so well up to 1893, after J. P. Morgan had shown the way during the West Shore–South Pennsylvania crisis of 1885.[7] The willingness and ability of the financial leaders to assume the consequences of two decades of widespread railroad anarchy was dramatically demonstrated after 1893. Morgan, for example, had welded an assortment of lines into the Southern Railway, thereby guaranteeing the Southeast a quality of transportation service which it had never known before, and saving

[5] Ibid., LXVIII (Jan. 7, 1899), 5.   [6] Ibid., LXVIII (Feb. 4, 1899), 6.

[7] Albro Martin, "Crisis of Rugged Individualism: The West Shore–South Pennsylvania Railroad Affair, 1880–1885," Pennsylvania Magazine of History and Biography, Vol. XCIII (April, 1969), passim.

many an investor's nest egg from extinction.[8] In the East the relations
of the Central and the Pennsylvania remained excellent as the conservative policies of the Vanderbilt sons, Cornelius II and William K., and of
Frank Thomson, nephew of the Pennsylvania's pioneer leader, were replaced by those of men with more expansionist attitudes. Morgan continued to oversee the eastern railroad situation, particularly the
anthracite roads, which were a constant problem. Having secured control of the Reading after it went bankrupt in 1893, he sewed up the
eastern terminus of a potential trunk line by acquiring, in 1901, a controlling interest in the Central Railroad of New Jersey, over whose
tracks both the Reading and the B. & O. had been accustomed to reach
the Hudson River piers opposite Manhattan. He promptly resold the
C.N.J. shares to the Reading, and in 1903 the Pennsylvania quietly sold
$25 million of its Reading shares to the New York Central. The claim
of the Central and the Pennsylvania to the dominant role in the Northeast was soon to be beyond challenge.

The rising star which most fascinated observers of the railroad
scene, however, had so far confined his efforts to the western half of the
country. With his slight figure, myopic eyes, and droopy bookkeeper's
moustache, Edward Henry Harriman hardly looked the part of the driving tycoon; but by 1900 he was well on his way to welding the transportation facilities of the Mississippi Valley westward to the Pacific
Ocean into a great community of interests to match those of the East. A
brilliant performance as a Wall Street trader had provided him with the
stake which his imperial ambitions demanded. He had bought into the
Illinois Central, whose blue-blooded president, Stuyvesant Fish, responded positively to the proddings of Harriman during the expansionist years of the 1880s. Ten years as vice-president of the Illinois Central, during which the Wall Streeter assiduously studied every aspect of
railroading, saw Harriman emerge during the lean years of the nineties
as a major railroad leader. When the Gould-battered Union Pacific ca-
reened into bankruptcy, he saw in that line a golden opportunity to exercise the leverage which his talents would lend to the small amount of
capital its control required. Within another few years he had also taken

[8] Edward G. Campbell, *The Reorganization of the American Railroad System,
1893–1900* (New York, 1938).

absolute control of the Illinois Central and replaced its low-gear management with a group of men more alive to its potential.[9]

Harriman's powers of "trustification" had long since caught the eye of representatives of railroad and banking capital, who had been quick to see in him the instrument for stabilizing the western half of the industry. Big news of a Harriman offensive came at the beginning of 1901. Ever since the death of Collis P. Huntington the previous summer the Street had been abuzz with rumors about the future of the controlling block of stock in the Southern Pacific which the western magnate's widow, his nephew, and the James Speyer banking family now owned. Front-page news was made, therefore, when it became known that Harriman, as the leader of a syndicate which included his erstwhile opponent, J. P. Morgan, as well as William K. Vanderbilt, George Gould (heir to his father's extensive southwestern railroad holdings), and Kuhn, Loeb, and Company, had put up $66.4 million and coolly walked off with the "octopus." Access to the S.P. was vital to the U.P., which could proceed west of Promontory Point to the Pacific only on the rails of the old Central Pacific, long since amalgamated into the S.P. It was no surprise, therefore, that control was to be exercised through the U.P., which was issuing forty million dollars in bonds to acquire the controlling interest.[10]

There were just two parties who might block Harriman's western empire: James J. Hill, and the federal government—in the person of Theodore Roosevelt. Both proved formidable enemies. Hill, who had realized for his Great Northern the potentialities which Jay Cooke had thought he saw in the weaker Northern Pacific back in the 1870s, was not happy as the balance of power shifted in Harriman's favor. Trouble came first over the Chicago, Burlington, and Quincy. Both men needed it because neither the Great Northern nor the U.P. had ever been extended eastward into Chicago. Hill, probably the only man who could have done so, beat Harriman in the struggle for the Burlington. But Harriman and his ally, Jacob Schiff of Kuhn, Loeb, and Company, had

[9] The best biography of Harriman is still George Kennan, *E. H. Harriman: A Biography* (2 vols., Boston, 1922). His impact on the Illinois Central is covered in C. J. Corliss, *Main Line of Mid-America* (New York, 1950).

[10] *NYT*, Feb. 2, 1901, 1; *CFC, QS,* LXXII (March 2, 1901), 13–14; Stuart Daggett, *Chapters on the History of the Southern Pacific* (New York, 1922), 426–28.

noted that Hill's hold on the Northern Pacific, which held one-half of the Burlington shares just acquired by Hill, was not secure, and they went after that line. Suddenly the nation found itself staggering under a stock market crash which "in the violence and extent of the decline . . . was undoubtedly the worst experienced since the Panic of 1873." Competitive buying of N.P. stock by Harriman and Hill forces had dried up the floating supply, and those who had sold the stock short were unable to buy shares to cover their obligations, even at a price of $1000 a share.[11] Railroad stocks were badly mauled, but this was the kind of confrontation and resolution on which the Street thrived, and prices recovered quickly. Even as the market raged in confusion, the principals in the drama were reaching the sort of compromise which one expects from sensible and evenly matched antagonists. When the titans sat down at the council table and wrapped up the Burlington and Hill's two lines, the Northern Pacific and the Great Northern, in a monster trust to be called the Northern Securities Company, all doubt that the leaders of American railroads could harmonize their interests (at least according to their lights) was laid to rest.

The Northern Securities affair, however, exceeded the limits to which the community-of-interests technique could be pushed in the trust-conscious America of the 1900s. The decisions of the Supreme Court in recent years had greatly weakened the application of both federal and state laws in controlling large corporations, to be sure. And the simultaneous arrival of prosperity and William McKinley in 1897 seemed to gurantee a maximum of freedom for the proponents of cooperation. An assassin's bullet, however, was to change these conditions drastically so that by the end of the decade trustification, for better or worse, would no longer be an available means for reconciling divergent points of view among industrial leaders. For in September, 1901, the heartbeat which Mark Hanna had said was all that stood between "that madman," Theodore Roosevelt, and the White House, was violently stilled. Roosevelt was far too intelligent, and headed too constructive and successful an administration, to be classed as a demagogue, but he never forgot the source of his strength, which was the extraordinary popularity of his crusader stance. To such a leader the hue and cry

[11] *CFC, QS,* LXXII (June 8, 1901), 19–20.

raised over the monopoly which the Northern Securities deal would give the Hill-Harriman interests in the West called for an energetic application of the antitrust laws. In three short years the government's demand for dissolution reached the Supreme Court, which, by a surprise five-to-four decision, ordered the combine dismantled. This was by far the most significant application of the restraint-of-trade concept in preventing the centripetal forces of high finance from placing the entire American transportation system under an oligarchy of three or four powerful men. Nevertheless, repeated threats to invoke the Sherman Act would prove to be a major unsettling factor in the financial climate in which the great railroad expansion of the 1900s proceeded.[12]

Not only their power to combine, but also the ability of the railroads to secure capital for their multitudinous projects seemed unlimited in these fat years. No stress, apparently, was great enough to stem the steady stream of announcements of bond issues, increases in capital stock, acquisitions of branch lines, and, above all, the great engineering projects which would rebuild America's railroads in this golden decade. The railroad labor unions, which by the end of the decade would be a major threat to railroad profits, were still only a cloud on the horizon.[13] The crucial test was passed, however, when weakness in the steel industry, the railroads' largest customer, failed to cause any appreciable pause in the railroads' forward march.[14]

[12] The Northern Securities affair is recounted in Balthasar H. Meyer, *A History of the Northern Securities Case* (Madison, 1906), which concludes that the case had no economic significance. A greater measure of competition appeared after the decision, particularly in the West. That the investment community valued stability more than competition, however, is seen in repeated troubled reactions to such developments as Harriman's departure from the N.P. board, George Gould's decision to push his lines on to the Pacific coast by building the Western Pacific, and the U.P.'s opening of its San Pedro line southwestward, through some of the most desolate country in the world, to salt water at Los Angeles. *CFC, BQS,* LXXX (May 6, 1905), 1777–78.

[13] The lack of coordination between railroad unions in these years is summarized in James W. Kerley, "The Failure of Railway Labor Leadership: A Chapter in Railroad Labor Relations, 1900–1932" (unpublished doctoral dissertation, Columbia University, 1959).

[14] The underlying financial strength of the railroads is a recurrent theme in this period. Cf. *CFC, QS,* LXXIII (Nov. 2, 1901), 19; LXXIV (Feb. 8, 1902), 22; LXXVII (Dec. 5, 1903), 2201–2. The steel companies had demanded a 50 per cent cut in rates to the East Coast to enable them to export their temporary surplus. They got a one-third cut. *CFC, BQS,* LXXVII (Dec. 5, 1903), 2202.

III

The Pennsylvania Railroad Company's nineteenth-century president, Frank Thomson, viewed the onrush of the twentieth century with trepidation in his 1898 annual report. He felt that the courts, in striking down the carriers' group, the Joint Traffic Association, had deprived the community of a "potent agency in enabling the Inter State Commerce Commission to . . . secure the results sought . . . by the Act," and he called for legislation to permit the railroads to be run efficiently.[15] The road had to press ahead with its improvement program, however, if it was to continue to accept the unprecedented volume of freight being offered it. Demands for capital funds, for everything from one thousand new steel gondola cars to new passenger stations, were coming in from all parts of the system and the subsidiary lines west of Pittsburgh. The $1.8 million "extraordinary expenditures fund" which had been set aside no longer looked very extraordinary.[16]

Frail, hard-working Frank Thomson passed out of the picture with his sudden death the following year. It seems unlikely that he would have met the challenges of the next seven years with quite as much strength, imagination, and courage to commit the Pennsylvania to long-term projects of great magnitude as his successor. Alexander J. Cassatt came late to the presidency of the Pennsylvania, a post for which he had given up hope nearly fifteen years before. Now he had only a short time to make his mark, and in his ambition and in the growing demands on the railroad, the times and the leader found their classic coincidence. Early in 1901 stockholders of the railroad were informed that at the annual meeting in March they would be asked to authorize an increase of $100 million in the capital stock of the company. Approval was easily obtained, the stockholders eagerly grasping the opportunity to subscribe for one-half of the shares even though they were priced ten dollars above the par value at which they would go on the books.[17] The reason

[15] P.R.R. Co., *Annual Report for 1898*, 24–25.   [16] *Ibid.*, 23.

[17] The ten-dollar difference was shown as an underwriting profit in the current accounting period, and was not added to the capital account. That railroad accounting practices were indeed conservative on the stronger lines is clear from this example. P.R.R. Co., *Annual Report for 1901*.

for their eagerness lay in the fact that the market price of their company's stock stood even further above par, fluctuating that year no lower than 137 and as high as 161, a record. This spectacular equity financing, moreover, was accomplished at a time when the Pennsylvania's best customer, the U.S. Steel Corporation, was decidedly in profit trouble and when other railroads were simultaneously increasing their equity capitalizations. Almost immediately thereafter the Pennsylvania paid out over six million dollars to acquire the Long Island Railroad, the first step in its grand design to invade New York City.[18]

This was merely the beginning. The magnitude of the Pennsylvania's capital needs had only begun to be apparent, but by early 1903, when stockholders were asked to approve another expansion of the equity capital (this time by nearly $150 million), the financial community was growing accustomed to these regular trips to the capital market. In fact, the Pennsylvania could not wait for the cumbersome process of issuing new capital stock. Reluctantly offering 4½ per cent, it borrowed $35 million dollars on six-month notes to finance construction work on additional freight lines east and west of Pittsburgh, where congestion had forced the humiliating decision to remove temporarily the famous twenty-hour limited trains which ran between New York and Chicago.[19] Approval of the new issue was given in March and stockholders took about $80 million dollars' worth at the usual premium, now somewhat less of a bargain as the stock was selling on the market at between 111 and 158 that year. Such large offerings did indeed tend to depress the market, so much so that J. P. Morgan granted an infrequent interview to cheer things up.[20] It was late summer, however, before the mild bear market which had ensued once again gave way before the fundamental optimism of the times. The first dividend distributions since the depression by a number of lines did the trick, and by early next year Kuhn, Loeb, and Company had "no difficulty" in getting the Pennsylvania another $35 million of short-term money from bankers in the United States and Europe.[21]

[18] *CFC, QS,* LXXII (April 6, 1901), 16. James J. Hill's Great Northern, for example, increased its capital stock from $100 million to $125 million at this time.

[19] *CFC, BQS,* LXXVI (Feb. 7, 1903), 4.   [20] *Ibid.,* LXXVI (April 4, 1903), 24.

[21] *Ibid.,* LXXVII (July 4, 1903), 23, and Aug. 8, 1903, 23; LXXVIII (March 5, 1904), 1034.

Under these onslaughts of financing, it was natural that the Pennsylvania's stockholders, if not the market, should show some exhaustion. Besides, these equity issues were expensive. While they did not technically increase the expenses of the road, the 6 per cent dividend was psychologically almost as much of a fixed obligation to the Pennsylvania in 1904 as interest on first-mortgage bonds was to ordinary railroads. Beginning in 1903, therefore, the Pennsylvania's financial experts turned to the device of the convertible bond, which the holder could exchange for shares of capital stock of the company at a stated price which, it was supposed, would become more and more attractive as the years passed. These securities were marketed at par at the then unheard-of low coupon interest rate of 3½ per cent, or less than half the rate which roads had frequently paid in the perilous years of the seventies and eighties. The issuance of $100 million of this security in the spring of 1905 was the occasion for noting that the leaders of the syndicate, J. P. Morgan and Company and Kuhn, Loeb, and Company, had been opponents just four years earlier in the Northern Securities affair. Nor did it escape notice that Pennsylvania stockholders this time took barely 10 per cent of the issue, instead of their customary 50 per cent, indicating that the mighty Pennsylvania would be depending more and more upon the open market in the future.[22]

Still the demands for new money continued. Almost no segment of the great system, from the new terminal rising in New York City to the Romanesque pile which the Pennsylvania shared with twenty-odd other railroads in St. Louis, was without concrete plans for increasing the capacity and efficiency of the system—and they all cost money. Again through Kuhn, Loeb, and Company, but this time at a net cost of 5 per cent, the road raised $50 million in eighteen-month notes and rumors ran through the financial world that Cassatt was in Europe seeking to tap foreign funds directly. That he was doing exactly that was confirmed in the company's annual report for 1906. It was revealed that the Girard Trust Company had placed fifteen-year bonds in France to the amount of 250 million francs, at a time when huge amounts of French capital were being sunk, much of it forever, in Russian railroads. The rate, moreover, was only 3½ per cent. These securities were for the

[22] *Ibid.*, LXXX (April 8, 1905), 1282, and June 3, 1905, 2262.

very restricted purposes of providing new water supplies for the Pennsylvania's great fleet of locomotives, and for acquisition of new steel freight cars of greatly increased capacity.[23] So great, in fact, was the need for new freight cars that almost at the same time the road issued directly $44 million in equipment trust certificates. This method of financing, whereby title to a specific piece of equipment remains with the lending institution until the trust has been paid off, was the medium by which the Pennsylvania showered upon the feast-or-famine railroad equipment industry orders for a total of 40,000 new cars. Such largesse was unprecedented. But the real blockbuster in the annual report for 1906 was the announcement that the management intended to authorize yet another $200 million capital increase, one-half to be in stock and one-half in long-term bonds which, the report noted, carried a much lower rate of interest.[24]

Into the Pennsylvania Railroad Company, in the nine years between 1898 and 1906, had gone a total of almost $375 million in new capital funds, consisting of nearly $180 million in fresh stock issues, $104 million in long-term debt, and $92 million in earnings retained in the business after payment of all fixed charges and 6 per cent dividends on the stock. Was it enough? There were many indications at the time that the Pennsylvania was, indeed, securing sufficient capital to meet its increasingly heavy obligations as a common carrier. The greatly increased volume of traffic was being carried more efficiently than ever before, resulting in a flow of earnings which management felt was sufficient to pay capital its customary reward and still provide an adequate surplus for growth. "Traffic . . . for 1906 [was] greatly in excess of that for 1905 and much the largest in the history of the Company," Cassatt proudly reported. "The flow of traffic, too, was easy and uninterrupted, showing that through the facilities furnished by the Company it had regained . . . efficient and economical operation." [25] But the management was confusing a temporary return to satisfactory conditions with adequacy for the future. Much greater demands would be made on the system in the years just ahead. As Cassatt's optimistic words were being written, the traffic crisis of 1907 was in the making.

[23] P.R.R. Co., *Annual Report for 1906,* 25. "The first important flotation of American securities in France," said the New York *Times,* Jan. 25, 1906, 10. *CFC, BQS,* LXXXII (June 2, 1906), 22.

[24] P.R.R. Co., *Annual Report for 1906,* 8, 21.   [25] *Ibid.,* 22.

IV

Fifty years of operation by the Illinois Central Railroad, and fourteen years of Stuyvesant Fish as its president, were the occasions for a banquet at Chicago's Auditorium Hotel on February 9, 1901. Good feelings flowed freely. Even John Peter Altgeld, no ally of the railroads eight years before during the Pullman strike, occupied a place at the speakers' table where, as ex-governor of Illinois, he automatically deserved a seat as a former director ex officio of the railroad. The very reticent Edward H. Harriman, warmed by the occasion, was persuaded to make a few remarks, during which he offered a toast to the railroad and its president. President Fish replied with a reference to the many adversities which he and Mr. Harriman had gone through together, adversities which, as he said, "try and test character." Mr. Fish was to have his character tried and tested quite harshly when, five years later, Harriman would lead a successful fight to oust him from the presidency. But in 1901 an impressive record of growth and development of the I.C. was his to savor.[26]

He savored it well in a personal "letter" as president which he enclosed with the annual report for 1900. While conservatively run railroads like the I.C. no longer paid the kind of dividends they once did, he noted (6.7 per cent annually, on the average, since the road's founding against only 5 per cent in the preceding ten years), the I.C.'s record was still better than that of most railroads. This was an understatement. The strategic location of the line, the superb management which it had received through the joint ministrations of Fish and Harriman since the early eighties, and its unmatched physical condition were all reflected in a market price for its $100-par-value stock, which ranged from a low of 96 in the recovery year of 1898 to an incredible high of 184½ in the pivotal year of 1906.[27]

The directors had resolved to put the I.C. in first-class physical condition around 1890, when the aggressive program of acquisition of other roads that made it an integrated Chicago–New Orleans line had

[26] Corliss, *Main Line of Mid-America,* 318–23, 325–28.
[27] I.C.R.R. Co., *Annual Report for 1900,* "Letter," 2.

been substantially completed. Financing was to be accomplished
through expansion of the capital stock in preference to increasing the
long-term debt. For the first several years of the 1900s this policy was
carried out with considerable success. From 1898 through 1906 the
stock was doubled by the issuance of $53 million while the long-term
debt was increased by $31 million. The first $10 million stock issue, announced in 1895, had had heavy going: very little was disposed of until
1899.[28] In 1901 and 1902, however, greatly increased demands for
equipment and improvements were easily met with issues totaling $30
million and the next year another $15 million was added. The market
greeted these developments by bidding the stock even higher.[29] By
1901, furthermore, control of the line had passed from foreign hands to
American investors; the management availed itself of every opportunity
to replace European with domestic capital, as in 1906, when £200,000
sterling of maturing 5 per cent bonds were replaced with one million
dollars of 3½ per cent gold bonds.[30] In the nine years 1898–1906, net
capital investment in the Illinois Central totaled just under $100 mil-
lion, of which more than one-half was equity financing. Of the other
$50 million dollars, only $15 million was contributed by earnings retained in the business. It was clearly time, stockholders must have
thought, for future growth to be more heavily financed internally. As it
would for most American railroads, in fact, this distribution between
equity, debt, and retained earnings would change remarkably.

V

When the rotten financial timbers of the old Atchison, Topeka &
Santa Fe Railroad gave way in the first years of the nineties depression,
the territory which it served stood on the verge of an unparalleled period of expansion. If Horace Greeley had been surveying the scene in
1898, he might well have advised young men to go *southwest*. The new

[28] I.C.R.R. Co., *Annual Report for 1899*, 2–3.

[29] I.C.R.R. Co., *Annual Reports for 1901–3*, 4; *CFC, BQS*, LXXV (July 5, 1902),
24.

[30] Corliss, *Main Line of Mid-America*, 319; I.C.R.R. Co., *Annual Report for
1906*.

management which took over the properties upon the reorganization of
the A.T. & S.F. Railroad in 1895 was headed by two of the most capable men in the business: the shrewd railroad lawyer and expert on antitrust matters, Victor Morawetz, as chairman and general counsel; and
Edward P. Ripley, late of the Chicago, Milwaukee, and St. Paul Railway, as president and chief operations officer. The road would need all
of the managerial skill it could get. Starting with an obsolete and largely
worn-out property, President Ripley and his men would face a never-
ending struggle to handle a flow of traffic which, in the years from 1898
to 1906, was to triple and then, by the start of World War I, to increase
by another 50 per cent—a quintupling of traffic from 1898 to 1914. In
these years the Santa Fe would become one of the most prominent railroads in the country, and frequent spokesman for the entire western
portion of the industry. In the annual report for 1897 the management
announced that among its projects for betterment of the property was
"the addition of improved labor-saving tools and the adoption of uniform economical methods in the handling of work and materials," thus
marking the adoption of the new principles of scientific management.[31]

If the large capital requirements of the road were to be met in the
coming years, the company would have to demonstrate not only efficiency in operation but shrewdness in the expansion of the system and
in its commercial relations with shippers and competitors as well. As
the twentieth century began, the historic evils of railroad competition
and community harassment weighed heavily on the minds of the Santa
Fe's leaders. "The relations of the Company . . . are in the main satisfactory and harmonious, with the exception of some unreasonable demands for the reductions of rates . . . relations to its competitors . . .
are as good as can be expected under laws which foster . . . unrestrained competition and forbid the formation of reasonable agreements." [32] The building of lines by others in Santa Fe country in advance
of any foreseeable needs was to be discouraged, but encouragement and
outright acquisition of such enterprises were not to be ruled out if protection of the Santa Fe's position called for them.[33]

Despite nearly continuous operation of the road at peak capacity,

[31] A.T. & S.F. R.R. Co., *Annual Report for 1897*, 12.   [32] *Ibid.*, 16.
[33] A.T. & S.F. R.R. Co., *Annual Report for 1898*, 16.

the Santa Fe quickly began to show the results of wise and frugal management. Even the relatively small scale of improvements in track and equipment which characterized the first five years of operation by the new team paid off rapidly. But heavier capital demands were in the near future. There seemed to be no let-up in the rapid growth of passenger and freight traffic and the management was almost apologetic for the burdensome prosperity, noting the following year that no recession had occurred to bring relief. "It is now apparent . . . that additional equipment must be provided, both for passenger and freight service, and that immediate action must be taken in that direction." [34]

No railroad as recently out of bankruptcy as the Santa Fe could hope to interest investors in its stock. Until late in the decade, therefore, the line would have to rely on borrowing and retained earnings to an unusual degree. From 1898 to 1901, in fact, the Santa Fe actually depended more heavily on plowback of earnings than on borrowed capital. When by 1902 large-scale borrowing could no longer be avoided, management still shrank from adding to the company's long-term interest burden. Instead, thirty million dollars was raised by the ultraconservative means of 4 per cent bonds which the company bound itself to pay off out of its earnings in twelve annual installments. [35] Financially speaking it was no way to run a railroad, at least not one with the Santa Fe's prospects. By 1905 the company was spending one million dollars a year on double-tracking alone, on the long, heavily-traveled "throat" which connected the Santa Fe at Kansas City with Chicago. Expenditures for locomotives and for passenger and freight cars were running between six million and eleven million dollars each year. By 1906, it was obvious that large amounts of outside capital would have to flow into the system if it were to continue to shoulder the burdens being placed upon it. "The lines have been taxed beyond their capacity resulting . . . in inadequate service, in additional cost . . . and the loss of some traffic that was offered," wrote Ripley in the annual report. [36]

A special meeting of stockholders, called for January 30, 1907, promptly authorized a $98 million increase in the capital stock to $250

[34] A.T. & S.F. R.R. Co., *Annual Report for 1901*, 18.

[35] A.T. & S.F. R.R. Co., *Annual Report for 1902*, 17.

[36] A.T. & S.F. R.R. Co., *Annual Report for 1904*, 21; *Annual Report for 1906*, 18.

million. The month before the company had offered stockholders $26 million in ten-year convertible bonds. Despite the convertibility feature, the 5 per cent interest rate, and incredibly prosperous conditions, however, stockholders had taken only $10 million dollars by July, 1907, when the remaining $16 million dollars were sold on the open market. The stock also moved slowly; at the end of 1910, only about two-thirds of the new shares had been issued. The Santa Fe continued after 1906 to provide one-third to one-half of its capital needs out of earnings.[37]

VI

American railroads were demanding capital funds at a record rate during the presidential election year of 1904. Edward H. Harriman took time from his busy schedule to write his friend in the White House about the railroads' needs:

I am of the opinion that an effective Interstate Commerce Commission could regulate the matter of rebates, and absolutely prevent the same, without any additional power of any kind. . . .

During the enormous development of the last four years, the railroads have found it very hard to keep pace with the requirements imposed on them, and the so-called surplus earnings, as well as additional capital, have been devoted to providing additional facilities and the bettering and enlarging of their properties. . . . This work of betterment must go on, and is all-important for the proper development of all sections of the country. There is little doubt that during the next decade every single-track railroad in the country will have to be double-tracked and provide enlarged terminal and other facilities, and any move that will tend to cripple them financially would be detrimental to all interests over the whole country.[38]

Roosevelt was cold to such arguments. He was only beginning to move toward that belief in positive regulation of large-scale enterprise which would ultimately constitute the core of the New Nationalism; but closer control of the railroads was being demanded from all sides and it was inevitable that the President, in his all-out drive to be elected to the

[37] A.T. & S.F. R.R. Co., *Annual Report for 1907,* 7, 15–16.

[38] Harriman to Theodore Roosevelt, Dec. 2, 1904, quoted in Roosevelt to James S. Sherman, Oct. 8, 1906, *Letters,* ed. Elting E. Morison (8 vols., Cambridge, Mass., 1951–54), V, 450–51.

office in his own right, could not resist a policy on which he and the mass of the electorate saw eye-to-eye. New legislation giving the Interstate Commerce Commission the power to set specific maximum rates, where it held existing rates to be "unreasonable," became one of the most prominent features of the President's campaign pledges.[39] The new term had not even begun before T.R. applied pressure to make good on the promise. Members of Philadelphia's Union League Club, assembled to hear the newly elected President, were treated on January 30, 1905, to an urgent call for greater regulatory power. Next day the House Interstate Commerce Committee reported out the Esch-Townsend bill, which provided for strict control of rates.[40] Railroad men were appalled at what happened next. The House, sensing the mood of the country, passed the bill by the overwhelming vote of 326 to 17. Only the deliberateness and conservatism of the Senate could be counted on to salvage the freedom which the roads had enjoyed during recent years. Certainly no such radical bill could be expected to pass by the time the short session ended on March 4.[41] What the Senate might ultimately do, however, could not be left to chance. As hearings by the Senate Committee on Interstate Commerce proceeded during an uncomfortably warm May, the railroads mounted an all-out campaign to swing sentiment away from the radical provisions of Esch-Townsend, if not from the idea of governmental rate-making power altogether.[42]

[39] John M. Blum, "Theodore Roosevelt and the Hepburn Act: Toward an Orderly System of Control," in *Letters,* ed. Morison, VI, 1560.

[40] *CFC, BQS,* LXXX (Feb. 4, 1905), 514.

[41] That businessmen looked to the Senate for more conservative legislation is apparent in *CFC, BQS,* LXXX (March 4, 1905), 915.

[42] The railroads' campaign against stricter regulation was widely noted, and with considerable damage to the roads' public relations. Cf. Theodore Roosevelt to Ray Stannard Baker, Nov. 22, 1905, *Letters,* IV, 88; to Lyman Abbott, Dec. 14, 1905, *ibid.,* 111; to Lincoln Steffens, Feb. 6, 1906, *ibid.,* 146; to William B. Allison, April 12, 1906, *ibid.,* 210; also, William Z. Ripley, *Railroads: Rates and Regulation* (New York, 1912), 496–98, and Frank H. Dixon, *Railroads and Government: Their Relations in the United States* (New York, 1922), 14. The campaign is discussed in one of Baker's most widely read muckraking articles, "Railroads on Trial," *McClure's Magazine,* XXVI (March, 1906), 539. Gabriel Kolko, *Railroads and Regulations* (Princeton, 1965), 118*n* and 128*n*, is at great pains to fit the railroads' attitude toward the course of legislation in 1905 and 1906 into his thesis that they favored governmental control of railroad affairs, but his conclusion that the publicity campaign did not take place flies in the face of evidence provided by authoritative contemporaries who followed events closely.

The story of how Theodore Roosevelt traded away tariff reform for a strong railroad rate bill has been well told elsewhere.[43] We shall confine ourselves to the fate of the provision to reserve full review of the Interstate Commerce Commission's decisions to the Supreme Court, which the railroads wanted so badly. It was in the Senate that the fight for the Hepburn Act ultimately centered on the question of whether the Commission's decisions would be final and not subject to review as to their substance (i.e., as to specific maximum rate orders); or whether the national government's actions on railroad questions should continue to be centered in the Court, which had forcibly argued in 1897 that the Act of 1887 had conferred no rate-fixing power. The Senate sought to the bitter end to maintain the idea of full court review against the House's concept of the independent regulatory commission. Notwithstanding the compromise reached by Senator Nelson Aldrich and President Roosevelt, the clause which would have secured independence to the Commission was thrown out just before the Senate, on May 18, 1906, passed the Hepburn bill with only three dissenting votes.[44]

Retention of broad court review of rate decisions was cheerfully noted by the financial press.[45] Cheer, however, shortly gave way to gloom. When the House-Senate conference committee agreed to reinstate the key clause, both bodies accepted the decision and the bill became law at the end of June, 1906, "containing," cried the anguished *Commercial and Financial Chronicle,* "most of the objectionable fea-

---

Kolko misrepresents Prof. Ripley's case. Ripley did not cite the article in *Collier's Weekly* for May 4, 1907, as the source of his statements about the propaganda campaign, but only as a "good resumé" of the affair. An undisputed authority on railroad financial matters, and Ropes Professor of Economics at Harvard, Ripley was writing only seven years later about events which he had followed with the keenest professional interest. Nor should one conclude, from Kolko's assertion that the Congress held no hearings on the Hepburn Act, that the Congress was indifferent. No one held hearings on the Hepburn Act, but on a sheaf of bills to amend the Interstate Commerce Act of 1887 which ultimately emerged as the Hepburn Act. The Senate, in fact, thoroughly ventilated the subject in five months and 1,716 pages of testimony during hearings in late 1904 and 1905. See 1905 Senate Hearings.

[43] Blum, "Theodore Roosevelt and the Hepburn Act," 1558–71.

[44] *NYT,* May 19, 1906, 1. Alexander Cassatt had come out strongly for rate regulation, but with the rights of all concerned to be guaranteed by broad judicial review, *Ibid.,* 2.

[45] *CFC, BQS,* LXXXII (June 2, 1906), 21.

tures grafted on the measure by the two houses." [46] The *Chronicle*'s editor bitterly denounced what the paper saw as the real attitude behind the newly bestowed rate powers:

> The whole movement against the railroads is predicated . . . on the idea that they are extremely prosperous and that some of their profits might as well be taken from them and appropriated for the benefit of shippers and the general public. No one would think of suggesting that the power [of the ICC] of revising or supervising rates will be used to advance such rates. The purpose is to reduce them and in some quarters there would be great rejoicing if [such policy should] make it necessary to forego . . . improvement and betterment work. . . . It is the large earnings of the railroads that are inviting attack. And yet how small a portion of these large earnings are coming to the proprietors—the shareholders—in the shape of increased dividends.[47]

The statement was not a very accurate evocation of the general mood of the country, but it turned out to be remarkably good prophecy. In 1906, however, it remained to be seen whether the new rate-making powers would indeed be applied repressively, or whether the lines would be permitted to continue their ambitious plans with their accustomed freedom. Ultimately the problem of whether (and more importantly, as it turned out, *how*) rates could be raised under the Hepburn Act would have to be faced. Meanwhile a host of new problems harassed railroad men and chilled the spirits of investors.

VII

Representative Oscar W. Gillespie, Democrat of Texas, looked at the nearly deserted Republican side of the House of Representatives and decided that his opportunity had come. "Mr. Speaker," he drawled, "I desire to present a privileged resolution." Before the leaders of the House could close ranks, the body had called up a resolution which few could go on record against once it came to a vote: a resolution asking the President, January 29, 1906, to submit to the House any information which the ICC might possess of a combination in restraint of trade

---

[46] *Ibid.*, LXXXIII (July 7, 1906), 22; *NYT*, June 30, 1906, 1.
[47] *CFC*, LXXXIII (Aug. 4, 1906), 240.

by the Pennsylvania Railroad and a number of other roads in whose stocks it had invested heavily, notably the B. & O., the Norfolk & Western, and the Chesapeake & Ohio.[48] The resolution had been introduced at the start of each session in recent years as a matter of party politics. Once adopted, however, it was economic dynamite because it struck at the most stabilizing influence in the railroad industry, the Pennsylvania's community of interests. Share volume on the Exchange shot up and prices were irregular. John W. Gates and his fellow bears were reported to have made a killing.[49] The awful realization ran through the community that not only was the government about to saddle the railroads with rate regulation, but the industry was likely to be sent, like other great combines, through the wringer of T.R.'s trust-busting program. Today it is reasonably clear to the nation's leaders that comprehensive government regulation of an industry precludes a literal application of the Sherman Antitrust Act. From our vantage point, nothing could seem more obvious than that government setting of prices for goods or services pretty well rules out any duty for, or, for that matter, possibility of, competition between firms, whatever the threadbare concept of "competition" is taken to mean. In 1906, however, especially with an ambitious man like Charles Joseph Bonaparte in the Attorney General's chair, no such light had yet dawned.

The Pennsylvania's ordeal had just begun. On the same day that the Senate passed and sent to conference the Hepburn bill—the same day, in fact, that President Cassatt's statesmanlike message in favor of government regulation was issued—the front pages of the newspapers carried the horrendous news that executives of the circumspect Pennsylvania had been receiving bribes. Even the late president, Frank Thomson, as well as a number of executives and clerks in the traffic department, had accepted "gifts" of stock in certain coal companies which were desperate to get scarce railroad cars allocated to their mines.[50] This was no time to expect a wise public to reflect that the root cause of these bribes was the fact that traffic was growing faster than the railroads' facilities. That, after all, was the railroads' problem, but any evi-

[48] *CR*, 59th Cong., 1st Sess., 1701–3.

[49] *NYT*, Jan. 30, 1906, 1–2; *CFC, BQS*, LXXXII (Feb. 3, 1906), 22.

[50] *NYT*, May 19, 1906, 1.

dence of discrimination in granting access to the nation's transportation facilities was the nation's business. The revelation could not have come at a worse time. The government was just then planning its suit against Standard Oil, and word was allowed to leak out that consideration was being given to direct criminal action against Cassatt under the antitrust law. Reaction was mixed. While westerners were generally favorable, more sophisticated groups wondered if anyone would benefit from such punitive measures. "Put everybody in jail," grumbled the New York *Times* editorially, pointing out that Secretary of Agriculture James Wilson might well be indicted, in the same spirit, for having allowed some interests to violate the pure-food laws.[51] It would not be necessary, however, for the Pennsylvania's community of interests to be dissolved in the heat of a court battle. Recognizing the way the antitrust wind blew, and realizing that the railroads whose policies it had been dictating through stock ownership were now strong enough to stand alone, the Pennsylvania's management informed the stockholders that the interests had been disposed of—and at a good profit, too. So well stabilized had the rate situation become, Cassatt reported, that the stock was no longer required for the purpose for which it had been bought. Besides, he might have added, the Pennsylvania could use the cash.[52]

Attorney General Bonaparte was stalking more exciting game than the prim Pennsylvania. No name among American railroaders was more frequently coupled with empire-building than that of Harriman. In early 1907 he was still under sixty years of age, in apparently excellent health, and besides being the absolute ruler of the U.P., the S.P., and the I.C., had a large and growing interest in the Santa Fe, the Chicago & Northwestern, the B. & O., and the New York Central. He was also disarmingly frank about his ability to get control of railroads and confident to the point of arrogance in his ability to run them wisely. Harriman went to Washington early in March, 1907, ostensibly to show his younger son, Roland, the sights. For such an old friend, a forgiving T.R. opened the doors of the White House, where father and son spent fifteen minutes getting the standard T.R. treatment: a discussion of the animal trophies which hung on the walls of the President's office. Whether Harriman got an opportunity to discuss what was uppermost in

[51] *Ibid.,* June 25, 1906, 1; June 26, 6.   [52] P.R.R. Co., *Annual Report for 1906,* 7.

his mind is not known, but on the same day Bonaparte's office let it be known that the government, by legislative and judicial means, was going to seek dissolution of the U.P.-S.P. tie, and to challenge the U.P.'s 80 per cent control of the I.C. as well. "I've been a pack horse all my life," said Harriman next day to reporters who descended on him in his New York office, "I guess I can pack this too." The day before, orders had gone out to cancel plans to build a twelve-story general headquarters for the U.P. in Omaha.[53] Harriman remained icily cool throughout the next few months, bravely announcing that any changes in the U.P.'s affairs would "be of his own devising and at his convenience." His associates were reassured. Banker James Stillman decided not to return from Europe. But from this moment on the Harriman community of interests, like the Pennsylvania's, began to decline.[54]

Harriman may have been cool, but Wall Street had a bad case of the jitters. If a settled near-term outlook is the key to stock market stability, the market had reason to be unstable, for what happened in the next few weeks indicated that businessmen clearly could not take the President for granted. J. P. Morgan, about to depart on his annual European trip, felt he could not go without a good talk with the President about the latter's increasingly hostile attitude toward the railroads. It is easy to imagine two such powerful personalities getting up from such a meeting with totally different ideas about what had been agreed upon. Any other interpretation implies extraordinary rudeness on the President's part. Morgan informed three of the top railroad men in the nation that the President wished to hear them out on the subject of government policy, and that they should stand by for an invitation to the White House. Immediately, Marvin Hughitt, president of the Chicago & Northwestern and dean of railroad presidents, Charles S. Mellen of the New Haven, and James McCrea of the Pennsylvania gathered for a preliminary meeting in New York on March 14. As they sat in their hotels it became apparent that no invitation from the White House was on its way. Queried on the affair, T.R. bluntly stated that he "never invited them nor even intimated that [he] wanted them to come." This was harsh treatment for a group of major corporation executives in 1907. The humiliated railroad presidents angrily announced that they were

[53] *NYT,* March 3, 1907, 1–2.   [54] *Ibid.,* May 3, 1907, 3.

going home. They did not think it was a good idea to go to Washington after all, because they had heard that T.R. was primed to lecture them, whereas they had done nothing wrong.[55] The episode was like a can of gasoline thrown into the already overheated economy of early 1907.

Nervousness gave way to disorderly retreat in the market. Stocks broke in "one of the worst collapses in prices . . . of which there is any record." U.P. fell twenty-five points. The Harriman-Roosevelt friendship suffered a telling blow when reporters asked the railroad man what had caused the sharp break. "I'd hate to name him," retorted the indignant Harriman, adding quickly that he was not selling stocks himself. Reporters rushed to the Lackawanna ferry slip to get the reaction of William Jennings Bryan, who was arriving almost unwelcomed after a change of travel plans en route. It was all the railroads' fault, of course, according to Bryan, whose Populist-style comments about dishonesty, inefficiency, and overcapitalization were beginning to be indistinguishable from those of Theodore Roosevelt.[56] The President himself was furious at the suggestion that he was unsettling the affairs of the nation. He was equally convinced that a few men of great wealth could and did call forth such gyrations as the market had just displayed, in order to embarrass his policies.

All summer the President's resentment festered and grew. On August 20 he sailed into Provincetown harbor at the tip of Cape Cod, his yacht *Mayflower* passing between two lines of eight battleships and fifty fishing boats. Along with such other notables as Senator Henry Cabot Lodge and Lord Bryce, the British ambassador, he was there to lay the cornerstone of the Pilgrim monument. But the eight battleships could not have fired a more telling salvo than T.R. was about to deliver. He praised the Pilgrims briefly, declaring that they were "no laissez-faire theorists," and then for the better part of an hour hammered at the great corporations. "Certain malefactors of great wealth," he said, were responsible for the decline in stocks, and were seeking to discredit his administration. These men, he said, might have combined "to bring about as much financial stress as they possibly can, in order to discredit the policy of the government and thereby to secure a reversal of that

[55] *Ibid.*, March 15, 1907, 1; *CFC, BQS*, LXXXIV (April 6, 1907), 22.
[56] *NYT*, March 15, 1907, 2.

policy that they may enjoy the fruits of their own evil-doing." The crowd of ten thousand interrupted with frequent cheers.[57] Two months later the obsolete monetary system of the country broke under the combined strain of economic growth and financial uncertainty. The boom decade which William McKinley had ushered in seemed to be at an end.

The panic of October, 1907, while it did not bring the protracted depression which the public, its memory of 1893 still fresh, had reason to fear, nevertheless shook the President badly. When recovery seemed assured, however, he returned to the offensive. He still apparently believed that a few powerful men were playing on the nation's finances like a great pipe organ. If he had studied page nine of the New York *Times* for January 30, 1908, he might have awakened to the fact that at least one notorious Wall Street speculator regarded the President himself as the mighty organist. Thomas Lawson, betting that the presidential message scheduled for the next day would be in the recent Roosevelt tradition, inserted a remarkable three-column display advertisement on the financial page:

PRESIDENT ROOSEVELT AND THE PEOPLE
During the recent panic after the System had surrounded the greatest President the American people have had since sainted Lincoln, I publicly went on record with two predictions [that Roosevelt would run again and would continue to fight "frenzied finance"].

Tomorrow comes his first thunderbolt. . . . It is a syrenated corker . . . shake [s] them [the frenzied financiers] as a tiger does a blood-stained meat bag . . . but . . . its every word means higher prices for American securities. . . . Buy stocks on tomorrow's message. . . . Buy Nevada-Utah now.[58]

Most Republican members, assembled in the House, remained silent as the presidential message was read, but western Democrats, especially the supporters of Bryan, applauded it paragraph by paragraph and let loose a rebel yell at the end. Calling for new laws to protect the rights of labor and further subject the railroads to government control, the message was indeed a strange document for a Republican president. Renewing his charge of a plot to engineer embarrassing panics, T.R. denounced "predatory wealth" and demanded laws to end "stock gam-

[57] *Ibid.*, Aug. 21, 1907; *CFC, BQS*, LXXXV (Sept. 7, 1907), 22.

[58] *NYT*, Jan. 30, 1908, 9. Nevada-Utah was a copper-mining concern in which Lawson was deeply involved.

bling." But in Wall Street (where traders had received ample warning) prices held firm.[59]

Less than a week earlier Bonaparte had filed his suit against the U.P. to require it to divest itself of stock in competitor western railroads. Harriman, not entirely to show his pique but also because business had slipped badly following the panic, immediately ordered all shops on the U.P. to retrench by shifting from a six- to a five-day week.[60] Things were not going to get better any time soon, it seemed. Secretary of War William Howard Taft, now enthusiastically playing the role of heir-apparent, called the President's message a "bugle call." "We have not quite enough regulation of railways," he declared; "other powers ought to be conferred on the ICC." [61] But the President had a balanced program in mind. Up to Capitol Hill on March 25, 1908, went yet another special message. Now he suggested that the railroads be permitted to enter into agreements among themselves, through an amendment to the antitrust law, to legalize contracts not in unreasonable restraint of trade—thereby anticipating the Supreme Court's "rule of reason" by a good three years. The ICC, he said, ought to be empowered to pass on railroad securities. "Good trusts" were all right. Reaction was guarded, although some optimist managed to start a rumor that as a corollary to his very pro-labor pronouncements the President was about to recommend a 10 per cent rate increase out of which, presumably, the higher wages which the railroad unions were demanding could be paid. T.R. in conciliation, however, was no match for T.R. on the attack. The message "went off with a noise like one of Maxim's new silent firearms," somebody said.[62]

VIII

The county jail at Asheville, North Carolina, had never expected such a distinguished occupant as W. W. Finley, president of the South-

[59] *Ibid.,* Feb. 1, 1908, 1.
[60] *Ibid.,* Jan. 26, 1908, 1; *CFC, BQS,* LXXXVI (Feb. 8, 1908), 21.
[61] *NYT,* Feb. 11, 1908, 1; *CFC, BQS,* LXXXVI (March 7, 1908), 22.
[62] *NYT,* March 26, 1908, 3; *CFC, BQS,* LXXXVI (April 3, 1908), 22.

ern Railway, but for a few hours on July 27, 1907, the institution seemed about to receive the honor. Finley had been arrested on orders of Governor R. B. Glenn of North Carolina for refusing to put into immediate effect the state's law limiting railroad passenger fares within the state to 2¼ cents a mile. Finley was determined to await the outcome of an injunction against the North Carolina Corporation Commission which a federal judge had recently continued in Asheville, following the arrest in June of two Southern Railway ticket agents. These unfortunate men had been rescued from thirty days on thc chain gang by a writ of habeas corpus. The confrontation dramatized the deteriorating state of affairs between the nation's railroads and many of the states in which they operated. The approaching confusion between federal and state regulation of railroad rates which such encounters presaged was a matter of deep concern to Theodore Roosevelt. He put an assistant attorney general to work on the state authorities, while simultaneously pressuring J. P. Morgan, still the real power behind the Southern, to direct the railroad to accede to North Carolina's demands pending further legislation.[63]

Efforts by the states, especially the Granger states, in the days before the Interstate Commerce Act of 1887, to exercise basic regulation of railroads are a familiar part of the history of the seventies and eighties. Even after the advent of the ICC, however, and especially after its rejuvenation in 1906, the states continued to level many a legislative blow against the roads, some constructive, some repressive, many demagogic, and almost all expensive. Going far beyond the unquestioned authority which they possessed to exercise the police power, the states were not content to require separate accommodations for the races (in the South), to demand separation of railroads and grade crossings where unwonted numbers of the new automobiles were being reduced to junk, or even to set specifications for locomotive headlights. Within their borders, the states still insisted upon the right to fix maximum rates for passenger, freight, and express movements confined to the state. One of the factors which kept average passenger rates low in the years before World War I was the maximum rate laws, frequently called "two-cent laws" after the maximum rate that seemed to have some sacred validity

[63] *NYT*, July 28, 1907, 1; *CFC, BQS*, LXXXV (Aug. 3, 1907), 21–22.

to state legislators. The merits of state railroad commissions, and the question of whether they made any sense at all after the maximum-rate amendments to the federal statute in 1906, were less of a question in these years than they deserved to be, in great measure because they were of such undoubted political value. Concerning the North Carolina spectacle, the New York *Times* commented sourly, "It is now almost certain that Governor Glenn will be elected to the Senate." Imitation was inevitable. A few days later the Secretary of State of Alabama flamboyantly revoked the license of the Southern Railway to do business in that state—a gesture about as meaningful as the threat to choke oneself to death with one's own bare hands.[64]

Rate rollback laws continued to be enacted in many states in the Progressive era, to the material and spiritual harm of the railroads. The drab annual reports of the era were made more depressing still by lugubrious comments on the dire results of state maximum fare laws. The I.C. excused the sharp drop in passenger revenues in 1908 not only by referring to the recession which followed the panic of 1907, but also by a blast at the rollback of passenger rates from three cents to two, "forced upon the roads" in Illinois and Iowa.[65] President Ripley of the Santa Fe waxed indignant on the ungratefulness of the people of Texas. "The State in most need of development was Texas and with one exception [was] the most severe and unjust . . . but the last session of the Texas legislature resisted practically all efforts [at] further radical legislation [and therefore] in view of the crying needs of West Texas [the Santa Fe will resume its expansion and improvement program] relying on the ultimate good sense of the people of Texas." [66] The Santa Fe was given to frequent threats to hold up its service improvement projects in retaliation against governmental actions which depressed income

---

[64] *NYT,* Aug. 3, 1907, 1; *CFC, BQS,* LXXXV (Sept. 7, 1907), 21. Gov. Glenn did not make it to the Senate; "Robert Brodnax Glenn," *Who Was Who in America, 1897–1942,* 461. Robert Louis Peterson, "State Regulation of Railroads in Texas, 1836–1920" (unpublished doctoral dissertation, University of Texas, 1960), is disappointing in his failure to discuss the cost of regulatory policies to the railroads, or their merits as legislation. Maxwell Ferguson, *State Regulation of Railroads in the South* (New York, 1916), 172–74, and *passim,* accurately foresaw the eclipse of the state commissions by the ICC.

[65] I.C.R.R. Co., *Annual Report for 1908,* 6.

[66] A.T. & S.F. R.R. Co., *Annual Report for 1909,* 17.

and raised costs. There is little evidence that any state legislators were moved by such outbursts.[67]

IX

Members of the board of directors of the U.S. Steel Corporation, gathered in the board room on the last Tuesday of January, 1909, for their regular monthly meeting, proceeded to the jolly ritual of playing heads-or-tails with the fifty-dollar gold pieces which they received for their attendance. They would have snorted disdainfully if one of their group had ventured to inform them that their gold pieces were now worth only about forty dollars, assuming that they had been worth fifty dollars at the first meeting in 1901.[68] After all, there was just as much gold in a fifty-dollar piece in 1909 as there had been in 1901, and hadn't the Gold Standard Act of 1900 guaranteed, once and for all, that the value of the dollar would not be tampered with? Such concepts as the purchasing power of the dollar, or the general level of prices, were rarely encountered outside the classrooms of political economists in 1909. The steel men's railroad executive brethren would probably have reacted just as indignantly to the suggestion that the dollar was being violated. Still, when they sat down to write the summary to their annual reports, their formal principles were apt to become pragmatic doubts.

The advent of positive government control of railroad rates occurred only a few years after the end of the longest period of price stability in world economic history.[69] Against such a monetary background a railroad executive surveying the scene on the eve of passage of the Hepburn Act in 1906 might have consoled himself with the thought that fixed rates would not be much of a drag on profits. There had been a gratifying increase in traffic since 1898, and it seemed reasonable that

[67] The full-crew law passed in Texas in 1905 was followed by one requiring many new depots in 1909. In 1917 Sam Rayburn energetically opposed extension of the Newlands Committee, which was considering emasculation of state regulation by the expedient of granting federal charters to railroads. Peterson, "State Regulation," 308, 415, 463.

[68] U.S. Bureau of the Census, *Historical Statistics of the United States: Colonial Times to 1957* (Washington, 1960), 127; F.R.B. of New York index.

[69] *Historical Statistics,* 115–17.

the massive investment in improvements and additions to capacity would continue to bring significantly lower operating costs. As for fixed rates, even without government regulation railroad charges since 1897 had climbed only a few percentage points above the level of the 1880s. Things could not have worked out more differently from what the railroad men expected. After the rude shock of the recession which followed the 1907 panic, annual reports of railroads and financial periodicals began to be filled with dark references to rising costs and retrenchments—real or threatened—of betterment programs.[70]

Nothing the railroads bought, however—not rails, nor crossties, nor coal, nor rolling stock, nor even investors' confidence—even when lumped together came anywhere near equaling human labor as an input to the nation's transportation mechanism. Nineteen-seven, in many ways the best year the railroads ever had, saw 1,700,000 men (and a few women) working on or for the railroads. Out of a total expense bill of $1.7 billion, workers received $1.1 billion, or 64 per cent of the total. In 1898 the labor share was 65 per cent; in the very good year of 1910 it was 61 per cent, and by 1914 it was back up to 64 per cent.[71] From these simple figures two conclusions may be drawn: the significant increase in productivity during the past decade was being absorbed, in large measure, by increases in money wages, preventing any reduction in relative labor costs; and the constant upward pressure on wage rates, as unions became more effective in pressing the workers' demands, absolutely necessitated further investment in better plant and equipment if labor costs were not to outstrip gains in productivity. As long as the railroads could keep the two factors in balance, and maintain profits, they were reasonably sure that the flow of new capital would be maintained. But it was dangerous to assume that labor would key its demands to actual gains in productivity (as dangerous then as now), for the rising cost of living was a guarantee of unrest. Railroad management and labor, in short, were on a treadmill in these years and the strain showed clearly after 1907.

---

[70] P.R.R. Co., *Annual Report for 1906,* 21–22; *Annual Report for 1907,* 20; I.C.R.R. Co., *Annual Report for 1908,* 6. The Santa Fe management was especially bitter at the turn of events and spoke grimly of retrenchment in the line's *Annual Report for 1907.*

[71] ICC, *Annual Statistics of the Railways of the United States.*

The success of the men in getting wage increases failed to guarantee serenity in the long run, for the simple reason that they never won any increase in *real* wages in the Progressive era. Paul Douglas estimates that real wages of railroad men never rose above the 1890–99 average in the years between 1896 and 1914 and, in fact, sank as low as 6 per cent below the average in 1907. Not until the substantial increase awarded by the government commission in 1918 did railroad workers achieve *any* improvement in their standard of living, and by then they had fallen behind workers in war-goods plants.[72] The wage question hung over the railroads like a black cloud in these years, pregnant with trouble.

Labor strife, however, fell short of becoming a crippling problem for the railroads until the eight-hour controversy in 1916. There were no nationwide strikes and, although there were a number of serious walkouts on individual lines, the eagerness of the railroads to move the mountains of goods that piled up in their freight houses even during normal delays, combined with a strong upper hand on the part of management, usually led to quick settlements or replacement of the striking men.[73] The more prosperous and enlightened roads made a real effort to anticipate the wage demands of their employees before 1907. President Cassatt announced in November, 1902, that the Pennsylvania's 100,000 men would receive wage increases of 10 per cent. "We have more business than we can handle and can't see our way out of that difficulty unless we keep our men loyal to the Company and help them while they help us," he said, opining that the cost of living had risen 25 to 30 per cent since the depression. The other trunk lines generally had to follow the leader.[74]

Concurrent with the growth of the American Federation of Labor, the large numbers of skilled craftsmen who labored to keep the railroads' overworked equipment running strengthened their union status markedly. When strikes were threatened in the spring of 1903, the New Haven, the Great Northern, and the Union Pacific quickly caved in and

[72] Paul H. Douglas, *Real Wages in the United States, 1890–1926* (Boston, 1930), 167–68. See Chapter I for conflicting views.

[73] *CFC*, LXXVI (March 21, 1903), 619.

[74] *NYT*, Nov. 14, 1902, 1; *CFC, BQS,* LXXV (Dec. 6, 1902), 24, and *CFC,* LXXV (Nov. 22, 1902), 1115.

settled.[75] The tough-minded management of the Santa Fe, however, chose to fight later that same year when the International Association of Machinists struck all of its shops. The cost to the company was estimated at $1.5 million, and months passed before normal operations were resumed, but the annual report for 1904 blustered that no difficulty had been experienced in filling the positions vacated by the strikers, and added, rather unconvincingly, that the shops were operating more efficiently than ever.[76]

Most significant in the railroad labor history of the decade, however, was the discovery of new strength in joint action by the occupation-oriented brotherhoods and unions. Industry-wide tactics had all but disappeared with the smashing of Eugene V. Debs's American Railway Labor Union during the Pullman strike of the nineties,[77] but in 1902 the conductors and trainmen on western lines formed the Western Association and presented demands for better working conditions and higher wages to all of the western railroads. That the move was successful is attributed to the fact that the pacesetter lines, the S.P. and U.P., were unprepared for the new solidarity of railroad labor.[78] The railroads in these years were generally favorably disposed toward arbitration of disputes, especially where a serious tieup was threatened, not only because they could ill afford a shutdown in the face of capacity traffic, but also because arbitrators were generally favorable to the companies.[79] (For the same reason, the railroad unions developed a strong aversion to arbitration which persists today.)

It was the railroads' prosperity in the years before 1908, however, and the willingness to pass some of this good fortune along to the workers in a time of rising consumer prices that kept labor problems gener-

[75] *CFC, BQS,* LXXVI (June 6, 1903), 24; May 2, 1903, 24.

[76] A.T. & S.F. R.R. Co., *Annual Report for 1904,* 19.

[77] Ray Ginger, *The Bending Cross: A Biography of Eugene Victor Debs* (New Brunswick, 1949), 181.

[78] Edwin C. Robbins, *The Order of Railway Conductors* (New York, 1914), 64; J. Noble Stockett, *Arbitrational Determination of Railway Wages* (Boston, 1918), *passim.*

[79] Kerley, "Failure of Railway Labor Leadership," 47; George J. Stevenson, "The Brotherhood of Locomotive Engineers and Its Leaders, 1863–1920" (unpublished doctoral dissertation, Vanderbilt University, 1954), 298, 306–8, 344–45.

ally below the boiling point. Announcements of dividend increases were frequent in late 1906. Wall Street watchers stared in amazement on August 17 at the news that the Harriman-dominated board of directors of the S.P. was not merely increasing the dividend but was doubling it to 10 per cent on the par value.[80] It remained for the Pennsylvania to lead the way, however; in November the company announced that the dividend was being increased from 6 to 7 per cent, and another 10 per cent wage increase was being awarded to about 185,000 employees throughout the system, subsidiary lines as well.[81] Despite such initiative, by 1907 the railroad unions and management were squared off against each other. The conductors and trainmen united against the western roads in a demand for a 15 per cent wage increase and establishment of the eight-hour day. The carriers offered 10½ per cent, but refused to discuss working conditions, which were still considered a sacred prerogative of management. Chairman Martin A. Knapp of the ICC, mediating under the Erdman Act of 1898, secured a 10 per cent raise for the men but no reduction in the workday for men working ten hours. He achieved a major breakthrough, however, in persuading the roads to reduce the maximum day from twelve to ten hours, with no reduction in wages, which meant that these men, who were for the most part in slow, local freight service, received a 20 per cent raise.[82]

In the same year an eastern association of conductors and trainmen was formed and in 1909 one in the South as well. In 1908 the Brotherhood of Locomotive Firemen and Enginemen also formed regional bargaining units. By 1910, therefore, the railroad unions were in a position to shut down the nation's entire transportation system in prosecuting their demands, although such concerted action would not become a reality until 1916. Advances of 25 to 50 per cent were secured for the rather poorly paid conductors and trainmen in the South in 1910 and the mighty Pennsylvania, which had sought to go it alone with voluntary increases, ratified a recent arbitration award which the brotherhoods had obtained against the B. & O. and were demanding be

[80] *NYT*, Aug. 18, 1906, 1; *CFC, BQS*, LXXXII (Sept. 8, 1906), 21.

[81] *CFC, BQS*, LXXXII (Dec. 8, 1906), 22.

[82] Kerley, "Failure of Railway Labor Leadership," 30–31; Robbins, *Order of Railway Conductors*, 170–71.

made general.[83] From this time on, demands from one railroad union or another were almost continuously before the railroads. As technological changes revolutionized railroading, they added to labor problems. In the fall of 1910, for example, the engineers demanded double pay for operating the giant new Mallet-type locomotives, on the grounds that they were really two locomotives in one! [84]

And so the railroads, which in 1906 had lost the power to price their product, were rapidly losing by 1910 the power to determine what they would pay for labor, their most important input.

X

Edward P. Ripley, president of the Santa Fe, foresaw the railroads' problems when they were still no more than a plume of smoke on a distant horizon. His vision was matched by that of a number of his fellow railroad presidents, who felt as strongly as he that the lines were hell-bent for trouble if the squeeze between rising costs and frozen rates was not relieved by restoring to the managers at least some of the freedom of action which they were rapidly losing. No one matched Ripley, however, in his willingness to disturb the tranquil pages of the annual report with indignant and threatening blasts at public policy. His magnificent moustache bristles and he shoots his Sunday cuffs at the stenographer to whom he dictates a statement to appear in the report for the year ending in June, 1907, a year in which the greatest freight and passenger burden yet had been heaped upon the railroads:

The power of the Railway Companies to obtain . . . additional capital has been greatly impaired by loss of confidence of investors in the stability and security of railroad investments; and this loss of confidence has been caused, in great measure, by the unfriendly attitude of a large part of the public towards the Railway Companies and by the arbitrary action of Legislatures

[83] *CFC, BQS,* XCI (Aug. 6, 1910), 20; Kerley, "Failure of Railway Labor Leadership," 51. The engineers on the Pennsylvania, who were the very cream of railroad labor, remained aloof from union activity until about 1907. "You will find that the men on the Pennsylvania lines . . . are perfectly satisfied with their conditions . . . and say . . . just leave them alone," Warren Stone, head of the Engineers, wrote a friend in 1904. Stevenson, "Locomotive Engineers," 328.

[84] Kerley, "Failure of Railway Labor Leadership," 53–54; Stevenson, "Locomotive Engineers," 319.

and Railway Commission in reducing rates and imposing burdensome restrictions.[85]

And he kept up the tone the following year. "For the first time in the history of the Company there are no plans in hand for the construction of extensions," he growled; "during the year there have been no advances in rates affecting your property. There have been sundry reductions." Less bitter, but no less lugubrious expressions of gloom appeared in other reports.[86]

It was the panic of 1907 and the ensuing short, sharp recession which had shaken railroad management to its roadbed. Once the money stringency which had been the primary cause of the disquietude had been relieved, the national economy made a fairly quick recovery. But the short-term liquidation of inventories at all levels, from manufacturer to retailer, translated itself into a sharp decline in the amount of freight being offered, while travel, especially by businessmen, was cut drastically. Freight traffic fell by 7 per cent from 1907 to 1908 (years ending June 30); but net income of all U.S. railroads sagged 32 per cent, reflecting the simple fact that the break-even point had increased in recent years. The result was that even moderate declines in the flow of gross revenues meant severe dehydration of net income. The recession continued to affect freight volume the following year, but drastic economies and a good recovery toward the close of the statistical year ending June, 1909, brought a partial recovery in net, which remained, nevertheless, 14 per cent below the banner year of 1907.[87]

Threats to hold up the expansion of the nation's transportation facilities, no matter how sincere, no matter how justified in view of the modest dividends which stockholders were receiving, could not be made good in the ebullient economic climate of the decade before World War I. Railroad men were learning, in some ways for the first time, just what

[85] A.T. & S.F. R.R. Co., *Annual Report for 1907,* 20–22; P.R.R. Co., *Annual Report for 1906,* appearing six months earlier, had expressed concern that rising operating costs, as well as higher rates at which capital was available, would soon require a cutback in expansion projects.

[86] A.T. & S.F. R.R. Co., *Annual Report for 1908,* 20; P.R.R. Co., *Annual Report for 1907,* 20; *Annual Report for 1908,* 20; I.C.R.R. Co., *Annual Report for 1908,* 6.

[87] ICC, *Annual Statistics of the Railways of the United States, 1907–9.*

it meant to be in a public-service business. Ripley snatched comfort where little could actually be discerned, and announced in his 1909 report that in view of a more reasonable tone from the Texas legislature, the Santa Fe would proceed with a major 500-mile extension (the Abo Pass low-gradient cutoff) in west Texas. The Pennsylvania, deeply involved in growth projects from its mammoth Manhattan terminal in the east to a similar, if somewhat less grandiose, undertaking which would become the line's western portal in Chicago, thought it saw a more conservative attitude developing on both the national and the state level.[88]

Demands on the railroad system, which for the greater part of the ten years since the return of prosperity in 1897 had exceeded the comfortable capacity of the roads, continued to grow rapidly. The panic of 1907 turned out to be the merest hiccup in the economic growth curve. By 1913 the burden was 39 per cent higher than in the 1905–7 period. Except for the aborted recession of 1914, in fact, the nation's railroads would get no relief from their heavy burden, to which, indeed, would be added the unparalleled loads of the war years. But the flow of capital into the railroad system slackened significantly at just this critical juncture. How, and why, and by how much, we must now consider.

In the nine years of feverish economic growth from 1898 to 1906, $4.2 billion of fresh capital flowed into the nation's railroads. (See Chart, p. 131.) During this period the annual level of investment, considered as a trendline, was rising in relationship to the trendline for demands on the system. By contrast, in the period 1905–7 the investment peak was reached and the curve turned downward. Because of the crucial events which occurred in 1906 in respect to the railroads' ability to increase their revenues on their own initiative, the level of investment in relation to demand for their services that was reached in 1905–7 was never bettered. In this sense it turned out to be the "optimum" level which the railroads had been striving to attain ever since 1897. Indeed, the amount invested each year had risen consistently, from $232 million in 1898 to $859 million in 1906, and then, in the hectic year of 1907, had nearly doubled to $1.5 billion. If the relationship between demand and investment which obtained in the average period 1905–7 had obtained in the 1898–1907 period as a whole (and there must have been

[88] A.T. & S.F. R.R. Co., *Annual Report for 1909*, 17; P.R.R. Co., *Annual Report for 1908*, 21.

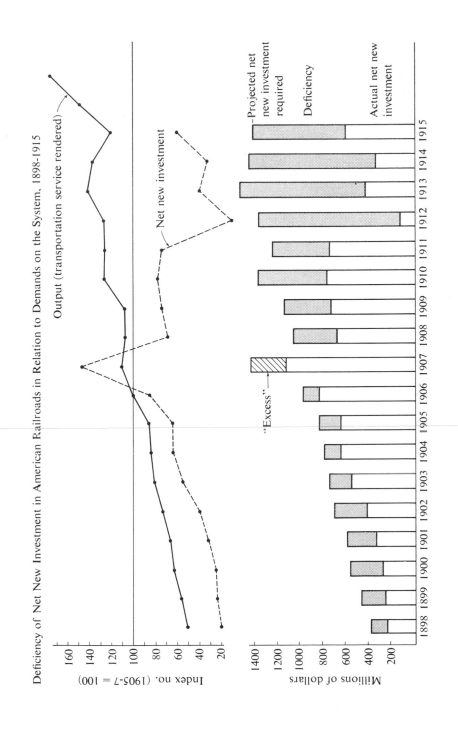

Deficiency of Net New Investment in American Railroads in Relation to Demands on the System, 1898-1915

many railroad men who wished it had when the freight crisis of 1906–7 hit them), an additional $1.9 billion would have been invested over what actually went into the system. The "deficit," if such one agrees to call it, would be much larger in the decade coming up.[89]

Did the passage of the Hepburn Act, the movement to apply the anti-trust laws to the railroads, the hostility of state legislatures, the rising demands of increasingly powerful labor unions, and the other slings and arrows which have been discussed in this chapter reduce the railroads' ability to bid for capital resources in a market which was growing ever tighter? Slowly, but inexorably, they did. At first the big change in the railroads' position was not fully appreciated. No really sharp cutback in new investment occurred (ignoring the highly untypical year of 1908) until 1912. (Much more significant, however, is the fact that investment did not turn upward on a trend basis.) Apparently very little of the "smart money" which is supposed to inhabit Wall Street saw these trends before the plight of the railroads became obvious after 1912. The fact is that in the decade before 1907 the railroads had become America's great growth industry, promising an almost endless opportunity for the profitable employment of a steady stream of investment funds. The annual statistical report of the ICC assured everyone that the golden opportunity was still there in 1906, painting a picture of an industry which, despite heavy investment, was still not abreast of rising traffic demands. Clearly, this Commission, which was about to assume the enormous new powers the people had given it, was acutely aware of the needs of the railroad industry and, one would assume, would see to it that the public continued to find that industry attractive to capital.[90] And, too, the roads were recovering rapidly from the 1907 panic: in April, 1908, there had been over 400,000 idle freight cars in the storage yards, but by October this number had dropped to little more than 100,000 and was declining rapidly. Good years lay ahead, it seemed, and annual investment, although it never equaled 1906 or even remotely approached 1907, remained at about the three-quarter-billion-dollar level through mid-1912.

One danger signal that turned up at this early stage in the new era

[89] See Appendix.

[90] ICC, *Annual Statistics of the Railways of the United States, 1906*, 28–29.

of regulation was the fact that the roads were forced to rely much more heavily on outside financing (stocks and bonds) than on retained earnings. They were able to do this by turning increasingly to foreign capital, by emphasizing new forms of financing, such as equipment trusts, and by paying a consistently rising price for the funds they raised. Sales of stock, which in pre-1907 years had averaged only 16 per cent of funds raised annually (including retained profits), were to average 25 per cent in the period 1907–14. In the pivotal year 1912 they reached 42 per cent of the total, when equities were expanded by $317 million, or nearly one-third more than in any previous year. Dividend rates were well maintained up to 1910, when they averaged 5.4 per cent, thus encouraging investment in railroad equities. But after the shattering events of 1910 and 1911, which we are about to consider, the story was different.[91]

Debt financing rose only slightly as a percentage of total capital inflow in the post-1906 period, but new sources and modes of raising money were resorted to. Good luck was encountered, as we have seen, in selling U.S. railroad securities abroad. It was not that foreign investors were less aware of what was troubling U.S. railroad management than their American counterparts. In the spring of 1907, in fact, the London *Statist* had condemned the new governmental policy toward American railroads. In the past, said the influential journal, the policy had been to provide adequate transportation, with the manner of raising capital a mere detail, and on the basis of results obtained the U.S. railroad policy had been the envy of the world.[92] But American railway bonds were increasingly attractive to European investors, all the same, not only as to yield but especially as to risk, in the troubled years before World War I. As we have noted, French investors had begun to turn away from Czarist projects in favor of opportunities in America. In 1908 the Pennsylvania management confessed that negotiations for the sale of $40 million in forty-year bonds had run into an American money market saturated with short-term, high-cost financings, and that

[91] It must be noted that in these years it was widely believed that the real capital of the railroads was much below the book value, and rates of return, correspondingly higher. Only in 1920, when the first estimate was released under the valuation program, was this notion dispelled. Dixon, *Railroads and Government,* 239.

[92] *The Statist* (London), LIX (March 16, 1907), 533.

only the willingness of the English to take one-half of the issue had made it possible to consummate the transaction.[93] By 1910 the *Commercial and Financial Chronicle* noted that the volume of foreign purchases of U.S. railroad securities had reached such proportions that a tendency for gold to flow out of the country had actually been reversed. Kuhn, Loeb, and Company achieved a major coup by selling $50 million of Milwaukee road bonds to a group of French banks by agreeing to issue them in franc denominations and to list them on the Bourse. Other investment bankers were keeping the transatlantic cable hot with similar negotiations.[94] And when in that same year the S.P. sold $25 million of bonds to an international syndicate led by Germans, the nationalistic press of Germany was highly insulted.[95]

The volume of financing in the form of equipment trusts, while small relative to bonds, is significant because such financing is a technique for raising capital which proud, conservative managements resorted to only under pressure. Under the terms of an equipment trust, the risk to the lender is low, since only rolling stock, which is easily repossessed and disposed of to another railroad in case of default, is involved. The most conservative of the roads looked upon this kind of financing as a form of weakness, although an outstanding exception was the Pennsylvania, which had millions of dollars of "car trusts" on its books by the turn of the century. The I.C. had consistently bragged that it had no car trusts, and when in 1908 the company found it necessary to pledge $30 million of new rolling stock in this manner, it was careful to label the items "first liens" on its balance sheet; and it did not mention the transaction in the text of the annual report.[96] From 1898 to 1914, American railroads increased their dependence upon equipment-trust financing tenfold, from $40 million to $419 million.

What, then, caused the sharp drop in the flow of capital funds to American railroads after 1912? The answer lies not alone in the psychological effects of repressive regulation after 1910, although they were real enough, but in the cold arithmetic of the profit-and-loss state-

[93] P.R.R. Co., *Annual Report for 1908*, 20.   [94] *CFC, BQS*, XC (June 4, 1910), 20.

[95] The Berlin *Tageblatt* editorialized that Germans had no good reason to send funds to America. Quoted in *NYT*, June 7, 1910, 7.

[96] I.C.R.R. Co., *Annual Report for 1907*, 7.

ment.[97] By 1911 gross and net were going in different directions, and the inability of the railroads to provide an increasing proportion of their capital needs through retained earnings (a phase which should follow a period of heavy investment) became increasingly apparent. Whereas in the nine years from 1898 to 1906 the roads had plowed back an average of $156 million a year from net income, meeting one-third of their growth needs in this manner, after 1906 the annual average plowback dropped to $122 million through 1914, and the share of new capital raised in this manner fell to 18 per cent. The apparent prosperity of the railroads obscured the crisis that was developing. Earnings in 1910 did not equal the banner year of 1907—an ominous development in view of the fact that the roads carried 10 per cent more traffic. What the general public and the Interstate Commerce Commission could not or would not see was that net income was not on the rise, although traffic, cost of materials, wage rates, and the demands of investors were soaring. The railroads were understandably reluctant to denigrate their own credit rating in public hearings, although they became less and less so. It would come as a great shock on the eve of the war, therefore, to learn that American railroads had turned to short-term bank loans in the amount of nearly one billion dollars. For many weaker lines, especially in the midwestern and plains states, the solution had been the promissory note or bankruptcy, and as we shall see, by 1914 not even that escape route was open to some.[98]

Retained earnings after 1907 never equaled the levels attained in 1904–7. In 1911 the railroads plowed back the smallest sum since 1898, and 1912 was even worse, despite the fact that the dividend rate —on stocks that paid *anything*—had been cut from 1910's 5.4 per cent. External financing dried up altogether or was greatly reduced in 1912 and 1913. It recovered nicely after the year ending in June, 1913, proved to be a good one, but, emphasizing the uncertainties of the entire situation, a major crisis was at hand just one year later.

[97] "Railroad credit declined in the half-dozen years before the [First World] War, not primarily because of the specific decisions of the Commission, but rather because the Commission had power to decide at all. . . . The investing public was brought to a sharp realization of the fact that the earning power of the roads was subject to public control." Dixon, *Railroads and Government*, 24.

[98] ICC, *Annual Statistics of the Railways of the United States, 1917.*

From 1907 through 1914 the deficiency in capital flow into the railroads, on the basis of pre-1907 relationships, totaled $5.6 billion. In early 1907 railroad management had stood on a peak of prosperity and everywhere surveyed an economy demanding transportation services far in excess of anything projected in the busy ten years after 1897. A burgeoning technology held out the promise of a hundred ways to hold down the operating ratio, that sacred guide to operating results which had been rising so disturbingly. The ratio was not supposed to go above 66 per cent, according to tradition, if adequate profits were to be made, and that is just where it stood (for the railroads as a group) on June 30, 1910. But no one expected it to stay there unless some way out of the cost-price squeeze was found. Nor did it stay there. It rose in 1911 to 68.6 and in 1912 to 69.3. Startlingly, despite a 10 per cent increase in traffic in 1913, it inched up to 69.4 and then, in the poor year of 1914, went out of control at 72.2, an unheard-of figure.[99]

XI

By 1909 it was obvious, to railroad men and not a few of the rest of American economic society, that rates had to be raised. The only question was how. The answer seemed to be a general increase. Rates, after all, had been frozen for all practical purposes at the 1906 level, which in turn was not far above the depression levels of the nineties. Could the ICC be persuaded to defrost them? There was absolutely no precedent for or against a general lifting of tariffs. Theoretically, the roads were as free as ever to raise any rate they wished, subject to investigation by the Commission after the increase, an investigation which would ensue only on complaint of a shipper who was materially affected by the rate. But new, more stringent regulatory legislation was almost certain to be passed by the Congress that had been elected along with William Howard Taft and that would convene in December, 1909. The hour was late for a test of the ICC's policy toward rate levels. Such a test would call for unity and the best leadership the railroads could find.

The leader of the American railroad industry in 1909 was still

[99] The operating ratio is simply total operating expenses expressed as a percentage of operating revenues.

Edward H. Harriman. His formal control of the system had been weakened, but by no means ended, by antitrust actions against him. The ul-
tramodern refinancings, notably of the Chicago & Alton Railroad,
which he and his associates had carried out in the previous ten years
had convinced many that his methods were immoral, if not illegal. But
when the subject was railroads, America hung on Harriman's every
word. As the Taft administration began, he was as prominent as ever.
The previous spring he had demonstrated his own brand of economic
statesmanship by pulling the Erie Railroad, of which he was a director,
out of a bad hole.[100] In December, 1908, his opposition to answering a
number of questions of a general nature, put to him by attorneys of the
ICC during the 1907 investigation, had been vindicated by the Supreme
Court.[101] The very next month his influence in the East had been
greatly increased as stockholders of the New York Central elected him
to their board, giving rise to the old rumors that a coast-to-coast railroad alliance was again in the works. Clearly, Harriman's leadership in
the railroads' approaching Armageddon would be an important, perhaps a crucial, factor in the outcome.

It was with intense interest, therefore, that the entire financial community and much of the general public learned that Harriman had
sailed to Europe for a rest cure necessitated, it was said, by nervous exhaustion brought on by his notoriously punishing work habits. As rumors multiplied concerning his plans for the New York Central, he was
reported taking the cure at Bad Gastein. Then, unexpectedly, he was reported aboard the *Kaiser Wilhelm II,* which was scheduled to dock in
New York City on August 24.

A small army of reporters and unusually aggressive news photographers were shocked by what they saw. They reported to the nation
that it was a very sick man, an invalid who had ominously lost ten
pounds from his slight frame, who gamely struggled to walk down the
gangplank. A tugboat stood by to take Harriman aboard and whisk him
across the Hudson to the Erie Railroad terminal, the reporters still in

---

[100] It was a bad time for the Erie's $5.5 million in one-year notes to fall due. The
line sought to exchange them for part of a new three-year, 6 per cent issue in the
amount of $15 million. When holders of the old notes balked at the exchange,
thereby threatening the marketability of the portion to be sold for cash, Harriman himself bought up the old notes. *CFC, BQS,* LXXXVIII (Jan. 9, 1909), 19.

[101] *Ibid.*

tow. There, the railroad magnate attempted to walk over to the party of newsmen, all but collapsing before taking the arm of Robert S. Lovett, general counsel of the U.P. and Harriman's closest lieutenant. "No, boys," whispered the sick man to the advancing photographers, "no, don't take me now." It was announced that as soon as the railroad leader had been made comfortable aboard the special train that was to take him to the Harrimans' country home, Tower Hill, at Arden, New York, a conference would be held with the members of the press who cared to accompany the train in a combination-smoking car which had been attached for their convenience. By the time he arrived at Arden Harriman had spent a total of four hours with reporters, but despite repeated efforts to draw him out on his plans for the Central, he refused to comment on the future. As to his physical condition, he declared that he was recovering from a condition which had caused him several attacks of acute indigestion.[102]

The stock market sagged alarmingly that day and continued to drop during the rest of the week. His Sabbath duties notwithstanding, the powerful financier, Jacob Schiff, traveled to Arden on Saturday, August 28. Describing his visit with his friend, Schiff declared that Harriman had had a nervous breakdown, but was recovering.[103] On Monday the railroad leader himself issued a statement that he was not seriously ill, that indeed he was continuing his recovery. Tension on Wall Street was greatly relieved, following "one of the most striking episodes in Stock Exchange history." The following Sunday the New York *Times* felt free to print a cartoon showing a wide variety of Americans trying to peek through a keyhole, with the caption, "How's Harriman?" That morning Mrs. Harriman and her two sons, Averell, twenty, and Roland, fourteen, went to church, smiling bravely for the inevitable reporters. Later that day something seemed to have gone wrong. No news pierced the walls of Tower Hill for two days. The front page of the *Times* was crowded with a rare three-column headline proclaiming that Peary had discovered the North Pole, but it found room for a bulletin about Harriman, who was reported to have suffered a relapse. Down went stocks again. But the well-laid plans of Schiff, Lovett,

[102] *NYT*, Aug. 25, 1909, 1–2; *CFC, BQS*, LXXXIX (Sept. 4, 1909), 19–20.
[103] *NYT*, Aug. 29, 1909, 1.

and William Rockefeller to protect the Harriman properties bore fruit and the market rallied on the tenth. Edward H. Harriman, railroad leader, had died the day before.[104]

[104] *Ibid.*, Aug. 31, 1909, 1; Magazine Section, Sept. 5, 1909, 12; Sept. 7, 1909, 1; Sept. 10, 1909, 1. *CFC, BQS,* LXXXVIII (Oct. 2, 1909), 19–20.

CHAPTER V

THE BATTLE JOINED

*We do not intend that this Republic shall ever fail . . . [by] the
poor plundering the rich or in the rich . . . exploiting the poor.*
—THEODORE ROOSEVELT, *1905*

*It is . . . patent to everybody . . . that the three months immediately
preceding a Presidential election offer a very poor time in which to expect
to get fair and reasonable consideration of such a matter as an advance
or readjustment of freight rates.*—THEODORE ROOSEVELT, *1908*

I

W. H. Hosmer, chairman of the Western Traffic Association, was
a braver man than he realized. The documents which he filed with the
Interstate Commerce Commission in Washington at the end of April,
1910, were a package of economic and political dynamite, for they constituted the jointly-arrived-at decision of the twenty-four railroads west
of the Mississippi River, which made up his association, to increase
their freight rates on 200 commodities throughout their territory. Multiplied by all of the mathematical combinations of shipping and destination points that were theoretically involved, the boosts represented literally hundreds of thousands—perhaps millions—of rate increases. The
decision thus inaugurated a radically new policy of making, not specific
rate adjustments a few at a time by individual railroads, but what
amounted to a general increase in the entire freight rate structure. The
increase, under the Hepburn Act of 1906, which was still the law of the
land regarding rate adjustments, would become effective within thirty
days and could then be challenged, rate by separate rate, by shippers
and other interested parties before the Commission. Not so brave nor so
brazen were the big eastern railroads. When they filed notice a few days
later of their intention to increase rates they did so as individual roads,

although their adjustments were identical, from road to road, within the Official Classification Territory in which they operated. But they did not stint themselves: their increases applied not only to one-half of the commodity rates but to all of the class rates in their densely populated and highly industrialized territory. The actual number of individual rates now involved was anybody's guess, but the total was astronomical. It was also anybody's guess as to the over-all average percentage increase involved, but data furnished by the roads and based on traffic in previous years suggested that the cost to the nation's shippers could be as much as 10 to 15 per cent more than what they had been paying.[1]

The hour was not merely late for this move by the nation's railroads; in almost every respect the hour had already passed. Except for the railroad men themselves and a painfully small coterie of Americans in public and private life, in the financial world, and in the industries whose prosperity depended so vitally on the railroads' having plenty to spend for betterments and expansion, and except for a very few large shippers who doubtless were more against strict government regulation in principle than they were for higher freight rates, American public opinion was arrayed almost solidly against a general increase in railroad rates. The move would be attacked for the increases involved, for its implication that the rate structure might be upwardly mobile after long years of relative stability, and most violently for the style, the very manner, in which the raise was sought. When President Taft's ambitious, antitrust-minded Attorney General, George W. Wickersham, heard the news of the western roads' joint application, he wondered aloud to reporters about "what was going on . . . he was surprised to find that all of the 24 companies' applications had been filed by one man." If the idea of having to pay more for transportation services to railroads that

[1] *NYT*, June 1, 1910, 3; June 2, 1, 3; *CFC, BQS*, XC (June 4, 1910), 20. The hearings of the Commission on these applications and the decisions of that body are in 61st Cong., 3d Sess., *Evidence Taken by the Interstate Commerce Commission in the Matter of Proposed Advances in Freight Rates by Carriers*, Senate Document 725 (10 vols., Washington, 1911), hereinafter referred to as "1910 Hearings." The eastern railroads, however, indicated that they expected only about a $27 million increase in their freight revenues, which totaled $727 million in the preceding year, or only about a 3.7 per cent increase. 1910 Hearings, 1634. Just how much the increase amounted to was as much at issue in the proceedings as any other question. The confusion arose from the fact that the size of any rate increase, in terms of its effects on railroad revenues, depends upon what it does to traffic volume, which can be measured only after the rate is in effect.

already appeared to be making exceptionally good profits did not rouse the public to arms, Wickersham can have had no doubt that the sinister implications of their obvious collusion would do so. Besides, requests for increases had come at a time when the broad question of additional, tighter legislation which Taft had promised during the campaign of 1908 was before the Congress.[2] Whatever room for maneuvering the railroads had had after the passage of the Hepburn Act in 1906 had vanished. In retrospect, the railroad men had allowed four precious years to slip by in which they might have tested the national sentiment in respect to general rate increases at a time of generally rising prices and swiftly increasing demands on their lines. What had happened to those four years?

When the railroads first found themselves subject to unequivocal governmental power to fix maximum rates upon finding existing rates "unreasonable," they had had little to fear, or so they thought. The past ten years had been good to them. The government had tightened its enforcement of the Elkins antirebating act of 1903 (not without some embarrassment to certain railroad executives on occasion) and thus the ancient practice of deferring to the superior economic power of large shippers was giving way to a greater ability to collect the published rates. By 1907, moreover, the railroads had more business than they could handle efficiently or satisfactorily at these rates and the competitive necessity of offering costly, unremunerative "services" to their customers had all but disappeared.[3] The strongest roads, in fact, had succeeded in greatly strengthening their rate structures by highly selective increases for manufactured goods which were well able to bear higher charges in the prosperity that followed the depression of the nineties. The development of communities of interests by many of these roads had made this practice possible.[4] Then came the panic of 1907 which brought, as we have seen, a slump in traffic and a much greater decline in profits at the very time that the railroads were engaged in a record expansion program. If financial results were no more than comfortable

[2] *NYT*, June 2, 1910, 1, 3.

[3] Commissioner Prouty did not fail to point this out in his decision in the 1910 rate case. 20 ICC 243, 284.

[4] The Pennsylvania Railroad was notably successful in this regard. "Alexander J. Cassatt," *DAB*, III, 566.

—at least in the view of free-spending railroad executives—in riotously prosperous times, it seemed obvious that in bad, or even ordinary, times, the existing profit margins were dangerously inadequate.

The financial community fully agreed. J. P. Morgan, in the 1880s and 1890s the investing public's best watchdog for its interests in the railroads, was soon to pass personally from the picture, but his sturdy lieutenant, George W. Perkins, took charge. Within four years Perkins was to break a spear in the interests of a scientific national economic policy in the Progressive campaign of Theodore Roosevelt. Meanwhile, what happened to his plan to get the railroads the additional income they seemed to need so badly would serve as something of a rehearsal for that great disappointment. In April, 1908, he organized most of the railroads in a plan to raise rates.[5] If the President could be persuaded of the constructive nature of the move, it seemed likely that the opposition which was sure to come from shippers, and especially from those agricultural interests so zealously represented in Washington by men soon to earn the title of Insurgents, could be neutralized. Roosevelt had spoken for the Hepburn Act in the most reasonable and objective terms. In June, 1905, as the movement to grant the Interstate Commerce Commission real rate-making powers gained momentum, he had told the Union League Club of Philadelphia:

In temperate, resolute fashion there must be lodged in some tribunal the power over rates, and especially over rebates . . . which will protect alike the railroad and the shipper on an equal footing. . . . We do not intend that this Republic shall ever fail . . . [by] the poor plundering the rich or in the rich . . . exploiting the poor.[6]

This was consistent with what he had said as early as his second annual message to Congress:

In curbing and regulating the combinations of capital which are injurious . . . we must be careful not to stop the great enterprises which have legitimately reduced the cost of production, not to abandon the place which our country has won in the leadership of the international industrial world.[7]

[5] Perkins to Morgan, April 21, 1908, quoted in Robert H. Wiebe, *Business and Reform* (Cambridge, Mass., 1962), 85.

[6] Henry F. Pringle, *Theodore Roosevelt: A Biography* (New York, 1939), 361.

[7] *Messages and Papers of the Presidents,* ed. James D. Richardson *et al.* (20 vols. and supplements, Washington, 1898–1925), XV, 6711.

Perhaps, therefore, his fury against the financial leaders whom he suspected (or so he said) of arranging the panic of 1907 to discredit his administration would not extend to so reasonable a Morgan man as Perkins. No one doubted that the attempt to raise rates had to be made.

But the recession and his suspicions were not what made this seem a bad time for an increase in railroad rates to Roosevelt. As the presidential election of 1908 approached, this man who already had begun to regret his resolution of 1904 not to seek a "third" term was determined to see his chosen successor elected. Summering at Oyster Bay, the President fired off a salvo of letters intended to stop the plans for a rate increase dead in their tracks. First he wrote to Perkins, whom he told that a general raise "is simply an invitation to an attack," adding the rather lame excuse that while to some of the roads a rate increase would be a relief, to others it would be a windfall.[8] At the same sitting he wrote to the Commission to inform that independent body to let it be known that if there were a general rise the Commission would be obliged to make an investigation.[9] To Charles Bonaparte, his aggressive attorney general, he wrote two days later, "I quite agree with you that the railroads ought not to raise their rates until December. I have not much sympathy with the shippers, however, as [they are mostly] wealthy concerns, many of them by no means of impeccable character in their own private business." [10] Thus did the President momentarily place his finger on the answer to the question of who would really benefit by clamping the lid on rates. Politics, however, overrode all other considerations and Roosevelt did not hesitate to cite this political fact as a reason for restraint when he wrote William C. Brown, president of the New York Central and one of the leaders in the fight for higher rates, that just before an election was no time to seek a general rise.[11] Perkins, disgruntled because word of his strategy had leaked out before he was ready to move, reluctantly dropped his plans.[12] Except for the

[8] Roosevelt to Perkins, July 23, 1908, *Letters,* ed. Elting E. Morison (8 vols., Cambridge, Mass., 1951–54), VI, 1140–41.

[9] Roosevelt to ICC, July 23, 1908, Roosevelt MSS, cited *ibid.,* VI, 1140n.

[10] Roosevelt to Bonaparte, July 25, 1908, *ibid.,* VI, 1143–44.

[11] Roosevelt to Brown, August 6, 1908, *ibid.,* VI, 1151–52.

[12] Perkins to Elbert Gary, July 28, 1908, cited in Wiebe, *Businessmen and Reform,* 85.

southern roads, which would shortly be locked in combat with the Commission, there would be no application for higher rates by the railroads as a group until 1910.

II

If the railroads' financial condition had deteriorated by 1910, the climate of public policy had deteriorated even more. The railroads faced a Congress in which their staunch friends were few in number and of a growing ineffectuality, while the ranks of those who would fight higher rates on the basis of pure principle were growing. In the White House was a man who felt that the nation had to "get back to competition" or else submit to socialism, who saw in both the letter and the spirit of the Sherman Antitrust Act a measure which had to be enforced. Not for another ten years would the patent nonsense of requiring the railroads to "compete" while at the same time requiring them to post notices of rate changes thirty days in advance be faced up to. Uniformity in rate structures had been made inevitable by the Hepburn Act; the existence, albeit uneasy, of the eastern and western tariff associations was therefore equally inevitable, and Hosmer was indeed no more than a messenger boy when he filed the western roads' joint application. But legal minds pounced on the "collusion" which was obviously involved, while those who had little enthusiasm for this retrogressive interpretation of the Sherman law nevertheless rejoiced at the opportunity for the President to mend his relations with the midwestern Insurgents.

In the Senate, the burden of protecting the railroads' interests had for some years rested on the shoulders of Stephen B. Elkins of West Virginia, chairman of the Committee on Interstate Commerce. A hugely successful coal producer whose business had taken him inevitably into railroad promotion, construction, and operation, Elkins knew the railroad business intimately (as did none of the Insurgents), and there was much about it of which he did not approve. He had fathered the Elkins Act of 1903, now finally being enforced, as a means of relieving railroads of the pressure which large shippers put on them to grant special rates. In 1905 and 1906 he had gone along with the idea of granting the Commission the right to set maximum rates and he had fought and lost the battle to reserve to the courts the right of final review. To the Hepburn bill he had seen added the commodity clause (which required carriers to divest themselves of manufacturing and mining concerns, the products of which they would be carrying) and the clause giving shippers an absolute right to have sidings built to their platforms. He had been hurt by President Roosevelt's lack of trust in him when the new legislation was introduced, and suggestions that he represented the railroads' interests alone (notably by Governor Albert B. Cummins, who was running for reelection in Iowa) angered him. "My interest on the side of the shipper is ten times greater than on the side of the railroads, and . . . my interest in railroads is confined to my own state," he asserted.[13] Ever since the Hepburn Act had enabled shippers to challenge specific rates before the Commission, support had been growing for an amendment which would empower that body to suspend any proposed rate changes for a period of time sufficient to allow it to investigate the reasonableness of the new rate. By such arrangement, shippers could continue to pay the old rate until the new rate had been given the Commission's blessing, and if the Commission took an uncomfortably long time to rule, the railroad and not the shippers would be the loser. In 1909 Elkins, as chairman of his committee, had written an adverse majority report on a bill which would have amended the 1906 act along these lines. He noted that the Hepburn statute had been on the books barely two years, and he doubted that Congress really wanted "to pass additional legislation which would invite and suggest such confusion and legal difficulties in the construction of an act which has not yet been put in full operation by the tribunal charged with that duty." [14] He doubted seriously that the Commission was capable of assuming the enormous day-to-day task of pricing the railroads' services for them. But what really bothered him was the essentially negative aspect of the suspen-

[13] Oscar D. Lambert, *Stephen B. Elkins* (Pittsburgh, 1955), 267–81. Lambert does not stress the point that failure to reserve to the courts the last word in rate cases constituted a defeat for Elkins and others who had wanted a moderate bill. It is often overlooked that while many railroad men supported rate-making powers for the Commission in 1905 and 1906, it was always with the understanding that the courts would retain the power to review specific rates thus established.

[14] "Concerning Advances in Railway Rates," Senate Report 933, 60th Cong., 2d Sess., *Report of Senate Committee on Interstate Commerce to Accompany S. 423*, Feb. 8, 1909, 22. (Hereinafter referred to as the "Elkins Report.")

sion idea. If the Commission suspended a proposed rate permanently as a result of finding it unreasonable, what then? Could it propose an alternative rate? Elkins concluded that it could not.[15] He also had evidence that the Commission wanted no such rigidity in the structure of the nation's railroad rates. In response to an inquiry from Elkins, Martin A. Knapp, chairman of the Commission, had cited that body's recent annual report on this subject, and declared:

> The Commission believes the highest duty of the Commission is to bring together shippers and carriers, to the end that each may see that neither can be permanently prosperous at the expense of the other. . . . The most sensitive spot in the great business dealings of the country is the railroad rate. This rate must be raised or lowered, not in obedience to a rigid statutory law, but in obedience to the varying conditions of trade and commerce.[16]

Unfortunately for the railroad men, who could not have expressed their position more eloquently themselves, neither Senator Elkins nor Commissioner Knapp would influence the outcome of the new rate-increase fight.

The fact is that public policy, as reflected in the attitudes of the President and many of the most energetic and determined members of Congress, was strongly in favor of stricter regulation than had been provided by the Act of 1906. The House of Representatives had gone over to what, on balance, has to be considered an antirailroad bias as early as 1905 when it had approved by an overwhelming margin the strict rate regulation envisioned in the measure authored by Republican Congressmen John Jacob Esch of Wisconsin and Charles Elroy Townsend of Michigan. Even James R. Mann, Republican party stalwart from Illinois, who would serve in the House from 1897 to 1922, ended up opposing Elkins' efforts to modify the rate-suspension bill in 1910 because, one of his colleagues said, he felt that "the bill should reflect the requirements of the times and the demands of the shipping public." [17] William Peters Hepburn could testify to the radical swing which public

---

[15] *Ibid.*, 6, 7.

[16] Knapp to Senate Committee on Interstate Commerce, Jan. 29, 1908, cited *ibid.*, 19.

[17] William H. Stafford, "Memorial Address Delivered in the House of Representatives of the U.S. in Memory of James Robert Mann, Late a Representative from Illinois," *CR*, 77th Cong., 4th Sess., Jan. 14, 1923.

opinion had taken on the question of how to deal with the railroads. His name is associated with the Act of 1906, one of the most important pieces of domestic legislation in the nation's history, but the relatively moderate position which he took on this and other issues was enough to defeat him in the election of 1906.[18] Iowans, who had sent him to Congress as early as 1881, were changing their minds on what they wanted from their representatives.

The Senate was rapidly taking on a radical complexion where the railroads, and much else about American economic life, were concerned. The kind of man midwesterners now admired was someone like Robert M. La Follette, who, as governor of Wisconsin, had developed the state regulatory commission to a fine art and had shown a strong penchant for commissioners who were firmly dedicated to comprehensive control of monopoly enterprise. Voters in that agricultural state sent him to the Senate in 1905, and for twenty years he was to be the figure in whom Progressivism as a political philosophy would continuously reside.

A smart politician had to move adroitly if he would keep abreast of the times in those days, especially if he came from a highly indignant state like Iowa. A case in point is Jonathan Prentiss Dolliver, a walrus-moustached, old-fashioned orator and a politician of shrewd integrity. Dolliver had no high opinion of the railroads. In 1904 he had agreed with an Iowan back home that "it was the railroad people who destroyed the meat-packing industry in Iowa 20 years ago." [19] And his increasingly radical stand on regulation was to make him very durable. A representative from 1889 to 1900, he then went to the Senate, where he died in office at the end of 1910. In the 1905–6 battle for rate regulation he still favored a provision for court review and so, he thought, did the President. He was prepared to become the father of the act which bears Hepburn's name. An Iowa politician had reminded him that they could always send "one Albert B. Cummins" to the Senate, because the people wanted relief from unjust railroad practices.[20] Senators Aldrich

[18] "William Peters Hepburn," *DAB*, VIII, 568.

[19] Dolliver to A. B. Stickney, Sept. 22, 1904, cited in Thomas R. Ross, *Jonathan Prentiss Dolliver: A Study in Political Integrity and Independence* (Iowa City, 1958), 196.

[20] *Ibid.,* 197.

and Foraker turned the rate-regulation bill over to "Pitchfork" Ben Tillman for presentation on the floor, but Dolliver was probably the most effective Senator fighting for what turned out to be a truly independent rate-making Commission. It developed that his desire to retain some form of court review stemmed from his fear that the law would be unconstitutional without it, but he opposed any "broad review" that would cover reasonableness of rates. "The thing I have objected to is framing the provisions so as to enlarge the jurisdiction of the circuit court and make it practically an appellate ICC," he said.[21] Few of his Iowa constituents could have wanted the courts in the picture in a substantive way, not after what the judges had done to the original ICC powers. Senator Aldrich saw that Dolliver's objective was to secure for the Commission the greatest possible amount of power, "by hook or by crook." [22] And when an amendment providing for court review was offered, the Iowan opposed it.[23]

By the spring of 1910 Dolliver was too sick to continue as an active member of the Commerce Committee, but when Attorney General Wickersham presented Congress with a prepared bill including exemption of the railroads from the antitrust law he was furious, especially when he heard that the railroad executives had decided to support it, suspension clause and all. He had, he said, "old-fashioned views about the Congress of the U.S. finding the work of Congress so elaborately mapped out by other departments of the Government." [24] He wanted a stronger bill than the President had in mind. What he and the nation got was even stronger, but it was primarily the work of another Iowan, tougher and even more determined than Dolliver.

If anyone in high public office truly hated the railroads in 1910, it was Albert B. Cummins, whom Iowans had sent to the Senate in 1909. He had cast his lot early with those who wanted the arrogant railroads of his state put in their place, and as a consequence he always faced bitter opposition from these interests. They had kept him out of the Senate in 1894 and again in 1899, and when he won the Republican nomination for governor in 1901 in a momentous struggle, he had resolved to

---

[21] *Ibid.,* 202–9.

[22] Nathaniel W. Stephenson, *Nelson W. Aldrich: A Leader in American Politics* (New York, 1930), 288.

[23] Ross, *Dolliver,* 211.   [24] *Ibid.,* 276.

bear down on them in earnest. Their taxes, which many had always considered too low (here was one instance in which lawmakers were willing to accept the railroads' stated capitalization), were raised, and their political power, which had become legendary, was greatly weakened by a primary election law. Venerable Senator William B. Allison had won the primary in 1908 but died before the general election, and Cummins had found it relatively easy to step into his place.[25] Once in Washington, he was to become the *de facto* leader in the development of national railroad policy, shouldering aside the less able La Follette. His accomplishments would embrace the entire spectrum of national policy, from the most repressive features of the Act of 1910 to a belated "apology" in the Transportation Act of 1920 which is sometimes referred to by his name. Without Cummins in the Senate, Hosmer's packet of rate increase applications would still have produced a loud report; under the circumstances it was pure dynamite. For this most insurgent Iowa Senator was determined that not only would many remaining railroad abuses—such as long- and short-haul discrimination—be ended, but the railroads' power to put up their rates at will, individually or in concert, would be destroyed once and for all.

III

Nearly everybody who counted himself a member of informed opinion during the Progressive era believed he knew what to do about the railroads. Outside the halls of Congress, college professors, editors of influential magazines, and public-spirited men from various callings wrote and spoke with varying degrees of effectiveness on such knotty problems as levels of rates, discrimination, standards of honesty, good business practice in the issuance of railroad securities, and that most controversial subject of all—government ownership. Sweeping changes

[25] "Albert Baird Cummins," *DAB,* IV, 597. As governor, Cummins had rebuffed the offer of a railroad executive to testify in favor of an anti-pass bill because it would destroy the image of the railroads as unanimously opposed to progressive legislation. Raymond L. Flory, "The Political Career of Chester I. Long" (unpublished doctoral dissertation, University of Kansas, 1955), 201. See also Ralph M. Sayre, "Albert Baird Cummins and the Progressive Movement in Iowa" (unpublished doctoral dissertation, Columbia University, 1958).

were taking place in the halls of higher learning. The social sciences were emerging as the handmaidens of the spirit of reform and good government which had survived the ignominious political miscalculations of the Populists, and which was so much in evidence among academic men, especially in the great land-grant universities of the Midwest. Economics led the way, but economics that was still emphatically "political economy," dedicated to the pragmatic study of historical and institutional parameters of problems affecting the material public welfare. It was a period in which the old nineteenth-century concept of *laissez faire* was finally mangled beyond all recognition as intellectuals condemned large-scale enterprise because it lacked the elements of free competition, and looked to government to reestablish, by the most direct and comprehensive means of intervention, that earlier and presumably happier state of affairs, the existence of which was a virtually unquestioned article of faith in all but a few doubting, searching minds.

If one could be against *laissez faire* for reasons that often seemed more sentimental than intellectual, one could also be for it on the basis of evidence that governmental controls over the important policies of a basic industry, such as railroad transportation, simply did not work. Not quite everyone believed that regulation would achieve that result which the intellectual and economic idealists could surely agree was the only legitimate end of a well-ordered society: the allocation of economic resources in such a manner as to maximize total output and ensure its equitable distribution to those factors of production most directly responsible for its production, after making some allowances for those members of society who were unable to take care of themselves. One *could* argue that such a result could not be reached through regulation, but in fact very few thinkers of the Progressive era did actually deny the ability of government optimally to achieve these ends. The remarkable era of prosperity which the nation had enjoyed since 1897 did not deflect informed opinion from the assurance that things could be a lot better than they were, nor had many had the time or the inclination to forget the highhanded practices of the trust-builders of the eighties and nineties and the cruel depression to which, it seemed clear, they had led. Few were in the mood to "let business alone." The exhilarating notion that men who lacked the experience, the economic power, and the enlightened self-interest of the leaders of big business could nevertheless establish the patterns by which such great aggregates of property fitted into the nation's economy popped up everywhere. The notion was, after all, only one aspect of a greater reform movement which meant to clean up the way things were done in politics at the same time. Reform was a well-established movement in America by the turn of the century and insofar as it reflected a widespread antipathy toward anything big, it was bound to grow rather than to decline during the prosperous decades before America entered the war.[26]

It was a lone voice, therefore, that had issued from the newly built collegiate Gothic walls of the University of Chicago in 1905 to warn the nation of the pitfalls of government regulation of railway rates. Its owner was a forty-year-old assistant professor of political economy at the university, Hugo Richard Meyer, who had studied the regulation of rates in Germany in the preceding several years, and who had not liked what he had seen.[27] The railroads, just then mounting a massive publicity campaign against the strong movement toward rate regulation which was to end a year later in the Hepburn Act, learned of what Meyer was saying about government rate-fixing in a book which he had almost completed on his German researches, and encouraged him to rush it to completion with the assurance that there would be many customers for it. It appeared late in 1905 and in the coming controversy over the publicity campaign waged by the railroads it was virtually the only scholarly statement of the case against rate regulation with which muckrakers like Ray Stannard Baker, who specialized in jabs at the railroads for *McClure's Magazine,* would have to contend.[28]

[26] Cf. Charles Forcey, *The Crossroads of Liberalism: Croly, Weyl, Lippmann, and the Progressive Era, 1900–1925* (New York, 1961), xv, for a theory of why so powerful an urge for reform appeared in such a prosperous period.

[27] "Hugo Richard Meyer," *Who Was Who in America, 1961–68,* 657. Meyer died in Melbourne, Australia, in 1923; Harvard University, *Tenth Report of the Class of 1892* (Cambridge, Mass., 1927), 26.

[28] Hugo Richard Meyer, *Government Regulation of Railway Rates* (New York, 1905). The book was reviewed, with due notice of its uncompromising stand against rate-fixing, by such other widely read periodicals as *Review of Reviews,* XXXII (Nov., 1905), 637, and *Outlook,* LXXXI (Dec. 16, 1905), 936. Baker reported, in his article on the railroads' publicity campaign against rate regulation, that Meyer's book "is being widely circulated by the railroads, and is regarded as one of the strongest arguments in their favor. . . . [Meyer] is perhaps the only economist in the country who appears as a thick-and-thin defender of present railroad conditions." "Railroads on Trial," *McClure's Magazine,* XXVI (March, 1906), 539.

What troubled Meyer was the fact that, to him, regulation meant the end of what Chairman Knapp had spoken of so highly in his letter to Senator Elkins: a rate structure that would be flexible and free to reflect changes in the conditions of trade. Meyer was so unorthodox as to praise what he called constructive discrimination in the pre-ICC years when, he said, there was a "heterogeneous mass of railway rates that knit the different producing, distributing, and consuming sections of the country into a more compact trading unit than was to be found anywhere else in the world and carried the exploitation of our resources farther than . . . any other country." [29] He praised the philosophy contained in the decision of the lower court in what eventually became the Alabama Midland case (in which the Supreme Court ruled that the Act of 1887 had not delegated to the Commission the substantial powers it was exercising): "The carriers are better qualified to adjust such matters than any court or board of public administration, and within the limits suggested [that discrimination in rates not be practiced where conditions were substantially similar] it is wise and safe to leave to their traffic managers the adjusting of dissimilar circumstances and conditions to their business." [30] Meyer had not found in the German railway system the well-run, rationally regulated system which others had seen. He observed that rates were being set which froze the country's trade in the geographical patterns in existence before the coming of the railroads. Eastern beet sugar, grain, and timber producers, for example, were shut out of the western market just as the Ruhr iron and steel industry was prevented from competing with that of the Saar. He noted that the Prussian Minister of Finance had declared, in the nineties, that "the system of government ownership of the railways will break down unless it shall prove possible to find refuge from the jealousies and conflicts of local and sectional interests behind the stone wall of a system of hard and fast railway rates which admits of no exercise of discretion." [31]

Meyer's position (and this is what made it so unacceptable to the Progressives) was that the government was simply incapabl of devising a rate structure that would ensure the most efficient economic growth of

[29] Meyer, *Government Regulation of Railway Rates,* 457.

[30] *ICC* vs. *Alabama Midland Railroad* (41 U.S. App. 453 and 168 U.S. 144), quoted *ibid.,* 459.

[31] Meyer, *Government Regulation of Railway Rates,* 450–53; 456.

the nation. It was not merely that government officials obviously lacked the practical, day-to-day knowledge of business conditions which it was the duty of the railroads' traffic managers to keep abreast of; public regulators, in fact, would be unable to resist the complaints of those who were losing out to "progress." He pleaded that regulation was as much a question of regulating different producing areas as of regulating competing railroads; "the invariable result in these countries [where railroads have been nationalized] has been to transfer from the field of business to the field of politics the perplexing question of trade rivalry and jealousy precipitated by the annihilation of distance by means of the railway." [32] Meyer claimed that before he began his study of German railway policy he had had "a strong bias in favor of State intervention in industry." Perhaps that was true, but nobody seemed to care. When he said flatly, "It is impossible for the State to conserve and promote the public welfare by intervening in the regulation of railway rates," he was, to most people, still back in the nineteenth century with Herbert Spencer.[33]

This unfashionable young professor published two more books on the evils of government ownership and operation of public utilities, but he never attained any stature as an authority on transportation economics in the United States. He shortly emigrated to Australia, where he spent the rest of his life. Much more in tune with the times, and possessed of an infinitely more effective sounding board, was William Z. Ripley, Nathaniel Ropes Professor of Political Economy at Harvard. No one else carried half the weight with makers of public policy that this persuasive, hard-working, idealistic political economist enjoyed. The very well-defined views on discrimination, rate regulation, and especially the practices and ethics of railway finance which he was conveying to his students would soon be embodied in two hefty and highly topical volumes.[34] Ripley severely condemned the stand which the rail-

[32] *Ibid.*, 449–50. He scored a telling point in noting that the vaunted canal system of Germany was built, for the most part, after the railroads were available, by interests who found that their natural advantages of production were being neutralized by an unenlightened rate policy; 450–51.

[33] *Ibid.*, vii, 472.

[34] William Z. Ripley, *Railroads: Finance and Organization* (New York, 1915), and *Railroads: Rates and Regulation* (New York, 1912).

roads had taken against regulatory legislation. To him there could be no question of the need for a commission empowered to pass on the reasonableness of rates.[35] His attitude toward the problem of the general level of rates and what the railroads could expect from the Commission if they wished to raise *all* or a substantial number of their rates, rather than adjust a few relative to other rates from time to time, is probably typical of most planners of rate legislation in the years from 1906 to 1910: that is, he *had* no attitude because he did not recognize that rising costs in a period of rising prices could or would make the historical rate level passé, thereby bringing carriers and shippers into conflict with each other. As late as 1913, moreover, he was still insisting that "it is a matter of far less concern to an individual merchant or group of traders that the absolute freight rate is high than that it (be it in general high or low) is higher than the rate enjoyed by a competitor. For even if it be unreasonably high, so long as it applies to all traders in the same market, the surcharge can immediately be levied upon the consumer by all dealers alike through an enhancement of prices." [36] Professor Ripley might have benefited by talking to men on the firing line, like Hosmer; as it was, the expert's deductive reasoning about shipper psychology was a poor guide for the future on the eve of the 1910 rate controversy, and by 1913 it was hopelessly divorced from reality. The question of whether rate increases would be passed along to consumers—and by what procedure, and whether in the short or long run—or would be absorbed by shippers, was to be argued back and forth in the coming months. Nor would it be subject to an easy solution. In fact, there would be no general solution at all, for the simple reason that every commodity, and every shipper of a given commodity, was a special case in respect to the competitive impact of a rate increase. Ripley's pure theory of rate-making apparently appealed to his students. How poorly it reflected the real world, we are about to see.

Other men in the academic world echoed Ripley's brand of thinking about the need to improve standards and procedures of railroad operation and finance. At the University of Pennsylvania, Emory K. Johnson taught a sober if unimaginative gospel of regulation to his students

[35] William Z. Ripley, ed., *Railway Problems,* 2d ed. (New York, 1913), xxviii–xxix.

[36] *Ibid.,* xviii.

of finance and commerce.[37] At the University of Wisconsin, fountain-head of Progressivism, young Balthasar H. Meyer (no genealogical or philosophical relative of the University of Chicago's Professor Meyer) had looked upon the European system of regulation and found it good. By 1910 he was making a brilliant career which had taken him from teaching into service on his state's regulatory commission, a mode of economic regulation to which he remained dedicated when, the next year, he was called to Washington in time to participate in the ICC's decision on the 1910 applications.[38] These men preached, on the whole, the policing of railroad corporations. They hardly envisioned a positive, creative role for the regulatory agency in the formulation of a national policy that would set rates for the railroads in advance, and never questioned that the railroads would remain private enterprises with full sovereignty over their properties except for those aspects of their business which had been specifically reserved to a public body, essentially judicial in nature. Surprisingly enough, the idealistic approach to government control of economic life came from quite a different quarter, from a little group of talented, earnest, and highly articulate writers and thinkers. Charles Forcey paints a vivid picture of the zest with which they approached these weighty matters: three men, seated before a great fireplace in the study of a solidly comfortable mansion on Long Island's north shore, earnestly discussing America's economic future until the small hours of the morning. They were the editor of the crusading little magazine, the *New Republic;* one of his most able writers, who was also a trained economist; and a former President of the United States who had just returned from a triumphant trip around the world, and

[37] Emory R. Johnson, *American Railway Transportation* (New York, 1903), and *Railroad Traffic and Rates* (New York, 1911). Although Johnson's influential textbooks were still coming out in "revised" editions after the general level of rates had become a leading issue, they continued to ignore the problem.

[38] Balthasar H. Meyer, "The Administration of Prussian Railroads," *Annals of the American Academy of Political and Social Science,* X, No. 3 (Publication No. 215) (Philadelphia, 1897), 389–423. Meyer also published treatises on the history of state regulation of railroads and spoke out strongly, if ineffectually, on the backwardness of the Supreme Court's economic wisdom in the Northern Securities case. (See Chapter IV above.) His conversion to a strong, centralized body for railroad rate policy-making is revealed in his *Railway Legislation in the United States* (New York, 1903).

who was already beginning to chafe at the state of affairs at home and his inability to do anything about it.[39]

Herbert Croly, editor of the *New Republic,* was the most original thinker of the three. In 1909, just before Theodore Roosevelt sailed away to Africa, the former President received from several quarters copies of Croly's new book, which the donors knew contained ideas that he would find most agreeable. Entitled *The Promise of American Life,* it was a clarion call to all who saw, not a disappearance of freedom, but a golden opportunity in the trend toward the centralization of economic power which was so unmistakably continuing in the twentieth century. Croly's concept of future American society was more Hamiltonian than anything else, but he sought to smooth off some of the rough edges of Hamilton's aristocratic views by balancing the call for a strong, centralized government and "constructive discrimination" between elements in the national economy, by a recommendation for the promotion of labor unions and the restraint, to be followed eventually by nationalization, of big business. The program would be carried out by a "democratic elite," apparently a halfway house, philosophically, between the nineteenth-century concept of the "career open to talent" and the "brain trust" of a Roosevelt yet to come. Croly worried about replacing the dynamic brilliance of American industrial leaders with the kinds of people he saw in government at that time. "The peculiar advantage of the organization of American industry which has gradually been wrought during the past 50 years," he said, "is precisely the opportunity which it has offered to men of exceptional ability to perform really constructive economic work." [40] He was cruelly contemptuous of the creative potential of the bureaucratic (as opposed to the entrepreneurial) approach to the running of big business which he saw in such legislation as the New York Public Service Commission law that was a standard of legal and social excellence to many people:

It tends to deprive the peculiarly capable industrial manager of any sufficient opportunity to turn his abilities and experience to good account. It

[39] Forcey, *Crossroads of Liberalism,* 3–4.

[40] Herbert D. Croly, *The Promise of American Life* (New York, 1909), 368; Forcey, *Crossroads of Liberalism,* 35–38; David Levy, "The Life and Thought of Herbert Croly, 1869–1914" (unpublished doctoral dissertation, University of Wisconsin, 1966), attempts no analysis of Croly's program of economic regulation.

places him under the tutelage of public officials . . . and in case this tutelage fails . . . (as it assuredly will) the responsibility for the failure will be
divided . . . [and] the constructive economic work of the past two generations will be undone. . . . Such obnoxious regulation has been not unjustly
compared to the attempt to discipline a somewhat too vivacious bull by the
simple process of castration.[41]

A majority of Americans in 1910 probably felt that, so far as the
railroads were concerned, a "little" castration might be a very good
thing, but for most of them Croly's metaphor could easily have been
countered with one about rings in noses. Few people in the Progressive
era felt that a loss of competitive drive toward higher profits was a real
danger. What they wanted was specific recommendations for dealing
with great aggregations of power. Croly could provide few. He noted
that the railroads had hastened the growth of national markets and that
"this natural process was accelerated by the policy which the larger
companies adopted in the making of their rates." [42] He felt the railroads
should continue to have maximum freedom in setting rates, and he proposed to solve one perplexing problem by abolishing the entire concept
of state supervision in favor of exclusive national regulation. He wanted
to encourage the natural development of the system by legalizing mergers and traffic agreements among the companies. But always he kept
trailing off into generalities: "Any such reorganization [nationalization
of the railroads] should aim at keeping the benefits of the then existing
private organization. . . . If agents of the national economic interest
cannot be trusted to fulfill their responsibilities without some system of
detailed censure and supervision they should be dispensed with." [43]
What did he mean? Did his plan amount merely to placing American
railroad executives in uniform (figuratively speaking) and then ordering
them to go about their business of making the nation great? *The Promise of American Life,* so far as formation of a national policy within the
framework of what the American people would accept is concerned,
seemed to add up to little more than a warning against punishing a
body of indispensable, if not entirely blameless, men, and against legislators who "endeavor to evade a fundamental responsibility by meeting
a superficial one." [44]

[41] Croly, *Promise of American Life,* 368.   [42] *Ibid.,* 110.
[43] *Ibid.,* 353–56, 365–66, 367, 378.   [44] *Ibid.,* 367.

Even more general, and therefore less helpful, was Croly's colleague, the economist Walter Weyl, who was the third man sitting before the fireplace that night at Oyster Bay. Weyl did not get his ideas into book form until the publication of *The New Democracy* in 1912. This is a far-ranging book, reflecting the breadth of its author's interests. Only one chapter, "The Industrial Program of the Democracy," bore on the nation's railroad problems. Written in very broad and often unconvincing style, it calls for a socialization of industry: "The most characteristic feature of the industrial program of the democracy . . . is the emphasis which is laid upon the state in industry . . . a true socialization of industry." [45] Weyl describes a wide range of government intervention, from monopoly to a situation in which regulation would be very restrained, where competition and especially the benefits of competition are still present. The objective, according to Weyl, was to retain the virtues of competition *within* a trust (i.e., one plant manager's performance would be judged against another's), but to do away with meaningless competition between trusts.[46] This is a program which not even a J. P. Morgan could dispute. The great financier had devoted nearly thirty-five years to eliminating meaningless competition (what is more, he could recognize it when he saw it) and he would not have put a red cent of his clients' money into any enterprise whose head did not pit his lieutenants against each other mercilessly. Where thinkers like Weyl lost the general public was in his threat of something in which most people had little faith: noting with approval the trend toward more regulatory power over the railroads, he warned that "the government may (and if regulation fails, it will) buy, own, and operate the railroads of the country." [47] What constituted failure of regulation to Weyl? Was it the failure of government to guarantee railroad service at existing or still lower rates, come hell or high prices and wages? Was it the failure of government to assure the railroads a "living rate"? Was it the failure of the railroads to raise and invest the sums necessary to provide constantly more and better service, without regard to their own financial performance? Weyl could offer no guidance on these critical issues. Still, even today not quite everybody would recognize his threat of government ownership as the refuge of ignorance it so clearly was.

[45] Walter E. Weyl, *The New Democracy* (New York, 1912), 278–79.

[46] *Ibid.*, 281–82.   [47] *Ibid.*, 284.

Falling somewhere in between the pragmatic academicians and the idealistic journalists was a man who felt he knew exactly what was wrong with American economic life, on the railroads and elsewhere: that it was, in the simplest possible terms, based on corporate organizations which were too big to be efficient. The descendant of European liberal intellectuals who had fled to America following the failure of the revolutions of 1848, Louis D. Brandeis was turning into one of the most doctrinaire, perfect-competition, Manchester-school economic thinkers in the nation. He hated the insulated, privileged existence which he fancied the administrators of great corporations enjoyed as members of an exclusive club from which many Americans (including, not incidentally, men of his own ethnic group) were systematically debarred. By 1910 his earnings as a highly successful lawyer, supplemented by a tidy inheritance from his father, had made it possible for him to select causes to prosecute rather than cases to handle and he allowed himself to become known as the "people's lawyer." He possessed in great degree the dramatic skill and instinct for in-fighting which mark the successful trial lawyer. His frequent articles on the meaning and the implications of a rapidly industrializing America attracted widespread attention and were eventually published under the eye-catching titles of *Other People's Money* and *Business—a Profession.* He ripped into the greatest and most dignified corporations with a conviction of their inefficiency that sometimes bordered on prejudice. Even the "generally well-managed" Pennsylvania Railroad, he charged, seemed to be suffering from "excessive bigness." [48] He scorned the role of bankers, especially investment bankers, claiming that really powerful, well-run enterprises ought to raise their own capital. A corporation like the Pennsylvania Railroad "with its long-continued success and reputation for stability should have much wider financial support [than its own stockholders in marketing new securities issues] and should eliminate the banker altogether. With the 2,700 stations on its system, the Pennsylvania could, with a slight expense, create nearly as many avenues through which money would be obtainable to meet its growing needs." The ticket agent at the window of the station in Altoona, apparently, was considered by Brandeis to be equally competent to sell stocks,

[48] Louis D. Brandeis, *Other People's Money* (New York, 1914), 126; *Business—a Profession* (Boston, 1914), *passim.*

bonds, and upper berths to Akron. Obviously, either Brandeis knew less about corporation finance than he should, or the mighty Pennsylvania was paying for something it was not getting or did not need and was therefore stupid as well as inefficient. Brandeis was willing that his readers should decide that the problem was indeed big-business obtuseness. It was not unusual for critics of high finance to ignore the underwriting risks which investment bankers shouldered and on which they were primarily dependent for their reason for existing. Brandeis' talent for obfuscating the real issue, which was the need for capital for expansion and improvement of service, was even more considerable where it afforded an opportunity to demonstrate what he considered the sterility of the banking community. His treatment of the Union Pacific situation is a case in point. Here is a railroad, he said in summary, which in the fourteen years up to 1912 issued $375 million in securities. But the "extraordinary improvements and additions that raised the U.P. to a high state of efficiency" were financed out of earnings except for about $1 million a year. Most of the enormous financings, he noted, had gone to acquire the securities of numerous other roads. The U.P.'s actual need to raise capital, therefore, was very slight in Brandeis' opinion. Thus he seems to have confused his argument against giantism, as exemplified by the railroad holding company, and his argument against the investment banker's role in society. As a lawyer, however, he must have appreciated the myriad advantages of the acquisition of one company by another through purchase of its capital stock rather than its assets. It is significant, therefore, that he assigned no importance to the investment banker as underwriter, whose function was to assume the risks which always attend a financial reorganization—risks which the railroad management could not calculate, and had no business assuming. There seems to have been a certain intellectual coarseness in Brandeis' grasp of the workings of the capitalistic economy, in which he never seems to have lost faith as the best form of organization of American life; but he could really build a case in the strict legal sense, and the public, whose comprehension of financial realities was even coarser, loved it.

The possibilities of lighting into the big, bloated railroad companies, however, had hardly been touched. Back in 1906, Brandeis recalled, he had been greatly impressed by an article in the *American Engineer and Railroad Journal*. Written by one Harrington Emerson, it told of the enormous possibilities for improving efficiency which he and his fellow efficiency experts had observed in a pilot application of their ideas and procedures in the shops of the Santa Fe Railroad. Brandeis filed this one away for future reference. It would soon be time to roll into battle against the railroads. He could see the light shining far down the tracks.[49]

IV

The engaging gentleman who was addressing the members of the American Railway Guild so earnestly at their New York meeting in May, 1914, went by the highly improbable name of Ivy Lee. In another few years he would be recognized as the father of corporate public relations, a field in which he had been working for nearly a decade. His message to the assembled railroad men in 1914 contained all of the conviction and emotion of one who had spent most of that decade watching the railroads outclassed by virtually every enemy of a better deal for the carriers. Now he was a prophet with considerable honor in his own land, and he preached freely the central doctrine of the public relations man: the job is to change or cultivate public opinion, not to crusade for the truth in and of itself. "You can not argue with the public," he told these men who were so sure of the virtue of their cause. "Mr. Roosevelt, in his speeches, gives us holes through which one can drive a coach and four. Mr. Bryan doesn't reason, but he moves multitudes powerfully. Such men, and quite legitimately, say what they have to say with a view to its emotional effect upon the imagination of the people they are seeking to reach." Righteous indignation, appeals to logic, and the like were out when the opinion of the masses was involved. The railroads must adopt this strategy, too, if they were to live down the prejudices which sixty years had accumulated against them, and if they were to gain the sympathy of enough of the American people to change the bias of their elected representatives in dealing with the corporations.[50]

[49] O. Kraines, "Brandeis' Philosophy of Scientific Management," *Western Political Quarterly,* XIII (March, 1960), 192.

[50] Ivy Lee, *Human Nature and the Railroads* (Philadelphia, 1915), 18.

Lee was very frank with the railroad men. There were three evils, he said, which the public believed implicitly about the railroads, and all of them were based on ignorance and misunderstanding. Take the old chestnut about the vast amount of watered stock on which dividends are being paid, he said. Here is a myth which has plagued the railroads for half a century, and yet in England, where 15 per cent of the capitalization is water, Lee said, the myth that watered stock raises rates or makes for unjustly high returns to stockholders does not exist. Yet Americans, he noted, were just then spending a lot of money to conduct, through the Interstate Commerce Commission, a comprehensive study of the actual physical value of the railroad facilities of the nation, as if such knowledge, when gained, would solve the rate-making problem. Almost as crippling, Lee said, was the belief that bankers in a few large cities, in their roles of absentee landlords, were draining off big profits from the localities in which the railroads did business. Railroad men who could not understand the readiness of politicians and businessmen to underpay the railroads for carrying the mail, for example, or to force them to build handsome new depots, ought to consider how much support for such unfairness people could find in the conviction that they were merely returning the favor. But the biggest public relations problem was the power which the railroads exercised over people, by virtue of the fact that they were far and away the largest employers of men and therefore the first whom the public could accuse of heartlessness in hard times.[51] These were beliefs which only years of skillful public relations effort could change, and the hour was late in that lovely, deceptively peaceful month of May, 1914.

Not that the railroads had been entirely without friends over the years. As far back as 1869 the pioneer reporter of financial information about the railroads, Henry Varnum Poor, had delivered a powerful blast in favor of private enterprise in the further development and expansion of the nation's transportation system. Democracies, he warned, had a special need for private organization even of such great undertakings. "Their incompetency to carry out an elaborate scheme requiring years for its accomplishment, or to redress abuses, he said, is one of the striking characteristics of all free governments. . . . They have no

[51] *Ibid.*, 9–11.

'vested right' either in their places or honors, which any day may fall to another, and very little sense of personal interest in the results of their services. . . . No government is capable of properly executing or administering commercial enterprises." [52] Many would continue to agree with Poor well into the twentieth century, but after 1906 nothing was to be accomplished by that line of reasoning. Other financial journals and trade papers, however, seemed to offer little help. Periodicals like the *Commercial and Financial Chronicle,* for example, although generally honest and tolerably fair, influenced only a very small segment of the public, and their dedication to serving the financial community was manifest. Trade papers like the *Railroad Gazette* found the day-to-day affairs of the railroads, in this period of rapidly unfolding technological progress and high level of railroad activity, more to their taste than the long-range transportation problems of the nation. As for the general magazines, the candidacy of the railroads for any editorial policy based on the highly effective muckraking formula was so obvious that such periodicals, influential as they were in these years, had to be considered among the enemy. This bias would melt away very slowly as the second decade of the new century wore on.

  Railway World, however, undertook a project in 1909 which was designed to marshal public opinion behind a sober consideration of the effects of changing economic times on the railroads. There is no evidence that this substantial undertaking had any marked effect on the course of events. It is interesting primarily for what it reveals about the primitive character of economic thought in those days, and as an example of very early public opinion research.[53] The editor noted that the inflationary effects of the rapidly rising price level had been perceived as early as 1905, when Arthur Twining Hadley, president of Yale and a leading economist, had observed in an article in the Boston *Transcript* that the small increases in rates which had been instituted since the return of prosperity, when increases in prices were taken into account, amounted to "a tremendous and gratifying decrease." [54] In fact, the rail-

[52] *Poor's Manual of Railroads, 1868–69* (New York, 1868), 31.

[53] *Railway World,* "Depreciated Currency and Diminished Railway Rates" (Philadelphia, 1909). The articles based on the survey were collected and published in this pamphlet.

[54] *Ibid.,* 8.

way trade press had been pushing this issue for a year before Hadley's pronouncement, and in 1906, the *World* noted, the Hart, Schaffner, and Marx essay contest had been won by Dr. Albert N. Merritt, who revealed a similar philosophy. It seemed important, therefore, to find out just how widely these views were held among professional economists.[55] In September, 1908, *Railway World* mailed a questionnaire to a list of such men, which was accompanied by an impressive array of data that could hardly lead to any other conclusion than that rates had not risen as much as prices, whatever implications the economists might choose to see in this situation. Is there such a thing, asked the *World,* as a distinction between real and nominal wages and prices? Has this distinction any importance for railway rates? Have real railway rates, in fact, risen or fallen since 1897?

The economists responded in the manner the *World* expected, but those who chose to comment on the practical significance of their theoretical observations were not optimistic. Joseph F. Johnson, professor of political economy at New York University, growled that "the forces bringing about the rise of prices will necessarily lead to a rise of railroad rates—or to railroad bankruptcy." [56] From Burlington, Vermont, Charles W. Mixter predicted that "if real rates continue in the future progressively to decline . . . it will first check improvements and ultimately bankrupt the roads. . . . We are really at present in a revolutionary economic state and the public mind has great difficulty in getting its bearings. . . . This is but the third time, since modern history began, when there has been inflation on a specie basis." [57] Gloomiest of all was Jesse E. Pope, former professor of economics at the University of Missouri. "We need improvements and we need extensions [but] the general public do not easily grasp the importance of the above distinction [between real and nominal increases in rates] and . . . prejudice is sure to be the outcome of any upward movement of rates." [58]

The railroads were far from being without friends who had a deep personal interest in their fight to raise rates. The most active such group was the Railway Business Association, whose members represented, ac-

[55] *Ibid.;* Albert N. Merritt, *Federal Regulation of Railway Rates* (Boston and New York, 1907).

[56] *Railway World,* "Depreciated Currency," 44.   [57] *Ibid.,* 45–46.

[58] *Ibid.,* 49.

cording to their president, George A. Post, $800 million in capital and one and a half million workers, all devoted to supplying the railroads. Meeting at New York's Hotel Belmont in June, 1910, at the height of the excitement that surrounded the passage of the new rate-suspension bill by Congress, the Association drafted a plea for public support of the railroads' application, declaring that the railroad equipment industry, notoriously one of feast or famine, had but recently emerged from "a period of closed shops and idle men." [59] Clearly, however, the group whose support would be most dramatically helpful to the roads were the shippers themselves. Sentiment in favor of higher rates as the best guarantee of improved service was not entirely unknown. Representatives of some of the largest shippers in the country served on the boards of major railroads in the post-rebate era. [60] And many an industrial tycoon had substantial personal investments in the railroads. Not surprisingly, this concern among industrial interests was centered in the leader of the financial community, J. P. Morgan and Company, whose chief trouble-shooter, George W. Perkins, undertook to see that there was peace, or at least no open warfare, between shippers and carriers. Following a meeting at the Trunk Line Association offices in New York on June 10, 1910, it was announced that "the spirit was friendly," that representatives of shippers in Philadelphia, Boston, and elsewhere in the East did not oppose the railroads' drive for increases, so long as they were not put at a comparative disadvantage with the West. [61] Financial editors began to take heart. "Public opinion was beginning to manifest itself in fair treatment of the railroads," wishfully wrote the editor of the *Commercial and Financial Chronicle* in his summary of the hectic month of June, noting that sympathetic expressions had come from the National Association of Clothiers, in session in Baltimore, from the Chicago Board of Trade, and from "some other mercantile bodies." On June 21, the *Chronicle* said, Perkins had actually got the big meat packers to agree to an 11 per cent increase in rates. [62] Where these shipper-friends of the railroads would be when the hearings began before the Commis-

[59] *NYT,* June 4, 1910, 2; June 9, 2.

[60] Henry H. Rogers of the Standard Oil Co., for example, was a director of the Santa Fe at the time of his death in May, 1909; A.T. & S.F. R.R. Co., *Annual Report for 1909*, 21.

[61] *NYT,* June 4, 1910, 2; June 11, 5.   [62] *CFC, BQS,* XCI (July 2, 1910), 20.

sion later that summer would be quite another story. The same might be wondered about the 3,000 members of the Brotherhoods of Railway Trainmen, of Locomotive Engineers, and of Locomotive Firemen and Enginemen, and the Order of Railway Conductors, all of whom voted, at their New York meeting in September, to take political action against those who were unduly antagonistic toward their employers.[63]

Men like Ivy Lee, however, had already begun to convince the railroads that an organized, professional program of public relations was a necessity. Lee's firm of Parker and Lee had been retained by the Pennsylvania Railroad in 1906 to help that far-reaching enterprise in its mammoth job of maintaining cordial relations with its enormous public. Lee saw to it that the newspapers at least got their facts straight, especially when such delicate matters as accidents were involved, and arranged for the company's executives to address business and civic clubs at every opportunity.[64] Other early believers in corporate public relations were William W. Finley, president of the Southern Railway, which called the turn for all of the railroads in the Southeast; and Daniel Willard, president of the prestigious Baltimore & Ohio.[65] The railroads had already had considerable experience in joint public relations activity; in 1905, when they were resisting Theodore Roosevelt's drive for rate regulation, they had operated a "news bureau" of forty-three employees in the Orchestra Building in Chicago.[66] This organization almost certainly had done the railroads more harm than good. Operating as a propaganda machine, whose output was often difficult for busy country editors to identify as to source or merit, it drew the well-deserved fire of muckraking journalists and serious intellectuals as well. When the railroads decided to renew their efforts to maintain a joint voice in rate affairs in 1910, they organized the Bureau of Railway Economics, as we shall see, along entirely different lines. This unit, armed with the mandate to produce calm, serious reports of facts and figures about the na-

[63] *Ibid.,* XCI (Oct. 8, 1910), 20.

[64] Alan R. Raucher, *Public Relations and Business, 1900–1929* (Baltimore, 1968), 34, 37.

[65] *Ibid.,* 99; Wiebe, *Businessmen and Reform,* 99, 203–4; Edward Hungerford, *The Story of the Baltimore & Ohio Railroad, 1827–1927* (2 vols., New York, 1928), II, 265.

[66] Baker, "Railroads on Trial," 537.

tion's transportation situation that would be above professional reproach, was one of the forerunner organizations of the Association of American Railroads.[67]

A pioneer in the field of industry-wide railroad public relations was an old-time newspaper man, Slason Thompson. Originally a lawyer, he had turned to journalism around 1875 and after nearly thirty years of practical experience in midwestern newspaper work had joined the General Managers' Association in 1903. This Chicago-based organization of the operating heads of twenty-three eastern and midwestern railroads had been the spokesman for major U.S. railroads since the riotous days of the early nineties. In 1907 Thompson set up his own "Bureau of Railway News and Statistics," which the twelve leading railroads represented in the General Managers' Association supported. In addition to carrying on a general news bureau, Thompson brought out annually a bound volume of reprinted articles, speeches, and similar material bearing on railroad problems. A generous budget enabled it to be circulated without charge to libraries and newspaper publishers.[68] The volume for 1909, for example, carried a surprisingly scholarly article by C. C. McCain, chairman of the Trunk Line Association and former ICC auditor, which included many statistics on increases in material prices and wages that might have provided the basis for a railroad "cost of living index" if the Commission had been in the mood to develop such a measure. McCain found that nearly everything the railroads bought— except, he noted laconically, putty, portland cement, and Ames shovels —had gone up drastically, so that, even taking into account an average 4.83 per cent increase in rates over the still-depressed level of 1899, the nation's railroads were earning 25 per cent less in purchasing power with each unit of transportation service they sold.[69]

Railroad men themselves, however, had always been the founda-

[67] Raucher, *Public Relations,* 42; Frank H. Dixon, *Railroads and Government: Their Relations in the United States, 1910–1921* (New York, 1922), 13–14; Logan G. McPherson, "A Concerted Movement of the Railways," *North American Review,* CXCVII (Jan., 1913), 40–49; Michael C. Douglass, "A History of the Association of American Railroads" (unpublished B.S. thesis, Wharton School of Finance and Commerce, University of Pennsylvania, 1962).

[68] 1910 Hearings, V, 2992–94; Slason Thompson, ed., *The Railway Library and Statistics* (Chicago, 1909–15).

[69] C. C. McCain, "The Diminished Purchasing Power of Railway Earnings," in Thompson, ed., *The Railway Library, 1909,* 165–98.

tion for the public's attitude toward the railroads, and they would continue to be the focal point of public opinion. But the colorful personalities were passing, while the new men often showed themselves as efficient managers but poor copy. Of the earlier breed, only James J. Hill remained in 1910, and his dim views of where public regulation of the railroads was tending commanded widespread attention. His own position—that the nation needed even more basic rail facilities than it possessed in 1910, as well as more and better equipment—was widely quoted. As he approached the end of his long career, he was more convinced than ever that government had to take a more sophisticated view toward combinations and large aggregations of capital. A barn-raising is a combination, he reminded the reformers, and "all progress is the development of order . . . [and] uniform method is the highest form of order." To Hill, the entire combination movement was merely the industry's response to a demand for service at lower rates which the call for regulation, beginning in the 1870s, had reflected.[70] By late 1910 his tone was darkly negative. In what a financial writer called a "depressing interview," Hill predicted great unemployment the following year because of a decline in railroad investment. Coming on the eve of the Commission's decision in the rate case, the old man's remarks must have caused the new public relations men to gasp: "It isn't because they [the railroads] haven't the money but because there are no inducements . . . for them to invest it." [71]

It was in the executive offices of the Santa Fe Railroad in Chicago that one would find the emerging leadership of American railroads in this new era of professional managership. This rapidly expanding railroad was playing a leading role in the fast-growing Southwest, and had a generally good record of government relations. One of the Santa Fe's top vice-presidents, Paul Morton, had served Theodore Roosevelt as Secretary of the Navy and had obliged the President, during his drive for tighter regulation, by testifying before the ICC that the 1903 Elkins antirebating law was not working, and that attempts to enforce it had resulted in "violent opposition from the great bulk of railroad men." [72]

[70] James J. Hill, *Highways of Progress* (New York, 1910), 114, 129.

[71] *CFC, BQS,* XCI (Dec. 3, 1910), 20.

[72] Roosevelt to Paul Morton, June 12, 1905, *Letters,* IV, 1213.

Until 1909 the general counsel of the road was Victor Morawetz, an urbane and highly eligible bachelor who wrote intelligent popular articles on the government's antitrust policies.[73] It was the Santa Fe's hardworking, dynamic, and deeply concerned president, Edward Payson Ripley, who would carry most of the burden of the railroads' drive for higher rates in the coming months. By 1910 Ripley had been president of the Santa Fe for fourteen years and was responsible to a considerable degree for the vast improvement in the physical and financial condition of the road since its reorganization in the late nineties. He had seen government regulation of rates coming after the turn of the century, and had counseled his fellow railroad leaders not to oppose it.[74] Few recognized as clearly as Ripley what an uphill fight the railroads faced in seeking to improve their reputation with the general public. In his frequent addresses to the public, he acknowledged the heavy burden which such unfortunate gaffes as William H. Vanderbilt's "public be damned" remark had laid on the railroads. He counseled his brethren to steer clear of the inflammatory phrase, "what the traffic will bear," for while the railroad men knew what they meant by it, the public was likely to interpret it as meaning *all* that the traffic would bear. In a major speech in November, 1909, at the annual dinner of the Railway Business Association, Ripley pointed to two handicaps which the railroads had to overcome: their reputation for negativism on the subject of rate regulation, and the misguided activities of "reformers," a category into which he lumped the railroads' Progressive antagonists. He was not optimistic on either point:

In all the controversies that have led up to this almost complete control of railroad earnings and railroad policies by governmental agencies, the railroads have, as a rule, acted in active opposition. They have not been unanimous—some of us were willing to accept it long before it became a fact . . . but the scars of the conflict remain, and a large section of the public still suspects and misjudges us. . . . Our troubles are with this class [reformers] of well-meaning men who have zeal without knowledge and enthusiasm without sanity; these we may not reach, but the great mass of the solid and substantial citizenship may perhaps be induced to stop and con-

[73] "Victor Morawetz," *Who Was Who in America, 1897–1942,* 863; *NYT,* Oct. 9, 1910, VI, 2.

[74] "Edward Payson Ripley," *DAB,* 620–21.

sider whether . . . this greatest of all the country's industries is being fairly treated.[75]   ·

The conviction among railroad leaders that they were misunderstood and misjudged sometimes produced poignant results. In the summer of 1910 that prime thorn in the railroads' side, Senator Cummins of Iowa, was working overtime at his pain-producing activities. He had made a speech at the Chautauqua Assembly in Peabody, Iowa, in July in which he bore down on the old charge that the railroads were capitalized at $17 billion whereas the highest estimate of their real value he had seen was $8 billion. Another Iowa boy, who had made good in the railroad business, found this too much to take. W. C. Brown, president of the New York Central, wrote the Clarinda, Iowa, *Herald,* Cummins' home-town newspaper, recalling that many years before he and Cummins had been friends when the future Senator was a clerk in the express office at McGregor, Iowa, where Brown had held his first job as telegraph operator. Brown pleaded that the Senator at least quote the ICC reports correctly. The reports clearly stated that the *net* securities in the hands of the public totaled only $12 billion, the rest being accounted for by securities of subsidiary companies which were already represented in the securities of the parent companies. The Senator ought to know, Brown went on to say, that the railroads could not possibly be duplicated in 1910 for $12 billion.[76] There is no evidence that Cummins ever replied to his onetime friend's indignant appeal for fairness. Nothing, in fact, could reveal more dramatically the great gulf which had opened between railroad leaders and the Progressive era politicians.

President Brown's concern for the truth was all the more acute for the reason that the Central had been spending freely that fall on an advertising campaign designed to coincide with the rate case hearings then getting under way.[77] But the indignation of railroad executives was on

---

[75] Edward P. Ripley, "The Railroads and Public Approval" (speech before the annual dinner of the Railway Business Association, New York, Nov. 10, 1909), in Thompson, ed., *The Railway Library, 1910,* 199–210.

[76] *NYT,* Oct. 6, 1910, 8.

[77] The newspaper advertisements, four columns wide by 12 to 20 inches in length, emphasized the importance of the Central as an employer and the greatly increased cost of the new equipment which it was putting into service. *NYT,* Sept. 8, 1910, 6, and Oct. 29, 9.

the whole quite ineffectual. The Erie's president, Frederick Douglass Underwood, who was cast in the mold of the self-made American man if ever there was such a mold, reacted to the new rate-suspension legislation then pending by harrumphing that there were too many lawyers and not enough businessmen in Washington. "It would be well," he said, "for the railroads of the country to go on strike against the politicians, and then they would wake up." [78] It was enough to make a public relations man cry out loud.

Improving the public image of the railroads turned out to be even more of an uphill fight than the public relations men could have imagined. One bad apple could spoil the entire barrel, and that summer several bad apples had turned up on one of the nation's most conservative and circumspect railroads. Several years before the Illinois Central had closed its largest car repair shop, asserting that it was convinced that it could get the work done more cheaply by outside contractors. The road, like most of the others, subsequently began to grumble about the rapidly increasing cost of running the railroad. Rumors meanwhile began to fly which could not be downed. In June, 1910, the news broke that in the preceding four years a "graft ring," centering in the Illinois Central's former superintendent of transportation and three other trusted employees, had defrauded the company of nearly two million dollars in excessive payments to the repair firms. The damage to the railroads' case was incalculable. It looked as though Louis D. Brandeis, who continued to preach the doctrine of the inefficiency and unmanageability of big business, had a telling point.[79]

[78] *NYT,* June 4, 1910, 2; "Frederick Douglass Underwood," *Who Was Who in America, 1943–50,* 542.

[79] I.C.R.R. Co., *Annual Report for 1910,* 6.

CHAPTER VI

TIGHTENING THE SCREWS

Chairman Hepburn: What is the method pursued by the Commission in ascertaining what is a reasonable rate? . . . Is there any mathematical method of determining it?
Commissioner Clements: There is absolutely none, I think. There is no method by which you can work out to a mathematical demonstration that a particular figure is a just and reasonable rate.—1905 HEARINGS
*All charges made for any service rendered . . . shall be just and reasonable [and] whenever there shall be filed . . . a new . . . rate . . . the burden of proof to show that the . . . proposed increased rate is just and reasonable shall be upon the common carrier.—*MANN-ELKINS ACT, *1910*

I

The gloomy, ugly, faintly Romanesque old building still stands in the 1300 block of F Street in Washington, D.C. Now the home of a nondescript covey of lawyers, lobbyists, and trade publications, it conveys no sense of the magisterial wisdom which the classic elegance of the Federal Triangle is supposed to lend nowadays to such bodies as the ICC, which holds its deliberations there. Built in the early 1880s primarily to house the American National Bank, the building was a forerunner of a number which began to spring up as private enterprise recognized that a growing federal bureaucracy would need more space. Its present tenants can hardly realize what matters of such great importance to the rapidly growing American economy were fought out within the confines of this building, from 1887 to 1917 the home of the Interstate Commerce Commission. The modesty of the surroundings would prove all too appropriate to the modest conception of their mandate which the Commissioners would assume at this critical stage in the economic growth of American railroads. Hard-working, honest, generally determined to be fair, the men who made up the Commission in these years also turned out to be unimaginative, narrowly legalistic, right-eously indignant, and, in the final test, hopelessly biased against the idea of freeing the competitive strengths which the railroads possessed within the framework of the American economic system. From the ac-tual phraseology of the legislation of 1910, down to the emotional and historical make-up of the men who were to decide the rate cases of the prewar years, the cards seem almost inevitably to have been stacked against the possibility of the general rate increases which the railroads felt they needed so badly. The Commission was legally able, and psy-chologically likely, to reject any and all applications for general rate changes. A constructive and creative national transportation policy was needed, but at no time would these men ever be in a position to supply it. The reasons are to be sought not only in the men themselves but also in the swift-moving events which brought this particular group of men into public life at this critical juncture.

From the beginning, the Interstate Commerce Commission had tended to see itself not as a creator of rates but as a controller of rates. In its early period, when its strength had not yet been drained by the se-ries of Supreme Court decisions of the nineties, its first chairman, Thomas M. Cooley, had made this clear. During a proceeding before the Commission, President A. B. Stickney of the Chicago, St. Paul, and Kansas City Railroad, one of a number of midwestern railroads which had found themselves unable to enforce rate-maintenance agreements among themselves, suggested that if that body could order rates low-ered, it could order them raised. Cooley had answered the argument with the observation that it was logically correct. But he went on to say that the Commission had to interpret its mandate in the light of its his-tory, which provided abundant proof, at least to him, that its purpose was to protect the public and not the railroad companies.[1] And Cooley wanted a strong Commission, which would be able to carry out such a policy of rate control on a national basis with a minimum of confusion or interference from state commissions. In support of his program, he traveled extensively in the late eighties despite his rapidly deteriorating health. His valedictory in the 1890 annual report of the Commission is

[1] A. Jones, "Thomas M. Cooley and the ICC: Continuity and Change in the Doc-trine of Equal Rights," *Political Science Quarterly*, LXXXI (Dec., 1966), 618–19; 2 ICC 231, 259–60.

a plea for a strong Commission, a stand which was widely popular with such generally conservative men as Arthur Twining Hadley.[2]

Fortunately for the Commission in those days, if unfortunately for the guidance of the post-Hepburn panel, the body had never had to develop an unequivocal position on general levels of rates in the Cooley era. Competition, technological improvement, and a secular downtrend in prices had combined to produce a consistently declining level of rates from the seventies onward, and the depression of the nineties virtually demoralized rate levels.[3] The first decades of the Commission's existence were a period in which the fairness of rates vis-à-vis one shipper and another, or one location and another, was the great problem. During this period there was a real need for an agency to protect society in general from the life-and-death powers of railroads to discriminate between persons and locations, and from the all-too-human arbitrariness in setting rates which malice, obtuseness, ignorance, and just plain indifference can produce. The nation's philosophy of what the Commission was and what it was supposed to accomplish was firmly established in this period, so much so that after 1900, when the railroads were attaining a remarkable degree of self-control against shippers' demands for favored treatment, legislative efforts (notably those of 1903 and 1910) were still colored by this Populist-Progressive psychology. Not until the rate cases of 1910 and 1914 would the Commission be forced to turn from the consideration of individual rates in isolation to a judgment of rate levels in general. How completely—how inevitably, in fact—the Commission would fail this first great test of its administrative powers, we shall see.

The two men who were most closely identified with the policies of the Commission at the time of its rebirth in 1906 were determined that it should take an aggressive, positive stance in the development and implementation of a railroad regulatory policy. One of these men was Martin Augustine Knapp, who had joined the Commission in 1897 at the nadir of its influence and had become its chairman the following year. The other was Theodore Roosevelt. As the new era began,

[2] *Annual Report of the Interstate Commerce Commission for 1890;* Arthur Twining Hadley, "The Legal Theories of Price Regulation," *Yale Review,* I (1892), 66.

[3] I. L. Sharfman, *The Interstate Commerce Commission: A Study in Administrative Law and Procedure* (4 vols. in 5, New York, 1931–37), IIIb, 14.

Knapp's ears rang with the admonition of the President: "Your Commission should . . . lay greater stress upon the administrative side of its functions. . . . If your body becomes simply a court, then it had better be abolished. The only justification for [it is] its active exercise in constantly increasing measure of administrative supervision and control over the railroads." [4] Knapp agreed. Having spent ten years on the Commission during which its activities consisted of little more than gathering statistics, he supported the investigative functions of the body and launched it on its own full-scale investigation of the railroads' earnings and investment situation when the 1910 rate case was pending. Only five feet tall, he commanded attention by reason of a pleasing personality combined with a candor and frankness rare in government officials who customarily saw themselves as judicial functionaries. [5] Inevitably, his friendly and sympathetic attitude toward the railroads occasioned criticism by those who did not look upon the Commission as a source of aid and comfort to railroad executives. Addressing the dinner of the Railway Business Association at the height of the 1910 rate hearings, he attracted widespread publicity with his friendly mien. "Gentlemen, and members of the society for the prevention of cruelty to railroads," he began, to nervous laughter from the railroad suppliers who were crowded into the Waldorf-Astoria ballroom, "must we not in the larger public interest, whatever may be thought by this or that shipper, make the business of furnishing railroad transportation so desirable to the investor that the necessary funds for betterments and extensions will be forthcoming?" Then, departing from his prepared text, he invited the storm. Railroads should become regulated monopolies, he asserted; competition cannot be forced where it is not natural. The only substitute for trust methods was government ownership. "Knapp flouts our railroad laws," complained the New York *Times* the next morning. Little notice was taken of Knapp's idealism concerning the nation's attitude toward its railroads. Continued improvement was in order, he said, "in accordance with that enlarging spirit of altruism which manifests itself in public as well as in private life, and which impels the present assumption of burdens that might be escaped or deferred, in order that

[4] Roosevelt to Knapp, Jan. 24, 1907, *Letters,* ed. Elting E. Morison (8 vols., Cambridge, Mass., 1951–54), V, 566.

[5] "Martin Augustine Knapp," *DAB,* X, 450.

another generation may have an easier task and a larger opportunity." [6] Theodore Roosevelt, Herbert Croly, and the other New Nationalists would never put it better. But as the rate case reached a decision early in 1911, Roosevelt would be far from the scene of battle and Knapp would be effectively shut off from any further influence over railroad rate affairs.

There were two other old-timers on the Commission when the 1910 rate case decision had to be made. Judson C. Clements, when he died in office in 1917, had served twenty-five consecutive years since his appointment to that body in 1892. A southerner, former Congressman, and one-time lawyer for the Rome and Northern Railway Company, he hardly reflected the idealistic view of the Commission which Roosevelt entertained. Of much greater consequence for the rate case was Charles A. Prouty, who had been on the panel since 1896. Testy, peppery in speech, short-tempered and caustic, certainly no man to suffer fools gladly, this onetime Vermont Republican who would switch over to the Progressive party in 1914 was destined to write the decision in the eastern railroads' application. No doctrinaire when it came to the question of holding down railroad rates at all costs, Prouty did have one overriding obsession. He believed that until a definitive physical valuation had been made of the railroads' properties, it was useless to talk of rate levels and rates of return. This belief would be armor enough against the railroads' assault in 1910. In 1913 Congress finally authorized such a study and Prouty resigned to become Director of Valuation. The results of that study, attained after the expenditure of millions of dollars of government and railroad money, were a full vindication of the railroads' balance sheet valuation, but in 1910 no such data were at his disposal and without them Prouty would not be able to see any basis for an increase in rates. [7]

The man who would play an equally decisive role in the western railroads' case was a West Coast Progressive who, although himself conspicuously unsuccessful in California and San Francisco politics, had endeared himself to Theodore Roosevelt. Franklin K. Lane, a capable

[6] Martin A. Knapp, Speech before the Railway Business Association, New York, Nov. 22, 1910, in Slason Thompson, ed., *The Railway Library and Statistics, 1910,* 157–58; *NYT,* Nov. 23, 1910, 4; *CFC, BQS,* XCI (Dec. 3, 1910), 20.

[7] "Charles Azro Prouty," *DAB,* XV, 248; 1910 Hearings, 5439.

man of considerable charm and limited means, whom conservatives considered a radical on railroad and trust matters, was delighted to be appointed to the Commission by Roosevelt in 1905. There he would remain until President Wilson made him Secretary of the Interior in 1913. President Benjamin Ide Wheeler of the University of California had recommended Lane to Roosevelt as someone who would protect the interests of the shippers of the Golden State, then chafing under the domination of the Southern Pacific. Lane clearly believed that the problem was one of protecting the people against the all-powerful combinations, which, he had no doubt, possessed virtually all of the real power. "It does look to me," he wrote to a friend shortly after his appointment, "as if the problem of our generation is to be the discovery of some effective method by which the artificial persons whom we have created by law can be taught that they are not the creators, the owners, and the rightful managers of the government. . . . The President . . . has determined to prove to the railroads that they have not the whole works and the policy that they have followed . . . will lead to the wildest kind of a craze for government ownership of everything." [8] Lane got enthusiastically behind every project for making the railroads toe the mark. In 1906 Elihu Root, firmly seconded by Knapp, advised the President against a sensational investigation of the affairs of Edward H. Harriman, but Lane supported the course recommended by Attorney General Bonaparte, Secretary of War Taft, and Frank B. Kellogg. He strongly supported the philosophies that led to the rate-suspension law of 1910. To a fellow Californian he had written at the end of 1908, "You are protesting against increased rates. I have outlined to you the only remedy [a change in the law] that I see available against the continuance of just such a policy on the part of the railroads." [9]

As the nation looked forward to the inauguration of William Howard Taft, Lane spoke darkly about the treatment which the railroads could expect from the new administration, writing to his brother, "The Harriman crowd seems to think that they will all be on good

[8] *The Letters of Franklin K. Lane* (Boston and New York, 1923), 49–50; Lane to Edward B. Whitney, Nov. 13, 1905, *ibid.*, 51–52. Keith W. Olson, "Franklin K. Lane: A Biography" (unpublished doctoral dissertation, University of Wisconsin, 1964), does not probe Lane's rate-making philosophies.

[9] Lane to E. B. Beard, Dec. 19, 1908, *Letters*, 67–68.

terms with Taft, but unless I'm mistaken in the man they will be greatly fooled." [10] He thought the idea of a Commerce Court was a good one. Regulatory laws, no Progressive could forget, had not fared well in court tests in the past. With the special court, he explained to Lawrence F. Abbott of the *Outlook,* "the question of nullifying our [i.e., the Commission's] orders will be brought up before men who have special experience. The . . . courts know nothing about the question. . . . It is not law but economics that we deal with. The fixing of a rate is a matter of politics." [11] If Lane had been more of a lawyer, he might have sensed the self-contradictory nature of his observation. Taft, at least, would be able to claim consistency on the Commerce Court question inasmuch as he so clearly believed that the regulation of railroads was essentially judicial in nature. Yet Lane was the man who would conduct much of the hearings on the western railroads' rate application and who would write the decision for the Commission.

At the time Lane's appointment to the Commission was before the Senate, Roosevelt had pledged himself to make his next two appointments from the ranks of the Republican party.[12] Accordingly, when the Hepburn Act increased the membership of the panel from five to seven in 1906 the President submitted the names of two members of his party. But they were hardly men who could be expected to uphold the interests of big capital. One of them had learned the doctrines of liberal Republicanism at the knee of his famous father, for he was James S. Harlan, son of the man who, as an associate justice of the Supreme Court throughout the period of conservative reaction in the last quarter of the nineteenth century, had written some of the most notable dissents of that period. It was John Marshall Harlan, for example, who had opposed the court majority in the narrowly reasoned Knight sugar-trust case, in which manufacturing was held not to be commerce within the meaning of the Sherman Antitrust Act, and in the income tax decision. It was Harlan who had spoken for the bare majority in the Northern Securities decision after the twentieth-century trust-busting era had begun. And, most significantly, it was the father of the new Commissioner who had dissented bitterly in the Alabama Midland case in 1897, when the

[10] Lane to George W. Lane, Feb. 13, 1909, *ibid.,* 68–69.
[11] Lane to Abbott, Sept. 22, 1909, *ibid.,* 71.   [12] Lane, *Letters,* 49–50.

Commission had been stripped of most of its powers.[13] The other appointee was Edgar Erastus Clark, one of the leaders of the rapidly growing railroad labor movement. A trainman and conductor on the railroads for sixteen years, in 1889 he had joined the staff of the fledgling Order of Railway Conductors and by 1906 was Grand Chief Conductor.[14] As events would so forlornly demonstrate, Clark's qualifications for passing judgment on so complicated a question as an increase in the general level of railroad rates were slim indeed.

As the railroads' applications for rate increases approached the day of decision late in 1910, the Commission stood four antirailroad, one prorailroad, one uncertain (labor leader Clark), and one vacancy. Before the Commission would reach its decision, however, the climate was to be even less favorable to the railroads. At the same time that Taft shunted Chairman Knapp onto the Commerce Court, he sent in two names to bring the Commission up to full strength. Both appointees were firmly in the tradition of state regulatory commissions, a breed which had learned to make it tough indeed for the railroads in the frustrating days of Populism and early Progressivism. Charles C. McChord, who would spend fifteen years on the Commission, serving as its chairman from time to time, came to Washington after more than a decade of service on the Kentucky Railroad Commission, and was the author of that state's railroad rate law.[15] From Wisconsin came a forty-five-year-old scholar who had distinguished himself as a member of the faculty of the University of Wisconsin, as member and then chairman of the Railroad Commission of Wisconsin, and as author of a number of books on transportation subjects. Balthasar Henry Meyer, born in Wisconsin of German immigrant parents whose like had helped people that state in the mid-nineteenth century, had earned his Ph.D. at the state university in 1898 with a thesis on the history of early railway legislation in Wisconsin.[16] No doctrinaire partisan of one side or the other in the epic struggle between capital and "the public," in the midst of which he had grown to manhood, he spoke for an enlightened, scientific public policy.

[13] "James S. Harlan," *Who Was Who in America, 1897–1942*, 520; "John Marshall Harlan," *DAB*, VIII, 269–72.

[14] "Edgar Erastus Clark," *Who Was Who in America, 1897–1942*, 222.

[15] "Charles Caldwell McChord," *ibid.*, 800.

[16] "Balthasar Henry Meyer," *Who's Who in America, 1948–49*, 1704.

His volume on *Railway Legislation in the United States,* which appeared in 1903 as one in a series edited by Wisconsin's Professor Richard T. Ely, was remarkably outspoken for reforms in public policy as well as in railroad practices.[17] He saw that lack of uniformity in state regulation was leading to a wider scope of federal legislation. He refused to agree that long-haul–short-haul discrimination by railroads was always undesirable, and he decried the one-sidedness of the struggle in which shippers had built up impressive pressure groups to prevent rate increases. Rates, in fact, were the heart of the railroad problem, according to Meyer. He warned that the concept of "reasonableness" of rates, on which regulation was based in law, would be useless in a question involving the general level of rates. And he decried the outlawing of agreements between railroads which had as their purpose the ending of wasteful or meaningless competition; this policy, he said, only encouraged consolidation of railroad corporations, and in discountenancing these agreements the ICC had "signally failed in accomplishing the purpose for which [it was] enacted." [18] While the Northern Securities decision of the Supreme Court was being hailed as an unqualified victory for Theodore Roosevelt and the people, Meyer was quietly dissenting from the negative, unconstructive public policy which it heralded:

This undiscriminating opposition to all forms of open concerted action on the part of the railways is in my mind the greatest single blunder in our public policy toward railways. . . . Some legislation which will enable companies to act together under the law, as they now do quietly among themselves outside of the law, is imperative. . . . We should have cast away more than fifty years ago the impossible doctrine of protection of the public by railway competition.[19]

The application by America's railroads for general rate increases was unprecedented, and offered this scholarly man an opportunity for the

[17] Balthasar H. Meyer, *Railway Legislation in the United States* (New York, 1903).

[18] *Ibid.,* 11–12, 13, 35, 151–52, 205–6, 211, 242.

[19] Balthasar H. Meyer, *A History of the Northern Securities Case* (Madison, 1906), 305–6. Meyer's service on the Wisconsin Railroad Commission just prior to his moving to the federal body revealed a bold willingness to rule in the railroads' favor on occasion, in the face of growing resentment on the part of the legislature. Stanley P. Caine, *The Myth of a Progressive Reform* (Madison, 1970), *passim.*

fullest exercise of his talents in the field of national government regulation of industry. It would be interesting to see how he would use them.

The question in most minds in late 1910 was whether the Commission would give basic consideration to the railroads' earnings in reaching its decision on the rate applications. There would be no "affirmative public responsibility in the matter of financial return," as the historian of the Commission has called it, until 1920, but the Supreme Court, in its decision in *Smyth* v. *Ames* in 1898, had laid down the general rule that rates which deprived carriers of a fair return on fair value were confiscatory.[20] The Commission had settled six cases in late June, however, which (while they depressed the railroads and the financial community) at least showed that the panel recognized a duty to consider profit levels. The decisions, involving rates between the Mississippi River and the Pacific Coast, ordered reductions ranging from 20 per cent to as high as 50 per cent. "The effect was naturally in the highest degree demoralizing," grumbled one editor. "The roads had been planning to raise rates. . . . In the stock market the result was an immediate and utter collapse of values, and everywhere throughout the financial world there was consternation."[21] Recent publicity concerning the prosperity of Harriman's Southern Pacific had not helped: the Commission cited excessive earnings as the basis for the decision. The honor of writing the major decision against the "octopus" had gone to Franklin K. Lane.[22]

II

Heading into the lengthening shadows of a beautiful June afternoon in 1910, the gleaming special train of the Michigan Central Railroad flew northeastward toward Detroit at a steady speed of more than seventy miles an hour. In the swaying parlor car at the rear of the short train a great mountain of a man boredly fingered the manuscript of a speech which he was to deliver that evening before the Detroit Board of Commerce. William Howard Taft, twenty-seventh President of

[20] Sharfman, *ICC*, IIIb, 7; 169 U.S. 466.   [21] *CFC, BQS*, XCI (July 2, 1910), 20.
[22] 19 ICC 156, etc.; *NYT*, June 30, 1910, 4.

the United States, had just performed the same task in Toledo and was being whisked at record-breaking speed from that city to Detroit, where he was due at 7:00 P.M. He made it, and his speedy trip made the front pages of the newspapers next day. But the greatest interest centered on his reaction to the Senate's passage that day of the new railroad rate legislation for which he had been pressing. Informed of the event, and of the fact that Senator La Follette's attempts to add further amendments to the measure had been voted down, Taft exclaimed, "Bully! Bully!" [23]

The President had reason to rejoice. Now at mid-term as President, he could reflect that nothing to date had seemed to go right. The members of his party from the Midwest and West were being rapidly alienated after a series of events in which he had seemed to desert them at the critical moment.[24] The speech-making trip on which he had so reluctantly set out had been undertaken to shore up his hold on the party. Taft had great hopes, furthermore, that the bill which had been before Congress all spring, and which the Senate had just passed by the decisive vote of 50 to 12, would convince the Insurgents that he was not "soft" on the railroads. Soon, he was sure, the ICC would have the new powers to prevent long-haul–short-haul discrimination, to pass on railroad securities issues, and to hold up rate increases pending investigation which he had promised.

None but the most rabid Insurgent could accuse the President of favoring the railroads since he entered the White House. At the very moment that one of their trains was so efficiently carrying the President to his speaking engagement, the nation's railroads were being made to play the role of criminals. Their applications for rate increases, recently filed with the Commission, had created a furor which threatened to remain at fever pitch indefinitely, or at least until the new legislation could be brought up to sink its sharp teeth into the fat belly of the railroads. From the very beginning of George Perkins' latest campaign to get the roads a rate increase, the prediction of Franklin K. Lane about

[23] *CR*, 61st Cong., 2d Sess., 7375; *NYT*, June 4, 1910, 1.

[24] The deterioration of relations with the Progressive wing of his party, culminating in the Insurgents' revolt after 1910, is summarized in George E. Mowry, *The Era of Theodore Roosevelt and the Birth of Modern America, 1900–1912* (New York, 1958), Chapters 12 and 13.

their relations with Taft was being confirmed. This time, the railroads had been determined to go about their drive for an increase in the right way. Hats in hand, the top leaders of the industry had traveled to Washington early that year for a meeting with the President. J. P. Morgan, unaccustomed as he was to asking for anything, even from a President of the United States, had urged Taft to hear the railroad men's views before he sent in the special message which they all feared. Deferring dutifully to the nation's financial leader, the President leaned back in his overburdened swivel chair as they had their say: W. C. Brown, of the mighty New York Central; James McCrea, of the gargantuan Pennsylvania; R. S. Lovett, caretaker for the Harriman interests in the Union Pacific; George F. Baer, Morgan's "man" and head of the Reading; Charles S. Mellen, who, as time would show, was even then in the process of helping to ruin the New Haven; and W. W. Finley, of the Southern, who spoke for all the roads of the Southeast.

Taft had heard the railroad men's story before: demands for transportation services were continuing to grow at a great rate; the needs of the railroads for more money for improvements and additions to their facilities were not being met at existing profit levels; competitive conditions were sapping efficiency; and the companies needed freedom to enter into agreements to eliminate certain practices. Unmoved by their passionate pleas, four days later Taft asked Congress for new legislation which would do all that the railroad men had feared, and more: the ICC was to initiate rate reductions where it felt they were warranted; advances in rates were to be suspended pending investigation; ownership of stock in other roads was to be prohibited, thus doing away once and for all with the community-of-interests technique; and, perhaps worst of all, the application of the antitrust law to railroad affairs was not to be compromised.[25]

The legalistically-minded man who currently strained the Presidential chair was strongly attracted to an even more comprehensive system of regulation than that to which the Hepburn Act of 1906 had subjected the railroads, and he was indisposed to discriminate between the railroads and the industrial trusts in the application of the antitrust law. But behind him, like a goad to a slow and ponderous ox, was that most radical of midwestern Insurgents, Senator Albert B. Cummins. As ru-

[25] *CFC, BQS,* XC (Feb. 5, 1910), 19–20; *NYT,* Jan. 3, 1910, 3; Jan. 4, 1910, 1.

mors of the railroads' intentions to raise rates spread late in 1909, Cummins cleared the decks for action. He went to see Taft at the White House in November but could not get the President to agree to the kind of rate-freezing legislation which the Iowan demanded.[26] Rate suspension pending investigation was fine, the Commerce Court no insurmountable obstacle to compromise, and strictures on railroad securities a must—but with all these provisions enacted into law, there was still no guarantee that rates would not be raised, and that, after all, was the heart of the controversy. When it became apparent that the nation's elephantine leader was once again crashing dangerously through the political underbrush by directing Attorney General Wickersham to draft a bill embodying the administration's policies, Cummins was as furious as Dolliver. Into the Senate hopper went Cummins' own bill, which called for complete and final divorcement of the judiciary from any consideration of the reasonableness of a rate set by the Commission, and for the freezing of any rate which the railroads desired to increase at the old level until the Commission could investigate it.[27] There could no longer be any question of where he and his fellow Insurgents stood, and when, a month later, Senator Elkins introduced the administration's bill the elephant crashed into the trap.[28] Why, Cummins exclaimed during a four-day speech in the Senate, the bill contained "the most startling proposition, the most destructive proposal that has been heard in regard to this subject in years." Sure enough, once again the President had thrown the wrong switch at the wrong time and had allowed himself, all of his prior protestations to the contrary notwithstanding, to be persuaded to approve a clause permitting the railroads to enter into traffic agreements without prior approval of the Commission. This was nothing but legalized pooling! [29] Not while the midwestern granger spirit still lived could such a thing be permitted. Chairman Elkins, now mortally sick with cancer, suffered in silence while Cummins presented the Commerce Committee with over 100 amendments to Wickersham's bill.

[26] Ralph M. Sayre, "Albert Baird Cummins and the Progressive Movement in Iowa" (unpublished doctoral dissertation, Columbia University, 1958), 352.

[27] *CR,* 61st Cong., 2d Sess., 77.   [28] *Ibid.,* 501.

[29] *Ibid.,* 3341–52. Possibly with his friend and one-time fellow employee, Brown of the New York Central, in mind, Cummins closed his devastating speech with a nod to the railroads for their value to the country, and to their managers as his friends.

Once again the President stood alone, for no one on the committee was in favor of the bill: not the Insurgents; certainly not the Democrats, who joyfully watched the splitting of another rafter in the Republican edifice; and, finally, not Elkins himself.[30] The West Virginian and the Iowan laid the Taft-Wickersham bill to rest in their majority and minority reports and sat down to write a new one. The Insurgents were now in complete control of the situation.[31]

What would satisfy Cummins? The answer was soon apparent, when Elkins at the beginning of April meekly offered the Progressive's amendments to the committee. He wanted the period of time in which the Commission could freeze rates while investigating proposed increases doubled from 60 to 120 days, and he wanted full provision for shippers to appear as parties to all rate proceedings regardless of whether the judges of the proposed Commerce Court should deem their interests to be materially affected. This, it may be noted, would ensure that Commission hearings would retain the forensic qualities of an adversary proceeding and not become routine administrative affairs. He was adamant on the question of pooling agreements, and willingly sacrificed Taft's cherished securities regulation provisions in a compromise which meant that the railroads would remain bound by the antitrust laws.[32] But this was not all he wanted. His real "stopper" was still to come. For the present, however, his credit was exhausted. As the bill struggled through the complex legislative process, there would be plenty of time to play his strongest card. He smiled benignly as an unhappy Elkins labored to advance the bill to the floor, which he was able to do only by trading the Democrats statehood for Arizona and New Mexico in return for their approval.[33] Tough as the new bill was, it seemed that real fireworks had been avoided.

Not quite. The team of Taft and Wickersham, having lost the initiative in the legislative arena, seized it on the legal front. Shippers were hopping mad as news seeped out about Hosmer's heroic act of filing a rate increase jointly for the hated western roads. On May 30, two days before the new tariffs were to take effect, the powerful Illinois Manu-

[30] *Ibid.*, 2780, 3361–62.   [31] *Ibid.*, 2817–23; Sayre, "Cummins," 359–60.

[32] Sayre, "Cummins," 371–72.

[33] George E. Mowry, *Theodore Roosevelt and the Progressive Movement* (Madison, 1947), 101–2.

facturers Association demanded that the Attorney General invoke the
antitrust act. Frantic conferences at the White House ensued next morning. Taft, once he saw that the law had at least been badly bent, nodded
his approval of a dramatic procedure. That same evening David P.
Dyer, judge of the U.S. District Court at Hannibal, Missouri, was
handed a telegram from Wickersham telling him what he must do. A
few minutes before midnight the judge issued an order enjoining the
railroads from putting their new schedules into effect pending the outcome of a suit which charged them with conspiracy in violation of the
antitrust law.[34] Apparently the new rate-suspension legislation was required primarily to ensure elderly federal judges of a good night's sleep,
for the injunction achieved everything which the new law could provide
and, at this point, more. Shippers' representatives declared they were
elated because now the roads would have to bear the burden of justifying the increases, if they wanted the injunction lifted. The deepest
gloom pervaded railroad and financial circles. "They've got the pins set
up against us," sadly commented Ripley of the Santa Fe. The serious-
ness of the fight which the railroads faced now began to be realized. But
Wall Street had not waited for news of Wickersham's pyrotechnics. The
day that the antitrust complaint was filed was also decision day at the
Supreme Court. Stocks had broken "violently" on the news that the
court had ruled that the Interstate Commerce Commission had acted
within its powers in ordering reductions in the Missouri River and Denver rate cases, thus removing all question about the constitutionality of
the Hepburn Act.[35] Any grant of additional powers by the Congress
surely would be anticlimactic. What more could Cummins and his band
want? The answer would not be long in coming.

First, however, this new step in the President's continuing dance
of political death needs to be followed to its conclusion. While adding
little to his fading popularity in the West, the injunction episode
brought forth a storm of criticism from eastern Republicans. Henry

[34] *NYT,* May 31, 1910, 6; June 1, 1, 3; *CFC, BQS,* LXXXIX (June 4, 1910), 20.

[35] *NYT,* June 1, 1910, 3, 12. The court rendered split decisions. *ICC* v. *C.R.I. &
P. R.R. Co.* (218 U.S. 663), and *ICC* v. *C. B. & Q. R.R. Co.* (218 U.S. 641). The
most actively traded stock that day was Reading Railroad, down 5¼. Union Pacific and Southern Pacific each lost four points. Lest anyone suppose that the
court was careening to the left, it may be noted that on the same day the court
refused to hear a test case of the Jim Crow laws.

Phipps, sailing on the *Adriatic* for two months in the Austrian Tyrol, growled to a shipboard reporter, "You just wait until I get my hands on Wickersham and I'll tell him a few things." [36] The New York *Times* pilloried the President in an editorial, declaring that "the action strips the Administration of all consistency, and leaves . . . business . . . in . . . doubt regarding the legality of the simplest acts from which the President has undertaken to deliver [the country]." Only three months before, the exasperated editorialist wrote, Taft had asked for a clause in the new railway bill to permit joint determination of rates; and when, just a fortnight before, the Congress had rejected such a provision, had wailed, "This was declared for in the platform and recommended to Congress in two or three messages of President Roosevelt." No one, the *Times* said, suggests antitrust actions to prevent agreements which have to be made regardless of what the law may say. The ICC ought to be left to handle these affairs, but the trouble with that body, said the editor sarcastically, is that "after it hears evidence and argument on the law it is likely to follow the facts and the law as far as it can." And then the paper made a very wise, if in those days almost entirely neglected, point: an injunction is a proceeding in equity in which the party which seeks it is attempting to better himself; in this case shippers seek bigger profits than they would have if their rates were raised. The shippers, then, and not the government, are the real complainants; should not their profits, as well as those of the carriers, be investigated? It was a point of legal wisdom which would escape some of the best minds in the country when the railroads set out to support their increases. Two days later the *Times* admitted the folly of looking for logic in what was essentially a political move. "An injunction suit is . . . a spectacular proceeding. . . . It shuts out the uncomfortable Ballinger case . . . tends to make [people] forget about the tariff case . . . will please Insurgents . . . may help in the fall elections . . . will check the sale of securities abroad . . . [and] has the effect of a June frost upon business and enterprise." [37]

Such criticism, however, missed the real point entirely. What Taft thought about the reasonableness of the laws on the books had nothing

[36] *NYT*, June 2, 1910, 3.   [37] *Ibid.*, June 1, 1910, 8; June 3, 6.

to do with what he thought about his duty to enforce them. As things stood, what the railroads west of the Mississippi had done in filing a single application for rate increases through their Western Traffic Association was clearly in violation of the law. Of course, freight rates charged by competing railroads tended to become uniform for carrying identical goods between identical points; [38] they didn't just *tend* to be uniform, in fact, they *were* uniform, because the requirement that any tariff change be publicly filed with the Commission thirty days before its effective date meant that reductions would be quickly matched by competitors, while increases, if business conditions warranted, would also be matched or else the railroad desiring the increase would have to back down. This state of affairs, which merely demonstrated the law of competition that two prices cannot exist for the same good (or service) in the same "market" at the same time, was not challenged. The expedient of having all of the roads file the same tariff changes at the same time might have been considered as no more than a simple telescoping of the market mechanism just described. The law would have been wiser so to have considered it, but the law did not and, wise or not, the President was sworn to execute the laws. Taft's legalistic mind and judicial view of human affairs would serve him well in later years as a great chief justice, but they weakened his effectiveness as chief executive.

Railroad men recoiled in horror at Taft's injunction move. What they said about him in the privacy of their clubs probably came near to melting the brass cuspidors, but in public their attitude became one of peace at any price. Like the President, they had acted on principle so far and as a consequence everything was going wrong. The fact that there was no rate-suspension law on the books yet was beside the point. Future transportation policy for the nation was obviously going to be worked out under the new law that would ultimately emerge from the House-Senate conference. The only thing to do was to put the best face possible on the railroads' position. Brown of the New York Central

---

[38] As time would reveal, however, there were still plenty of techniques besides crude price cutting which competing railroads could use to jockey for the traffic of a steady, heavy shipper, and the frantic scramble for volume to compensate for declining profit margins in these years of frozen rates ensured that they would be used.

saw this as clearly as anybody. His company was already under heavy criticism for trying a little economic blackmail—there was a strong rumor that the Central was about to announce the cancellation of a six million dollar order for freight cars, which Brown denied.[39] The Central, he declared, would push ahead with its expansion program. The efforts of George Perkins and others to round up sympathy from the shippers were redoubled.[40] Brown came out for dropping the railroads' struggle against the injunction, and offered to suspend the increases until the Commission had had a chance to rule on them, a concession which Franklin K. Lane admitted would pretty well make legal proceedings unnecessary.[41]

This time the swivel chair in the President's office held a beaming Taft, as he welcomed the delegation of western railroad presidents who had come to see him: Ripley of the Santa Fe and, for good measure, Walker D. Hines, its chairman, who was working night and day to plan the carriers' new strategy; Frederic A. Delano of the Wabash; and S. M. Felton of the Chicago Great Western. With Wickersham at his side, Taft accepted what the conciliatory railroad men had come to offer: withdrawal of the rate application until the railroad bill had become law. Hosmer, at least, was off the hook. Next day, June 7, the scene was reenacted with McCrea of the Pennsylvania (accompanied, significantly, by his general counsel), Brown of the Central, and Finley of the Southern. All the railroads of the country were now pledged to follow the new regulatory procedure. One financial editor sighed that it meant that the carriers would have to get along on the old rates indefinitely even though the higher wage scales negotiated recently were already in effect; but, after all, good relations with the government were important, and "the proposition for better rates possesses so much merit that the Commission will be forced to grant some increases, no matter what its predilection might be." [42] The western railroad men claimed they were satisfied that the Commission would do the right thing, and reviewed the continuous record of wage increases going back to 1902.[43] Thus ended "the picturesque business of private treaty making between

---

[39] NYT, June 3, 1910, 3.   [40] Ibid., June 5, 1910, 1.   [41] Ibid., June 6, 1910, 1.
[42] CFC, BQS, XCI (July 2, 1910), 19–20.   [43] NYT, June 7, 1910, 1.

the President of the United States and the presidents of the great railway systems." [44]

The railroad leaders now saw all too clearly what they were up against. The bill which the Senate had passed on June 3 was a killer. Immeasurably aided by the wave of antirailroad feeling which followed in the wake of the injunction high-jinks, Senator Cummins had resumed the offensive. The suspension period had grown from 60 days to six months—plenty of time for the Commission to find a judicious way to say no. But the Senator's greatest achievement, which at the moment lay hidden like a scorpion in a stalk of bananas, was a clause which placed the burden of proof of the reasonableness of any increased rate (*not*, as would be recognized only later, just the increase, but the *entire rate,* taking no account of the historical legitimacy of the pre-increase portion) on the railroads.[45] The Insurgents were delighted. Pass it, pass it now, they demanded. All that was needed was for the Senate to accept the House's amendment, offered by Representative Irvine L. Lenroot of Wisconsin, to make rate suspension immediate.

But where was the President's cherished provision for the regulation of railroad securities issues? Sacrificed, as we have seen, on the altar of compromise. The President had salvaged nothing but the Commerce Court. Senator Winthrop M. Crane of Massachusetts and Representative James R. Mann, advocates of moderate railroad legislation, appealed to the President to send in a special message asking for a House-Senate conference. He did so. The regular Republicans rallied to his side, as did six Democrats who were horrified at Cummins' handiwork, and over the cries of Insurgents that the bill would be murdered, into conference it went.[46] Nobody, however, wanted a tough securities clause at this juncture. Senator Aldrich abominated the idea, and Elkins resented its implications. The Insurgents had bargained it away in the process of having virtually everything else their way and were not about to pull at this loose string in the fabric of compromise. While the other conferees waited, Aldrich, Elkins, and Mann went to the White House

[44] *Ibid.,* June 8, 1910, 1.

[45] *CR,* 61st Cong., 2d Sess., 7374–75; Sayre, "Cummins," 376; *Nation,* XC (1910), 620.

[46] *CR,* 61st Cong., 2d Sess., 7537, 7564; *NYT,* June 8, 1910, 1; June 9, 1.

where they "collided" with Taft and Wickersham on the issue. Aldrich proposed as the only possible compromise a study—that familiar substitute for action which politicians love—of the securities situation. The President reluctantly yielded.

The Insurgents turned the conference calamity into another golden opportunity. It was hardly a fair fight. The subtropical Washington weather sapped the strength of the two conservative leaders, Aldrich and Elkins, who were nearly twenty years older than their major Insurgent adversaries. "We saved the bill from mutilation by the conference committee," bragged Senator Joseph Bristow to a friend, "by notifying the Senate conferees that if the bill was materially changed we would stay in session all summer before we would permit the conference report to be adopted; and . . . some of us every day warned Elkins that if the bill was materially changed he and Aldrich could cancel their European trips and spend the summer in Washington." [47]

The cruel tactics worked. That young giant, the suspension period, grew another two-thirds, from six months to ten. Into the text went, word for word, the House's tough version of the clause outlawing all long-haul—short-haul discrimination except with the express approval of the ICC. Appalled, the Democratic members of the conference refused to sign the report. The majority members, badly split between regulars and Insurgents, adjourned several meetings to the White House where Mann, almost despairing of getting a bill at a time when the entire nation was watching expectantly, "used a club" to get agreement. "It's *our* bill now," chortled an unidentified Insurgent when news of the agreement reached the Capitol. An exhausted Congress, which had been in session for six weary months while one of the hottest mid-term election campaigns in years was shaping up, was in no mood for further controversy, and adopted the conference report on June 16.

The exhilaration of the midwesterners contrasted dramatically with the dejection of the conservative Republican leaders. Senator Cummins, in an expansive mood with reporters now that he had got every-

[47] Kenneth W. Hechler, *Insurgency* (New York, 1940), 176–77. The average age of six Insurgents (Dolliver, Cummins, La Follette, Bristow, Borah, and Beveridge) was 51. The oldest, at 60, was Cummins. In contrast, Elkins and Aldrich were both in their seventieth year. Otto Kahn recalled this aspect of the struggle with bitterness in *Our Economic and Other Problems: A Financier's Point of View* (New York, 1920), 72–73.

thing his group wanted, and more, predicted a short life for the Commerce Court, but about the new bill in general, he "crowed lustily." [48]

[48] *CR*, 61st Cong., 2d Sess., 8026–33, 8237–41, 8391; Sayre, "Cummins," 377. The new law, by general agreement, was named for its nominal sponsors, the heads of the House and Senate committees, Mann and Elkins. Subsequent scholars, including Elkins' biographer, have assumed that the law was a great achievement for the West Virginia Senator, a judgment with which the dying legislator would have heartily disagreed. Oscar D. Lambert, *Stephen B. Elkins* (Pittsburgh, 1955), 320–21.

CHAPTER VII

THE FIRST DENIAL

I don't disguise my belief that the Sherman Act is a humbug based on economic ignorance and incompetence, and my disbelief that the Interstate Commerce Commission is a body fit to be entrusted with rate-making. . . . The Commission naturally is always trying to extend its power. . . . However, I am so sceptical as to our knowledge of the goodness or badness of laws that I have no practical criticism except what the crowd wants. Personally, I bet that the crowd, if it knew more, wouldn't want what it wants.— MR. JUSTICE HOLMES, *April 23, 1910*

I have been somewhat surprised to see the space that has been given in your newspapers to the criticism of your railways. It has been my opinion that in actual economy of operation the railways of the United States are first in the world. . . . Your railways have reached a higher standard in international comparison than your farmers or your government and under greater difficulties.—SIR WILLIAM M. ACWORTH, *1910*

I

Standing at the entrance to New York's fabled Broadway, the United States Custom House occupies as prominent and expensive a piece of real estate as any official architectural landmark of the big city. Cass Gilbert designed it almost seventy years ago and, with the help of sculptural embellishments by Daniel Chester French, gave the nation one of its finest examples of the Beaux Arts eclectic style. This style— and particularly the impressive main hall—has probably secured for the building whatever immortality the troubled American city of the late twentieth century has to give. None of these thoughts, of course, are likely to have crossed the minds of the men who crowded into one of the Custom House's meeting rooms on August 15, 1910. Drably and almost uniformly dressed in the modest male fashions which, Edwardian period or not, were all but mandatory in the financial capital of America, the shorthand reporter who had not yet opened his notebook and the general counsels of some of the nation's leading railroads were barely distinguishable.

This outwardly unimpressive group had gathered to begin the proceedings in which the profitability and future growth of more than $14 billion of capital, invested in America's greatest industry, would be determined. The Interstate Commerce Commission, proceeding under the newly passed Mann-Elkins Act, was beginning hearings on the increased tariffs which the eastern trunk line railroads constituting "Official Classification Territory" had filed earlier in the year, and which the Commission had suspended. The Commissioners had yet to meet on their own to discuss the provisions of the act. The railroad men, who for the first time were being asked to justify as a group what had always been a routine decision for them as individuals, had barely begun to work out the content of their argument and the procedure by which they would present it. The Commissioners stayed away, sending special examiner George Brown in their stead. A phalanx of grim-faced attorneys for a long list of shippers' organizations waited expectantly for the railroad men to show their hand before this unimposing gathering. After conferring briefly, the railroad lawyers asked for a three-week postponement and the assemblage quickly deserted the hot, smoky, crowded room.[1]

The room was no less crowded, if somewhat cooler, when an even larger group hopelessly attempted to crowd into it on September 7. Among the men attending for the first time were two representatives of shippers' groups who would play prominent roles in this and subsequent hearings in the new decade. After the Commission examiner, in desperation, adjourned the hearing to the oddly ornate environment of the Waldorf-Astoria's Astor Gallery (the Custom House had no larger room available), these two men and a "host of others" made their formal appearances before the Commission. One was a Boston lawyer who had already made a reputation for himself as the "people's lawyer" since giving up a lucrative practice in order to take cases on the basis of his view of their importance to the general welfare. The other was a brilliant young attorney who sported also a Yale Ph.D. in political sci-

[1] 1910 Hearings, 1630.

ence, who gave his home as Washington, Iowa, and who had drawn considerable favorable comment for his pioneer work on state railroad commissions. The Bostonian was appearing in behalf of a number of eastern organizations, including the Chamber of Commerce of New York State, who were challenging the rate increases, while the midwesterner represented not only a number of farm marketing organizations but also the state regulatory commissions of Iowa, Illinois, Missouri, Kansas, and several other neighboring states. Both men were profoundly aware of the importance of the hearings, to their own careers as well as to the causes which they represented. The names of Louis D. Brandeis and Clifford Thorne would dominate all others in the weeks to come.[2]

The railroad forces, ready or not, now had to move into the spotlight. Still there was no Commissioner ready to hear their case. No Commissioner, in fact, ever came up to New York to these hearings although Clements and Lane had journeyed to Chicago to preside over the presentation of evidence by the western roads. No one could have been more aware of the intense publicity which these proceedings would draw once the shippers began their indignant interpositions. If the railroad lawyers fretted that a Commissioner would hew to a line of greater judicial impartiality than a mere special examiner, however, they were shortly to be corrected on that score as reports of Commissioner Lane's off-the-record remarks began to reach them from Chicago. If this was the way it was going to be, then they would have to make the most of it.

From the beginning, the railroad men chose to stress not their great achievements of the past ten years but their financial position. They sought to demonstrate that the proposed increases in rates were very small in comparison to the increases in wages and material costs of recent years. Under the new law, they had to make such a strong case that the Commission would have to approve the higher rates. How this was to be accomplished—just how the assemblage of high-priced legal talent was to know when the magic point of persuasion had been

[2] *Ibid.*, 1633–34; *NYT*, Sept. 8, 1910, 5; Clifford Thorne, "Principle versus Precedent" (unpublished doctoral dissertation, Yale University, 1901); *Who Was Who in America, 1897–1942*, "Clifford Thorne," 1236; Alpheus T. Mason, *Brandeis: A Free Man's Life* (New York, 1946); see also Clifford Thorne's obituary, Chicago *Tribune*, Nov. 14, 1923, 10.

reached—no one could even pretend to know. They had to sing their song to a most unsympathetic audience composed of their customers, who did not want their charges raised, and the Commission, which was under a virtual mandate from Congress not to see rates raised except under the most compelling circumstances. As it turned out, the railroad men's presentation was a series of earnest but mediocre "numbers," without a single outstanding tune in the lot. Still gun-shy as a result of the accusations of illegal combination, the railroads avoided choosing a single spokesman. The tactic which they adopted was to place an appropriate operating executive or employee of an important railroad on the stand and have him interrogated by the line's general counsel. On the first day, therefore, Hugh L. Bond, Jr., head lawyer of the Baltimore & Ohio, began to draw out his company's general auditor and ex officio statistician, J. T. Leary, on the subject of the cost of materials, wages, and the raising of capital. The two men agreed that the cost of running a railroad was indeed rising rapidly, and a few examples were given, but the lack of general price statistics was almost embarrassingly obvious. Then the shippers' strategy began to be apparent. Francis B. James, representing the Shippers' Association and the National Industrial Traffic League, went at Leary in a manner which fully justified the shorthand reporter's calling it a "cross-examination." Bond's statement that the eastern roads' total freight revenues were $727 million, while the increases were estimated to total only $27 million (implying a less than 4 per cent increase), impressed no one. On and on went the monotonous process, as executives of the Pennsylvania, the New York Central, and the Erie recited virtually the same litany to their companies' lawyers. Only the sarcasm of the shippers' representatives, who questioned the very accuracy of everything the bookkeepers said, enlivened the dull proceedings.[3]

II

The hearings moved into a new phase as the important executives of the railroads began to make their appearances. The shippers, it soon became apparent, had been reserving their heavy ammunition for their

[3] 1910 Hearings, 1635–1894.

counterparts, the railroads' traffic vice-presidents, who were, in a sense, the most important and most vulnerable executives scheduled to appear before the Commission. When Charles F. Daly, vice-president in charge of freight traffic for the far-flung New York Central, took the witness chair the time was ripe. Like his own counterpart from the Pennsylvania Railroad, who had just preceded him, Daly recited at the promptings of his company's lawyer the by now familiar proposition that the increases were very modest in total. The shippers then moved in to show that such testimony might be very true but that it was entirely beside the point. James, one of the most militant opponents of the increase, began a cross-examination which considerably stirred up the proceedings:

> James [to Daly]: You have qualified to tell this Commission what would be a just and reasonable rate on every piece of goods, wares and merchandise included in these six classes, have you not?
> O. E. Butterfield [assistant general solicitor of the Cincinnati, Hamilton & Dayton Railroad, a Baltimore & Ohio subsidiary] (interrupting): I take an exception to any intimation of that sort. The witness has not intimated anything of that sort and it is not a fair treatment of the witness. He distinctly stated that he did not undertake to distinguish between all the commodities, and distinctly stated that it was not a perfect schedule. Now he [James] undertakes to put into the mouth of the witness the words that he has sworn as to every commodity that the rate is reasonable and proper.[4]

Good enough, as far as the shippers were concerned. Butterfield could not have been more helpful if he had let James draft a statement along these lines. If the traffic representatives of the railroads could not certify to and support—at least up to the extent of the Commission's ability to receive and absorb the testimony—the reasonableness of each and every rate included in the revised schedules, and if, on the other hand, the law clearly was based on just such a rule of rate making, why, then, the invalidity of the procedure the railroads were engaged in was obvious. What the railroads were doing was a mere waste of the Commission's time. It mattered not that the Commission, and certainly not the shippers, were unable to demonstrate that the proposed increases were *not* reasonable. They did not have to do so under the law. What the railroads were doing, then, was virtually making a plea of *nolo con-*

[4] *Ibid.,* 1989.

tendere. Brandeis, perfectly briefed on the shippers' strong legal position, joyously seized the baton from James. He skewered Daly on the railroad man's lack of data on the reasonableness of some of the most frequently applied rates in the schedule. "So far as the rates you do make are concerned," he demanded, "all you know about it is that inner feeling that comes in the experienced man as to what is high enough and what is not?" The question had drawn blood. "It comes from that same experience that teaches you to be such a learned lawyer," the unhappy witness angrily responded.[5]

Others were content to stick with the old strategies. Railroad accounting methods had always been at the very heart of the problem of effective regulation as far as many midwestern Progressives were concerned. No one had arrived at the hearings better prepared to question the validity of the railroads' figures than Clifford Thorne. At that moment he discovered that the Pennsylvania's traffic vice-president planned to leave on a trip to Europe as soon as his testimony was completed, and he objected bitterly to such a procedure. In a motion obviously prepared in advance, he asked that all of the man's testimony be stricken from the record unless the shippers got a chance to cross-examine him. In fact, the young Progressive wanted *all* testimony on costs, no matter which railroad had offered it, stricken unless and until the Commission made "an original investigation, through its proper agents, of the records, officers, and employees of the *defendant* carriers [because] such matters can be easily manipulated by the general policy of the road as to improvements, replacements and betterments." [6] This was pretty tame stuff after Brandeis' performance.

On these minor notes the New York hearings came to an end. The tone of the affair had reached the point where it was absolutely necessary that the Commissioners take over the proceedings. It was mid-September, almost five months since the railroads had first attempted to post their new rates, when their executives returned to their offices to await the call to Washington.[7] Few if any of them could agree with the

---

[5] *Ibid.*, 2024–25; *NYT*, Sept. 14, 1910, 5.   [6] 1910 Hearings, 2226. Italics added.

[7] *Ibid.*, 2251. On the last day the Baltimore & Ohio introduced a nostalgic note by presenting to the examiners their general traffic manager, C. S. White. Forty-five years a railroad man, and now about to retire, White was one of two surviving people who as young men had helped prepare the freight classifications which the eastern railroads had originally filed with the new ICC in 1887. What he had

Commercial and Financial Chronicle, which tried to cheer them up with the plaintive assertion that "everyone thought that [the railroads] made a good case." [8]

III

The western railroads meanwhile had been subjected to similar treatment out in Chicago, although there the hearings had largely turned into a forum in which Commissioner Lane had aired his philosophies of railroad regulation. During the first recess in New York, many of the shippers' representatives, including Thorne, had shown up in Chicago when the Commission's examiners got things under way on August 29. The western railroads moved more directly into the thick of things, placing their leading advocate, Edward P. Ripley of the Santa Fe, on the stand first. Again the lack of any well-prepared, clear-cut, hard-hitting case showed itself almost from the beginning. Responding to questions put to him by his general counsel, T. J. Norton, Ripley recited the old story of low return on capital, poor credit standing (as evidenced by the recent shocking necessity of selling Santa Fe bonds below par), and the unreasonable, non-revenue-producing demands of localities for everything from new depots to additional train service. Of the greatly enlarged and almost wholly rebuilt railroad which hundreds of millions of capital invested in the Santa Fe had given the people of the rapidly growing Southwest, there was hardly a mention. Norton, realizing that one thing, and one thing only, would carry weight with the Commission under existing attitudes and statutes, raised the subject of reasonableness of rates. Ripley, with his immense prestige as an honest, efficient, hard-working railroad leader, might have scored a strong point for the railroads in their almost unconscious effort to lodge with the Commission the concept of a general test of reasonableness. Only his unfortunate choice of rhetoric prevented it. "There never was any better defini-

---

to say about the historical validity of the rates made news, but again it was Brandeis who offered newspaper men their best copy. Unmercifully, he challenged White to tell him how to separate terminal (i.e., switching) costs from transportation costs in justifying the need for rate increases. Of course the old man could not. *NYT,* Sept. 16, 1910, 4; 1910 Hearings, 2214.

[8] *CFC, BQS,* XCI (Oct. 8, 1910), 19.

tion [of reasonableness of rates] than that which was given many years ago by somebody and which has been used as a by-word and a reproach ever since, namely, 'what the traffic will bear.' " There they were, those ugly words, out in the open for all to hear. The earnest words of explanation which followed might as well not have been spoken: "That does not mean all the traffic will bear, it does not mean all that can be extorted or squeezed out of it, but what the traffic will bear having regard to the freest possible movement of commodities, the least possible burden on the producer and on the consumer. The middleman can take care of himself." [9]

Amid murmurs from the throng of middlemen in the room who were intent on taking care of themselves, Ripley pressed on. Under the freest possible conditions, he explained, the railroads would still carry much freight at less than the average cost per ton, simply because such traffic would bear no higher rate. "I deduce, then, that the rates have been reasonable?" said Norton, attempting to drive home his point. "They have been unreasonably low," was the railroad leader's rather unsatisfactory reply. John C. Atwood, representative of the Shippers' Association, was almost insulting in his cross-examination. Smarting under the suggestion that the railroads were reduced to selling some bonds below par, he asked Ripley if it were not true that other railroad securities sold well above their face value. The railroad man, himself no financial expert, pointed out the perfectly obvious fact that some men speculated—gambled, in fact—on railroad securities. He might have taken the wind out of his inquisitor's sails by pointing out that the market value of a security reflected its investment value, and had nothing at all to do with its par value. As it was he could only redden and fight back his indignation as Atwood turned away with the sarcastic remark, "I regret to think that your railroad even in a remote degree lends itself to gambling interests." [10]

[9] 1910 Hearings, 19–27.

[10] *Ibid.*, 36. The patience of the railroad lawyers was sorely tried a little later when Atwood tried to bully the chairman of the Trans-Missouri Freight Bureau. Despite the high-sounding title, the position was little more than clerical in nature and the witness, W. A. Poteet, was a young man still in his twenties. There was something ridiculous in Atwood's attempts to get Poteet to incriminate himself under the antitrust laws for compiling the western railroads' proposed new tariffs. Norton demanded that these "speeches to the bleachers" be ended. *Ibid.*, 226.

Quickly the presentation of evidence by the western railroads fell into the same repetitious pattern that marked their eastern colleagues' case. Representatives of the Rock Island and the Wabash put their executives and accountants on the stand. The same generalities were expressed about the modest size of the increased revenues expected from the new rates in the face of cost increases which were already a certainty.[11] The railroad men were repeatedly questioned on the cost-saving possibilities of the many new railroad devices then being introduced. William L. Park, vice-president and general manager of the Illinois Central, explained that the new automatic block signals, while they greatly increased safety of operation on single-track lines, did not greatly increase the maximum traffic capacity of such lines because their primary function was in permitting minimum spacing of trains operating in the same direction on double-track routes. In other words, block signals were no substitute for the program of double-tracking which had absorbed so many of the billions of dollars invested by the railroads in the previous ten years. Warming up to the promising theme that higher traffic volume was more likely to mean higher costs than higher profits in the near future, William Ellis of the Chicago, Milwaukee, and St. Paul Railway ran head-on into a hornet's nest. By now Commissioners Lane and Clements were presiding over the hearings. Lane grew impatient as Ellis pontificated that every additional ton of freight was a burden which raised operating costs for railroads operating at or near capacity. "As the country develops," he blurted out, "there will be more freight delivered to you and therefore . . . rates have got to be increased. Now, I regard that as a serious matter to this whole western country. If there is to be a progressive increase in railroad rates and no stability, then certainly we have got to find some basis upon which we can work this problem out upon another line." The outburst, through which the gestating philosophy of the Commission could be plainly discerned, cast a chill on the friends of the railroads.[12] But the bias which the statement revealed was no more depressing than the evidence of ineptness and indecision which was shortly to follow.

The men in Chicago had endured a month of desultory testimony

[11] *Ibid.,* Vol. I, *passim.; N YT,* Sept. 1, 1910, 10.

[12] 1910 Hearings, 751; *CFC, BQS,* XCI (Oct. 8, 1910), 19.

from the railroads when H. C. Lust, representative of the powerful Illinois Manufacturers Association, arose on September 29, 1910, to present the shippers' case. Fresh fireworks were anticipated by the jaded participants. It was well known that the shippers had marshaled some plain-spoken, long-suffering railroad enemies to speak for them, including the state of Iowa's most articulate citizen, Henry C. Wallace, publisher of the corn-belt bible, *Wallace's Farmer,* and the governor of Kansas. Few were prepared for the confidence with which Lust addressed the bench, which now included Commissioner Clark. He blandly moved that since the railroads had tried—and, obviously, failed—to justify the proposed increases, the show was all but over. "We move . . . to have the Commission in Washington set an early date for an argument," he announced. John B. Payne, general counsel of the Chicago Great Western Railroad, jumped to his feet, red-faced, and snapped sarcastically, "Next Sunday, do you suggest?" "If you can get away from the golf links, it will be all right," shot back the crafty Lust.[13] Norton, who had already accused Lust of "passing the puck [*sic*]" to the Commission, was even more indignant when Lust demanded that the proposed rate increases be permanently suspended then and there. Commissioner Clark, a good railroad labor leader but no lawyer and certainly no judge, raised his hands in dismay. Half to himself, he speculated aloud that the Commission could not suspend permanently. He clearly did not know where the case stood. He knew that the railroads were supposed to sustain the burden of proof of reasonableness, "which, as I take it, must go to each individual rate and not to a general schedule of rates under a general order." The Commissioners, he murmured, had not yet had a chance to consult on the new law. Lust was eager to help. "If they [the railroads] have not established that contention [that the new rates are reasonable], that ends the hearing, I take it," he insisted, and proceeded to lecture the Commission on procedure.

When Lust had finished, Clark leaned forward and spoke earnestly to him. Railroad hearts sank at his next words. "If we assume, just for the purpose of this argument, that the Commission should decide that the carriers had not shown a justification for a general increase in rates, what order would you suggest the Commission enter?" If Lust was

[13] 1910 Hearings, 1123.

taken aback at the Commissioner's ingenuousness, he did not show it. Permanent suspension, he shot back without hesitation. No, he corrected himself in some confusion, that wasn't right. Accentuating the positive, he decided that the thing for the Commission to do was to find the present rates reasonable for two years. Clifford Thorne, no doubt dismayed at the amateurishness of the entire proceeding, got the floor. He pointed out that the Supreme Court, in *Munn* v. *Illinois,* had waited a year after presentation of evidence to decide. The Commission, he said, had no reason to be in a hurry and plenty of precedent to take its time. It had not been a good day for this pioneer independent regulatory commission, from which the country was expecting so much. A month's recess was hastily called.[14]

The parties reassembled in Chicago in October to hear the shippers' case which had been so unexpectedly interrupted. It turned out not to be a very impressive showing since the few days which they required were taken up with details of individual rates. No general case against the rate increases was made, a not surprising tactic since the shippers had steadfastly denied that the railroads could change their tariffs in such a wholesale manner. The tone of the Chicago hearings in their last days, when everyone was weary if not a nervous wreck, was set by Commissioner Lane while Henry C. Wallace was on the stand. Was it not true, he asked, half-jokingly, that Iowa farmers were actually buying automobiles? Wallace, who knew a great deal more than Lane did about what the new, cheap cars that Detroit was now turning out meant to the isolated farmer, shot back, "Unquestionably large numbers of autos have been purchased by the farmers—and paying cash for them!" [15] Payne, still holding the fort for the carriers, attempted to probe the question of farm prosperity. Eggs, he wondered aloud, were surely selling for considerably more than in the days when the existing railroad rates on eggs had been established. Wallace refused to bite. "I raise my own, and I don't know," he smirked.[16]

The shippers' tactics shifted to the question of how the railroads had fared under regulatory legislation passed in recent years. Atwood placed on the stand H. G. Wilson, revising clerk for the Commercial Club of Kansas City. The railroads, said Wilson, were now collecting much more of their published fares as a result of the Elkins and Hepburn

[14] *Ibid.,* 1125–28.   [15] *Ibid.,* 1159.   [16] *Ibid.,* 1173.

laws, since rebating had virtually stopped. But he refused to allow Atwood to place in his mouth the words that the net was as much as 40
per cent greater. On cross-examination, Payne managed to get Wilson to
admit that from time to time he had suggested that upward revisions in
certain rates were in order, an embarrassing admission for a man who
earned his bread by saving shippers money on their freight bills. Witnesses from commercial clubs in Minneapolis and Omaha followed with
similar testimony.[17] Hastily the shippers changed their tactics, placing
on the stand one in whose testimony they could be more confident. Governor W. R. Stubbs of Kansas occupied the chair long enough to make
a speech against the raising of railroad rates and to answer a few questions about railroad service in his state. His castigation of the Santa Fe
for the quality of service on its branch lines was given with relish.[18]

The proceedings now bogged down completely in a welter of detail on why and how specific rate increases were selected. Railroad men
and shippers wrangled over the reasonableness of specific rates, differentials between rates, general economic conditions, and anything else
that obtruded itself into the discussions. The hopelessness of making
any progress in the direction of an intelligent decision by discussing
reasonableness of specific rates was painfully apparent. The western
hearings ground to a halt, but not before Commissioner Lane made one
more headline and once again chilled the spirits of the railroad men.
Stanley H. Johnson, assistant freight traffic manager of the Rock Island,
had been answering question after question about the proposed increases when Lane suddenly tore into him. "Is it not true," he exclaimed impatiently, "that deep down in the mind of the traffic manager
he knows that even the present rate is too high?" The startled witness'
indignant response was drowned by a roar of laughter. Sadly, the railroad men closed their briefcases and made ready to depart for Washington to see how their eastern brethren were faring.[19]

[17] *Ibid.,* 1187, 1197. Revising clerks, whether they operated independently or as
members of commercial "clubs," made their living by examining the freight way-
bills of shippers and dividing with them any amounts which they were able to re-
coup from the carriers as a result of errors in classification, application of rates,
or computation.

[18] *Ibid.,* 1330.

[19] *NYT,* Nov. 2, 1910, 10. This revelation of prejudice against the railroads' case
is nowhere to be found in the printed transcript of the proceedings, which suggests that its author thought better of it later.

IV

Chairman Knapp was firmly in charge of things on October 12 when the eastern hearings were resumed in the modest conference rooms of the Commission's Washington offices. A party of railroad presidents, traveling together to the capital, were somewhat more cheerful than they had been when the New York proceedings were adjourned. A group of shippers in St. Louis and another in Wisconsin had released a statement favoring an 8 to 10 per cent across-the-board increase because "a fair advance could be well borne by the public at large." [20] The presidents had no illusions, however, about the uphill fight which they faced and the moral fervor of their adversaries. Their star witness, President James McCrea of the Pennsylvania, felt the pressure almost at once, as Louis Brandeis bored into him. The Pennsylvania, Brandeis noted, had just completed a $115 million investment program in the New York terminal and related facilities. Would not this soon bring big dividends? No, replied McCrea. "We have simply provided a new station to take the place of an old one, with improved facilities to the public. . . . But I do not look upon it . . . as showing any net returns that are worthy of consideration." McCrea emphatically explained that his management had simply felt that the greatest railroad in the world owed the greatest city in the country a better terminal than a shed in Jersey City which had to be reached by ferry. Brandeis let the point pass. If the president of the nation's largest transportation enterprise wished to show such a lack of sensitivity to return on investment and such a penchant for monumental enterprises as the new Pennsylvania Station, it fitted quite well into what he really wanted to establish.

What Brandeis was after was to show that the great railroads, where they were not actually corrupt (he had in mind the recent revelations of kickbacks on the Illinois Central), were inefficient and insensitive to the needs of the public. They suffered, in short, from what he liked to call "giantism." "Is it not a fact," he demanded of McCrea, "that the relatively poor showing of the recent years is due to the fact that your railroad has eliminated competition and all the stimulus that

[20] *Ibid.*, Oct. 12, 1910, 13.

came from it, and in the second place, [lacks] that greater efficiency
and economy of management which is a necessary incident to an institution growing so large that no human being is capable adequately to su-
pervise it?" McCrea, unsure whether his tormentor had just made a
speech or asked him a question, but growing hot under the collar nevertheless, snapped, "What is the particular point—the incompetency of
the management or the conspiracy by which they advanced the rate?"
Brandeis was willing to explain. He had discovered in the Pennsylvania's own records certain figures on the cost of locomotive repairs per
mile which were higher than those for other roads. McCrea's icy response showed that he was ready for that one. "The Pennsylvania Railroad Company has always tried to keep its expenses in such a way as to
know how much a thing costs, not how little," he retorted.[21] The Pennsylvania, after all, was the standard to which other railroads had learned
to repair. To those present who were familiar with the Pennsylvania's
achievements over the past two decades, it looked as though Brandeis
was getting beyond his depth. But the wiry little lawyer pressed on.
How do you know, he challenged McCrea, that you are not being
robbed in the same manner as the Illinois Central in the matter of car
repairs? The company's reporting system, said the executive, was their
guard. It told them how much was a normal cost. Brandeis leaped on
this, for it led him precisely in the direction in which he wished to go.
You only know how much something has cost in the past, he pointed
out, not how much it ought to cost. What he was driving at would become painfully clear when the people's lawyer presented the shippers'
case.[22]

McCrea shuffled the pages of a prepared statement which he
wished to read. Seeking to maintain the role of economic statesman
which he felt his position and the importance of the matter before the
Commission justified, he turned to a consideration of the public interest.
What the country looks to all of us for, he asserted, is a rate policy
based on "the needs of the country as a whole and [influenced] by the

[21] 1910 Hearings, 2301–4. It is difficult to believe that Brandeis did not know
that maintenance expenditures were one of the first to be cut in lean times, and
that such charges were bound to be lower for almost any railroad than the relatively prosperous Pennsylvania.

[22] Ibid., 2307, 2314; NYT, Oct. 13, 1910, 5.

conditions under which those needs can be supplied." Higher charges for everything were justified to a certain extent, he felt, by the general rise in the cost of living. The net profits retained by the railroads were becoming less and less adequate to meet their needs. Since 1887, in fact, the Pennsylvania alone had plowed back a quarter of a billion dollars of profits that the stockholders, it was becoming painfully clear, would probably never see. He predicted a lower growth rate for eastern railroads in the future while noting that wage demands were based on past trends.[23]

The second and third largest eastern trunk line railroads were next heard from in testimony by Brown of the New York Central and Willard of the Baltimore & Ohio. They entered much the same pleas as McCrea had. Brown described current investment programs, at that time about one-half completed, totaling $230 million on the Central and its major subsidiaries. New York City, he reminded the Commissioners, was forcing the company to rebuild its entire freight line from Spuyten Duyvil down the west side of Manhattan to the St. John's Park freight terminal, a project which would cost millions and yield virtually nothing in additional revenue. When the Michigan Central had recently tried to sell $17.5 million in 4 per cent bonds, Brown said, the best offer the company had received was 87 cents on the dollar, indicating that investors wanted more than 4.5 per cent return on a gilt-edged security in the investment climate of 1910. It had been a rude shock indeed for a railroad which had been financed at par with securities which for decades had been eagerly bid up on the exchanges to a stiff premium.[24] Willard sought to shore up the railroads' plea that they had to find a way to increase their income in the face of rising costs. It was the wrong move with Commissioner Lane back in the chair. The California Progressive, to whom the idea was anathema that rates should be automatically responsive to increases in costs, showed little of his usually

[23] 1910 Hearings, 2325; *NYT*, Oct. 13, 1910, 5.

[24] 1910 Hearings, 2428–30; *NYT*, Oct. 14, 1910, 8. The West Side freight line improvements were over and above what the Central was spending to develop Grand Central Terminal in response to legislation outlawing steam trains in tunnels within the city. Although the Central was spending only a few millions less on its own monumental terminal project than the Pennsylvania, the circumstances were so familiar to all that Brown did not even go into this aspect of his company's investment program.

sunny disposition when Brandeis pushed Willard into the inevitable logical corner on this point. He demanded to know whether the Baltimo-
rean thought rates should go up every time wages did. Willard, somewhat taken aback by the Commissioner's belligerent tone, replied
weakly, "In my opinion the two things will be found to be very closely
related to each other in the future." [25] Indeed they would be, but just
how closely few were able or willing to see in 1910.

The Central executive's quiet, measured tones, however, and the
sobering financial facts which he commanded so well had drawn the re-
spectful attention of the large assemblage. When Brown continued the
next day his words were closely noted. His frankness concerning the
size of what the eastern railroads were presently asking was impressive.
"I do not think that the increases in rates asked for are all that we
should have but . . . the sentimental effect of the allowance . . . would
be worth as much as the practical advance in sustaining our credit."
The Central, he reminded his listeners, paid an average dividend of
only 4.7 per cent on the par value of its stock. Smiling ruefully at his
colleague from Baltimore, he noted that his company had not been able
to do even as well as the B. & O., which was putting one-third of its
profits into improvements while the Central could manage only one-
quarter. Lane demanded to know why such a state of affairs existed in
such rich territory. "We can't earn it," said Brown. The bonded debt of
the Central and its subsidiaries was $254 million, he noted, and despite
the fact that every cent of it had been raised at par, and at an average
interest cost of only 3.5 per cent, the fixed costs of running such an enterprise as the Central were staggering. The proof? So far was the Central from being a watered property that the reproduction cost of the
railroad was actually close to twice what the books showed, and nearly
every mile of the vast system demanded constant enlargement and improvement. Brandeis quickly sought to break the spell which Brown's
testimony had produced. He demanded to know of the startled executive
whether J. P. Morgan was still connected with the New York Central
and then, as if to emphasize the rhetorical nature of the question, hastened on to his next shaft. The Central, he reminded Brown, had recently raised its dividend from 5 to 6 per cent. Didn't he think that, in
view of the need for funds, the managers ought to have lowered the div-
[25] 1910 Hearings, 2363–64.

idend? "No, sir," emphatically responded Brown, "we raised the dividend to the rate which a person could get on a first-class mortgage." Then Brandeis announced to the Central's leader that he was going to put men on the stand who would show how the problem could be solved via greater efficiency of operation, thereby eliminating the need for rate increases. Brown was not impressed. "When you find the men," he replied, "send me a list of the first five or ten of them. . . . I will assure them a good position as soon as you can send them to New York." [26]

V

By the middle of November the small group of reporters who were covering the hearings for the newspapers, wire services, and financial journals had grown bored with their assignment. Their editors kept them at their posts, all the same. Experience showed that Brandeis was eventually good for a front-page story. He certainly was not in this fight for his health, and he had hinted at revelations to come. When he asked leave to address the Commission on November 21, therefore, the reporters were ready with pads and pencils. The people's lawyer began on a lofty plane. He demanded that the guardians of the American transportation system take some other approach to their problem of rising costs than the bankrupt idea of raising rates correspondingly. That, he said, was only a "vicious circle":

Now there, precisely, is the point at which we take issue most largely with the railroads. We say that this situation, this practical declaration of hopelessness which comes from the railroads, this incompetence to deal with the great problem of labor and the great problem of costs, is due to a failure to regard that which the most progressive manufacturers in competitive lines of business have been led to adopt, namely, the science of management.[27]

He announced that he was about to present witnesses who would show that this "science of management" could save the carriers as a group a million dollars a day—more than they had any thought of getting by raising rates. He did not abandon, but rather reiterated, his original points that the railroads had not met the legal requirement of proving

[26] *Ibid.*, 2512; *NYT*, Oct. 15, 1910, 10.   [27] 1910 Hearings, 2617.

the reasonableness of the proposed rates, that the increases would be burdensome to consumers, and that they would upset transportation practices which had been in effect for a generation. But now he was obviously ready to take a new and exciting tack. The New York *Times* moved its daily piece on the hearings from its usual place on the financial page to page six.[28]

Brandeis had finished his opening remarks and was preparing to announce his first witness when Joseph Ramsey, Jr., garrulous president of the Ann Arbor Railroad, demanded the floor. He objected to what Brandeis was about to do. He lectured the Commission on scientific management, saying that "a railroad cannot install piece work like an industrial establishment can. There is nothing in these ideas [Brandeis] has put forward this morning." The railroads were perfectly aware of the advantages of piece work, he asserted. For years they had been seeking ways to install such a system of paying employees for the amount of work actually performed. Having done with Brandeis, the wound-up Ramsey blundered ahead while the Commissioners, eager to see what the people's lawyer had up his sleeve, fidgeted in their chairs with growing impatience. "This question [of rate increases] should be treated not on the simple basis of whether the railroads can stand it or not but whether both of them can stand it—both the shippers and the railroads. It is a joint matter between the two, and it is not fair to put the whole burden on the railroads and let those shippers that are declaring an average of fifteen per cent a year go free." Here was an echo of a New York *Times* editorial during the injunction excitement of earlier that year. What Ramsey was saying was that there was an inescapable question of equity involved—the carriers' material welfare versus the shippers' welfare. Carried to its logical conclusion, this line of thought would leave little room for a regulatory body which placed all of the burden of proof on one of the two parties. It was all true (at least in principle), all embarrassing, and all entirely out of order. Chairman Knapp brusquely informed Ramsey that his time was up.[29]

That afternoon Brandeis began his parade of experts on scientific management. First came Horace K. Hathaway, plant manager of the Tabor Manufacturing Company, a Philadelphia maker of machinery. Startlingly young in appearance, Hathaway further impressed the gath-

[28] *NYT*, Nov. 22, 1910, 6.   [29] 1910 Hearings, 2628–36.

ering by his "clean cut, incisively direct answers." He described the repetitive operations of the workmen at their machines, and explained
that the basis of scientific managment lay in determining what was a
reasonable amount of time for a given operation or suboperation, and
then setting hourly rates and bonuses accordingly. The men, he proudly
declared, had been making only eighteen dollars a week before the system was installed. Now they were averaging twenty-seven dollars a
week and the company was more prosperous than it had ever been. Up
stepped O. E. Butterfield, canny legal head of the Cincinnati, Hamilton
& Dayton, who would soon move to the New York Central. How many
workmen were on the payroll before the system went in? A hundred
and ten. And how many are on the payroll now? Ninety-five. And is
that just the operatives themselves, or does it include foremen, clean-up
men, and the like? It includes everybody who works in the plant. That's
a reduction of about 15 per cent, Butterfield pressed the witness. But
how much have you reduced the workmen who were directly affected by
the new system? Too late, young Hathaway saw that the lawyer had maneuvered him into revealing that the system had its Darwinian aspects.
Actual operatives had been reduced by 40 per cent, he murmured.[30]

Next came James Mapes Dodge, chairman of the board of the
Link-Belt Company, a manufacturer of industrial products which were
assembled in large quantities from numerous identical small compo-
nents. He spoke in glowing terms of what the new techniques had done
for his company. He also took the opportunity to scold the railroads,
who used great numbers of products like those his company made, for
making their own equipment rather than buying in the open market. He
was followed by Henry V. Shields, in charge of manufacturing at Bright-
on Mills, Passaic, New Jersey, producers of cotton duck. Then Frank
Gilbreth, whose name would come to rank just behind that of Frederick
W. Taylor as a synonym for scientific management, took the stand
briefly. All that Brandeis wanted from Gilbreth was to repair the damage which young Hathaway's remark about employment reductions had
done. Yes, indeed, replied Gilbreth, scientific management could be ap-

---

[30] *Ibid.*, 2655, 2688; *NYT*, Nov. 22, 1910, 6. If "scientific management" was to
make progress in American industry, such delicate points as its effect on total
employment would have to be handled in a much more diplomatic manner than
the goldfish bowl situation to which Brandeis had exposed it.

plied in union shops. In fact, "we have always made it a point to deal with unions by preference," he asserted.[31] It wasn't much, but it was something, and Brandeis, who already suspected where the real opposition to scientific management lay, was grateful for it.

But what had all this to do with the peculiar problems of railroads? It was one thing to say that shoveling coal, or stacking pig iron, or feeding metal blanks into a punch press, or replacing bobbins on a cotton-spinning machine was reducible to standard operations. So much was obvious. But Commissioner Prouty was growing impatient. He reminded Brandeis that unless he had some evidence on the practical application of scientific management to railroading, the hearings would have to pass on to other matters. Brandeis forged ahead. He placed Charles B. Going, editor of *Engineering Magazine,* on the stand to tell the gathering about the experiment which had been under way for several years on the Santa Fe, and which he had written up in his magazine. The experiment, Going explained, had been carried out in the railroad's locomotive shops, where many procedures similar to those of a manufacturing plant were involved. The Santa Fe, according to his information, was saving a million dollars a year by 1908 and was thinking of extending the system.[32]

Harrington Emerson, consulting mechanical engineer and the man directly in charge of the work at the Santa Fe, followed. Charming and highly persuasive, Emerson practiced a brand of scientific management that was very much his own, and considerably less "scientific" than that of Frederick W. Taylor.[33] Brandeis asked him if he was the person who was responsible for the statement that the railroads could save $300 million a year, or a million dollars a day? Emerson was proud to acknowledge that he was. What did he base it on? Merely the assumption that labor is always 5 per cent inefficient under ordinary circumstances. Brandeis, sensing perhaps that such a response was on not much firmer ground than the railroads' "feeling" that the proposed new rates were reasonable, hurried on. Where had Emerson first got the idea of apply-

[31] 1910 Hearings, 2776–77.   [32] *Ibid.,* 2822.

[33] Samuel Haber, "Scientific Management and the Progressive Movement" (doctoral dissertation, University of California, 1961), 75–77. [Published as *Efficiency and Uplift: Scientific Management in the Progressive Era, 1890–1920* (Chicago, 1964).]

ing scientific methods to the railroads? As far back as 1870, Emerson
answered, when he had observed the railroad operations of the Prussian
army in the war with France. Had American railroads, then, neglected
the scientific approach in comparison to European railroads? Indeed
they had, Emerson asserted, as shown by the fact that their costs were
up. Angry murmurs arose from the railroad men, who were hard put to
contain themselves at this point. Emerson hastily backtracked. Of
course, he acknowledged, the rapid change in design and the growth in
size of rolling stock, especially locomotives, entailed unusual costs.
Roadbeds, for example, frequently had to be rebuilt to take the newer
locomotives. At this stage Emerson had served his purpose and Brandeis excused him.[34]

VI

Railroad men, at first amused at Brandeis' blundering into an area
which they felt he and his witnesses could not possibly know anything
about, were thrown entirely off balance by the sensation which the tactics of the people's lawyer had produced. The obviously deep interest
with which the Commissioners had followed the proceedings had
wounded their egos profoundly. No group of businessmen in America
had more right to be proud of their accomplishments, or so they sincerely believed. The fact that they were not very articulate about their
achievements, and that the public at large and even the Commission
seemed to take these accomplishments for granted, did not make them
any less real. Yet here was one of the country's most skillful lawyers,
performing in a publicly provided forum attracting the widest possible
attention, casting the gravest doubt on the effectiveness with which they
had discharged their stewardship to the investing community and the
public at large. Their bitterness was beyond control. Brandeis' sincerity
was challenged. Vice-President W. L. Park of the Illinois Central called
him "a fool." A group of western railroad men composed a sarcastic

[34] 1910 Hearings, 2823–38. Emerson, if given the opportunity, might have cited
other examples of the higher costs involved in an industry whose technology was
changing rapidly. The situation of the railroads at this time was strikingly similar
to that of the airlines in the 1960s when they were converting to jet equipment.
The phenomenon, of course, is much better recognized today.

telegram and sent it, over the signature of O. L. Dickinson of the Burlington, inviting Brandeis to come to work for them, "allowing you to name your own salary," if he could indeed point out to them just where they were "wasting" a million dollars a day. The wire ended with the snide remark that the offer was made "in the same spirit of sincerity in which you rendered your statement to the Commission."

Such reactions were far from unwelcome to the people's lawyer, for the opportunity to turn the other cheek to the haughty railroad moguls was priceless. Brandeis grandly offered to work for them for nothing. He would arrange "conferences" with their representatives to show them just how scientific management could save them what he now referred to hedgingly as "a substantial portion of this amount." His real reason for working for the shippers without compensation, he insisted, was that the increased rates sought by the railroads "will ultimately be borne in large part by the consumer through increasing the cost of living, mainly of those least able to bear added burdens." There is little doubt that Brandeis sincerely meant every word of what he said, and the devastating effect of his remarks was to cause the railroad men to lapse into a sullen silence. Meanwhile millions of indignant Americans who knew nothing of the merits of the case and, in fact, had heard virtually nothing about the case up to then were now reading about it on the front pages of newspapers across the country.[35] The railroads had lost whatever popular support they had salvaged from the injunction proceedings of the previous spring. Whatever the Commission thought of the scientific management argument, Brandeis had provided the panel with all of the support it could conceivably need for a decision against the carriers.

Behind the adulatory chorus, however, was a group of doubting Thomases. Edward L. Suffern, president of the American Association of Public Accountants, declared in an interview with the New York *Times* that there was not much opportunity to apply industrial plant experience with time and motion studies to the railroad problem. Suffern's main criticism of Brandeis was that he ignored the "intermittent charac-

---

[35] *NYT*, Nov. 23, 1910, 4; Nov. 24, 8; Nov. 30, 1. The details of Brandeis' participation in the rate fight of 1910, and of the reaction of various groups to his scientific management ploy, are summarized with little critical understanding in Mason, *Brandeis*, 315–34.

ter" of railroad operations, which deprived them of one of the most fundamental bases for the routinization of repetitive manufacturing operations. But there was criticism of a more powerful nature than a group of accountants could offer. John M. Mitchell, the widely respected ex-president of the United Mine Workers and now a member of the National Civic Federation, attacked the people's lawyer for the manner in which he wanted to save money for the railroads. Mitchell claimed high esteem for Brandeis, but asserted, "I do not believe that the workmen employed by the railroads should do any more work than they are now doing. . . . If there is a waste of $300 million a year it lies outside the sphere of cost occupied by the workmen. And I am against the premium or bonus system and too much specialization." A psychologist, said Mitchell, had discovered recently that the monotony of labor could cause insanity.[36] This was the first major blast which organized labor was to level against Brandeis' philosophy that the productivity gains of scientific management could only benefit the worker, rather than exhaust him or put him out of work. The following month Warren S. Stone, Grand Chief Engineer of the Brotherhood of Locomotive Engineers, told the National Civic Federation with brutal frankness that the bonus system and his organization could not exist together on the same railroad.[37] In the next few years Louis Brandeis would fight this attitude in articles and speeches before workingmen. Had it been the only cause for which he was fighting it probably would have broken his heart, because the unions never in his time forsook their conviction that the new techniques were the speed-up in disguise, and that higher wages were unwelcome through a system which meant fewer jobs.

And what of the embattled railroad men, who had been so effectively ambushed? It seems to have come as a complete surprise that anyone could make a case against them out of something which had shown so little promise for their operations. They deeply mistrusted Brandeis'

[36] *NYT,* Dec. 11, 1910, 6. In their third-volume continuation of John R. Commons' *History of Labor in the United States,* covering the period 1896–1932 (New York, 1935), Don D. Lescohier and Elizabeth Brandeis condemn the labor theories of Frederick W. Taylor, and note that the railroads' protests that their workers would not permit scientific management to be introduced were borne out a year later when the unions successfully resisted its installation in the War Department's arsenals.

[37] Quoted in William J. Cunningham, "Scientific Management in the Operation of Railroads," *Quarterly Journal of Economics,* XXV (May, 1911), 555.

motives and resented the knight-errant role which he had taken upon himself. Some were inclined to attribute his lethal dedication to ambition and to the natural desire of a good lawyer to use whatever ammunition is at hand to win a case. There was probably much truth in this assessment. But what they seem to have failed to see in Brandeis—probably because it was such a common failing—was a devotion to a set of economic and social doctrines which were at best rather old-fashioned and at worst distinctly inimical to the interests of the very people whom he claimed to represent. The assumption that all rate increases would be automatically passed on to consumers was not warranted. As we have seen, transportation charges had become such a relatively small factor in the retail prices of a wide range of consumer goods, while market conditions and simple custom were such transcendent factors, that it is much more likely that increases in rates would have come out of manufacturers' and middlemen's profits. The zeal with which these interests fought the railroads throughout this period cannot be explained away as merely the industriousness of professional lobbyists or the self-serving actions of ambitious Progressive politicians. The railroad men, with just a little more economic sophistication than they could command from within their own organizations, could have demonstrated that the real costs of railroad transportation had been brought down dramatically since the turn of the century. If they were somewhat behind in the systematization of such repetitive processes as railroading embraced, account must be taken of the fact that labor cannot always be "mixed" with capital in the ideal manner when the qualitative nature as well as the quantity of that capital is changing as rapidly as it was in the railroad industry.[38] It was a far greater achievement, they might have pointed out, to have remained flexible and open to innovations which promised far greater savings in unit costs—or distinct improvements in the quality of the service—than to have inaugurated an extensive time and motion study program which might well have resulted in a freezing of attitudes and work procedures. Small gains in efficiency, theoretically, would in such circumstances have come at the expense of big innovative

[38] For a devastating indictment of economic history which is based on the altogether insupportable assumption that inputs in a "production function" are a "homogeneous jelly," see Edward Ames and Nathan Rosenberg, "The Enfield Arsenal in Theory and History," *Economic Journal*, LXXVIII (Dec., 1968), especially 831–35, 842.

improvements. But the most devastating rebuttal which the railroad men might have made was missed completely.

The remarkable fact is that the railroads, notwithstanding the abundance of legal talent with which they were supplied, were unable to see how the question of the efficiency with which they had discharged their stewardship to their stockholders and the public could possibly be made the subject of a public investigation carried on in the goldfish bowl of an ICC hearing. They were proud of their accomplishments in the preceding decade and they could not bring themselves to see where they were in any degree answerable to the sensational charges of a brilliant trial attorney. They lacked the creativeness, moreover, that was required to turn their hands to a rebuttal of the claims of Brandeis' witness, Emerson. Had they been able to do so, at the moment when the subject was front-page news, they could have put the people's lawyer and his "high priest of scientific management" to complete rout. A few minutes' work with the latest annual statistical report of the ICC was all that was required to demonstrate that the million-dollars-a-day argument was indeed, as the editor of the *Railway Age Gazette* had called it, the "merest moonshine." [39] The talented O. E. Butterfield, so soon to become general counsel of the vast New York Central system, might very quickly have made the mental calculation that an annual saving of $300 million, if predicated on labor's being 5 per cent inefficient, implied an annual wage bill of six billion dollars. Such an astronomical figure would have sent him hurrying to the statistical report where he would have discovered, to his immense satisfaction, that in the fiscal year ended June 30, 1910, the sum paid in wages had totaled barely one-sixth that amount: $1.1 billion. Emerson's 5 per cent could have amounted to no more than about $50 million a year, not much beyond

[39] "Railway Rates and Railway Efficiency," *Railway Age Gazette,* XLIX (Dec. 2, 1910), 1035. The editor cannily put his finger on one of the striking contradictions which marked the positions of the various groups who were fighting the rate increase: "It [Brandeis' theory] involves the abandonment of the theory on which the shippers heretofore have opposed advances in freight rates. Their contention has been that the railways have so greatly increased the efficiency of their plants and operating methods during the past ten years that, in spite of the advances . . . in the costs of labor and materials, they do not need higher rates." The shippers felt that prosperity precluded a rate increase; Brandeis argued that failure to follow an alternative path to prosperity precluded an increase. When two parties reach the same conclusion through diametrically opposed arguments, the inference is that they have prejudged the issue.

the $34 million which the railroad unions were already demanding in raises. To save $300 million the railroads would have had to eliminate nearly one-third of all their employees, even if they could have kept wages at existing levels. Such an abrupt "giant step" forward in industrial productivity hardly deserves consideration with a straight face, but to carry Emerson's testimony to its logical conclusion the point must be noted that the *gross* savings which he had in mind must have been even larger inasmuch as the entire system of scientific management is based on the payment of some of the savings to the men in the form of bonuses.

VII

Six months after the scientific management furor, when all of the news value had gone out of the allegations of inefficiency of railroad management, William J. Cunningham, professor of political economy at Harvard, published a sober, scholarly article in the *Quarterly Journal of Economics* which cast the gravest doubt on the assertion that the techniques of time and motion study were widely applicable to railroad operations. The economist completely demolished the idea that the possibility of great savings in a short period of time was being ignored by railroad men. Cunningham's first step had been to go to see Emerson. That gentleman, having had plenty of time since the hearings to revise the inconsistencies in his testimony, gave the Harvard professor a vastly different story. His experience at the Santa Fe, he said, had revealed that various departments of railroad operation were from 50 to 80 per cent efficient. Fuel consumption, he pontificated, was only 50 per cent efficient.[40] Cunningham's calculations showed clearly why the efficiency expert had so radically changed his position. The famous one million dollars a day amounted to 23 per cent of the railroads' entire wage bill

[40] Cunningham, "Scientific Management," 546. Note the efficiency expert's tendency to confuse potential savings in the use of labor with potential savings through technological advances. Unless Emerson really believed that firemen were carelessly slinging half of their coal about the cabs of their locomotives, he must have known that the problem of wringing more energy out of a pound of coal was one of equipment design and had almost nothing to do with work practices.

and anticipated discharging 310,000 men out of about 1.5 million then working on the railroads. The implied decline in the operating ratio was from 66 per cent to a fabulous 51 per cent! The professor wasted no more time on Emerson's data but proceeded to consider the engineer's qualifications to criticize the efficiency with which railroads in general conducted their work.

It had escaped everyone's attention, he said, that Emerson had been retained by the Santa Fe in 1904 to bring order out of chaos in a maintenance shop which the railroad had been attempting to operate in the face of a protracted machinists' strike. Santa Fe executives had blustered at the height of the strike that they were managing quite well without the union men but the fact is that skilled machinists were (and still are) among the scarcest of workers and the strikebreakers who had been hired were, in a word, "incompetent." Add to this, Cunningham pointed out, the fact that the Santa Fe had not got around to using high-speed drills (Frederick W. Taylor's great contribution to industrial productivity) until Emerson's sojourn there, even though they had been in general use on the railroads almost from the beginning, and you had a field observation which was totally unrepresentative of the situation on American railroads in general.[41]

Cunningham had two more points to make about the real possibilities of introducing time and motion techniques to railroading. He detailed a number of hard facts about the nature of railroad operations which the inarticulate executives had tried to bring out during the hearings. To these he added the comment that the ICC's requirement that railroads compete with each other led inevitably to underutilization of cars, which were one of their most important items of equipment. Cars were frequently sent away with light loads, and they often sat on sidings while valued customers took their time about unloading them.[42] A much greater obstacle to the introduction of scientific management, however, lay in the attitudes of "militant" labor leaders.[43] The professor showed a greater practical familiarity with the accomplishments of American railroads than many a man charged with formulation of national policy had revealed during the rate hearings. "The history of American railways," he wrote, "shows that their progress has been steady and substantial." They were, in fact, as acutely aware of the

[41] *Ibid.*, 547.   [42] *Ibid.*, 552.   [43] *Ibid.*, 555.

rapid flow of technological change as any branch of industry. Professional organizations devoted to the application of the latest ideas abounded, he said, mentioning the Car Efficiency Committee of the American Railway Association and the Railway Signal Association, among others.[44] He might have made one more point, his most telling, had the concept of labor productivity been as well developed then as it is today. Employment on the railroads had nearly doubled since 1898, but traffic carried had risen even more. In terms of output of transportation services per employee, American railroads were 20 per cent more efficient in 1910 than in 1898. At the very moment when railroad men were allowing themselves to be roasted at Brandeis' inefficiency stake they had behind them a twelve-year history in which they had actually bettered their performance four times over by the magic 5 per cent which the devastating little lawyer had pulled out of the air.[45]

Brandeis' use of the scientific management argument in the 1910 rate hearings is comfortably within the tradition of Anglo-Saxon trial procedure, which conceives of litigation as an adversary proceeding. It was not his fault that the Commission, almost without any reflection that it was doing so, conceived of its proceedings in that light. He had clients who believed that they stood to lose by higher rates, and he served them well in their equity proceeding by searching tirelessly for the best foundation for his case. When he had found it he guarded it well until it could be used most effectively. With greater legal and statistical resources at their command the railroads had made no legal case for a rate increase, and had failed miserably even to spread on the record the true story of their considerable accomplishments. A general rate increase was probably a political impossibility in 1910. Even if the railroads were bound to lose their case, however, they might have done so with style and dignity. The question of whether Brandeis' tactics were appropriate for a "people's lawyer," with all that the term implies as to the taking of a broad, long-range view of the economic needs of society, is one with which the great jurist's future biographer must wrestle. That the episode provides an opportunity to portray the man as more of a human being and less of a saint seems beyond question. Louis Brandeis was a prodigiously creative lawyer in the sense that he knew how to look far beyond the boundaries of conventional legal

[44] *Ibid.,* 557, 559.   [45] See Chapter III above.

knowledge for the foundations of his arguments. He does not seem, however, to have possessed the analytical mind of the economist or the statistician which, even in 1910, would have led him to see that Emerson's claims were pure hokum. Perhaps he was not of a mind to try too hard to test his evidence. To a person of Brandeis' background the moral superiority of old-fashioned, perfect-competition, small-firm liberalism was bound to be as much a religious conviction as a scientific fact, and his eagerness to employ the crushing power of government to bring back a past that never was is poignantly self-contradictory in its authoritarian, father-knows-best fervor.

This stage of the people's lawyer's career, finally, will have to be judged on the question of whether his work in the 1910 case served the American people in their quest for a bigger and better transportation system. It seems to have served that purpose very badly indeed. The scientific management argument and the floor speeches about the evils of "giantism" were a tragic obfuscation of the main issue, which was the economic reasonableness of the proposed rate increases. There was no logical link between Brandeis' claim that the railroads could operate more efficiently and the fact that in being bypassed in an inflationary economy their substantial productivity gains were being absorbed into other areas of the economy when they should have been plowed back into the railroads, where they were being produced and where opportunities for still more gains abounded. When the time came for these truths to be apparent, Louis Brandeis would be among the first to recognize them.

When the Commission reassembled the parties in January to hear the final arguments, Brandeis outshone everybody in his three-hour summary. By now it was his show. Even Clifford Thorne, who had his own political future to consider, was unrestrained in his deference to Brandeis, who he agreed should be the last to speak for the shippers.[46] As for the railroad men, they had little enough to be gay about. Only one man, Chairman Knapp, of all the Commissioners before whom they had appeared, seemed to them to have a real understanding of what the

---

[46] Mason, *Brandeis,* 333. Thorne's argument that the railroads were overcapitalized and their return on investment fictitiously low, which he had presented at the end of November, was pathetically "old hat" in comparison to Brandeis' high-voltage arguments. *NYT,* Dec. 1, 1910, 8; 1910 Hearings, 5182, 5251.

railroads had accomplished in the past decade, and of what was needed in order to keep up the pace. They had just learned that even this one friend at court would not participate in the decision—that his seat and, in fact, the existing vacancy on the panel would be taken over by two men who had made careers of state regulation of railroads. This was bitter news indeed. President Taft, now that he had his beloved Commerce Court, was determined to give it every chance of success. He urged Knapp to head it. With considerable misgivings as to the future of the court, but with the prestige of permanent rank as a federal judge to make up for whatever might befall, the veteran Commissioner consented. A few days before Christmas the Senate Judiciary Committee singled out the appointment for special attention. A few hours later the Committee on Interstate Commerce confirmed the nominations of Balthasar H. Meyer and C. C. McChord to be members of the ICC. Not a single Insurgent voted against Knapp's appointment, although there had been some rumblings about his being "friendly" to the railroads. If one was an enemy of the railroads in 1910, however, one could have wished for no better place for a friend of the railroads than a seat on the Commerce Court.[47] The ordeal of the railroad executives, in any event, would soon be over, for the Commission had promised an early decision. As they stole back to their offices at the end of the arguments in January, few of them can have believed that they had much to look forward to.

VIII

A harried railroad executive who sought escape from his cares with the Sunday New York *Times* for February 26, 1911, would have had his mind drawn abruptly back to recent disappointments by the painting which decorated the cover of the rotogravure section. It was a sentimental genre picture, as usual. This one portrayed a great dog benignly keeping watch beside a crib in which an angelic baby lay sleeping. Beneath the reproduction was the title: *"In Loco Parentis."* The railroad man might never have noticed the picture, much less have known what the title meant, had it not been for the fact that he would

[47] *NYT*, Dec. 21, 1910, 5.

have just finished reading the adverse decisions of the ICC in the rate cases. Franklin K. Lane had emphatically declared that the Commission did not stand *in loco parentis* to the railroads. Their argument, he wrote, had been, "We need the money," but "the government has not undertaken to become the directing mind in railroad management." Besides, he reasoned, twisting the knife, the roads had done better under strict government control than before. Whatever the Commission was, it was certainly no watchdog for the interests of the railroads.[48]

The decisions, the western one by Lane and the eastern one by Prouty, shocked the railroad men by their uncompromising tone. Lane took 78 pages—an extraordinary length for an ICC decision—to declare over and over again that the railroads had never had things so good. He cited the testimony of Ripley of the Santa Fe, "which, it may be said, was the broadest and most statesmanlike of any given herein," to the effect that rates before regulation were too low and that now that strict regulation prevailed, the Commission ought to put rates "upon a paying basis." Lane all but taunted the roads for asking for something from regulation which they had never been able to achieve on their own.[49] But, he insisted, while costs had gone up, earnings were up, too.[50] It is true that 1910 had been a good year for the roads, possibly the best year since the record year of 1907. Apparently any factor making for a high level of earnings, no matter how exceptional in light of previous years' experience and no matter how temporary the peak volume giving rise to it, would be sufficient to justify a ruling against the railroads where their case was based, as this one was, on insufficient earning capacity. And, the Commissioner added significantly, thinking no doubt about Brandeis' sensational revelations, "cost figures furnished

[48] 20 ICC 307, 316–17.

[49] *Ibid.,* 318. Lane, who had headed the investigation of Harriman which President Roosevelt had ordered in 1906–7, knew perfectly well that the railroads had been making great progress toward tightly knit communities of interest before Attorney General Bonaparte threatened them with criminal prosecution for violation of the antitrust laws in 1906. The period from 1897 to 1906, when the Commission exercised no substantial powers, was the most favorable in railroad history. Lane knew that it was the carriers' stronger position that had brought on the demand for strict regulation, and not the reverse.

[50] The Commissioners could not make up their minds on what had happened to costs. Actually, prices of materials had fallen sharply, but very temporarily, following the 1907 panic; while wages only went up.

would indicate that under skillful management an additional tonnage may be handled under a higher wage schedule without increasing the cost of the service given." [51]

Lawyers scanned the decision for clues as to what the Commission would consider proof of reasonableness of rates in the future. They found some arid legal verbiage, but little that was concrete to guide them. Lane did make clear one thing: proof of reasonableness was to be defined much more rigorously in the United States than in England. In that country, when Parliament had passed the Railway and Canal Acts in 1891 and 1892, it had declared that in future a railroad would have to justify only the increase in a proposed new rate. In other words, as interpreted by the English courts, the maximum rate act automatically endowed all of the existing rates with the aura of reasonableness.[52] Not so in the case of the U.S. Congress. Under the Mann-Elkins Act the rate as a whole had to be justified, and the burden of proof, furthermore, was on the carrier. Each rate was open to question in its entirety, not just in respect to the proposed increment. This meant that what had been before the Commission all the time had been not the question of the increases which the roads sought but the entire rate, including the pre-increase component, even though it might have been in effect since before 1887 and never have been challenged by a shipper before. The carriers were forced to conclude, therefore, that their efforts to get the Commission to consider a general increase, even though it applied to only a portion of the total tariff, had had no legal standing throughout the proceedings.

Having thus dramatized to the railroads how magnanimous the Commission had been to entertain the railroads' request in the form presented, Lane went on to leaven his legal lecture with some common sense. "It is doubtless true that in its control over the charges which the railroads make this Commission exercises a power so extensive as to justify the broadest consideration of the economic and financial effects of its orders, but the government has not undertaken to become the directing mind in railroad management. This Commission is not a general manager of the railroads, and no matter what the revenue the carriers

[51] 20 ICC 307, 307.

[52] *Mansion House Cases*, 1894 (9 *R. & C. T. Cases*, 58), cited in 20 ICC 307, 312.

may receive there can be no control placed by the Commission upon its expenditure, no improvements directed, and no economies enforced." Here was Herbert Croly's fear about emasculation of the "vivacious bull" made real, and without any recognition of the duty of the castrater to fatten the animal into something useful.

If the railroad men looked hard enough, however, they could find some kind of a rule of rate-making—at least, one that made sense to a westerner like Lane. "It appears," he wrote, "that these commodity rates already paid their due share of the value of the service rendered by the carriers. Many of them, in fact, are now twice as high for the haul immediately west of Chicago as corresponding rates for a similar haul immediately east of Chicago." There was no mention of the fact that the volume of traffic on eastern roads more than made up for the lower rates. The generally higher rates on western roads had their origin in the extremely thin traffic of the early days and to some extent were still justified; but resentment of the differentials would explain in great measure the even tougher stand which the Commission was to take against the western railroads in the next few years.[53]

Wherever the railroad men turned in the lengthy decision, their way was blocked. Where practical economics did not serve, Lane cited the law of 1910, poorly conceived as it was. If the railroads complained about insufficient earnings to support needed capital programs, he reminded them that 1910 had been a very good year and ignored the implications of the fact that 1910 was, indeed, exceptional. As far as business conditions were concerned, the Commission's attitude was one of wait-and-see. If the carriers represented their increases as low in comparison to the general inflation, they were reminded that they had to justify the entire rate—hundreds of thousands of rates though there were—and not just the increase. The law might have been a bad one, but the interpretation of it was excellent. Just to make sure that no one should expect the Commission to take the bit of social progress in its teeth, Lane closed with a statement that was conservative indeed for him: "The railroads may not look to this tribunal to negative or modify

[53] 20 ICC 307, 308. Just how much of a differential was still justified is impossible to know, but the fact that the financial condition of the western railroads was worsening more rapidly than that of the eastern roads indicates that it was, if anything, too small.

the expressed will of the legislature. They have laid before the Commission the facts . . . but to the mind of the Commission their justification has not been convincing." [54] It was enough to make strong men weep. But the bitterest pill of all was the westerner's altogether gratuitous observations on the carriers' motivations in bringing the application for higher rates before the Commission in the first place. When the investigation began, he wrote, it had been the impression of the Commission that higher costs had impelled the proposed increase. It became manifest, he said, that the purpose of the carriers was not so much to secure approval of these specific rates "as to discover the mind of the Commission with respect to the policy which the carriers might in future pursue and to secure if possible some commitment on our part as to a nationwide policy which would give the carriers loose rein." The intensely political Lane, who had no intention of remaining an Interstate Commerce Commissioner forever, could not pass up the opportunity to show the folks back home that these city slickers were not putting anything over on him.[55] And so he portrayed the railroads as seeking, in bad faith, something which they did not need and which they had no legal right to ask for. Could anyone be *that* bad?

Commissioner Prouty's goals were more modest than Lane's, and 48 pages sufficed for him to give the *coup de grâce* to the eastern railroads' hopes. He managed to put in a few words for some favorite themes of his own, however. His attitude was kind compared to Lane's, even if his awareness of the crisis which the railroads faced was no more realistic. "There is no evidence before the Commission . . . for higher rates. The probability is that increased rates will not be necessary in the future . . . [but] if actual results should demonstrate that the Commission's forecast of the future is wrong, there might be grounds for asking a further consideration of this subject." The Brandeisian lance was revealed firmly stuck in the eastern railroads' hides: "We cannot escape the impression that the railroad operators have not given to this important subject [scientific management] the attention it deserves." Prouty wanted it clearly understood that he did not believe that the applicability of time and motion techniques to the railroads had

[54] *Ibid.*

[55] *Ibid.*, 316. This brutal blow at the railroads drew widespread attention. *NYT,* Feb. 24, 1911, 1–2.

been proved, but that the possibility had been duly taken note of by the Commission. He seemed to feel that the fact that business had "adjusted itself" to the existing rates over a thirty-year period was important, although just why the typically nimble American businessman should receive this consideration was not made clear.

Prouty seized the opportunity to renew the plea for a comprehensive physical valuation of the assets of American railroads which he and many other Progressives had been voicing for years. It was obvious that he believed that any decision on reasonableness of rates was a makeshift as long as profits could not be related to actual value of plant. "It is plain," he wrote, "that a physical valuation would introduce into the calculation a new element which might lead to a different conclusion. Congress ought to authorize a reproductive valuation of those railroads subject to Federal jurisdiction." [56] The crusty Vermonter then stiff-armed what the railroads had considered perhaps their most powerful argument—the demands which organized labor was making on them: "This Commission certainly could not permit the charging of rates for the purpose of enabling railroads to pay their laborers extravagant compensation as measured by the general average compensation paid labor in this country as a whole." To the Commissioner, apparently, labor relations on the railroads were still a fair fight and a private matter.[57]

But Prouty knew that there was something wrong with the way the American transportation system was developing, and he thought the fault lay in the railroad men's understandable desire not to overexpand. This philosophy, he breezily informed them, they must forsake. The scandalous situation of 1907 must not be permitted to happen again:

There had been for 12 years a rapid and constant development of business, but the feeling had been that this increase would not continue. Railroad operators as a whole had not felt justified in making the outlay which would be required if the growth of business was to continue. In consequence the facilities of all kinds in that year were inadequate to the traffic offered.

[56] 20 ICC 243, 243, 279. As we have already noted (Chapter IV), a valuation project was authorized in 1913. After fifteen years of work and hundreds of millions of dollars of taxpayers' and railroads' money (which revealed just what a Pandora's box Prouty had pried open), it was concluded that the fair physical value of the railroads (at prewar prices) virtually equaled their capitalization.

[57] 20 ICC 243, 278.

The business of 1907 was, in fact, handled, but not in a way satisfactory to the public. As this Commission will understand from its own investigations, transportation conditions were deplorable. A continuance of these conditions should not have been and would not have been tolerated. It was the duty of our railroads to provide at once improved facilities. That should have been done at once even though the traffic of 1907 was not to be exceeded.[58]

The Commissioner was not attracted, however, to arguments that improvements should be paid for by charging to current expense (even if the improvements did not add to earning power) or out of surplus. The present should not be charged, under any circumstances, for benefits that would accrue only in the future. "Each generation may well be required to bear its own burden, and the stockholder should not obtain both an adequate dividend upon his stock and an addition to the value of his property." Rates, in other words, need not be high enough to ensure a surplus. Shippers (not to mention consumers) should not have to pay anything toward expansion of the transportation plant; that was the role of the investor.[59] Thus was the aging railroad Samson given the jawbone of an ass and sent out to slay the Philistines.

The *Commercial and Financial Chronicle,* always anxious to show businessmen its powers of indignation, declared that "the character of the decisions proved a complete surprise." The editor could not have been more wrong. Ever since that chilling episode in Chicago when Commissioner Clark had asked the shippers for advice on how to proceed to deny the increases, railroad men had had few grounds for optimism. They had been sulking in their tents ever since Brandeis had insulted them on the front page of every newspaper in America in respect to the one thing they held most dear after their wives and children. They could take little comfort from the *Chronicle*'s assurance that it was Taft's moving Knapp to the Commerce Court and his appointment of Meyer and McChord which had "served to solidify the radical element in the Commission, leaving no recognized conservative representatives on the Board." [60] As far as they could see, the issue was settled. It

[58] *Ibid.,* 283.

[59] *Ibid.,* 266. Although modern economists will smile at such childlike ignorance of the dynamics of saving and investment, it was entirely typical. But compare it to Knapp's philosophy as expressed in his speech before the railroad suppliers (Chapter VI).

[60] CFC, BQS, XCII (March 4, 1911), 19.

would be three years before the railroad men would take Prouty's hint
and try again. Reports of retrenchments began to pour in. The Central
cut its dividend from six dollars to five. The Harriman roads were reported to be economizing. Chairman Elbert Gary of U.S. Steel agonized
publicly that the railroads, which usually bought about a third of his
output, were now taking only 7 to 8 per cent.[61] Investors began to
doubt that the railroads would ever get an increase. They almost turned
out to be right.[62]

[61] *Ibid.,* XCII (April 8, 1911), 19; May 6, 19; XCIII (Sept. 2, 1911), 19.

[62] The historian of the ICC believes that the panel acted reasonably in the absence of any knowledge of what lay ahead. "These proceedings, in themselves,
evince no evidence of an unduly restrictive approach, however unsatisfactory their
outcome may be deemed in the light of subsequent developments which could not
be anticipated. The full import of the Commission's policy will appear only after
the later advanced rate cases of this decade have been analyzed and appraised." I.
L. Sharfman, *The Interstate Commerce Commission: A Study in Administrative
Law and Procedure* (4 vols. in 5, New York, 1931–37), IIIb, 48. But if any group
connected with these proceedings had the responsibility of courageously interpret-
ing the decline in railroad profits in 1908, the approaching demands of labor to
share in the increased productivity of railroads, the continued upward trend in
demands on the system, and the rampant inflation itself, it was the ICC. It is not
unreasonable to suppose that the philosophy which caused the Commission to adhere to its basic policy of no increases (with minor exceptions) right down to the
wartime transportation crisis was already at work in 1910. There was nothing
which interposed itself between 1911 and 1914 to create such a policy where
none had existed in 1910. In view of the legislative history of the Mann-Elkins
Act, and the unsettled political atmosphere in which it was passed, it seems fair
to conclude that such a policy was implicit in the act itself.

CHAPTER VIII

THE SHIFTING SANDS OF
PUBLIC OPINION

How long halt ye between two opinions? I KINGS, *18:21*

By their fruits ye shall know them. MATTHEW, *2:20*

I

"They may experience a little difficulty in finding other meat that is quite so tender, but it is to be hoped they won't starve to death." A band of cannibals flees in terror from a troop of federal soldiers who rescue, in the nick of time, a ragged missionary tied to a tree near the pot in which he was about to be boiled. To a young artist named Jay N. Darling, who had a great future before him as the nation's leading newspaper cartoonist, the cannibals were the railroads, who had just been thwarted in their horrible plan to devour the nation's shippers by the dramatic arrival on the scene of the Interstate Commerce Commission. His cartoon on the ICC's decision in the 1910 rate case fitted the editorial policy of the Des Moines, Iowa, *Register and Leader,* perfectly.[1] And the Iowa newspaper's viewpoint probably reflected the attitudes of an overwhelming majority of westerners. Their elation at the smashing success of insurgent regulation in turning back the depredations of eastern capitalism was hardly to be measured. The inferiority complex which the isolated populations of the Great Plains and the Pacific slope had felt for decades was blissfully soothed by the victory in which one of their own sons (adopted, to be sure, as a good many sons of the West were) had participated so prominently. There was in the air west of the Mississippi and especially west of Kansas City the heady feeling that the center of gravity in national affairs was finally moving

[1] "Future Effects of the Rate Decision," *Literary Digest* (hereinafter referred to as *LD*), XLII (March 11, 1911), 441.

toward the land of those humble, plain-spoken, rugged people who fed
and clothed the nation. They had much to be proud of, and they beat
their drum in a concerted manner which the effete east seemed incapable of emulating. A year before *Collier's* magazine had shown the nation how the West felt in an article built around an insulting cartoon
from the Denver *Post*. A fat, elderly schoolboy, squeezed behind his
desk, listened attentively to a lecture being delivered, apparently in uni-
son, by a group of cap-and-gowned professors representing Judge Ben
Lindsey, who had captured the nation's admiration for his juvenile
court work in Denver; Senators La Follette and Dolliver, leading senatorial Insurgents; Joseph Polk, municipal reformer; and George
"Freight Rate" Kindel, whose efforts to get freight rate reform for "a
wide-awake and oppressed section" was the main point of the article.
"Go west, old man, and get educated," sneered the *Post*.[2]

The nation as a whole had been relieved, if not exactly elated, at
this reprieve from higher transportation costs. " 'The public gains and
the railroads don't lose,' seems to be the majority verdict of the newspapers," said the editor of an influential weekly, noting that the bad drop
in the market which followed the decision was erased and completely
forgotten within two days. Henry Clews, aging chronicler of Wall
Street, chose to look on the bright side. "It averts a possible congestion
of the security market by the flood of new issues which would certainly
have followed had the railroads secured what they wanted," he rationalized. The *Journal of Commerce* sought to assure businessmen that the
setback was certain to improve sentiment for the railroads by showing
that they were not beyond control, and hoped that this assertion of absolute federal power would "check the aggressiveness of state commissions." The Columbus, Ohio, *Ohio State Journal* lauded Brandeis' efforts with the observation that "the truest progress has a strain of
economy running through it." [3] Brandeis himself could not resist one
more contribution to the dyspepsia of railroad executives by declaring
that "the time is not far distant when it will be recognized by them to
have been a great blessing," by introducing them to scientific management. The professional managers of shipper organizations moved
quickly to collect their kudos. " [The Commission's action] assures the

[2] *Collier's,* XLIV (Jan. 15, 1910), 19.
[3] "Future Effects of the Rate Decision," 441.

roads prosperity at the present rates," concluded John M. Glenn, secretary of the powerful Illinois Manufacturers Association, which had led the industrial shippers in their opposition to the increases. "This talk of business depression is ridiculous. Business will take a big jump as a result of the decision," trumpeted the Association's Director, John W. Wilder. The New York *World* said the decision was the "beginning of a new era; railroad rates are no longer to be juggled to suit the purposes of Wall Street. . . . It halts the agitation for government ownership by proving that there can be effective government regulation for protection of shippers and the public." Even the New York *Herald,* a strongly conservative friend of business, said that the failure to obtain a moderate increase, even though one should have been granted, was no reason to be "panic-stricken," and it betrayed a characteristic unawareness of the absoluteness of the Commission's new powers by declaring that "it is not the court of last resort." [4]

Nobody paid much attention to the railroad men's disappointment, although George F. Baer, who had served well as sensational copy since his famous remark about the God-given role of capitalists during the anthracite strike a few years before, received some unneeded publicity. The decision, he grumbled, was "a great blow to the railroads," and in true pessimist style he went on to say, "I do not see how some of them will get along." L. W. Hill of the Great Northern could not hide his bitterness. "I will take a trip to Europe this year," he threatened, "as there won't be much use of my staying around here next summer; there won't be much done in the way of extensions and improvements." [5] There was one segment of the economy rapped by the decision, however, which did not intend to take the implications of the decision lying down. Railroad labor had no feeling of impotence and frustration to match that of their employers, and the comments of one of their number should have signaled the crisis which was coming. "Employees will be the ones to lose through it," grunted W. G. Lee, head of the trainmen, who foresaw a movement to reduce wages. Prouty's pot-shot at labor in his eastern decision had stung badly. "The decision establishes a dangerous precedent," Lee continued. "At this rate we will ultimately have a Commission empowered to prevent the workingmen of the country from de-

[4] "Railroads Forbidden to Take More," *LD,* XLII (March 4, 1911), 389–91.

[5] *Ibid.*

manding increased pay." Here, if anywhere, is the point at which trade union policy on the railroad question crystallized.[6]

II

In the excitement and relief over the rate-increase proceedings, it almost escaped notice that in the Mann-Elkins Act the conservatives in the badly split Republican party had salvaged something, even if not very much. There were, after all, the commission for the investigation of railroad securities flotations which Senator Aldrich had managed to substitute for a provision vesting the ICC with the power to regulate such issues; and the Commerce Court, just getting into operation under the leadership of former ICC Chairman Knapp. Late in 1910 a distinguished commission was appointed under the Act of 1910 and charged with preparing a report on the railroad securities situation, with recommendations. It was headed by Arthur Twinging Hadley, president since 1899 of Yale and one of the earliest academic writers on the subject of railroads and their regulation. Frederick N. Judson, a lawyer who had helped the government prosecute the Santa Fe for rebating, provided the shippers' viewpoint, and Frederick Strauss, a prominent Wall Street investment banker, represented the financial community. From Wisconsin came Balthasar H. Meyer, who ably represented the midwestern state-commission philosophy. Walter L. Fisher, a Chicagoan who had protected the city against predatory traction interests and who would shortly become Secretary of the Interior, completed the panel.

Hearings were held that fall and winter and in February a report of modest dimensions was filed. It was in most respects a very conservative document, particularly in its philosophy on the old question of public versus private control of business. But in its stand on the several controversial technical matters before the commission, notably the question of no-par-value stock, it was elegantly professional and far-seeing in contrast to the general level of economic thought at that time. The report first of all took an emphatic stand on the importance of the railroads to the nation and the acuteness of their financial needs:

[6] "Future Effects of the Rate Decision," 441.

There is a widespread belief, based on imperfect examination of the evidence, that the amount of capital needed for the future development of our railroad system is small . . . and that we can therefore fix attention predominantly if not exclusively on the needs of the shipper. . . . The building of additional mileage will be far less rapid . . . but the capital needed for the development and the improvement of the mileage already existing is enormous. . . . As our population grows denser, we shall need more and more to approximate European standards. . . . The average capital per mile in Germany is $109,000, in France $137,000, in Belgium $177,000, in Great Britain $265,000 [and in the United States $60,000]; and contrary to the commonly received opinion, much of this excess of cost . . . is due to other causes than the price of real estate . . . [but rather] to improvements which we have not yet made and many of which we must make in the future.[7]

The Hadley Commission did not believe that as things stood the nation was going to get that ample development of its railroads which the future demanded. "Neither the rate of return actually received on the par value of American railroad bonds and stocks today, nor the security which can be offered for additional railroad investments in the future, will make it easy to raise the needed amount of capital." [8] The national banks, the report noted, were accustomed to paying 10 to 11 per cent on their capital, whereas the railroads could manage only 4.5 per cent. And there was a question of risk to be considered. The railroads, especially the major lines, were well situated to make money, but they were hardly risk-free. In fact, the Commission hinted, the stringent new regulatory laws could become, if not administered wisely, an artificial form of risk which could drive away capital. "A reasonable return is one which under honest accounting and responsible management will attract the amount of investor's money needed for the development of our national railroad facilities." Risk and profits must be commensurate. "If rates are to be reduced every time dividends are raised, investors will seek other fields." [9] In other words, if investors were to be asked to assume the usual risk of loss without any hope of a handsome return should the investment prove to have been especially productive, then America's railroads could no longer expect to be financed through cus-

[7] *Report of the Railroad Securities Commission to the President,* House Document 256, 62d Cong., 2d Sess. (Washington, 1911), 32–33. (Hereinafter referred to as the Hadley Commission Report.)

[8] *Ibid.,* 33.   [9] *Ibid.,* 34.

tomary financial channels. "No attempt," the Hadley Commission declared, "should be made by statute to limit railroad profits to a fixed percentage." [10]

The Commission took note of the imperfect state of financial sophistication which still existed in respect to the distinctions between bonds and common stock, that quaint confusion which led investors and lawmakers to talk in terms of the percentage yield on common stock (of which the actual value might be far above or below par), and public bodies to complain of rates "based" on excessive capitalization. "Your Commission believes that the amount and face value of outstanding securities has only an indirect effect upon the actual making of rates," said the panel, "and that it should have little if any weight in their regulation." [11] But the general public, it noted, was determined to go to any length to keep the railroads from earning a return on capital not actually invested. This determination exceeded even the normal concern with what the public was getting from its railroads. "To most people the danger of these financial consequences [bankruptcy, poor service, inability to raise capital] seem a less serious thing than the danger that the railroads will tax the users of the road for the sake of making profits on capital not actually furnished." If common stock was to be issued with a par value—that is, with a dollar denomination displayed on the certificate—then certainly the government should make certain that it was fully paid in. [12] But why bring the subject up? Why not recognize, as was recognized in the proceedings on the stock exchange day after day, that no specific dollar value attached to an equity security; that it was, in fact, merely a percentage share in the going value of the business? "We do not believe that the retention of the hundred dollar mark, or any other dollar mark, upon the face of a share of stock, is of essential importance." And the Commission startled the financial world by recommending a law encouraging the issuance of no-par-value stock. [13]

[10] *Ibid.*, 27.   [11] *Ibid.*, 36.

[12] *Ibid.*, 37. This preoccupation with the idea that adherence to the rules was more important than the practical results attained is, perhaps, the quintessence of the spirit of the "age of reform."

[13] *Ibid.*, 25. Just how radical this recommendation was can be appreciated by reading the impassioned plea for par-value stock which William Z. Ripley made in his highly influential volumes, *Railroads: Finance and Organization* (New York, 1915), 89–94, and *Railroads: Rates and Regulation* (New York, 1912),

Those who felt that the railroads had not got a completely fair deal in the 1910 rate case could hardly fail to be pleased with the Hadley Commission's report. It asked nothing of the railroads and their bankers which they had not long since become accustomed to reveal, and which sophisticated investors had not long since come to demand anyway. What the public had a right to, and what the government had a duty to extract from the railroads, was "accurate knowledge of the facts concerning the issue of securities and the expenditures of the proceeds." All that needed to be done to make certain this information was accurate should be done. Beyond that, the government should not attempt a detailed regulation of railroad securities flotations.[14]

Where the report was lacking was in a discussion of that knotty question of the surplus. As the next few years would reveal, the men of this period had a most imperfect understanding of what the surplus was, to whom it belonged, and what could legitimately be done with it. In our day of full acquaintance with the concept of internal financing of expansion or improvement of business enterprise through the plowing back of profits not needed for dividends, it is virtually impossible to understand the prejudice which existed against allowing an increase in the stockholders' equity at the expense of the shipping public, as the operating surplus was widely viewed. It is difficult to escape the conclusion that the Hadley Commission itself lacked an understanding of the role of internal financing as the handmaiden of external financing, and especially of the function of innovation—from whence surplus profits flow, if they flow at all—in economic growth. Nor can we really believe that even if it had dilated wisely upon these points, such concepts would have made much headway in the world of 1911.

Progressives, archaic and otherwise, and the railroad world itself, watched fishy-eyed as the new Commerce Court took up its duties in 1911. No one had any idea what to expect from it. It is doubtful that even President Taft, whose pet idea it was, could have explained in more than the most unsatisfactory general terms just what it was to do. If it was to have more than mere procedural review powers over the

---

575–76. A decade later, moreover, there was still considerable support for par-value stock; cf. James C. Bonbright, *Railroad Capitalization: A Study of the Principles of Regulation of Railroad Securities* (New York, 1920), 111–24.

[14] Hadley Commission Report, 37.

ICC, it was obvious that it was going to have to fight for them. The Commission was feeling its oats, and if it is too colorful to say that that group of sobersides was drunk with power, at least it was acutely aware of the tremendous power which resided in the term "independent regulatory commission." Heading the new court, however, was a man who had taken his cue for the formulation of a national railroad policy from Theodore Roosevelt, and who was no archaic Progressive or midwestern Insurgent on fire with the determination to whip the railroads into dumb submission. How much longer Martin A. Knapp, with his ideas about the need to finance improvements out of current earnings, the wisdom of freeing the railroads from the anomalies of the antitrust law, and the urgent demand for a workable concept of reasonableness of rates, would have lasted on the Commission is anybody's guess. Certain it is that he would have felt increasingly lonely in the company of the Meyers, Proutys, Clements, Clarks, and McChords who now constituted the majority. But he still knew a great deal about government regulation of railroads, and his ideas were still very much in demand. In the fall of 1911 he was invited to deliver a series of lectures at the University of Pennsylvania. What he said to the students and professors in mid-November constituted a warning of the crunch between the Commerce Court, the Commission, and the Congress which was to come sooner and more dramatically than anyone realized. The genial little judge was uncharacteristically pessimistic about the existing system of regulation. It was "on trial," he said, and sooner or later the inconsistencies of the situation would have to be reckoned with. He made clear what they were:

I see constant dangers in the present condition. Congress is constantly agitated. So are the legislatures of all the states. Forty state commissions are wrestling with the subject. There is the menace of stubborn conflict between the railroads and their two million organized employees. Finally there is the menace of political influence. . . . The shipper is not always the underdog. Too often it happens that he is dishonest and that the carrier is wronged. *The selfishness of human nature is apparent in all of these trials.* . . . It is much better to make improvements from present earnings so that the lives of those that follow us may be easier than ours have been.[15]

[15] CFC, BQS, XCIII (Nov. 18, 1911), 1346–47. Italics added.

III

Judge Knapp's disquiet was shared to an increasing degree by the small band of thinkers who made up the eastern intellectual and academic community. The political economists were not having much luck conveying their ideas to an ICC dominated by lawyers who saw themselves as judges rather than makers of policy. As early as December, 1909, on the eve of the great controversy which ended with the Mann-Elkins Act and the first denial of increased rates, Columbia University's faculty of political science had asked C. C. McCain, a man with considerable experience on both the commission and the railroad side of the question, to write an article for the *Political Science Quarterly* on the economic aspects of the rate adjustment matter. McCain, formerly an auditor for the ICC and now chairman of the Trunk Line Association, had been wrestling with the problem of articulating the railroads' needs for several years. First he sought to emphasize the incredible interdependence which characterized the thousands of units of American business. It was not sufficiently appreciated, he said, that in contrast to Europe, U.S. business enjoyed "absolutely free trade over an extended area . . . with the most efficient transportation system in the world, offering its services at the lowest rates, [which] has brought about the highest degree of local specialization and the greatest dependence upon territorial exchanges of surplus products." Adam Smith could not have put it better. Then McCain wrote at length on the concept of the real, or purchasing, power of the money in which rates were paid, a concept which was taking so long to ascend to the policy-making level. The problem to McCain was that rates, even without regulation, were actually unresponsive to a host of factors which demanded their rise. Rates, he asserted, "have been so effectively controlled by custom and by law, *principally the former,* that they have far too sluggishly responded to the alteration in the value of the medium in which they are paid." [16]

But it was on the seemingly simple question of whether rates had

[16] C. C. McCain, "Necessary Adjustments of Railroad Rates," *Political Science Quarterly*, XXIV (Dec., 1909), 623–24. Italics added.

risen or fallen in the preceding decade that McCain's frustration showed most clearly. Knapp's remark about the selfishness of human nature was reflected in the fact that whereas the railroads could point to thousands of rates which had been cut over the years owing to Commission orders or, in many cases, competition, shippers held up instance after instance of rates which had been raised or which they thought, for one reason or another, ought to be lowered. It should be possible to agree on some broad, general measure of average freight rates. McCain pleaded for recognition of the simple revenue-per-ton-mile figure. Certainly it was free of trickery: a railroad had to report its ton-mile traffic and its total freight revenues, net of any rebates it might still be giving, and any duffer could readily divide the one by the other. To an opponent of the railroads, however, the ton-mile figure had two highly undesirable characteristics: in the first place, it produced a figure on the order of seven mills ($0.007), which made railroad service appear ridiculously cheap; and in the second, it was a figure which had unmistakably trended downward. The standard rebuttal of shippers' representatives had been that the trend reflected, not the cutting of rates on specific articles, but rather a trend in the "mix" (as we would call it today) of freight such that low-rated articles were rising as a percentage of the total.

McCain set out to disprove that theory. He noted that the percentage represented by the various categories of freight had actually varied little during the decade, and that while low-rated commodities like coal had indeed risen somewhat, so had high-rated manufactured articles. "The aggregate ton-mileage," he concluded, "is made up of such a multitude of separate services that it is necessarily governed by the statistical generalization sometimes called 'the law of large numbers.' " Thus, he concluded, "It would be difficult to conceive of a more satisfactory use of the statistical method than in the determination of the average rate per ton-mile." [17]

Yet even the professors could not agree on the seemingly elementary question of whether the railroads had been putting up or lowering their rates. In the same learned journal in the summer of 1912, Professor William Z. Ripley summarized the railroad situation in a thoughtful article. It was his contention, from which he would not recede when his highly influential volume on railroad rates was published the following

[17] *Ibid.*, 625.

year, that rates were going up, not down.[18] If the economists and statisticians could not agree on what was happening, it is probably asking too much to have expected the Commission to take a stand on this point.

But about this time others were wondering why all of this sudden concern with the general level of rates, when the history of railroad problems had for decades been one of concern with discrimination—between persons and between places—and not with how much the railroads charged in the aggregate. Why had the threat of increased rates suddenly pushed the more traditional concerns into the background? In the first of a series of articles for the *Quarterly Journal of Economics* in which he sought to review the entire subject of railroad regulation, M. B. Hammond put his finger on what was really upsetting many people about their railroads.

The probable explanation for this neglect is . . . in the shifting of interest which has taken place from problems . . . of railroad competition to those due to threatened monopoly. . . . A couple of decades ago the fear of railway monopolies was not seriously felt . . . [since] all dangers from that source, it was believed, were effectually forestalled by the legislative prohibition of pooling . . . [and] the public turned its attention to the more urgent problem: how to prevent discrimination between competing shippers. Railway managers, finding their efforts to maintain high rates at non-competitive points [thus] blocked, and compelled at the same time to continue their struggles with rival roads at competitive points, began to seek relief from this situation by bringing about a consolidation of competing roads. The question of whether a given rate is equitable . . . has given way . . . to the question as to whether or not an entire schedule of rates is too high.[19]

It was therefore critically important for anyone who was concerned with operating the nation's railroads to ascertain the Commission's philosophy of what made a rate too high. What was the Commission's recorded position? In its very first annual report, Hammond

[18] William Z. Ripley, "Present Problems in Railway Regulation," *Political Science Quarterly,* XXVII (Summer, 1912), 428–53; and *Railroads: Rates and Regulation,* 411. In its review of Ripley's book, the *Nation* noted that the Harvard economist "displays an unwavering loyalty to the ICC," that he believed the railroads should be permitted to earn an adequate surplus, and that he was not impressed by the scientific management argument. But the reviewer disagreed sharply with Ripley's contention that rates had risen sharply since 1900. *Nation,* XCVI (April 10, 1913), 361–62.

[19] M. B. Hammond, "Railway Rate Theories of the Interstate Commerce Commission," *Quarterly Journal of Economics,* XXV (Nov., 1910), 2.

noted, Judge Cooley had placed the panel squarely on record against the cost-of-service principle and firmly in favor of the value-of-service principle (our old friend, "all-the-traffic-will-bear," in company clothing), and this was still the Commission's official position. But, Hammond noted, "the Commissioners . . . have made much greater use of the cost of service principle than their preliminary utterances would lead us to expect." [20] Could it be that the Commission was incapable of promulgating its own rate-making philosophy? Would the criterion of railroad compensation take on more and more of an accounting quality and partake less and less of economic theory? It could, and it would.

A year later, in the fall of the highly prosperous year of 1911, the influential *Yale Review* issued the first number in its new series. The editors chose to include a perceptive article on the nation's policy toward its railroads. "No other country," wrote Morell W. Gaines, "is so dependent on railroads. . . . Freight transportation in the United States is thirty times the world's average [per capita] and nine times Europe's. . . . In our material development they always have been, and always will be, the prime force. . . . Stocks and bonds outstanding per mile of line are a little over half the average amount per mile on the foreign railways." [21] Since the nineties depression, Gaines observed shrewdly, capital had gone into the railroads in search of decreased costs instead of the competitive goal of increased traffic. One had only to look at the record to note two fundamental developments in the first decade after the depression: growth in mileage of track was replaced by growth in the form of improvements of existing routes, especially on heavy-traffic lines; and railroad management had found the way to bring competition under control so that the long-term decline in rates which marked the last quarter of the nineteenth century had been replaced by steady rates. But those who concluded that just because mileage expansion had all but stopped, the flow of fresh investment funds need not be continued, simply did not know what they were talking about. "They [the railroads] have added nearly as much to facilities in the last fifteen years as they had accumulated by 1894 during all their previous existence." [22]

[20] *Ibid.*, 65.

[21] Morell W. Gaines, "A Living Rate for the Railroads," *Yale Review* (n.s.), I (Oct., 1911), 65.

[22] *Ibid.*, 67–69.

And what of the future? How much new money would the railroads need, and what were their chances of getting it in the new order of things? Gaines was pessimistic. Capital requirements, over and above normal replacement needs, would be at least $500 million a year in the next five years. This money would have to come primarily from surplus. And this resort to surplus was a highly virtuous development in the mechanism of corporate growth, Gaines claimed, which was uniquely American. In England, where it had long been customary to pay out all earnings in dividends, successive new issues of debt and equity securities had expanded the capital accounts ridiculously. If the English railroads had experienced the relative rate of growth which the originally much more primitive American lines had had to contend with, the story would have been quite a different one. But the ICC, Gaines declared, was unable "to take any but an academic view of the actual facts." Its philosophies were hopelessly unattuned to the American situation. Thus it had lent the weight of its authority to the idea that the surplus is an unjustified burden on shippers. Nor could the members bring themselves even to entertain the thought that the value of the railroad properties by 1910 was probably "measurably near" the book value of the securities which reflected them, so durable was the old shibboleth of watered stock.[23]

IV

America's rapidly growing middle class subscribed to a wide range of magazines in the golden years before World War I. These long-since-dead periodicals maintained a lively and often surprisingly intellectual debate on issues which in our day never find their way onto the 11:00 P.M. television newscast, and as the editorial potential of muckraking declined it was replaced with a more balanced and certainly more sophisticated tone. One of the first to take a both-sides-of-the-question attitude toward the railroads was the *Outlook*. Its distinguished, white-bearded editor, Lyman Abbott, had recently scored a coup by signing as contributing editor America's most exciting citizen, Theodore Roosevelt, just returned from his grand tour of lion-hunting

[23] *Ibid.*, 72, 74, 76.

in Africa and being lionized in Europe. Teddy, if the truth were told, needed the money but he valued the opportunity to express himself even more. His influence is apparent in an article which the magazine published in May, 1910, just at the height of the controversy over the railroads' attempt to raise rates. What were the merits of their case? Would the increase tend to stifle trade? Would it be a crushing burden on shippers and consumers? Just what was the truth about the trend of recent years in freight rates? "The railways of the United States," said the *Outlook* in its very first sentence, "are receiving practically the same money return for transportation services today that they received ten years ago. Freight and passenger revenues are practically the only commodity prices in which there has been no advance from the general level which prevailed a decade ago." There followed a number of examples of the rise in prices of common consumer items which would follow a 10 per cent increase in freight rates.[24] Readers might well have stared in disbelief at the miniscule changes. And railroad men, then preparing for the great rate-increase battle, might well have added some such analysis to the exhibits which they would offer.

The *Outlook,* of all the voices then being heard on the problem, provided the best clarification of the dependability of ton-mile average rates as a measure of freight rate trends. The recent increase in low-rate freight was beside the point, the author declared, because when compared with the make-up of traffic at the start of the inflationary period such traffic was actually a smaller percentage of the total fifteen years later. The resourceful editor dug back into the hearings which the Senate Committee on Interstate Commerce had held in 1904 when the question of maximum-rate regulation was white-hot. One of the witnesses had been the able economist and statistician, Henry Carter Adams, who had been responsible for most of the Commission's significant work in the pre-Hepburn decade. He had settled the question of rate trends, one would have thought, once and for all. There had been a small percentage increase, he reported, which, when the rise in the general level of prices was considered, amounted to a decline.[25]

[24] E. W. Harden, "Effect of Increased Freight Rates," *Outlook,* XCV (May 7, 1910), 31–32.

[25] Adams, *Digest,* 77–78. See Chapter II above.

Ah, yes, the reader might respond, but everyone knows that the railroads' ploy had not been to raise rates. Nothing that unsophisticated would go once the Hepburn Act was on the books. What they had been doing was to upgrade the classification of a given article. Was this true? Many people took it for gospel. But in 1909, said the author, digging once again into the record, W. C. Brown, president of the New York Central Railroad, in a speech before the Albany Chamber of Commerce, had reported the findings of "ten months of the most thorough, painstaking analysis" of all of the reclassifications (1,773 of them) which his railroad had made in the ten years from 1898 to 1908. In 897 cases, the change had been upward, but in almost the same number of instances (876) the change had been downward, and the net result in the average rate for the nearly 2,000 commodities involved was a decrease of 10.69 per cent. Some of these changes had been initiated by the railroad in the normal course of its traffic solicitation efforts; some were the result of orders of the Commission.[26] And against this background of decreasing rates, the *Outlook* exclaimed, the operating ratio had risen only from 67.1 in 1897 to 69.7 in 1909. Then the author hit the spike of the controversy squarely on its head: "It is obvious that . . . rising prices [in the face of declining rates] have practically deprived the railways of the direct pecuniary benefits . . . of a generation of progress in the science of transportation." [27] This was powerful medicine for the railroads' public relations ailments, but it would work painfully slowly.

Most others were not so ready to pick up the railroads' standard, although a distinctly less hostile tone could be discerned. The man who opened his copy of *Everybody's Magazine* for May, 1911, must have been startled to note that an article entitled "Facing the Railway Facts" was prefaced by a lengthy note in which the editor virtually ordered him to read it. Despite the fact that the article which followed, wrote the editor, was full of dull facts and figures, it was everybody's duty to read it and understand the facts concerning the much-talked-about railroad problems. The magazine's farewell to muckraking was taken early in the article: "The mass of antiquated railway scandal will not be used

---

[26] Harden, "Effect of Increased Freight Rates," 32–33.   [27] *Ibid.*, 35.

here for the purpose of making people lay aside the magazine to say, 'Well, I'm dumbfounded.' A dumbfounded man is a poor thinker." [28] The author did not think much of the ICC's current policies because "it is still guessing whether rates are too high." Nevertheless, the railroads needed watching closely. The magazine took an uncompromising stand on the question of the surplus. It was, said the author, a way of hiding profits the owner wasn't supposed to have. "Instead of buying a steam-yacht for himself, he bought more railroad." Seldom had the popular confusion between personal property and mere private property been more clearly revealed. Still, "rates that are too low are worse than rates that are too high." But the government must know all the details of rail-road financing, and the public must be protected from unfair public re-lations activities. [29] The magazine continued its awkward and confusing straddling of all aspects of the controversy in a follow-up article which took over the scientific argument in its entirety, likening the railroads' "lack of efficiency" to an "open bunghole in the railroad barrel." [30]

On a somewhat higher intellectual plane elsewhere, readers' atten-tion was called to the startling increase revealed in the powers of the Interstate Commerce Commission by recent events. "The plain purpose of the [1887] law was the abolition of unjust rates and discrimina-tions," said the *North American Review* late in 1910. But recently, "in a unanimous opinion which has won public approval for its clear and convincing discussion of the issue, [the Commission] held that the carriers did not sustain . . . the burden of proof that the advances were necessary." Whether one approved of the decision or not (and it was clear that this respected old periodical, then approaching its 200th vol-ume, had not yet made up its mind), it was well for everyone to stop and reflect on the tremendous power which had suddenly been lodged in a panel of seven men. [31] The same issue contained a tart piece by a man whose taste for baiting his fellow businessmen reminds one of the Cyrus

[28] Richard W. Child, "Facing the Railway Facts," *Everybody's Magazine*, XXIV (May, 1911), 633.

[29] *Ibid.*, 639.

[30] Richard W. Child, "The Open Bunghole in the Railway Barrel," *Everybody's Magazine*, XXIV (June, 1911), 733–82.

[31] J. W. Crook, "The Interstate Commerce Commission and the New Railroad Law," *North American Review*, CXCIV (Dec., 1911), 859.

Eaton of more recent times. Currently enthralled with the idea of a court for everything from international peacekeeping to price fixing, Andrew Carnegie declared that the idea of commission regulation, even down to the day-to-day details of business, was now fully established. "There is nothing revolutionary in creating an Industrial Court," insisted Carnegie, who had always had more faith in the power of intellectuals than the average uneducated man. "We have the Interstate Commerce Commission, which fixes railway rates, and the Court of Commerce, its court of appeal. The greatest of all organizations, the Pennsylvania Railroad, appealed recently to the former for permission to advance a rate and was denied. It sought no appeal, thus setting a good example to others," concluded the retired ironmaster naïvely.[32]

A year later another gentleman of rapidly advancing years, who had also lived through the days of rugged individualism when the railroads had attempted to solve the problem of unrestrained competition by pooling agreements, took Carnegie's theories to task in an article in the same periodical. Albert Fink denied that the ICC's new-found power to suspend a proposed rate until it could investigate and pass on it was a precedent for an industrial court which would set prices on goods. Why was it, Fink wondered, that so many people had difficulty in understanding that "the authority to say a rate is unreasonable, or to fix a maximum rate, is still not the authority to fix a specific rate?" The reason should be clear to any thoughtful person. "A rate which is perfectly reasonable today may be . . . unreasonable next week or next month [thus] it follows that any law granting to a commission the power to fix such rates . . . for any length of time . . . will result in the imposition upon carriers of a rate admittedly unreasonable."[33] It was virtually the same argument that Senator Elkins had used against depriving the railroads' traffic managers of the freedom to change rates according to the state of business.

[32] Andrew Carnegie, "The Industrial Problem," *North American Review*, CXCIV (Dec., 1911), 914. Carnegie, who always felt acutely his lack of formal education, frequently revealed his contempt for what he took to be the narrow-mindedness of the typical businessman. His remark about the Pennsylvania takes on added significance in the light of his frequent run-ins with that railroad in the hotly competitive days of the 1880s. Cf. Burton K. Hendrick, *The Life of Andrew Carnegie* (2 vols., Garden City, 1932), I, 214.

[33] Albert Fink, "Trust Regulation," *North American Review*, CXCVII (Jan., 1913), 63–64.

Informed public opinion began to change more rapidly from late 1912 onward. Men who had never heard of a price index, much less reflected on the abstract qualities of the purchasing-power concept of money, found themselves reading a cleverly written, intelligent article in *Harper's Weekly* which said that the ICC was "the modern King Canute, bidding the sea of higher prices to go back." The time had come, said the author, when rates had to be raised or dividends had to be reduced. The second alternative meant simple starvation for the "golden goose." [34] By the end of 1913 it was clear that the nation was in for a painful recession, if not indeed a major business depression. Again the pattern was repeated. So prominent a role did the railroads still play in the national economy that their plight soon became that of everybody. The *North American Review* turned to a former University of Chicago political economist, now chief examiner of the new U.S. Tariff Board, for an updating of the situation. W. Jett Lauck showed his devotion to all the old shibboleths as he repeated the threadbare story of excessive capitalization, stock-watering, and the "economic crime" of capitalizing actual and potential earnings. But when he turned to the real problem —rapidly rising costs versus declining rates, which had resulted in an unheard-of operating ratio of 71—his tone changed. Operating expenses per train-mile now stood 42 per cent above the 1901 figure, he noted, while revenues for the same train-mile were up only 33 per cent. Increases in productivity—more powerful locomotives, bigger freight cars, longer trains, faster speeds—which had enabled the railroads to turn out more ton-miles per train-mile were no longer compensating for rising unit costs of operation. The increases for which the railroads were asking should be granted. "The sins of the past can not be rectified." It was an ungracious remark, blackening the just and the unjust alike, but to the hard-pressed railroads it was a step in the right direction.[35]

By the summer of 1914 *Collier's* magazine, whose reform-minded editor, Norman Hapgood, had departed two years before, had got the new religion. "A few years ago," confessed the magazine, "the average

[34] George D. Mumford, "How Many Golden Eggs Can the Starved Railroad Goose Continue Laying?" *Harper's Weekly,* LVI (Sept. 7, 1912), 4; LVII (May 17, 1913), 22.

[35] W. Jett Lauck, "The Plight of the Railroads," *North American Review,* CXCIX (Jan., 1914), 42–44, 51–52.

man's feeling toward the great steam common carriers was one of un-
friendliness, even hostility. Now . . . he wants them to be let alone, to
have a fair chance for existence, and he feels that when the great systems undergo the pinch of poverty he, too, must suffer." [36]

V

In 1912 this swirling stream of public sentiment toward the nation's railroads encountered the complicating shoals of a three-way
presidential election. By now the Insurgents—those midwestern and
western senators, congressmen, governors, and just plain politicians
yearning for such offices, who had demonstrated in 1910 the vote-get-
ting strength of that blend of Populism and reform which I have labeled
"archaic Progressivism"—were through with William Howard Taft.
That gentleman had revealed himself as basically conservative, the
staunch friend neither of the trans-Appalachian reformers nor of the
growing band of eastern Progressives who crowded around the neo-
Hamiltonian doctrines of Herbert Croly, and who were best epitomized
by George Perkins. The third party, which was to out-poll the regular
Republican candidate in 1912, took most of its grass-roots strength
from men of the stripe of Robert La Follette and Albert Cummins even
though, ironically, neither of these men would end up supporting the
man it would nominate. These men lived and slept the doctrine of public against private welfare, of agrarian virtue against eastern urban de-
cadence, of the breakup of large aggregations of propertied power if
possible and of its strict regulation if necessary. If the effete East was
going to play any part at all in the new party's great expectations (and
men like J. P. Morgan's "right-hand man," Perkins, would never be entirely welcome), it would have to make a truly significant contribution.[37]
And so it did: the most popular man in America, the one man who
could transform the Insurgents' parochial little bundle of grumbles into
the first significant third-party movement since the election of 1860.
This man's position on the railroad question was well known in

[36] Isaac F. Marcosson, "How Is Business?" *Collier's*, LIII (Aug. 15, 1914), 6.
[37] John A. Garraty, *Right-Hand Man* (New York, 1960), 271–74.

the America of 1912. He had had quite a bit to do with getting the first really effective maximum-rate law on the books in 1906, and he had stymied the railroads' first tentative efforts to increase their rates in 1908. He had spoken of the "malefactors of great wealth," and he reveled in the nickname of "trust buster." But he could speak most uncomfortably about fair play, and his insistence on being called a "progressive" rather than an "insurgent" could not please a Cummins man.[38] When he went west in 1910 he delivered a speech at Osawatomie, Kansas, by way of helping to dedicate a monument to a man who in the days of "bleeding Kansas" had done the nation the service of murdering five defenseless farmers. The speech became famous as the first formal enunciation of the New Nationalism, but it did not escape notice that a few weeks earlier, Theodore Roosevelt had drawn a most unflattering comparison between John Brown and the radical wing of the Insurgents. And the speech itself was not exactly reassuring, with its disturbing references to "local legislatures attempting to treat national issues as local issues." [39] What the real Insurgents wanted was for the national government to treat local issues as though they were national issues, and they had done a good job of securing their ends, at least as far as keeping freight rates down was concerned. This easterner did not seem quite to have the hang of Progressivism, western style. What about the letter he had written to Herbert Croly, telling him that "I do not know when I have read a book which I felt profited me as much as your book on American life. I shall use your ideas freely in speeches I intend to make"? [40]

Now, anyone who saw himself in a direct line from Alexander Hamilton had a lot to learn about what folks whose sons had to break their backs to go to the state university, and who had never heard of Harvard, thought was wrong with the country. This man thought the

[38] William E. Leuchtenburg, *Theodore Roosevelt: The New Nationalism* (New York, 1961), 8.

[39] *Ibid.*, 10, 36.

[40] This letter has had an interesting history. There is no record of the original except for a copy made by Croly himself. Apparently both the original and the writer's copy, if any, were lost. David W. Levy, "The Life and Thought of Herbert Croly, 1867–1914" (unpublished doctoral dissertation, University of Wisconsin, 1967), 343.

rich needed protection, too! "If there was danger of an assault on the property or person of any very rich man," he declaimed at Sioux Falls, South Dakota, in September, 1910, ". . . I would count myself a worthless American citizen if I did not come myself to his protection, and I would think the same of you." [41] But this man was Theodore Roosevelt, and he could win. The Populists had had a point, after all, when they swallowed some of their principles back in 1896 for a chance to run with what they thought was a winner. Get in with Teddy and change him afterward seemed to be the Progressive strategy. [42]

William Howard Taft never thought much of his chances in the 1912 election, and his lack of confidence was not misplaced. His various positions on railroad regulation had managed to alienate just about everybody in the political spectrum from Henry Phipps to Albert Cummins. [43] For an understanding of the guiding philosophy of the conservative Republicans whom he theoretically represented, one had better consider the ideals of such a man as Elihu Root, who was something of a bridge between the emotional New Nationalism of his close friend and the hard-shell remnants of stand-patism like Nelson W. Aldrich. "Root believed," says his biographer, "that there were evils in the practice of big business . . . and that labor should be treated more fairly. What he did not have was the passionate sense of grievance, the conviction that

[41] Leuchtenburg, *Theodore Roosevelt*, 92

[42] There were two junctures at which Theodore Roosevelt's presence in the White House might have vitalized Commission regulation of the railroads. One was the third term which he prematurely denied himself. The other was the third term to which he failed to be elected in 1912. His position on regulation was more scientific than that of any other man in public life (Woodrow Wilson had hardly given any thought to the matter in 1912) and he had the leadership ability to get a pill swallowed when necessary. The year after his permanent retirement to private life he wrote in the *Outlook*, "The living wage and the living rate are interdependent. . . . It is just as much the duty of the Commission to permit rates to be raised when the rate is justifiable as to require them to be lowered. Its control should not be hostile to that which it controls." Theodore Roosevelt, "The Living Wage and the Living Rate," *Outlook*, CIV (July 5, 1913), 501–2.

[43] Taft seemed quite pleased with the outcome of the battle that ended with the passage of the Mann-Elkins Act, although he grew to detest the Insurgents, especially La Follette, Dolliver, Clapp, and Bristow. Stanley D. Solvick, "William Howard Taft and the Progressive Movement" (unpublished doctoral dissertation, University of Michigan, 1963), 211, 220–23, 229. But in 1910 neither Taft nor anyone else knew what an unworkable piece of legislation the Mann-Elkins Act really was.

the American social order was manifestly unjust, which inspired some of the popular leaders." [44] What troubled Root, although he did not put it that way, was the threatened extinction of liberalism in American economic life, the attempt to attain social justice by coercing one branch of economic leadership for the benefit of another:

We are moving along toward a situation in which we are compelling agreements. Railroads are compelled to enter into agreements with their employees, not their own employees but the employees of universal organizations [the unions]. . . . The railroads are compelled to agree with a common bargainer, representing labor, regarding the most essential and important element affecting their rates. . . . No railroad acts for itself alone, the rates of no railroads are questions merely between that railroad and its employees . . . the rates they fix, the wages they pay, the arrangements they make, are all mutually interdependent. [45]

Late in August of that presidential year an unprepossessing little man finished his breakfast at New York's Albemarle Hotel, then walked the few blocks to the city's magnificent new Pennsylvania Station. One of the frequent trains which the Pennsylvania ran over the New York and Long Branch Railroad jointly with the New Jersey Central whisked him to the fashionable resort of Sea Girt, where the Democratic candidate, Woodrow Wilson, awaited his visit. Louis Brandeis knew that the "severe schoolmaster," who was being propelled at such dizzying speed from the frustrations of a college presidency and the governorship of a normally Republican state toward the White House, was in some trouble with his campaign. His first speeches had been "more polished than moving." He was aground on a reef between his abiding belief in a strong presidency and his conviction that local government and individual decision-making were superior to a "government regulation [which] will enslave us." At this stage Wilson's brand of progressivism was difficult to distinguish from the opposition. The man, in fact, who had expected to lead the new party and who was the linchpin of the radical Insurgents, Robert M. La Follette, had bitterly expressed the hope that Wilson would "make no mistakes that would result in Roosevelt's elec-

[44] Philip C. Jessup, *Elihu Root* (2 vols., New York, 1938), II, 185–86. See also Richard William Leopold, *Elihu Root and the Conservative Tradition* (Boston. 1954).

[45] Quoted in Ivy Lee, *Human Nature and the Railroads* (Philadelphia, 1915), 36–37.

tion," and by election day was firmly in the Democrat's corner.[46] That old rallying cry of the Democrats, opposition to the protective tariff, seemed to lack the spark that it had once had when times were not so good as in 1912. Brandeis' earlier letters to the candidate, therefore, gave strong promise that the meeting would profit Wilson beyond a few hours of conversation between two scintillating minds.

The people's lawyer had continued since the 1910 rate hearings to make friends and enemies at a prodigious rate. His bias against big business had grown into a full-fledged doctrinaire stand which his resourceful, pragmatic mind was nevertheless capable of advancing in most convincing terms. In 1911 he had revealed a talent for demagogy and questionable taste which fortunately was never matched in the future, when he publicly scourged Judge Gary, chairman of the U.S. Steel Corporation, for giving Mrs. Gary a $100,000 string of pearls at Christmas.[47] He continued to preach his peculiar doctrine of state-enforced liberalism wherever he thought "competition" and efficiency were threatened by overgrown corporations. The extremeness of his views on this point was dramatized in the impassioned objections which he raised to the plan approved by the Supreme Court for breaking up the American Tobacco Company into just four successor firms. Brandeis wanted the trust atomized into the numerous small concerns from which it had originally been put together, even if such a policy should result in a reduction in the value of the properties.[48] The little man, in fact, had had his share of newspaper headlines in recent years, and it

[46] Arthur Walworth, *Woodrow Wilson* (2 vols., New York, 1958; rev. ed., 1965), I, 240, 242; Alpheus T. Mason, *Brandeis: A Free Man's Life* (New York, 1946), 377.

[47] Mason, *Brandeis*, 361. Gary, apparently more in sadness than in anger, grieved that he had thought Brandeis "a bigger man." Brandeis attempted to justify his action on the ground that at a time when socialism (which he sincerely detested) was making such headway, Gary's behavior was to working men like waving a red flag in front of a bull. In view of the individualistic philosophy of the great majority of Americans in 1911, however, it is likely that many must have felt that what Gary did with his money was his business. In any case, Brandeis only succeeded in bringing the matter to the attention of millions who would never have heard of it otherwise. Ironically, the string of pearls was, in those inflationary times, a more conservative investment than the gilt-edged securities in which Brandeis preferred to invest the bulk of his own substantial fortune. The incident did much to swell the resentment which men of means felt toward Brandeis.

[48] Richard B. Tennant, *The American Cigarette Industry* (New Haven, 1950), 64–65.

was indeed a pair of celebrities who sat, deep in conversation, as the Atlantic broke relentlessly on the fine North Jersey beach.

Woodrow Wilson reacted to Brandeis' clarification of the issues as though to an injection of adrenalin. *Of course* there was a role for a strong central government, although that most certainly did not mean a big bureaucracy. Such a government was to root out unfair or inordinate privilege, whether its source was legislative, as in the case of the tariff, or conspiratorial, as in the case of the trusts. The important thing was to preserve opportunity of entry and growth for that small entrepreneur who, in Wilson's mind, was still the present strength and future hope of the republic. The particularly responsive chord which Brandeis' doctrine of smallness and localness struck in Wilson's mind was the hope it held out against America's becoming a nation of employees after all. Brandeis' doctrine made an outstanding appeal, and hit Theodore Roosevelt where he was weakest. When Labor Day arrived Wilson told a thousand working men at Buffalo that he did not "look forward with pleasure to the time when the juggernauts [of monopoly] are licensed and driven by commissioners of the United States." [49] The candidate repeatedly expressed his contempt for the intellectual in government and condemned the rise of government by commission. "I have lived with experts all my life," he said, thinking of the Princeton faculty which had characteristically been so sure of everything, "and I know that experts . . . don't even perceive what is under their nose." [50] The people's lawyer, himself the intellectual in government par excellence, may have winced on more than one such occasion as Wilson moved to give these ideas the stamp of his own individuality, but he knew, as did most other Americans by election day, that he was helping to make a president. That he had failed to make another ally in his war against the "giantism" which he believed was at the root of the railroad problem would be revealed gradually as the carriers' predicament became more and more acute.[51]

[49] Walworth, *Woodrow Wilson*, 244.

[50] William E. Leuchtenburg, *Woodrow Wilson: The New Freedom* (New York, 1961), 13. Wilson's manning of the Federal Trade Commission early in his first administration suggests that he expected little from it.

[51] A recent evaluation of Brandeis' economic philosophy states, "Although he, too [in addition to Wilson], misunderstood the forces that had fostered industrial concentration, Brandeis was consistent in his views of the trusts, as well as his

VI

Samuel Spencer's career as president of the Southern Railway and leading opponent of government regulation of railroad rates was abruptly terminated by a locomotive which crashed into his private car at a wayside station early of a November morning in 1906. But the role of president of a great American railroad, especially one which dominated the economic and cultural life of an entire region, as did the Southern, was already changing rapidly. What his work consisted of in large measure is revealed in two volumes of speeches and letters, totaling nearly 800 pages, which Spencer's successor, William W. Finley, wrote to the general public or delivered throughout the territory his line served, and at national gatherings as well.[52] Even busier was Howard Elliott, who faced the monumental task of rebuilding the reputation and the physical facilities of the grossly mismanaged New Haven. Also before the public in those days, but in a somewhat more scholarly manner befitting his position as one of the senior railroad statesmen, was Edward P. Ripley, along with such men as Daniel Willard of the B. & O., Samuel Rea of the Pennsylvania, William C. Brown of the New York Central, and Julius Kruttschnitt of the Southern Pacific. These men were constantly in the limelight in their quest for what they considered a more enlightened regulatory policy at both federal and state levels. Virtually all railroad presidents, however, even those occupying considerably less Olympian positions, found that more and more of their time was given to talking before a wide variety of civic and commercial organizations as the idea caught hold that in the future the railroads would have to fight for their position in the rapidly shifting economic and political scene.

Placing their case before the American people had been a matter

---

program for combatting them. . . . Brandeis believed that giant industries were detrimental to the country." Melvin Urofsky, "Big Steel and the Wilson Administration: A Study in Business-Government Relations" (unpublished doctoral dissertation, Columbia University, 1968), 70–71. It was a petty consistency, however, and one in which the man at the helm was less and less able to join as time wore on.

[52] *Addresses and Letters of William Wilson Finley, President of the Southern Railway Co.* (Compilation of the Bureau of Railway Economics, Association of American Railroads, 2 vols., 1907–10 and 1911–13.)

for considerable experimentation by railroad men ever since the hectic days of the Esch-Townsend bill crisis in 1905, and by and large the experimentation had proved highly ineffective. The railroads had begun at the bottom of the spectrum of public relations methods with a clumsily sly publicity campaign. Masterminded by a staff of newspapermen-turned-publicists, the plan had been to foist well-disguised "news releases" upon small-town newspaper editors who were easily impressed and almost always desperate for something with which to fill their gaping columns. During the 1910 rate fight the railroads had stepped up one notch by trusting their efforts to the advertising industry, which, in characteristic fashion, deflected a large percentage of the carriers' regular promotion budgets into a special campaign timed to the hearings. That they had been totally upstaged by an ambitious young radical midwestern Insurgent and a shrewd, resourceful eastern lawyer may have been due more to the large "image" deficit with which the railroads started than to their opponents' skills. Nevertheless, it was clear that in setting out to rebuild their public relations standing the railroads would have to proceed painstakingly and in a radically different manner. They began by establishing in Washington a permanent bureau of research and information which, by virtue of its intellectual stature and open-handedness, would give no ground for a continuation of the dark accusations which had been made against them in the past.

Late in 1910 the foremost among the committees into which railroad men were constantly organizing themselves was the Executive Committee of Six, composed of W. C. Brown, W. W. Finley, Daniel Willard, E. P. Ripley, B. L. Winchell, and Darius Miller (the last two being the heads of the Frisco and Burlington railroads). These men established the Bureau of Railway Economics, to which almost all of the railroads eventually contributed and which was ultimately to constitute one of the main branches of the Association of American Railroads. The Bureau, which was to have a fully qualified staff of economists and statisticians, was given the mission of "allaying the popular hostility to the railroads of the United States, its immediate function being the ascertainment and diffusion among its subscribers of accurate information in regard to the broader economic questions that are of general interest to the railroads in common." Translated, this early example of bureaucratese meant that the Bureau was to seek, first, to remove "local irritations" by responding to community grumbles in as objective a manner as possible. Then it was "to restore contact with the public" in whatever manner seemed most promising. And finally, it was to end the railroads' "silence in the face of injustices," that is, to substitute scholarship and analysis, which had worked so well for the railroads' opponents, for the sputtering indignation which had passed for rebuttal by railroad men. The Bureau was to do nothing to incur "the stigma attaching to the so-called 'publicity bureaus' that have developed during recent years and have justly excited the antagonism of the newspapers." [53]

In its first months the fledgling research unit was all but over-whelmed by a "whirlwind of antagonism instigated by advertising agents who had besought the railroads to make a large expenditure for the pur-pose of educational propaganda in newspaper and magazine advertising space." Sticking to its guns, however, and with the firm backing of the Executive Committee of Six, the Bureau achieved a vigorous and ade-quately financed start in life. Down from Hanover, New Hampshire, came Frank Haigh Dixon, professor of political economy at Dartmouth College, to direct the organization of the statistical department. Dixon recruited as director Lloyd G. McPherson, who had provided the eco-nomic brains for Samuel Spencer in the 1905–6 publicity campaign.[54] Not so ivory-tower as their titles might indicate, however, these men re-alized from the beginning that they would have to prove their worth to the railroads. The day the doors opened, McPherson began a log of vis-itors. The idea was to show the railroads as eager to reveal their souls, and, incidentally, to be helpful to whoever should walk through their doors, whether he be a senator, a railroad president, a representative of a shippers' association, or a local schoolboy seeking help in an essay contest. Friend and foe alike were welcome. Still fastened to the log with a rusty paper clip is the script-elegant calling card of Clifford Thorne, who also left behind his compliments for the quantity of infor-mation he was able to gather and the speed with which it was furnished. Similarly nice things were recorded as coming from Professor William Z. Ripley, who was a long way from being in the railroads' corner. The little bureau had, in fact, worked furiously during its first months to as-

[53] Bureau of Railway Economics, *First Report of the Director* (Washington, 1911), pages unnumbered.
[54] *Who Was Who in America, 1897–1942*, 823.

semble what quickly became the best reference library on railroad subjects in the country and to compile an extraordinarily comprehensive
bibliography of the holdings of railroad items of leading American libraries. Like the north wind in the fable, expensive and bombastic publicity had failed to remove the overcoat of prejudice from the American
public. Now the warm sun of the truth was to take its turn. It was a
slow process, but in the years to come the Bureau would turn out to be
the best public relations bargain the railroads ever had.[55]

Meanwhile there were more prosaic services which a permanent
Washington office could provide. The director was proud to report that
the Bureau had persuaded the ICC to end the notoriously "easy relations between employees of the ICC and members of the press" which
sometimes resulted in derogatory remarks, such as one which an auditor
had made about expense account padding by railroad executives. Commissioner Prouty had publicly apologized for that lapse. Most incredible
of all, however, was the episode of the carriers' exhibits in the 1910
rate hearings. Senator La Follette had introduced a resolution providing
for the printing of the complete record of the proceedings, a costly undertaking which was considered to be justified by the widespread interest which the case developed. As volume after volume appeared (there
would be ten in all), there was no sign of the supporting exhibits which
the railroads had submitted. When the exhibits of the shippers, who had
testified after the railroad men, appeared, it was evident that something
not quite right was going on. The chief clerk of the ICC, queried po-
litely by McPherson, replied coldly that he had not thought it worth-
while to subject the taxpayers to the expense of reproducing these admittedly very bulky documents. Into the Commissioners' offices sailed
McPherson. Called on the carpet, the chief clerk lamely explained that
he had not wanted the documents to suffer the mutilation which their
being processed by the Government Printing Office would entail. The
public printer, being consulted, assured the Commission that the documents would be returned, as was all copy entrusted to the GPO, in as
good condition as it was received. Satisfied, the Bureau waited. When
the ninth volume appeared without the exhibits, McPherson laid his
case before the chairman of the Senate Committee on Interstate Commerce. The documents, which were discovered to be still reposing in the

[55] Bureau of Railway Economics, *First Report of the Director.*

chief clerk's office, were sent off to the GPO in haste and appeared, eventually, at the very end as volume ten. Better evidence that the railroads needed a friend and watchdog in Washington would have been hard to imagine.[56]

VII

The ICC had been living on borrowed time ever since it told the railroads in 1911 to come back at some future time when the present record prosperity should disappear. Nineteen-eleven and 1912 were good years for the railroads by conventional criteria. They enjoyed continued growth in traffic, and if labor costs showed an increasingly clear trend to go up, at least the productivity gains of the past fifteen years were enabling the roads almost to hold their own. After maintaining their usual dividend levels, the railroads as a whole continued to carry over a modest surplus which, combined with the proceeds of security issues (floated, like all other securities at that time, at substantially higher interest rates and on much shorter terms than in the good old days), enabled them to continue with their more pressing improvement projects. Meanwhile they would watch the further development of the regulatory picture, ready to press again their case for rate relief if conditions should turn favorable. Late in 1911 the Commerce Court provided the railroad men with a thrill. In June the Commission had rendered one of its most famous decisions in the Spokane case, decided under the revitalized long-haul–short-haul provisions of the Act of 1910. The entire compromise structure of tariffs in the Pacific Northwest, and wherever else short-haul discrimination had been practiced in the face of long-haul competition, was in danger.[57] In November the Commerce Court issued an injunction against application of the decision. Intensely partisan financial journals were jubilant. At last, said one, the question "will be settled by the courts and not dictated by demagogues or politicians." [58] Alas, such optimism was premature. The court, after all, was only a first-level federal body and its decision would not stand. The Commission, moreover, would prove to have more friends at court than this judicial upstart. The following year peppery Commissioner Prouty,

[56] *Ibid.*   [57] 21 ICC 400.   [58] *CFC, BQS,* XCII (Nov. 18, 1911), 1345.

serving his turn as chairman, threw down the gauntlet. Members of the Pittsburgh Traffic Club, assembled for their annual dinner, were assured by Prouty that the Commission would fight any court review of his and his colleagues' actions that took place in the guise of efforts to uphold the Constitution.[59] The collision was not far off.

There were other developments that bothered railroad supporters. "The Commission," whined one, "is all the time making orders, whittling rates down to a lower basis." At the same time the railroads, it was noted, were having additional financial burdens dumped on them by other public bodies which were blissfully free of any responsibility for railroad finances. Take the employer's liability and workmen's compensation bill then pending before the Senate. Sure, the law is desirable, wrote a financial editor, but has any provision been made for revenue to cover it? Take that Pandora's box, the valuation project, which Prouty and the Commission were about to spring open, to what end no one could say. The project would cost far more than Prouty had promised, one could be sure; and, added the voice of doom, "a valuation lower than is just is probable." [60] As the election of 1912 drew near, the editor snorted indignantly at a piece of Republican campaign literature which bragged that the ICC "has steadfastly refused rate advances since its powers were enlarged." True, too true, said the editor: the box score since 1910, in fact, totaled 167 cases, out of which 85 were pending; 63 represented proposed advances which had been refused or withdrawn; and 19 were cases in which advances had been approved, for the most part only partially. "The Commission has conceived its function to be, not to hear cases open-mindedly and establish justice, but to put down rates and keep them down." [61]

But the editor rose to new heights of indignation the following month when the commission appointed to arbitrate the eastern locomo-

---

[59] *Ibid.,* XCIV (May 11, 1912), 1282–84.

[60] *Ibid.,* XCIV (June 8, 1912), 1537, 1539. Senator La Follette had been trying for seven years to get this pet project through Congress. By early 1913 he was determined to push through his latest draft, which had benefited considerably from the attentions of economist John R. Commons. La Follette's threat to filibuster several appropriation bills to death as Congress approached automatic adjournment on March 4 did the trick. Belle C. and Fola La Follette, *Robert M. La Follette* (2 vols., New York, 1953), I, 455–56.

[61] *CFC, BQS,* XCV (Oct. 19, 1912), 1010.

tive engineers' wage demands awarded an increase which would cost the eastern railroads two to three million dollars a year. The commission members had made the same error that ICC Commissioner Lane had made in his 1910 decision: they had blandly included in their data on dividends paid by railroad companies the amounts which the railroads had "received" from subsidiaries, thus counting them again when toting up what the parent corporations had paid. What should have upset the editor even more, however, was the utter confusion in which public policy now stood revealed. Prouty had declared in his 1910 rate decision that the ICC would not raise rates to finance higher wages. Now the arbitration commission declared that it was not going to pass on the railroads' ability to pay, but merely on their moral obligation (and, by implication, the nation's obligation) to do so. Charles R. Van Hise, president of the University of Wisconsin and chairman of the commission, wrote:

Therefore, considering the uncertainty of many of the factors involved, the arbitrators feel that they should not deny an increase of compensation to the engineers merely on the ground that the roads are unable to pay. If they are not able to pay . . . there is just cause for them to open again the question of an increase in rates with the ICC.[62]

Between Prouty's Scylla and Van Hise's Charybdis, the railroads could not hope to survive.

The railroads, however, had plenty of problems closer to home. With rates frozen at the dollar level of thirty years earlier, and with the costs of all inputs, most notably labor, rising inexorably, railroad management had but one dimension left in which to maneuver. The competition for volume became more intense than at any time since the lean days of the seventies and eighties. The Illinois Central revealed in detail how it was adjusting to the new rules of the game. It announced the appointment in 1911 of a "commercial agency" in Minneapolis and a freight and passenger agency at Sacramento. Contracting and soliciting forces were being enlarged at New York, Boston, Pittsburgh, Evansville, and Portland, Oregon, while an "assistant industrial and immigration commissioner" was assigned to the I.C.'s regular traveling repre-

[62] *Ibid.*, XCV (Nov. 30, 1912), 1432–33. *Report of the Board of Arbitration on the Matter of the Controversy between the Eastern Railroads and the Brotherhood of Locomotive Engineers* (Washington, 1912).

sentative in the South. The following year commercial agencies were added in Houston and Buffalo and traveling freight and passenger agents were hired out of San Antonio and Little Rock.[63] Only one of these places was actually on the line of the I.C. The companies were reaching out for business as they never had before. Under the new conditions no traffic manager could any longer assume that his line would get its share of traffic at transfer points, or, to be more realistic, no longer would his employers be satisfied with the historical "share" they had enjoyed. The spotlight had shifted, in the late 1890s, from the "wheeler-dealer" who could "pass the drinks, tell a good story, undercut his competitor, and write some business" to the financial and engineering technicians who faced the urgent task of rebuilding the railroads. Now the spotlight was shifting back. Ahead lay a repetition of some of the worst inefficiencies decried by Charles Francis Adams in the previous century. Rebating was a thing of the past, but there were many other ways to favor shippers: longer loading time, lower minimum carload weights, longer unloading time, to mention the most common. Financing, too, was becoming desperate by prudent investment standards. Whatever the reason, the long-term securities market was dead, and just at the time when old mortgage bonds were coming due. The I.C. attempted in 1913 to refinance $16 million of such obligations. Only one million dollars was taken on long term; the proud organization settled for $15 million in secured gold notes (at 4½ per cent) due just a year later. It was the best it could do. And the line now had to turn to equipment trust financing in a big way. The management could not postpone any longer the purchase of a "considerable number of large locomotives and freight cars as well as additional new steel passenger cars," so eight million dollars in trust certificates were issued. The twentieth century was going to be expensive. Could the railroads afford it? The same year the I.C. cut its dividend, a development which may well have been a financial hardship to many of its stockholders, of whom there were now nearly 11,000.[64]

[63] I.C.R.R. Co., *Annual Reports for 1911 and 1912.* From 1910 on, the lists of freight and passenger representatives which precede the timetables of the railroads in the *Official Railway Guide* grow longer and longer.

[64] I.C.R.R. Co., *Annual Report for 1913.* The *Journal of Political Economy,* XXII (Jan., 1914), 87, called its readers' attention to the financing situation, "which [has] not been generally recognized. The banks . . . have for some years

Stockholders of the Pennsylvania were presented with much the same story in their annual reports. The company laconically detailed the factors which were pushing up costs: the declining profitability of mail traffic, of which the Pennsylvania moved a small mountain every day in the year; higher wages; the extra-train-crew laws being passed by several states; higher coal prices; submission of wage demands to arbitration; and, of great concern to a railroad operating in such a highly built-up area as the Pennsylvania, the threat of the state of New Jersey to require it to eliminate every one of its grade crossings.[65]

The Santa Fe meanwhile continued the indignant mutterings which had become a regular feature of its annual reports since the dark days of 1907–8. The company simply would not pay the interest rates now being charged, it said, and in the future would make no further betterments except out of current income.[66] No surplus, no growth. What would Messrs. Thorne and Brandeis say to that?

VIII

Nineteen-thirteen began inauspiciously for the railroads. The worst floods in memory beset the Ohio and Mississippi River valleys. The Illinois Central had two bridges across the Ohio. The older one, at Evansville, Indiana, was washed away completely on March 29 and no service of any sort was reestablished until April 12. But—horror of horrors—the pride and joy of the railroad, the magnificent bridge at Cairo, Illinois, just above the confluence with the Mississippi, which had been designed with especial care for service at one of the most notoriously flood-menaced spots in the world, was awash at its northern approach. This aorta of the Midwest was blocked on April 2; with service barely restored on April 10, it was another several days before normal traffic could be resumed. When the ground dried, the road could

---

past been obliged to finance the current needs of the railroads by short loans, because of the inability of the latter organizations to borrow from the general public."

[65] P.R.R. Co., *Annual Report for 1912*. The automobile age had burst upon a society that was totally unprepared for it. Grade-crossing accidents became so common that they were soon relegated to the inside pages of the newspapers.

[66] A.T. & S.F. R.R. Co., *Annual Report for 1914*.

begin the expenditure of a tidy sum in raising the tracks.[67] Farther east
things were even worse. Dayton, with the railroads leading into it, was
on an emergency footing for days. The Baltimore & Ohio found that a
major bridge over the Allegheny would have to be replaced because it
was no longer adequate for the much heavier coal cars then coming into
use. The three million dollars for a new bridge would not be easy to
find. Republic Iron and Steel Company and more than a dozen other independent steel companies in the Pittsburgh-Wheeling-Youngstown area
chose this moment to demand that the ICC lower rates on coal, coke,
and ore. That, the railroads screamed, would be a step in the wrong
direction.[68] They had far different ideas about what should be done
with rates on these commodities, which formed so large a part of the
eastern railroads' traffic.

By the wet spring of 1913 it had become uncomfortably obvious
that all was not well with the economy. By fall it was clear that a recession, most noticeable in the railroad equipment industry but spreading
rapidly, was in full swing. Was the delicious prosperity of the past two
decades about to be replaced by a depression? The physical volume of
business activity, which had been at an all-time high in January, slumped
badly in March and continued downhill until a year later it was off 13
per cent. Factory employment had skidded 7 per cent by the year's end,
but meanwhile pig iron production—a critical index for the eastern
railroads—had tumbled by one-third.[69] And true to form, when the
economy sneezed the railroads got pneumonia. The efforts of prudent
businessmen to adjust to what appeared to be an inevitably lower level
of activity were reflected in the usual sickening decline in traffic and the
even more alarming drop in net income. These measures of railroad
well-being were down 4 per cent and 35 per cent, respectively, by mid-
1914. Nineteen-eight all over again? Well, it was an ill wind . . . And
this wind blew toward Washington.[70]

The Hotel Astor, now departed from the Times Square scene, was
in its prime in 1913 when the Economics Club met there for its annual
dinner. The honored guest was to have been Walter Hines Page, but

[67] I.C.R.R. Co., *Annual Report for 1913.*   [68] *NYT,* May 14, 1913, 2.

[69] U.S. Bureau of the Census, *Historical Statistics of the United States: Colonial
Times to 1957* (Washington, 1960), 329, 330, 333. Seasonally adjusted.

[70] ICC, *Annual Statistical Report for 1913 and 1914.*

President Wilson's new ambassador to the Court of St. James's could not be present. The meeting turned out to be a railroad show. Brown of the New York Central told the hundreds of railroad men and industrialists, and a sprinkling of academicians, that the time had come for the unfair treatment of the railroads to stop. The ICC originally had worked to the benefit of the railroads, he said in a conciliatory tone, when unrestrained competition had made them as much the oppressed as the oppressor. "In practically every instance where an unlawful pass or rebate had been granted the hand was held out to receive it before the railroad offered anything. . . . I do not think there is a railroad president in the United States today who if he could . . . would repeal the Interstate Commerce law." But to continue to make ICC policy on the assumption that the conditions, or, for that matter, the opportunities, of 1887 still existed was hurting the railroads and the nation. Among those who took a few words to second Brown's sentiments was Professor William Z. Ripley. As the plates were removed the audience buzzed with conversation about the secret that everyone knew: the eastern railroads had decided to ask the ICC to reopen the rate case. Daniel Willard of the B. & O. and Samuel Rea of the Pennsylvania would lead the fight. And this time, with wages and taxes up sharply since 1910 and the economy sliding rapidly, they expected to prove their case.[71]

One reason for railroad optimism was the belief that the tide of public opinion was finally beginning to turn. The renewed efforts to raise railroad rates thus became an important milestone in the history of public relations counseling in the United States. There was virtual unanimity among railroad men that publicity had been badly handled during the 1910 proceedings. The light had finally dawned that the public would have to be won to the railroads' side not by cold facts presented in a take-it-or-leave-it manner but by rebuilding the average citizen's opinion of the roads. The carriers had to develop an emotional, rather

[71] *NYT*, April 30, 1913, 2; May 6, 1913, 12. The railroad men were well aware that Prouty had practically ruled out any rate adjustment in the absence of a physical valuation of the properties. But that project, just beginning, would obviously take years and the railroads, said Rea, just could not wait. He now had a price tag for the grade-crossing eliminations which New Jersey was insisting upon: sixty million dollars. And, to stop further loose talk about rate increases enriching the few at the expense of the many, he released a closely guarded figure: the Pennsylvania Railroad now had 100,000 stockholders and 200,000 bondholders. *NYT*, May 11, 1913, II, 3.

than an intellectual, case. They had to show themselves as vitally interested in the public's opinion of them, their service, and the way they
did business. They had to show the nation that they were suffering from
repressive, unwise, and in fact highly confused regulation which was seriously undermining their ability to do the nation's work in the years to
come. The new campaign was set in motion by the Railway Executives'
Advisory Committee, originally organized for the 1910 effort but
greatly expanded and renamed the Supervising Board in 1913. Leadership fell to the three big eastern trunk line carriers. The Pennsylvania,
the New York Central, and the B. & O. combined their public relations
staffs under the Pennsylvania's head public relations man, Ivy Lee, and
despite the predictable reactions of midwestern Progressives the publicists forged ahead energetically, taking the greatest pains to make it
clear to the public just what they were trying to do.[72]

[72] Lee, *Human Nature and the Railroads*, 34–42, 57; Michael C. Douglass, "A
History of the Association of American Railroads" (unpublished B.S. thesis,
Wharton School of Finance and Commerce, University of Pennsylvania, 1962),
65; Alan R. Raucher, *Public Relations and Business, 1900–1929* (Baltimore,
1968), 43. The director of the railroads' Bureau of Railway Economics described
the enthusiasm with which the carriers embraced the concept of good public relations; Logan G. McPherson, "A Concerted Movement of the Railways," *North
American Review*, XCXVII (Jan., 1913), 40–49. Lee summarized the railroads'
fervent appeal to shippers in a speech before the Traffic Club of Pittsburgh in
December; Lee, *Human Nature and the Railroads*, 34–42. The savage reaction of
the archaic Progressives is revealed in the report of La Follette's investigation of
the campaign, which he made on the floor of the Senate the following spring.
Posturing dramatically beside a small mountain of pamphlets, press releases, telegrams, and letters piled upon his desk, La Follette demanded unanimous approval to print it all in the *Congressional Record*, in which it ran to 358 pages.
CR, 63d Cong., 2d Sess. (April 27 to May 8, 1914), 7735–8093. For evidence
that La Follette was badly out of touch with the regulatory situation even in his
home state, see Stanley P. Caine, *The Myth of a Progressive Reform* (Madison,
1970), *passim*.

CHAPTER IX

THE SECOND DENIAL

A foolish consistency is the hobgoblin of little minds, adored by little statesmen and philosophers and divines. —RALPH WALDO EMERSON

The greatest dangers to liberty lurk in insidious encroachment by men of zeal, well-meaning but without understanding. —LOUIS DEMBITZ BRANDEIS

I

When Franklin K. Lane turned his back on Horace Greeley's advice and left the Pacific slope for the East in 1906, he brought with him a young protégé for whom he had great hopes. The warmhearted Lane had been impressed by the young man's qualities that had enabled him to rise from linotype operator on Lane's newspaper, via night school, to the first rung on what promised to be a successful legal career. John H. Marble jumped at the chance to come east as Lane's private secretary, and it was not long before the enterprising Californian had secured for him the secretaryship of the Interstate Commerce Commission. "Great it was in that day to be alive" (especially if you were a Democrat and a westerner), "but to be young was very heaven." Marble was only forty-five when the confusions of Progressive politics swept Woodrow Wilson, the first Democratic President in sixteen years, into the White House. The day after the inauguration the President officiated at the swearing-in of the members of his new cabinet. The man standing before him who was to be his Secretary of the Interior was Franklin K. Lane, who had delivered his resignation as Commissioner to Marble's office a few hours before. Five days later Marble proudly took the oath as Lane's successor, at that time the youngest man to be appointed and the first to rise from within the Commission.

A good omen for the railroads? Perhaps. Marble was thought to have some pretty youthful ideas which did not entirely coincide with

archaic Progressive theology. On November 18, just before the hearings
on the eastern railroads' rate application were to begin in Washington,
he had been sent into the field, as one of the junior members of the
Commission, to preside over special hearings at Harrisburg, Pennsylvania, on the knotty question of anthracite coal rates. Reporters in that
important railroad town sought his views on the eastern railroads' prospects. "The appointment of the ICC was an experiment," said the
young Commissioner. "If we fail in the work we set out to do, the country will find some other way to solve the problem." What the Commission was going to do, he said, was "to try to help the railroads." He advised the reporters not to attach too much importance to talk about
government ownership. Eastern newspapers, by now largely in sympathy with the railroads, headlined the remark as an "intimation of higher
rates." The next day, without explanation, Marble told reporters that he
wished to "recall" his statement. He had learned, apparently, that antirailroad comments might pass unnoticed (oldtimers like Prouty seemed
to have no compunctions on that score) but a newcomer who happened
to feel that there were two sides of the question had better tread lightly.
Later that day Marble became violently sick at his stomach, and against
doctors' orders returned to Washington for treatment. Two days later
this promising young civil servant was dead of acute indigestion. The
other members of the Commission, who had been unanimous in their
affection for Marble, were thunderstruck with grief.[1]

There were more changes ahead for the ICC. Early in March,
1913, as one of his last official acts, President Taft had signed the bill
directing the ICC to conduct a comprehensive study of the market value
of the physical assets of the nation's railroads. As the first few months
of the new administration wore on, the true dimensions of the undertaking began to be apparent. Charles A. Prouty, who along with Senator
La Follette had been largely responsible for the new program, was
meanwhile casting doubt on his impartiality as a Commissioner. He
made no bones about his lack of faith in the future of the railroads as
they stood. Government ownership, he said to the Baltimore Traffic

[1] *NYT,* Nov. 19, 1913, 2; Nov. 21 (editorial); Nov. 22, 4; C. A. Miller, "Lives of
the Interstate Commerce Commissioners and the Commission's Secretaries," *ICC
Practitioners Journal,* XIII (June, 1946), Sec. 2, 71.

Club in February, 1914, would be "the great issue in the near future." The railroads were not giving good service, he crabbed, because they lacked money. But under government ownership Congress would simply vote whatever money was required, just as it was beginning to do in the good-roads program. The idea was not new, but neither was it particularly popular in 1914.[2] It had been apparent for some time that Prouty, who had made a long study of physical valuation accounting, could be more useful elsewhere. He resigned that month as Commissioner, to become head of the newly created valuation division of the ICC.

That made two vacancies for Wilson to fill. The President first named another western Democrat, Henry C. Hall, who offered political loyalty and a record as a successful lawyer in Colorado (where he had moved years before for his health), and not much more. The other seat was filled through one of the best appointments Wilson ever made. In their halcyon days at Princeton in the nineties, schoolmaster Wilson had made a lasting friendship with Winthrop M. Daniels, professor of political economy. The professor had acted as intermediary between the stubborn college president and the equally determined Dean Andrew West in the controversy over whether to build the new graduate college in ivory-tower seclusion a mile from the university library, or down the hill in the thick of things. And when he became governor of New Jersey in the reform landslide of 1910, Wilson besought Daniels to sit on the Public Utilities Commission, where the learned man's impassioned support of the recognition of intangible values in establishing utility rate bases created considerable stir.[3] Daniels was the first economic theorist, in fact, to sit on the ICC. With the possible exception of Knapp he was the only member who saw the panel primarily as an economic commission rather than as a judicial tribunal. A graduate of Princeton who had followed the nineteenth-century tradition of postgraduate study in Europe, he had been back at the New Jersey college teaching the boys the principles of neo-classical economics for twenty years when Wilson

[2] *NYT*, Feb. 19, 1914, 8.

[3] Arthur Walworth, *Woodrow Wilson* (2 vols., New York, 1958), II, 70, 122; Arthur S. Link, *Wilson: The New Freedom* (Vol. II of a biography of Woodrow Wilson) (Princeton, 1956), 449–50; Henry W. Bragdon, *Woodrow Wilson, the Academic Years* (Cambridge, Mass., 1967), 322–406 *passim*.

called him to Trenton. Daniels was the break with the past and its neo-Populist prejudices, a break which the nation so desperately needed in a Commissioner.[4]

By the time the eastern railroads' petition for a reopening of the rate question had been formally lodged with the Commission in May, there was little enough for the railroads to be optimistic about. Rumors had come out of Washington that the Commission did not believe (of course, it did not really *know*) that the cost of hauling the nation's freight had gone up for the railroads in the past twenty-six months. Then, there was the question of the extra services provided by the railroads for big shippers, which looked especially bad to a nation still enthusiastic over the New Freedom.[5] The railroads, nevertheless, felt they could ask for a couple of favors. First, they wondered if they could not somehow be relieved of the expense of formally printing the proposed new tariffs. That would save them $250,000. Second, they urged an early decision. The Commission promised to consider both requests, but as to the second, no assurances of a decision before the summer recess could be given. (As it turned out, the Europeans would be removing the covers from their field guns the following year before the decision would be reached.) It took the Commissioners five weeks just to agree among themselves whether to reopen the case. Again they tripped up in their own red tape. On June 21 the rehearing was granted, although three members (Clements, McChord, and Marble) complained that they had not had sufficient time to study the petition. Immediately it was discovered that a rehearing under the 1910 rate-increase proposal would demand printing of the new tariff schedules, so out went an order canceling the previous order. More wrangling ensued the following week, but finally, on June 26, 1913, the Commission agreed five to two (Clements and McChord were the diehards) to conduct an investigation on its own. Despite the legal fog, the decision was something of a con-

[4] Miller, "Lives of the Interstate Commerce Commissioners," 75; *Who Was Who in America, 1897–1942*, 143. La Follette and the other archaic Progressives, who were bitterly opposed to Daniels, seemed about to sway enough Democrats to deny confirmation, when Wilson let it be known that he particularly wanted the professor, and that "the time had come to let up on the railroads." Belle C. La Follette and Fola La Follette, *Robert M. La Follette* (2 vols., New York, 1953), I, 490.

[5] *NYT*, May 1, 1913, 10.

cession to the railroads.[6] But things were not looking too good. The source from which the railroads had hoped for support, the Commerce Court, was on its last legs and the Commission would have nothing to fear from that quarter much longer. It had become apparent that there was no area in which the court could exercise its supposed powers which had not long since been vouchsafed to the regulatory Commission, while it had not even speeded up the procedures of the Commission. That fall Congress heatedly debated the court's future. Then, without a tear shed, that body voted to include a clause in the Urgent Deficiencies Appropriation Act of October 22, 1913, abolishing the court as of the first of the coming year.[7] It having been finally established that the regulation of railroad rates was a delegated legislative function, rather than a judicial procedure, the ICC was now free to go on acting like a court of law.

II

"All rates on railroads should be increased, and at once." How gratifying to a railroad man to hear such sentiments from J. Ogden Armour, whose meat-packing plants made him one of the largest shippers in the United States. The occasion was the announcement that the ICC would hear the eastern railroads' plea. Shippers in St. Louis joined in approval. The New York *Times,* in the first blast of an unusual editorial barrage which would continue unabated throughout the rate controversy and, in fact, right down to the government's takeover of the railroads at the end of 1917, insisted that "the decision marks the turn of the tide of opinion on this important subject." Noting that railway securities had declined substantially, the *Times* said: "If this movement of capital away from the railways is not checked, the supply of railway facilities will be insufficient, and shippers who can not get their business moved will lose in profits more than the difference between the rates they pay and the rates the railways need. . . . The law may be muddled, but finance and

[6] *Ibid.,* June 27, 1913, 9.

[7] *ICC Activities, 1887–1937,* 39. The court had suffered a telling blow when one of its judges resigned under fire at this time.

economics are crystal clear." [8] Daniel Willard, by now the leading railroad statesman, told the New York Merchants' Association later that
year, just as the rate hearings were beginning, that if there was any
question of whether the railroads had risen to the efficiency challenge
Brandeis had thrown down in 1910, he was prepared to show that the
B. & O. was now hauling 650 tons per train, 47 per cent better than the
442 tons it averaged in 1910. How fast a railroad had to run, in fact,
just to stay in one place was dramatized by Willard's statement that
without the increased efficiency the B. & O. would have failed to cover
its dividend by three million dollars. The reception of the shippers was
"hearty." [9] Even more gratifying was the news that the Illinois Manufacturers Association, one of the most effective opponents of the 1910
proposal, would not appear in opposition to the 5 per cent raise, which
it had decided was justified. "The ICC," editorialized the *Times* a few
days later, "may easily overstay its time in dalliance with theories of
popular opinion and public interest which are no longer true." [10]

In the midst of all this cheerful news, Commissioner Harlan,
whose turn as chairman that year placed the investigation under his
direction, announced that the ICC would retain special counsel during
the hearings. The man, however, was not to be regarded as counsel for
the Commission as such, but as someone who had been charged with
the development and adequate presentation of all sides of the controversy. Who needed special help, then? "Doubtless certain protestants
will have their own attorneys," said Harlan, "but Mr. Brandeis will be
the general channel through whom the views of others opposing the proposed advance may be presented of record." [11] Railroad men and their
supporters were virtually speechless. "It may seem odd that a court
should employ counsel . . . that the case might seem prejudged by the
selection of a counsel who is not judicial to advocate a case on which
the court's mind is already made up. . . . If Mr. Brandeis pleads in his
former successful manner it will show to the country that the Commis-

[8] *NYT*, June 28, 1913, 6.

[9] *Ibid.*, Nov. 9, 1913, VIII, 7. The increase in tons per train, of course, is not to
be considered all a net gain in productivity. Greater input, mainly of capital in
the form of heavier locomotives, was obviously involved. But the reduction in
man-hours of labor per ton-mile hauled was dramatic and, to a railroad labor
leader, further justification for higher wages for the men who were driving the
new steam monsters.

[10] *Ibid.*, Nov. 10, 1913, 8; Nov. 15, 1913, 10.   [11] *Ibid.*, Oct. 10, 1913, 10.

sion is prosecutor rather than judge. . . . If the Commission is less open-minded than the country, the country will find a way to change the mind of the Commission, just as it is changing its own mind." [12] And so it would, but not until the whips of archaic Progressivism had been applied several more times.

The Boston lawyer had wanted to minimize his participation in the case. He had a number of other projects under way, and as events would prove he was beginning to believe that the railroads really did need rate relief. It would not do to get the same reputation as an out-and-out radical, socialistic railroad-hater that rash young Clifford Thorne was acquiring. On the other hand there was still work to be done in increasing the effectiveness of the railroads and protecting consumers from what might well be only the first in an endless succession of blanket rate increases. There was little Brandeis could do for the present to keep the press from assuming that he was being hired to fight the railroads, although Commissioner Clark did oblige with a letter saying that Brandeis had been appointed to "elicit the facts," not to represent any one group. The people's lawyer might have started a little earlier to let Thorne down. That gentlemen had written to him joyously, upon learning of his appointment, "I think this method of procedure is wise. There should be a head to the public's presentation. I firmly believe that the success of our case is now going to rest with you." Everywhere it was rumored that Brandeis was out to seek revenge for the business community's opposition to his appointment as Secretary of Commerce in Wilson's cabinet. Some such men did not bother to hide their feelings. "The Interstate Commerce Commission! They seem to be a clumsy, inarticulate lot, with a penchant for shady lawyers," wrote the president of the Third Avenue Railway to the *Times*.[13]

[12] *Ibid.,* Oct. 19, 1913, II, 14.

[13] Alpheus T. Mason, *Brandeis; A Free Man's Life* (New York, 1946), 336–37, 337*n*, 340, 342. Brandeis actually brought to the investigation some of the economic inquisitiveness which the Commission was so incapable of supplying on its own. Although his strategy would be to look for other means than a rate increase to improve the carriers' financial situation, and although in the end he would show himself as willing as anyone else to deny increases to the trunk lines on purely legalistic grounds, his participation added considerable depth to the proceedings and was well worth the $13,750 fee which he was paid. But time had run out on his scientific approach to the railroad problem. Brandeis' first service had been to draft a long questionnaire, covering services furnished to shippers, corporate organization, interlocking directorates, losses on passenger, mail, and

What with long-drawn-out conferences within the ICC, the summer recess, and the time required for the Commission and its special counsel to arrange the agenda, May had become November by the time the hearings began. What faced the Commission was almost entirely a decision in principle, for the request of the eastern railroads was modest indeed. While they had sought a relatively small increase three years before, this time they filed proposed tariff changes which averaged out to only about 5 per cent, despite the tact that costs, notably wages, had continued to rise since 1910. The new rates, if allowed, would generate additional revenue of barely fifty million dollars, which, in the face of demands made or expected to be made by the railroad brotherhoods, was a mere token. There is no doubt that the railroads were after only a token at this stage: a token of the ICC's conversion to the position that rates could be raised *en bloc;* that blanket proof of reasonableness would be acceptable, in the face of the obvious impossibility of proving each individual rate; and that historical rate levels which dated from the beginning of a twenty-year worldwide inflation of price levels no longer were meaningful and should be superseded. If the Commission took such a stand it would mean that it had moved onto new regulatory ground and had somewhere found the wisdom and the courage to recognize that it had a creative administrative function to perform. The smallness of the award would not matter, for once the ICC had successfully exorcised the repressive spirit of the Act of 1910 a brighter future, bringing realistic rate increases, would surely dawn. But if the ICC stood fast on the narrow legalistic ground of the 1910 decisions, then the appeal would have to be taken, not by the railroad executives themselves, acting as representatives of "private" property, but by the sweep of events, to the people and their lawmakers. Under the circumstances, it was no wonder that the Commissioners felt acutely the need for special counsel.

---

express business, and railroad efforts to date to increase efficiency, which the ICC mailed to all of the eastern railroads at the end of the year. The railroad executives, horrified at the time and clerical cost which assembly of the data would require, rushed to Washington to plead to be excused. Harlan impatiently threw out Brandeis' questionnaire, saying that "the roads need not turn their archives inside out; they are showing poor earnings." *NYT,* Jan. 8, 1914, 13. This apparently was the end of Brandeis' project to start a bureau of railway standards which would compute standard costs for future rate-making purposes.

III

It was a somber Commissioner Clark who rapped for order on the first day of the hearings.[14] He and his colleagues, he said, had just returned from the sad duty of attending the funeral of their youngest and most recently appointed associate. If duty did not demand that they get under way the consideration of one of the most pressing problems then facing the nation, they would have delayed the proceedings out of respect for the late Commissioner Marble. George S. Patterson, general counsel of the Pennsylvania Railroad, began the railroads' case with a discreetly short opening statement. He brought to the stand Daniel Willard, who summarized the situation facing the railroads in Official Classification Territory.[15] Willard showed the Commissioners how the roads east of Buffalo and Pittsburgh had fared in the three years since the Commission had left them to their own resources. Net additions to property (investment) totaled $660 million, he said. After making this investment, the railroads in the fiscal year ended mid-1913 showed a gain in gross revenues of $187 million, a rise in operating costs of $203 million, and a net profit (as one could quickly calculate) that was $16 million dollars less than in 1910. Rates, Willard said, continued to be whittled away (not only by the Commission but also by competitive conditions surrounding certain commodities), while an award just an-

[14] The hearings were published, pursuant to a resolution of Senator La Follette, as Senate Document 466, 63d Cong., 2d Sess., in fourteen volumes, hereinafter referred to as Five Per Cent Case Hearings.

[15] The "eastern" railroads, who were bringing this appeal while the "western" railroads watched with the deepest interest, were those lines operating north of the Ohio and east of the Mississippi rivers. They were subdivided, for rate-making purposes, into Official Classification Territory, which, as its name implies, was the oldest part of the nation's railroad network, the busiest, and the most prestigious, lying east of Buffalo (in the case of the New York Central) and Pittsburgh (in the case of the B. & O. and Pennsylvania); and Central Classification Territory, lying to the west of those cities. The eastern trunk line railroads had many years before integrated their operations throughout the two territories, and the survival of the classification system is dramatic evidence of the fact that railroad rate structures were based more on custom, modified by locally applied common sense, than any "scientific" rate-making principle. The typical freight traffic manager would have smiled at the idea of an over-all, "scientific" reform of railroad freight rates.

nounced by a board of arbitration would give conductors and trainmen in the territory six million dollars a year more.[16]

Willard's minor-key presentation was followed by an even shorter statement by Frederic A. Delano, president of the Wabash Railway. In his territory, where $175 million had been invested in the railroads since 1910, operating results were even worse. Traffic was not growing so fast as in eastern territory: it rose from $239 million in 1910 to $275 million in 1913 and net profit had slumped by $16 million.[17] These results, the railroad men would claim, were due to a number of factors, including the need for even greater efficiency all along the line, but the main reason was that rates had now fallen far behind costs and would do so even more rapidly in the foreseeable future unless rates were raised. If investment in the railroads continued to produce such negative results, they would preach, who could be expected to invest in their business in the future?

That afternoon the Commission adjourned the hearings until December 10, on which date they would resume in the mezzanine parlor of the new Willard Hotel. (The Commission was still hopelessly short of space in its own quarters.) Only Commissioner Harlan was present on that date to hear an expert witness whom the railroads had retained to teach the Commissioners a little monetary theory. George F. Brownell of the Erie pleaded with Harlan to introduce the concept of the purchasing power of money into the Commissioners' deliberations. He presented Charles A. Conant, a consulting economist of 34 Nassau Street, New York, whom Taft's Secretary of State, Elihu Root, had sent to the Philippines to reconstruct that country's currency system. Conant had also served Mexico's Porfirio Diaz and the heads of Panama and Nicaragua in the same capacity, and had helped Congress draft the Gold Standard Act of 1900. "Few persons outside the circle of professional economists are fully conscious of the principle that value is not a quality inherent in the article itself, in the same sense as size or color, warmth or cold, but is only the expression of a relationship between that and some other article," explained the expert. He cited Stanley Jevons, pioneer English economist, on the point; and America's Irving Fisher, who, in a lecture to the Alexander Hamilton Institute on the

[16] Five Per Cent Case Hearings, 12, 14.   [17] Ibid., 23.

instability of gold, had declared that the dollar had declined by one-third of its value in fifteen years.[18]

"What would have been said if it had been proposed by law in 1896 to require the railways to reduce their rates 35% to 50% within fifteen years?" Conant demanded to know. Yet that was just what had happened. "We have substituted statute law for economic law," he scolded. Index numbers of purchasing power (which he first had to explain) revealed that a shipper was paying, on the average, 37 per cent less to have a ton hauled a mile than at the end of the nineteenth century. The shippers, who were free to raise *their* prices, in fact, "have transferred an unearned increment to their own coffers at the expense of the railways." (If he had wanted to press the subject, he might have added that this had taken place at the expense of the larger economy as well, inasmuch as investment by railroads out of surplus had been limited accordingly.) Meanwhile, said Conant, other developments, such as industrial consolidations, the building of thousands of miles of electric traction lines, and heightening of competition in general, had reduced the railroads' ability to grow with the nation. Conant quoted the Hadley Commission's warnings about the great need for further capital investment in the railroads, and expressed doubt that it could be raised under the existing rate level. The urbane theorist apologized for the fact that a document he had in his hand, a reprint of an article by Professor Clement Colson in the *Revue Politique et Parlementaire,* was in French, but he promised to translate it for inclusion in the record. It was valuable, he said, because it summarized recent rate developments in both the state-owned and private railroads of Europe, where increases had taken place almost without exception.[19]

Clifford Thorne had arrived at the hearings just before the noon recess. In his formal appearance before the Commission, he made a statement by way of answering an embarrassing question which people had been asking recently: how could he represent the official regulatory commissions of eight western states and, at the same time, appear as counsel for a number of shippers' organizations? "I am simply here to help Mr. Brandeis and the others," he said. "In selecting someone to present the side of the public in these States, the [state] commissioners

[18] *Ibid.,* 691, 693–95.   [19] *Ibid.,* 699, 702, 705, 709, 711–13.

have gone no further than did the ICC in the appointment of Mr.
Brandeis." [20] In other words, to Thorne everybody not connected with
the railroads *was* the public, whether they were shippers engaged in private business for profit, or state commissioners. Their interests were
identical, while the railroads were merely private interests who had to
look out for themselves. His principle was a kind of prairie-grown
theory of class conflict. When it later became apparent that the thinking
of the people's lawyer had matured somewhat on this point, even if the
Populist-Progressive's had not, sparks would fly. Thorne and Frank
Lyon, counsel for the coal producers' association, made a cursory
cross-examination of Conant, but it was clear that such theorizing was
not their cup of tea.[21] If they based their lack of interest on the belief
that the economist had not penetrated the Commission's philosophy, the
decision in the case would show that they were not deceived.

The railroads now proceeded to show the Commission just what
they were up against in labor relations. John G. Walker, professional
wage negotiator for the B. & O., ticked off the dull, percentage-laden
list of increases since 1910. Now, he said, they were getting into a period in which wage increases were to be further removed from the railroads' discretion under the arbitration system. If labor was willing to
arbitrate, the railroads had to go along, or suffer condemnation for pulling the switch on a crippling strike. What reason did the brotherhoods
give for demanding wage increases if the eastern railroads were in poor
financial shape? Was it productivity increases in which they wished to
share? Nothing to do with it, explained Walker. To a wage earner there
was no more concrete argument for a raise than the fact that someone
else was getting more for the same job, and it was the union's argument
that western railroad men were enjoying higher wage scales. Lyon
wanted to know if increased rates was the answer to increased wages.
Definitely, replied Walker. "We have no recourse but to have someone
give us the money, which we can pass on to somebody else." Brandeis
jumped at this opportunity. "Or to save it through some other process!"
he exclaimed.[22]

The remark of the people's lawyer was the first concrete evidence
of the strategy he intended to employ in these hearings. After the new

[20] *Ibid.*, 729.   [21] *Ibid.*, 723–29.   [22] *Ibid.*, 755–69.

year he began to introduce testimony, supported by voluminous exhibits dutifully furnished by the railroads, on the "extra services" provided to large industrial shippers in the form of switching and spotting of cars at private sidings. These services, Brandeis calculated, cost the railroads about fifty million dollars a year—the same amount, coincidentally, which the railroads wanted to exact from shippers, large and small, in rate increases. The railroads, Brandeis asserted, should be collecting the cost of these services from the shippers who benefited by them. What he was complaining about was the use of railroad switch engines, manned by railroad employees, not just to switch freight cars onto these sidings (after all, they had to get there some way, and no one seriously suggested doing away with private sidings), but subsequently to move them to the exact spot on the siding where it was most convenient for them to be loaded, or to take out a car which had been loaded ahead of one which blocked its path.[23] This was an issue which fitted Brandeis' needs to a "T." The favor was a very simple one, practiced in the open for all to see, and it illustrated what the people's lawyer still firmly believed was the major evil of "giantism," the power of a large shipper to demand services which the little fellow could not.

In one sense, Brandeis' argument was sound. The traffic of a large, steady shipper was worth almost anything a railroad had to do to get it, and the assurance that cars would be furnished and spotted at his beck and call was frequently an important factor in the industrialist's decision to locate a plant upon a specific railroad in the first place. Railroads had special representatives whose job was to smell out plans for new factories and get them onto their lines. But as often was the case in Brandeis' arguments about "giantism," the argument produced initial indignation followed by the nagging feeling that there must be more to the matter than his simplistic explanations would indicate. Indeed there was. There were great economies to the manufacturer in not having to load his product onto a dray wagon, cart it to a public "team track," and reload it onto the railroad cars. (In many cases such a procedure was simply out of the question because of the size, weight, or other characteristics of the product.) Were these not savings to the economy as a whole? Furthermore, as a map furnished by the B. & O. at Bran-

[23] *Ibid.,* 1025.

deis' request showed, urban land on which to build team tracks had sky-
rocketed in cost and taxes in the past fifteen years. It was a great saving
to a railroad to be able to decentralize a large part of its freight transactions by shifting operations onto real estate owned by someone else. It
could be argued, although the bête noire of rebating ensured that it
would not, that such shippers deserved rate concessions, if anything. At
the very least, a railroad so fortunate as to acquire such a customer
could hardly refuse to put the freight cars where he could get at them.
Nevertheless, the impression was created that here was a source from
which the railroads could get additional revenue, if they really wanted
to. That was Brandeis' real objective. The issue of "free" services again
revealed the hopelessly confused state of public policy regarding railroad charges. In its very first decision, the Commerce Court had reversed an order of the ICC which had forbidden the S.P. and the Santa
Fe from making an extra charge for delivering cars to a jointly owned
industrial siding. The court, in other words, agreed with the ICC's special counsel while the ICC did not. The Supreme Court, as it would
most of the Commerce Court decisions which reached it, unanimously
reversed the decision, thus affirming the immunity of ICC rate rulings
from appeals to the judiciary.[24]

The railroads sought this time to demonstrate their achievements
in hauling the nation's freight and passengers. Patterson and the New
York Central's Butterfield spoke at length on how much had been done
and how much remained to do.[25] Following the 1910 debacle, the Central had hired William C. Wishart, former statistician for the state of
New York, to study its accomplishments. The period from 1896 to

---

[24] 1 Commerce Court 1 and 3 (188 Fed. Rep. 241), and 234 U.S. 294 and 315.
This matter is worth the space devoted to it here, because it illustrates the shaky
economics on which Brandeis founded some of his most ardent social convictions. Whereas he considered the free services merely a favor which large firms
could exact and small ones could not, the fact is that the social savings which
private sidings represented simply would not have existed in an economy composed of small factors of production. It is a simple case of the economies of
scale. Brandeis' summation, beginning on page 5259 of the Five Per Cent Case
Hearings, reveals that he could never get very far from his prejudice against
bigness. The question of the spotting services dragged into many pages of testimony and exhibits. A number of the latter were reproduced at great expense in
the printed record, including a bulky engineering drawing of a substantial portion
of the B. & O.'s main line.

[25] Five Per Cent Case Hearings, 5022, 5038.

1902, Wishart had discovered, was the most prosperous in the Central's history, because the enormous traffic gains had been possible without any substantial additions to plant. From 1903 to 1913, however, the story was quite different. Growth had taken place primarily by expansion of a plant which had been at capacity in 1903; furthermore, there had been an increase in output per employee of 16 per cent. As to prices, it was true that the recession had temporarily lowered the cost of certain commodities, just as the 1907–8 recession had temporarily lowered costs immediately before the 1910 hearings, but that was not the whole story. Take rails, for example. It was misleading to talk about the cost per pound of rail (it was up, anyway), when the Central was busily ripping up perfectly serviceable steel rail and replacing it with new, heavier rail (110 pounds per yard and more) demanded by the vastly heavier locomotives then coming into use. As for labor, the price of that commodity went only one way, and the records showed, asserted the statistician, that all goods which had a high labor input were now selling for much more than just a few years ago—all, that is, except railroad services. Brandeis, who would argue inaccurately that few prices had risen except food costs, could not afford to let this statement go by. But under cross-examination Wishart stuck to his point, and the people's lawyer ended up being bested by a lowly statistician.[26] The railroads then offered for the record extensive exhibits on recent gains in productivity.[27]

Nineteen-fourteen was a repetition of 1910 as far as the creativeness among the opposition was concerned. Again, only Brandeis had thought of anything new to say. The shippers, and particularly Clifford Thorne, acted as if they had learned nothing and forgotten nothing. Lyon had found a former New York University economics professor, Frank J. Warne, who had also worked for *Railway World* and as a statistician for the Order of Railway Conductors and Brotherhood of Railway Trainmen, and who had done considerable work on the sensational issue of interlocking directorates. Warne exhibited some hopelessly complicated charts which revealed the altogether unexciting fact that the names of members of a railroad's board of directors constantly popped up on the boards of the dozens of railroad corporations (most of them

[26] *Ibid.*, 4002–4.   [27] *Ibid.*, Vol. 5.

nothing more than names) which constituted the system—whose stock, in fact, was virtually wholly owned by the parent company. Challenged on the germaneness of these data, Lyon lamely replied that he wished to show that the railroads were "one big concern which is asking for a subsidy to carry on the transportation business of the country." [28] It was sheer legal puffery. Only the dignity of the proceedings must have prevented someone from reminding Lyon that he was delivering his antitrust evidence to the wrong address.

Thorne grasped at every straw. The dogmatic quality of his tone was astonishing. The great advances in productivity *must* have led to profitability, he blustered. Net earnings *can't* have declined. Reasonableness of return *can't* be established until the results of the valuation program are known. The railroads are still up to their old tricks, he argued. They are doctoring their books to show equipment maintenance costs far in excess of earlier years. Half of their securities are water. There is nothing wrong with railroad credit; there is simply a rise in interest rates which is affecting everyone.[29] The Iowa Progressive had wanted to appear last this time. When Brandeis' appointment as special counsel was announced, Thorne wrote the people's lawyer saying that such order would be in accordance with precedent established in 1910, but Brandeis gently reminded him that it had been the other way around.[30] The people's lawyer, however, chose a more dramatic way in which to reveal the course of his thinking than by playing the sphinx to the end. During a recess in the carriers' closing arguments, he had shown James L. Minnis, attorney for the Central Freight Association railroads, the brief which he had prepared. When Minnis was called to take the floor at the end of the recess, he was almost too excited to go on:

May it please your honors, an unforeseen circumstance has relieved the Commission of what might be termed an emotional scene. Had I presented my argument yesterday, I should have taken you to the ruins of CFA territory. I should have had my witness, Mr. Maxwell, accompany my description of that territory with his tears in order that I might have given some

[28] *Ibid.*, 2724–27.

[29] *Ibid.*, 2995–99, 3591. Italics added. Henry Varnum Poor would have been astonished at the durability of his thirty-year-old remark about watered stock.

[30] Mason, *Brandeis,* 342.

faint indication of the condition of the railroads in that unfortunate section of the country, but at adjournment yesterday Mr. Brandeis handed me a copy of his brief, and in that brief he makes a concession . . . that the CFA lines need more revenue.[31]

So it was not Brandeis' position, after all, that the railroads should have no relief whatever. They were, in fact, suffering from several injustices which should be rectified, in his opinion. For one thing, they were not being paid enough to carry the mail. The underpayment, he suspected, would amount to fifteen million dollars. The Post Office Department was rigidly adhering to the outdated law that the mails should be weighed only once every four years and the rate of payment adjusted accordingly. Not only was the volume of first-class mail rising steeply each year, but the flow now included packages mailed under the new parcel-post law, for the haulage of which no provision had been made in the statute! Another place where something would have to give, Brendeis asserted, was passenger service, which was one of the biggest leaks in the entire system. He adjured the roads to come back to the Commission with new passenger tariffs.[32] Finally, he counseled the Commission that the net earnings of railroads in Central Classification Territory were lower than desirable.

Brandeis spoke last, but the tone on which the proceedings were to end was more accurately set by George S. Patterson of the Pennsylvania, who had the last word for the railroad men. He ended his summation with an anguished cry of frustration which hinted that he believed the railroads east of Pittsburgh and Buffalo would come away with nothing:

Now, what is the conclusion of all this? I am worn out with figures . . . and hope this marks the end of an intimate relationship that I have had with the accounting department for the last six months [laughter]. But in these last three years—the real test, because they represent the field of legislative activity in full swing—the parties have expended $666 million and at the end find themselves $16 million worse off. . . .

The Pennsylvania system in three years has invested $207 million [yet] finds its net $11 million less. . . . In 10 years from 1903 to 1913 they invested $530 million upon which there was the munificent return of 2¼ per cent. And mark you, this was not in speculative enterprises . . . not in buy-

---

[31] Five Per Cent Case Hearings, 5073.   [32] Ibid., 5247.

ing the stocks of other companies . . . not for building any lines into a new country. It was expended in the intensive development of the richest traffic-producing sections in the world.[33]

IV

The senior senator from Wisconsin was furious. The railroad investigation was not proceeding in the way an archaic Progressive would like to have seen. The railroads' publicity efforts, of course, were old hat and easy to counter; if anything, they were welcome as grist for the Senator's journalistic mill.[34] But a disturbing flow of pro-railroad sentiment from other sources had become apparent. All kinds of people were delivering themselves of the opinion that the railroads deserved a rate increase and that it would be a good thing for the country if they got one. This being so, the ICC might be deflected from its duty, which, as a good Progressive, he saw as the prevention of a general increase in railroad rates in strict adherence to the Mann-Elkins Act. As the Commissioners retired into their chambers to consider the mass of evidence from the rate hearings, Robert M. La Follette rose in the Senate to propose an extraordinary piece of legislation. Anyone attempting to influence the ICC, except at a formal public hearing, he said, should be subject to a fine of $2000. This was "regulation gone mad," said one newspaper; "La Follette intends to imprison the ICC within the chamber where they give public hearings." [35] The bill was quickly buried in committee, and its sponsor's irritation revealed that the tide was beginning to turn against the repressive policies which the midwesterner and his followers had fastened onto the nation four years before. Albert B. Cummins, ranking minority member of the Senate Committee on Interstate Commerce (in energy if not in seniority), treated the chamber to one of his marathon speeches some days later. It was, said one observer, "extraordinary in its incomprehensibility," containing nothing more solid than the emotional accusation that the railroads were "sham-

---

[33] *Ibid.*, 5274–75.

[34] *La Follette's Weekly* (Madison, Wisconsin), quoted in "Are the Railroads 'Shamming'?" *LD*, XLVIII (April 25, 1914), 972–73.

[35] *CR*, 63d Cong., 2d Sess., 7727–8093; *NYT*, April 14, 1914, 14.

ming" before the ICC, and an assertion that the depression, although
real, was only temporary.[36] Cummins' speech was the beginning of a re-
actionary effort on the part of the radicals to stem the tide, which they
would continue right down to the federalization of the railroads at the
end of 1917.

   Clifford Thorne took a worse beating from the eastern press than
La Follette or Cummins. As the poverty of his arguments became apparent, he had shifted to an indictment of the railroad men's honesty, in
the best Granger-Populist-Insurgent tradition. His accusation of the fal-
sification of the books in the matter of maintenance costs backfired
badly as railroad men refused to take such allegations quietly. A horde
of Pennsylvania Railroad stockholders, gathered in Philadelphia's Hor-
ticultural Hall for their annual meeting, applauded Samuel Rea enthusiastically when he urged them to protest such unfair treatment to their
state and national representatives. Daniel Willard echoed the denial,
and condemned Thorne's attempt to show that his railroad's ability to
borrow money was unimpaired. A B. & O. bond sale which the Iowan
had cited, said Willard, was negotiated before, not after, the 1910 rate
decision. Meanwhile Thorne, attempting to extricate himself from
charges of "juggling" official data to suit his own purposes, hurt the
Commissioners' feelings with the lame excuse that their reports were so
confusing that he "misunderstood" them.[37] The New York *Times*
zeroed in on the ambitious young radical. His arguments, said the editor,
"are prejudiced by his personality. . . . His words reveal such a porten-
tous mixture of misinformation and malice that the prospect for any advance of rates seems postponed until after a change of political sentiments in the west." There was reason to believe, however, that Thorne
did not really represent the latest trend in thinking back home. Some of
his "constituents" had had some harsh things to say about him recently:

Now we find the same gentleman chasing up and down the country advocat-
ing all sorts of socialist ideas, such as government ownership of railroads,
and showing all kinds of statistics and compilations of figures. God knows
where he gets them. Certainly not from anything that has transpired on
earth, for neither his talk nor his figures represent the true conditions either

---

[36] "Are the Railroads 'Shamming'?" 972; *CR,* 63d Cong., 2d Sess., 6600 *et seq.*

[37] *NYT,* March 10, 1914, 3; March 11, 9; March 12, 8.

in this country or foreign countries where government ownership has been tried and inevitably has been proved a failure.[38]

"The Constitution," said the *Times*, "prevented the Thornes of the seventies from confiscating the railways, but at the cost of saddling the country with the doctrine that the rate which stops just this side of confiscation is reasonable." [39]

Not that there was any shortage of antirailroad sentiment. The farther west one went, the less sympathy with the eastern railroads one was likely to find. The Pittsburgh *Gazette* said that "the railroads are putting up the most stupendous hunger strike on record." The Chicago *Tribune* said that the railroads deserved the public's scorn because of their "shady past," but added prudently that railroad securities would in the end have to be made "secure." [40] In the same city *The Public* expressed Insurgent logic in the assertion that once the ICC gave the railroads a raise it would subsequently be subject to railroad control, and saw public ownership as the only remedy. The Boise, Idaho, *Capital News* hewed to the opposition line, although the old enthusiasm seemed to be lacking. In the East journalistic sentiment had generally swung over. The Philadelphia *Public Ledger* said that the ICC "has become a colossus. The Nation is investigation-mad . . . radicals and demagogues [are in control] . . . every new rate is assumed to be unreasonable unless proved to the contrary." The New York *Globe* said, "The public is with the railroads." The Baltimore *Sun,* contemptuous of the long-drawn-out proceedings, advised the ICC "to run this case by express and not by freight." The tramp, hat in hand at the housewife's back door, was a popular cartoonists' symbol for the railroads.[41]

Politicians could not escape the realization that what had been a Republican problem, and a very badly handled one at that, was now becoming a Democratic headache. President Wilson's preoccupation with Mexican badmen inspired the New York *Sun*'s Cesare to cartoon the ICC as a gang of bandits holding up a locomotive, with the barb, "They call this *revolutionary* in Mexico." Rogers, in the New York *Herald,*

[38] Resolution of the Mayor and Board of Aldermen, Fort Madison, Iowa, quoted *ibid.,* May 1, 1914, 12.

[39] *NYT,* May 1, 1914, 12.

[40] "The Bitter Cry of the Railroads," *LD,* XLVIII (April 11, 1914), 808–9.

[41] "Are the Railroads 'Shamming'?" 973.

showed the Democratic donkey, sledgehammer in hoof, beating the ar-
mored-knight railroads into a pile of junk.[42] What *was* the railroad policy of the Democratic administration? What *did* the new president think
of the way the ICC was running the railroads? Throughout 1913, during his whirlwind campaign to enact the New Freedom, Wilson had
seemed content to allow that body to make its own way. His faith in the
independent regulatory commission idea seemed complete, and his determination to keep hands off was a natural policy to expect from a
former professor of political science. By January of his second year in office, however, Wilson was deeply disturbed by the worsening economic
situation. He meant to be no Grover Cleveland, taking over the reins of
government on behalf of the Democratic party at the end of a period of
prosperity. He had reached the private position that rate increases
should be granted. On January 20, 1914, from the Speaker's rostrum of
the House of Representatives, he began what was to be a three-year effort to nudge the ICC into a more constructive frame of mind. Delivering his annual message to Congress, he removed all reasonable doubt as
to where he stood:

The prosperity of the railroads and the prosperity of the country are inseparably connected and those connected with the actual management and
operation of the roads have spoken very plainly and very earnestly with a
purpose we ought to be quick to accept.[43]

A month later things were much worse. The big eastern railroads
were threatening to cut back on service, thereby adding to unemployment, which was reaching crisis proportions in the steel and railroad
equipment industries. Wilson called Commissioner Clark to the White
House, ostensibly for a report on the progress of the physical valuation

---

[42] "The Bitter Cry of the Railroads," 808.

[43] *Messages and Papers of the Presidents,* ed. James D. Richardson *et al.* (20
vols., and supplements, Washington, 1898–1925), XVII, 7916. Winthrop M. Daniels, in whom the President confided more and more as the wartime transportation emergency worsened, later wrote, "During the long period of suspense
[while waiting for the ICC decision in 1914] Mr. Wilson said to me that he
would no more think of suggesting to the Commission how the case should be
decided than he would think of proffering suggestions to the Supreme Court. . . .
He felt strongly that the long delay was regrettable. . . . I never knew until long
after the Commission had denied the increase that his personal opinion lay in the
other direction." Daniels, *American Railroads: Four Phases of Their History*
(Princeton, 1932), 83.

program and to advise on Senate opposition to the pending appointments of Hall and Daniels to the Commission. During the early spring a
stream of callers talked to the President on railroad matters. To a delegation which had called to consult on the New Haven Railroad mess,
Wilson expressed deep interest in the urgency of their general financial
situation. The following week the major eastern railroads announced
that there would be no customary spring increase in operations. Instead,
nearly 100,000 men were being laid off. The Pennsylvania added that
one-third of the 125,000 men who were being kept on would be on
short hours, and that 118 trains on its lines east of Pittsburgh were
being "annulled." [44] In the Calumet industrial district of Chicago, 50,-
000 workmen in railroad equipment plants were preparing an appeal to
the President.[45] Vice-President Brownell of the Erie begged the ICC to
"sidetrack" Brandeis' interminable free-services investigation and proceed with the main subject. A. S. Smith, who had recently succeeded
William C. Brown as president of the New York Central, told the Commission, "It is very critical indeed; as I see it we are going to the devil
as fast as we can." By June 1 the New York *Times* flatly declared that
"the President's sympathies are with the railroads." [46] Meanwhile the
ICC plodded on.

V

Fourteen months were required for the ICC to decide whether to
allow the eastern railroads to raise their rates, and even then only three
Commissioners (Clark, Meyer, and Hall) agreed with the decision exactly as written. Clements remained a tower of strict-constructionist
strength to the bitter end, asserting that the Commission simply could
not consider the financial condition of the railroads in deciding whether
rates were reasonable. Commissioner Harlan, who ended up writing the
report as chairman of a badly divided panel, was only slightly less narrow in his position. The first job of the Commission, in his opinion, was
to correct inconsistencies and inequities within the rate structure.

[44] *NYT*, March 20, 1914, 1; March 28, 1; March 29, 6; March 30, 3; March 31,
15; April 2, 6.

[45] *Ibid.*, April 12, 1914, V, 4.   [46] *Ibid.*, June 2, 1914, 7.

Whether it would be proper afterward to raise rates generally was arguable, but to do so before revising the structure was "morally wrong." Two Commissioners, McChord and Daniels, joined with the contented three to make a majority of five to two, but neither was happy about it. As we shall see, McChord wanted to go somewhat further, and Daniels, a great deal further. In summary, the decision contained three important sections: (1) a 5 per cent average increase in freight rates in Central Classification Territory, where net operating income "considered as a whole, is smaller than is demanded in the public interest," but with important exceptions as to commodities covered, which drastically reduced the value of the award; (2) an extended remonstrance to the railroads against free services with suggestions for raising revenues otherwise than by increasing rates; and (3) a lecture on the role of the ICC in making national railroad policy.[47]

It took a great deal of agonizing for the Commission to rationalize the relief to the midwestern carriers. Reasonableness of a rate, the decision insisted, was a thing apart from the financial condition of the railroad charging it. A poor railroad would not be entitled to an increase if the rate were unreasonable, while a prosperous road would nevertheless be entitled to an increase if the new rate could be shown to be reasonable. But there was the matter of the public interest. If railroads in a specific geographic area were noticeably less prosperous than in other areas, and less prosperous than the public interest demanded, that might be a different matter.[48] Now, the Commission certainly did not think that the eastern railroads as a group were badly off, at least not in relation to the thirteen-year trend since 1900. Net income, as a percentage of total investment, was 5.36 per cent in 1913, better than in either 1912 or 1911.[49] But, acknowledged the Commission, when profitability

[47] 31 ICC 351. The decision is discussed in I. L. Sharfman, *The Interstate Commerce Commission: A Study in Administrative Law and Procedure* (4 vols. in 5, New York, 1931–37), IIIb, 33–48.

[48] 31 ICC 351, 357.

[49] But poorer, it might have noted, than any year before 1911 except for the panic year of 1908. The main weakness of the ICC's analysis, however, was that the 1913 figure, covering a fiscal year ending June 30, 1913, was a year old by the time the Commission decided, and failed entirely to reflect conditions in mid-1914. The panel ignored the obvious fact that the trunk lines were going to have a hard time carving a 6 per cent dividend out of a 5.16 per cent return,

was calculated by four categories of railroads, an interesting pattern
developed: [50]

Group I	(coal-carrying roads)	8.55%
Group II	(three leading systems) [51]	5.16
Group III	(New England lines)	5.56
Group IV	(the rest, 17 roads, of which 14 were in Central Classification Territory)	2.15

There was one bit of sophistry which the Commission certainly was not
going to fall for, and that was the railroads' efforts to have profitability
considered on the *increment* in investment from year to year or in the
three years since the Commission's power to suspend rate increases had
been granted. Net income, wrote Harlan testily, is earned as much by
one dollar of property as another. So much for economic sophistication.[52]

But, one might ask, how about all the improvements which the
railroads, especially the trunk lines, had made? How about the constantly rising trend in costs, especially wages? The Commission's reaction to these knotty problems was as infuriating to a railroad man as it
was incomprehensible to the general public. "Many improvements have
been made in railroad facilities, many economies in transportation have
been effected, and a general expansion and improvement in transportation conditions have taken place. Under the circumstances, if any
change in transportation rates were to be made, it would be logical to
expect a reduction rather than an advance." [53] But look at the operating
ratio, one might have spluttered: from 67.3 per cent in 1910 to 71.8
per cent in 1913—a disastrously high figure. Indeed, there were many

---

much less carry anything to surplus for reinvestment. Nor did it face up to the
fact that the small increase would be of little help to some midwestern roads like
the Alton which were barely covering operating expenses. 31 ICC 351, 367.

[50] 31 ICC 351, 384–86.

[51] Pennsylvania, 5.48 per cent; New York Central, 5.47 per cent; B. & O., 4.52
per cent.

[52] 31 ICC 351, 360.

[53] *Ibid.*, 353–54. This incredible statement reveals how totally the Commission
rejected the purchasing-power-of-money concept. In fact, the railroads had invol-
untarily lowered rates by some 30 per cent or more in this sense.

reasons for this, the Commission agreed. "In reconstructing their tracks and in changing and adding to their facilities . . . the carriers, wisely as we think, have endeavored somewhat to anticipate the future. . . . In some instances changes . . . have resulted in the practical rebuilding of lines, and there are few roads . . . on which work of this nature has not been done more or less extensively." All of this had naturally tended to increase the operating ratio, the Commission blandly explained, because the railroads increased their allowances for maintenance and depreciation concurrently, as was prudent. Some protestants who appeared before the ICC during the hearings had violently criticized these charges as excessive, but the Commission believed that they were still too low. Costs, the panel freely agreed, were rising. Coal was 7.7 per cent higher in 1913 than in 1910 and wages were 9.02 per cent higher, with another fifty million dollar increase not yet reflected in the data. Indeed, said the Commission without cracking a smile, the managements of the eastern railroads were to be congratulated that the operating ratio had risen no more than it had. Congratulated, yes—but not rewarded.[54]

The Commission, it seemed, was preoccupied with the many sources of revenue which the railroads ought to exploit before they could morally demand more from the nation's shippers. It had the passenger service very much in mind. The railroads were not charging enough for what everyone recognized was a vastly improved service. Yet the railroads had not asked for higher passenger fares. Why not? [55] Another thing you railroad men could do, said the Commission, would be to tidy up your rate structure. There were, it was sure, many unremunerative rates which had originated in "fierce competition" or under the "menace of . . . big shippers" which "have doubtless been continued through ignorance of the loss they entail." Most important, the railroads must start charging for services such as pickup and delivery, storage, furnishing of containers, excessive unloading time, and many others. Freight car utilization had to be increased. All of these factors

---

[54] *Ibid.*, 376–80.

[55] *Ibid.*, 392, 407. The answer, as the Commission should have known, was that as long as the states could control intrastate rates, which they were grinding down to two cents a mile, tinkering with interstate fares would only lead to an even more distorted fare structure than already existed. The Supreme Court, as we shall see, was to recognize this fact shortly in the Shreveport decision.

were tightly interrelated, a practical fact which the Commission recognized in its admonition, "The scramble for tonnage, which has led to so many abuses, should be succeeded by an orderly pursuit of profit-earning traffic." [56] Clearly the Commission could not comprehend a fact of life which any traffic manager could have explained: there was just not enough potential traffic, at the abnormally low rates in effect, to produce the gross revenues required to make operations more profitable, nor, as the events of 1916–17 would demonstrate, could the railroads carry such an enormous hypothetical volume efficiently anyway. If the railroads had followed the Commission's advice in 1914 and got tough with their customers, the weaker roads would simply have starved to death. There can be no mistaking the fact that the Commission held the key to the discouragement of wasteful competitive practices: higher rates.

Was there, then, no basis for the cries of alarm about the conditions of American railroads? No, the Commission concluded, there was not. "The credit of our railroads has undoubtedly suffered in recent years, but largely from causes that were independent of their rates. Their borrowing power has suffered relatively, because of the great competition for money by governments . . . public-service corporations, and industries [and] because of mismanagement." [57] Another factor which had certainly not helped was the railroads' own publicity campaign. And while it was on that subject, the Commission seized the opportunity to lecture the railroads and the nation on the uses of publicity where the deliberations of a government body were concerned. Many people, the Commission complained, thought it ought to act merely "to restore confidence" in business and "give things a start." The railroads had a perfect right to "get the facts across," as Daniel Willard explained the purpose of their public relations campaign, but frankly the Commission did not like being placed on the spot. The campaign, it said, "shows a widespread misconception as to our powers and duties." Happily, though, the railroads were getting more cooperative

[56] *Ibid.*, 408–9.

[57] *Ibid.*, 419–20. Events would prove that the ICC was hopelessly uninformed on this point, as was virtually everyone else outside the banking community. Nor did the Commission address itself to the working capital crisis which had already beset many weaker roads.

with the Commission all the time, and "the future is full of promises." [58]
So, unfortunately, was the past.

Commissioner McChord did not think much of the decision. If an increase was to be granted, there was no basis for preferential treatment of one geographic area over the other, either in law or in fact. The two territories, he noted, were industrially one. The relationship between rates in the two areas was historical, and should not be disturbed, at least not for the present reason. Furthermore, said the Kentuckian, perhaps recalling the sight of a Pennsylvania or a B. & O. freight train struggling over the Alleghenies east of Pittsburgh, "conditions of transportation are probably more favorable in the western area than in trunkline territory." [59]

Commissioner Daniels, however, spoke the wisest piece in this remarkable document. Not only should the increase apply to trunk line territory also, he said, but "the majority opinion falls far short of giving even the carriers in [the Central] region the relief to which the evidence clearly shows they are entitled." [60] And as long as the Commission insisted on computing net return on investment as a broad average, it was closing its eyes to a phenomenon which no investor would ignore: marginal return on marginal investment had not only declined but was actually a negative factor.[61] That this was an economist talking, not a lawyer or ambitious Progressive politician, was further underscored by Daniels' closing words of warning:

The world-wide phenomenon of rising prices is by this time no novelty. Since 1906 the average rise in the world's price level is estimated by competent statisticians at from 30 to 50%. It has mirrored itself in the rising cost of living; it has evoked, and most properly, advances in wages and salaries; it has coincided with an increase in the nominal rate of interest where part of the interest so-called is but compensation for the anticipated depreciation of the capital sum later to be repaid.

The rise in the price level must eventually be reckoned with in railroading. For a time its effects may be masked by adventitious increases in the volume of traffic, but this temporary relief in its very nature is uncertain, and sooner or later the difficulty is sure to reappear. For a time it may be

[58] *Ibid.,* 427. It was patently unfair of the Commission to lecture the railroads or the general public for misconceiving the panel's "powers and duties" when its members could not agree among themselves on what Congress expected of them.

[59] *Ibid.,* 432, 434.   [60] *Ibid.,* 437.   [61] *Ibid.,* 453.

circumvented by extraordinary economies, but in its nature it is inexorable. It must be faced, not trifled with. . . . A carrier without a sufficient return . . . can not permanently render service commensurate with the needs of the public.

Eventually it may come about that railroads will be owned by the government. . . . That a departure from . . . private ownership should be materially hastened by the reluctance of new capital . . . would seem to be a grave indictment of our present system of regulation and control.[62]

The Commission published its decision on July 29, 1914. In Vienna the people mourned the death of an archduke and prepared for war. In the White House a sorrowful President and his daughters watched the life of Ellen Wilson ebb away. Three days later the Germans crossed the Belgian border. The guns of August were about to blow archaic Progressivism into oblivion.

[62] *Ibid.*, 454.

CHAPTER X

THE THIRD DENIAL

Defeat of alfalfa and the Mariposa lily.
Defeat of the Pacific and the long Mississippi.
Defeat of the young by the old and silly.—VACHEL LINDSAY

The market yesterday illustrated the completeness with which the standard
railway issues have been eclipsed in the favor of traders by the industrials,
especially the group which is profiting from excellent business from home
and abroad. . . . There was not a single transaction in St. Paul Railway
[but] extraordinary activity of motor issues.—NEW YORK *Times,*
September 22, 1915

I

Excited traders, gathered on the steps of the New York Stock Exchange an hour before the opening bell on Thursday morning, July 31,
1914, were forming "bear pools" as thirty-six members of the Exchange's governing committee made their way into the building. All but
six of the membership had hurried back to town in response to an urgent telegram from Exchange President H. G. S. Noble, or were already
on hand for the unpleasant duty which they suspected awaited them.
After a month in which the Austrian archduke's assassination had been
shifted to the inside pages of newspapers and the possibility of war had
been minimized by numerous wise "authorities"—a month in which, it
was to be known only later, the chancelleries of Europe had labored
frantically to patch up the quarrel between Austria and Serbia—war
had come after all. By Wednesday, July 30, it was apparent that a general conflict was inevitable. All over the world trading in stocks and
bonds had been suspended. The price of gold mounted as holders of national currencies flew to the only "sure" storehouse of value in a world
gone mad. The pound sterling was so hard hit that few thought England

could continue to honor its commitment to the gold standard, while at this early stage few recognized that the dollar had suddenly emerged as the world's safest currency. As the full implications of the conflict dawned on businessmen and government officials, they foresaw ocean commerce at a standstill, with the great agricultural export surpluses of the United States rotting unmarketed in the farmers' storehouses. The stage was set for a financial catastrophe of snowballing proportions unless a hard decision was reached. A few seconds before the opening bell was due, word reached the floor that the Exchange was closed and all deliveries of securities suspended. Quietly the members drifted off the floor. They would not return for four months.[1]

A people whose views of the effects of world war were formed in 1939, when the economy of the United States had been limping along at a fraction of its capacity for ten years, cannot readily comprehend the depressing impact of the first several months of the 1914 war. Business, it is true, had been in the doldrums for upwards of a year, but the nation had been keyed to capacity output for almost two decades. Business had a long way to fall, and it had looked shaky ever since the new administration had taken over in Washington. To a nation still dependent upon a strong European market for its cotton and wheat, and so far as anyone knew still tied with golden cords to the international financial system headquartered in London, things looked disastrous. Certain it was that none of the developments the experts were predicting—the drying up of farm exports, the shutting off of strategic raw materials on which American chemical and metallurgical industries so heavily depended, the selling out of European holdings of the securities of American corporations to get gold—meant anything but disaster for the nation's already depressed railroads. A further decline in revenues could result in the disappearance of net income altogether. The first six months of the war were dark days for the railroads' customers. The physical volume of business, already well below the peak reached in January, 1913, had dropped another 10 per cent by November, 1914. Factory employment skidded another 4 per cent, while pig iron production (much more significant for the coal-, ore-, and steel-carrying business of the railroads) was in a full-fledged depression, at only one-half the level

[1] H. G. S. Noble, *The New York Stock Exchange in the Crisis of 1914* (New York, 1915), 9–10.

of early 1913. By the end of 1914, as a result, rail freight volume nationally was running nearly 20 per cent below the earlier period, but in the East, where export volume was down sharply and iron and steel production in such dire straits, the situation for the railroads, which had just been told by the ICC that they needed no rate relief, was bad indeed.[2]

War or no war, railroad men everywhere refused to accept the verdict in the rate case just settled. They were glad to get any indication from the Commission that rates could be raised across the board in response to general financial conditions, but to a man they agreed that the relief was too little and should have been extended to the eastern railroads as well. E. P. Ripley of the Santa Fe, whose role as a railroad statesman was being rapidly diminished by an ill-concealed disgust for the Commission and for the government's inept handling of railroad affairs in general, called the decision "a scolding which took the form of a stump speech . . . far from being the utterance of a judicial body." Frederic Delano, the more politic leader of the midwestern railroads which had just become the beneficiaries of the Commission's largesse, belittled the size of the grant. When one considered that coal and other minerals (50 per cent of total tonnage) were specifically excluded, said the Wabash head, and the fact that Buffalo-Chicago rates were effectively kept down by lake competition anyway, it was hard to see where the railroads would be any better off. Frederick D. Underwood, crusty president of the Erie, growled that his railroad was not interested in the decision "one way or the other. I predicted months ago that the Commission would give the railroads little or nothing."[3]

The considerably improved climate of public opinion seemed to make it certain that the railroad men would be back knocking on the Commission's door before long. During the long-drawn-out hearings the periodical press had had some very nice things to say about the railroads and their new stance. The railroads' presentation of their case, wrote the editor of the *Nation,* "is both temperate and impressive [in contrast to] the outcry against the government's injustice and the threats of business ruin which for a time made the episode of 1910 all but

[2] U.S. Bureau of the Census, *Historical Statistics of the United States: Colonial Times to 1957* (Washington, 1960), 329, 330, 333, 339.

[3] *NYT,* Aug. 13, 1914, 8; "Rate Decision," *LD,* XLIX (Aug. 15, 1914), 259.

farcical." [4] The *Review of Reviews* went on record in favor of an increase, and provided its readers with a photograph of the suddenly powerful Interstate Commerce Commission, sitting courtlike on its "bench." [5] The following month the same magazine featured an article by the "high priest of scientific management," the same Harrington Emerson who had provided Brandeis with his $300-million-a-year savings argument in 1910. Emerson went all the way for the railroads. He twitted the Commission for wasting so much time on questions like interlocking directorates, free passes, private cars, and the like. "Officers' business cars," he asserted, "assumed by the public to be abodes of luxury and ease, are generally the hardest-working centers of our American life." The real problem, Emerson said, was the multitude of meaningless regulations, state, local, and national. "One hookworm," said the colorful engineer, "would not count; a hundred thousand are depleting." As for scientific management, the ICC itself had a lot to learn. The Commissioners should remember that their reports were like eggs: "their value depends upon their freshness," but most of their reports were very old eggs indeed. More seriously, he noted that obsolescence, rather than simple wearing-out, was now the primary fact of railroad life, calling for much higher depreciation charges than in the past. The men in Washington, Emerson suspected, just did not realize this; at any rate, "The ICC does not bring into relief this tremendous change in conditions," he asserted. [6]

Newspapers generally found something, if not everything, good in the decision. The Philadelphia *North American,* consistent foe of any increase, rationalized that "there is a clear cut decision that the railroads must be operated not as private enterprises [but to ensure] fair dividends upon honest capital under efficient management." The New York *Herald* thought it a great step forward that the principle that "railways are entitled to a fair return" had at least been recognized, while the *Sun* cheered, "A day of fair play has dawned for the railroads after a long night of darkness." "A step in the right direction," granted

[4] *Nation,* XCVI (May 22, 1913), 533.

[5] "The Freight Rate Increase: A Crisis in Railroad Finance," *Review of Reviews,* XLIX (May, 1914), 562–65.

[6] Harrington Emerson, "Rate Decision," *Review of Reviews,* L (Sept., 1914), 345–48.

the Springfield, Massachusetts, *Republican*. But others felt that the ICC
had labored long and brought forth a mouse. "No one will ever be able
to compute the damage that has resulted to business of all kinds . . .
[the decision] comes at last when interest in it is reduced to a minimum," sneered the New York *World*. The height of contempt for the
Commission was reached by the Baltimore *News:* "It is not complete
proof of the success of regulation that the regulating agency unanimously agreed that more revenue was needed, and then by a divided
vote refused adequate relief." [7]

II

Winthrop M. Daniels had heard little from his old Princeton colleague since coming to Washington to sit on the Interstate Commerce
Commission, and now that a war was on in Europe he expected to hear
even less. He was surprised, therefore, to find in his mail one day that
summer a brief note from the President, enclosing a letter from Henry
L. Higginson, the Boston investment banker. The financier had written
to Wilson to solicit his direct support of the eastern railroads' efforts to
reopen their rate-increase case on the basis of considerably worsened
business conditions. The President had told Higginson that he had
doubts about the propriety of putting his personal convictions before
the Commission: "They are as jealous of executive suggestions as the
Supreme Court would be, and I dare say with justification." Still, he
thought Higginson's views "in the main true," and now he was sending
the banker's letter to his friend, who would shortly help to decide the
issue. [8] Whether such solicitousness would help or would turn out to be
the kiss of death for both the railroads and Commissioner Daniels was a
question that would not be answered for another two years.

Railroad men were looking for help wherever they could get it.
They had sent six of their number to plead personally with the President, and it was apparent that he wanted to help. They toyed with the
idea of going direct to Congress, but apparently decided that what

[7] "Rate Decision," *LD*, XLIX (Aug. 15, 1914), 259–60.

[8] Arthur Walworth, *Woodrow Wilson* (2 vols., New York, 1958), II, 409n.

might ultimately come out of the complex mechanism of compromise that had produced the Act of 1910 might leave them worse off than ever.[9] It was obvious that as long as the Commission was firmly in the driver's seat they would have to be careful how they criticized its driving.[10] In the end, they sought a simple rehearing of their case on August 25, 1914, and in less than two months the Commission was ready to hear testimony. The New York *Times* sarcastically commented in its editorial column that it was really the third beginning of a four-year-old case. This time, said the editor, there was hope, because by limiting their considerations to changed conditions since the end of July the Commissioners would not have to reverse themselves, and thus would not risk losing face.[11]

The hearings, which began on October 19 and continued through October 30, provided few surprises or new faces.[12] The railroad men pleaded that the surplus, which in past hearings they had described as inadequate, was now about to disappear altogether. The Commissioners seemed more hostile than ever. Clements asked querulously why the railroads thought they should get any different consideration from other industries affected by the war. Meyer questioned them rhetorically about foreign investors, and wondered if American shippers were not being asked to shoulder a burden which Europeans had thrown off. Daniel Willard, again carrying the ball for the railroads, was attacked by Brandeis for maintaining the B. & O.'s 6 per cent dividend even though the railroad was not currently earning it. This was logical: if the dividend was suspect when earned, it certainly was suspect when paid out of accumulated surplus. Willard missed the opportunity of pointing out to the people's lawyer that that was exactly what a surplus was for. Brandeis pressed on. The B. & O., he noted, had just issued $35 million in one-year 5 per cent notes. How did it expect to meet them when due,

[9] *NYT,* Aug. 26, 1914, 8.

[10] There were many who, although firmly in favor of rate regulation, could not understand why the Commission went out of its way to disapprove proposed increases to which no shipper had objected. The House Committee on Interstate and Foreign Commerce had just buried a proposal by Jefferson M. Levy of New York City that the House investigate such practices. *CR,* 63d Cong., 2d Sess., 7404.

[11] *NYT,* Sept. 20, 1914, II, 9; Sept. 21, 6.

[12] They were printed as Vols. 6 and 7 of the Five Per Cent Case Hearings.

since interest rates of 7 or 8 per cent were anticipated by some? "You defend here today a reduction of practically every expense except the dividend," said the people's lawyer. The railroads had no case, he asserted. In its decision in July the Commission had forecast a drop of $75 million in revenues, and a drop of $76 million had actually taken place. Where were the new conditions the railroad men talked about? "The Commission also forecast an improvement in business conditions," retorted Willard, "whereas there actually has been retrogression." [13] The following day a more serious note was introduced when Frederick Strauss, of J. & W. Seligman, investment bankers, warned of the outward flow of gold that would result from a loss of confidence abroad in American railroad securities.

Clifford Thorne made his customary appearance on October 23 and contributed his familiar arguments. "A number of years ago," he gravely informed the Commission, "a distinguished authority testified that over 75% of railroad capital stock was water." [14] The occasion for raising the ante on Henry Varnum Poor was the usual pointless discussion of the surplus. This time Brandeis consented to allow Thorne to speak last. The Iowan was to be so angry by the time his turn came, however, that the concession was a small one. For Brandeis had another of his dramatic changes of strategy to announce. He offered the startling proposition that, as long as rates were reasonable, the surplus could be any amount. A surplus was necessary, he explained, to provide for lean years and "to assure to the investor a sense of safety." Thorne had listened uncomfortably to all of this. He broke into Brandeis' reading of his prepared brief to remind him that he, Thorne, had, after all, only accepted the Commission's stand on surplus. Did Brandeis understand him to insist that *no* surplus should be allowed? Irritated at the discourtesy, the people's lawyer retorted, "I thought you were rather niggardly as to surplus," and swept on. Thorne was speechless with rage. Outside the hearing room he was unrestrained in his comments to reporters. "As an honest public servant . . . I resent most bitterly the unpardona-

---

[13] Five Per Cent Case Hearings, 5681–96; *NYT*, Oct. 10, 1914, 7. The *Times* felt it was "lamentable to have to explain to Mr. Brandeis" the importance of maintaining the dividend. It could well have been asked of the Boston lawyer whether he thought the short-term financing could have been placed at all if the dividend had been cut or passed. *NYT*, Oct. 21, 1914, 10.

[14] *NYT*, Oct. 24, 1914, 16.

ble attack made by Mr. Brandeis." He was chagrined, he said, finally to learn that the Bostonian had intended to take the railroads' side all along. Brandeis was, sneered the Iowan, "a second Daniel, well worthy of that distinguished ancestor." [15] It was the end of a beautiful friendship.

But Brandeis did *not* want the eastern railroads' plea for general rate relief granted. His entire case was based on the conviction that rates, taken as a whole, were *not* reasonable. He was surer than ever that the rate structure was badly flawed, and that inconsistencies and inequities in it should be corrected before any change was made in the general level. His continuing counsels of perfection in time of crisis were not well received. "Mr. Brandeis is wrapped up in the ideal railroad," editorialized the *Times;* "he has hitherto carried the Commission into the clouds with him, but the time has come for the Commission, at least, to come down to earth." [16] Sensing that the game was going against him, Brandeis showed himself willing to play the Progressive ace. "Does mere need force . . . your honors . . . to a finding that rates are just and reasonable because only with such increases can the necessary amount of money be raised?" [17] Brandeis' move was pure legal obfuscation, based on that flaw in the statute which was there to be used at times like this. But it no longer worked. Special counsel himself had cited "mere need" as the basis for his recommendation that midwestern rates be raised earlier that year. There was no turning back.

As the Commission retired to deliberate the issue, a voice came from out of the past which revealed dramatically how far that body had strayed from the original purposes of regulation. Still living in retirement up in South Lincoln, Massachusetts, was the man who, with his pioneer work on state commissions in the eighties and nineties, had done more than any other man to make the government assume some responsibility for what happened on the railroads. In an open letter to the President, Charles Francis Adams advised that the anomalies of regulation (he had the conflict between national and state bodies pri-

[15] Five Per Cent Case Hearings, 5260–61; Alpheus T. Mason, *Brandeis: A Free Man's Life* (New York, 1946), 345. Thorne was one of the bitterest opponents of Brandeis' appointment to the Supreme Court two years later.

[16] *NYT,* Oct. 21, 1914, 10.

[17] Five Per Cent Case Hearings, 6334; Mason, *Brandeis,* 349.

marily in mind) be cleared up before more harm was done. He recommended federal chartering of railroads, although not government ownership. Much, much damage had already been done, he asserted. "Personally, I have no financial interest in railroad securities. Watching the course of events and legislation, I long since ceased to feel confidence in them. . . . The situation is unbusinesslike, illogical, and absurd, as well as impossible. . . . The railroad candle has for some time past been burned at both ends." His statement was food for the most profound thought.[18]

A month later the Commission, by the same vote that had given relief to the midwestern railroads in July, now dropped a few crumbs to the faithful servant in the East. Harlan indulged himself in a legalistic orgy. No new facts had been introduced, he said. We agreed in July that the roads needed more income. But it couldn't be given in this manner then, and it couldn't be given so now. The law required the Commission to ascertain that rates were just and reasonable, he complained. For thirty years the first-class freight rate between New York and Chicago had been 75 cents per hundredweight. It was the "rate yardstick of this country." Now it was to be raised, although not a shred of evidence had been presented to show that that particular rate was unduly low. Clements shook his lawyer's head even more gravely. "If the legislative authority of the Commission is as broad as this [action of the Commission] then I must confess that I have gravely misunderstood the limitations upon our . . . authority . . . as well as the constitutional power of Congress to delegate its legislative power."[19] A growing segment of American public opinion would have agreed that that was exactly his problem.

Favorable reactions came from all sides. The New York *Times* could not resist the remark that the Commission had rather surrendered to the sweep of events than to arguments used, its original error having been its undertaking "to manage the railways rather than to regulate their rates."[20] Out in the Midwest the tone was set by the Chicago

18 *NYT*, Nov. 2, 1914, 11   19 32 ICC 325, 333, 338.

20 *NYT*, Dec. 19, 1914, 1. Nor could the editor resist one more dig at Clifford Thorne. "He represents sentiments which must be discarded if federal control is to prevail over that sort of Western populistic friendship for the people which has been defeated now thrice within a generation." Or at Brandeis: "Mr. Brandeis' error was an excess of zeal for reform and what he thought the public interest.

Tribune, which looked to the future: "It [the decision] gave the largest single order for the resumption of business, not on a normal but a super-normal scale." The Chicago *Herald* commented that "the war waked up the ICC—one of the war's benefits." Only Victor Berger's socialist Milwaukee *Leader* sounded an out-and-out sour note. Since its editor felt that the only problem was the inability of capitalistic society to force investors to put up the money the railroads needed, any other observations were beside the point. Cartoonist Harding in the Brooklyn *Eagle* portrayed the ICC as a white-bearded, stovepipe-hatted old man running breathlessly to hand a message labeled "rate decision" to the conductor of a departing train, as the sun disappeared in the west. "Better late than never," said the *Eagle.* The Louisville *Post,* however, applauded Clements' comment that the decision abandoned the philosophy of low freight rates on which the nation had been built; and the New York *Journal* saw the decision as merely a victory for railroad propaganda, "whose long and persistent campaign of misrepresentation has achieved its desired end." This time the *Post* and the *Journal* were in the minority.[21]

III

Herbert Croly proudly unveiled his new magazine, founded on the principles of the New Nationalism, in the fall of 1914. Besides Croly, editorial policy on the *New Republic* would be determined largely by Walter Weyl and Walter Lippmann. What the magazine had to say about the railroad problem revealed from the very beginning that these men had concluded that regulation, as practiced under archaic Progressivism, was a failure. "Regulation will never be a success unless more arduous, loyal and intelligent efforts are made to bring about success." [22] The idea that successful regulation was a matter not so much of legal form as of intelligence and idealism was probably Croly's. The hand of Walter Weyl, however, pushed the magazine's railroad

He is not likely again soon to press his views in public or to be retained anew by the Commission. It would be better without counsel of any sort."

[21] "Brighter Day for the Railroads," *LD,* L (Jan. 2, 1915), 6–7.

[22] "Railroad Regulation on Trial," *New Republic,* I (Dec. 19, 1914), 8–9.

policy in the direction of public ownership. Reaction to a burst of writings by Samuel O. Dunn of the *Railway Age Gazette* was sharp.[23] When Dunn, who was firmly in the railroads' corner, declared that nationalization would be a "disaster," the *New Republic* disagreed. Again, spirit, not form, was what counted. "Unless railway nationalization brings with it a new administrative *esprit de corps* similar to that which was shown in the building of the Panama Canal, and a much larger measure of expert administrative independence than that which now prevails, there will be substituted for the evils of the existing railroad situation others no less objectionable." [24] Failure of regulation extended just as clearly into the field of labor relations. Commenting on the arbitration award to the western engineers and firemen, the first under the Newlands Act which committed the government more firmly to achieving settlements than had the Erdman Act, the *New Republic* asserted that mediation had succeeded in the past because the mediators did not make any pretense of "settling questions on their merits," but merely acted as the confidential repository of what the parties would accept. As in the rate proceedings, it was a delusion to believe "that we can under present economic conditions find a basis for wages in any theory of ultimate reasonableness." Without the government, wages—and rates, too, in earlier days—were the results of bargaining skill and brute force. Now, "guesswork and compromise will play their part." [25]

Not all of the dark forecasts of nationalization came from those who were contemptuous of past efforts to regulate the railroads. Early in 1915 the *Journal of Political Economy,* thinking perhaps that eastern academic comment on the subject had been too one-sided, opened its pages to a brother economist who spoke unabashedly in the rhetoric of archaic Progressivism. In an article which was long on exhortation if

[23] Samuel O. Dunn, "Railway Efficiency in Its Relation to an Advance in Freight Rates," *Journal of Political Economy*, XXIII (Feb., 1915), 128–43; and "Political Phases of Government Regulation," *Atlantic Monthly*, CXV (Feb., 1915), 202.

[24] "An Innocuous Frankenstein," *New Republic*, II (March 20, 1915), 169–70. The contrast between the ICC and the Panama Canal as an example of the importance of *esprit* has an interesting contemporary parallel. In July, 1969, when man first set foot on the moon, a churlish minority leader remarked that the money might have been better spent on the poverty program. What the poverty program needed, commented the Vice-President, was not the space program's money but its spirit.

[25] "The Western Railroads' Wage Case," *New Republic*, III (May 8, 1915), 13.

short on analysis, J. H. Gray, professor of economics at the University of Minnesota, gave his impression of what the "public" thought of the railroads' need for a rate increase.[26] In a nationwide tour, undertaken for the National Civic Federation, he had become convinced that the American people would not countenance rate increases as long as the railroads were being run by "Wall Street," even if this meant retarded development and poor service. The American people, said Gray, preferred depression to railroad speculation, just as the Belgians preferred death to German enslavement. All of the Populist shibboleths were called forth, all of the archaic Progressives' ignorance of modern finance (the more shocking in a professional economist) was revealed. Harriman was condemned for amassing a fortune, thus revealing once again that characteristic inability to distinguish between personal property and private property. "If [the operating management] could be liberated entirely from the financial control of Wall Street they would doubtless operate the railroads chiefly as instruments of transportation . . . [but the financiers have] flooded the market with railroad bonds mostly for speculative purposes." Gray had no patience, however, with what was happening on the labor front. Clearly, the archaic Progressives did not feel that, just because the railroads had lost control over what they could charge, they should be deprived of control over what they paid their workers. Gray suggested no way of persuading railroad labor not to lay claim to productivity gains which frozen rates had passed along to shippers, but he closed with a dark syllogism the conclusion of which was easy to see: regulation, he said, may well be inconsistent with private ownership, but regulation is here to stay. On what did Gray base these conclusions about public opinion of the railroads? On interviews with state railroad commissioners, as he said, "from New York to California, and from Massachusetts to Texas"! [27]

In this atmosphere of growing tension about the present and future of railroad regulation, the western railroads filed their expected application for rate increases. Optimism ran high that they would get at

[26] In 1917 Gray came to Washington to help Prouty out from under the mountain of work which the physical valuation project had flowered into. He saw this prodigious job to completion in 1928, fifteen years after it was undertaken. *Who Was Who in America, 1897–1942,* 219.

[27] J. H. Gray, "Public View of the Railroads' Need for an Increase of Rates," *Journal of Political Economy,* XXIII (Feb., 1915), 111, 121–22.

least as good treatment as the eastern railroads, but they took no chances. Their lawyers examined the 1914 decisions minutely for guidance. They asked for no blanket percentage increase in rates, but instead combed their tariffs for inconsistencies in the rate structure, and grouped their proposals into fourteen commodity categories. Reacting to the Commission's complaints about the inefficiency with which the nation's fleet of railroad cars was being used, they proposed in a number of instances to increase the minimum weight that would constitute a "carload," which had the effect of raising rates on the commodities involved. With alacrity they took the Commission's advice that passenger fares were too low, and proposed increases to three cents a mile in interstate travel without regard to the fact that most intrastate fares in the West were held to two cents by state commissions. Taken altogether, the proposals amounted to an increase of no more than an estimated 2 per cent of gross revenues, or about ten million dollars in added charges to shippers and travelers, an even more obvious exercise in tokenism than the eastern railroads' modest request had represented.[28] Any law student could see that the western railroads, under these circumstances, were going to win their case in a walk.

Hearings began before Commissioner Daniels on March 4, and dragged on to the end of June. "A superfluous record," said the New York *Times,* as it sharpened its editorial axe for Clifford Thorne and his cohorts. Thorne had shown up, this time representing, in addition to more than half a dozen state commissions and several farm marketing cooperatives, the broomcorn growers, whose rates were among those to be raised. The railroads were represented primarily by the heads of the Missouri-Kansas-Texas, Chicago Great Western, and Chicago & Northwestern railroads. These executives told the Commission straightforwardly that under existing circumstances they needed to pay 7 per cent in dividends, and to earn a surplus besides, if they were to attract the capital necessary to keep them abreast of traffic demands on their systems. Meanwhile, they testified, pressures at the state and local level were out of control. S. M. Felton, whose Chicago Great Western was one of the smallest roads using the magnificent new Union Station in Kansas City, described what had happened when he and his fellow rail-

[28] 35 ICC 497, 500, 504.

road executives had proposed to unify that city's chaotic passenger facilities in a union depot of modest design which would have cost two to
three million dollars. No, sir, the city fathers of this up-to-date metropolis had objected. New York had just been given monumental terminals
by its great railroads. Kansas City would have one, too, one big enough
for all time to come. It cost the railroads ten million dollars before they
were through.[29]

The archaic Progressives, Thorne at their head, made an all-out
attack on the statistics which the railroads presented. In the first place,
he asserted extravagantly, the increased cost to the public would be
$100 million, not ten million. Then he showed his talent for stepping
on the Commissioners' toes by informing them that the operating ratios
of the roads had not really risen, it just looked that way because of the
changes which the ICC had made in its reporting methods.[30] (The Commissioners, who were really upset at the fact that the western railroads
were showing a disastrously high ratio of just under 80 per cent, later
set the rash young Iowan straight on this point.)[31] Everett Jennings,
counsel for the powerful Illinois Public Utilities Commission, tore into
a St. Louis banker who had spoken contemptuously of state commissions. "Don't you think," he asked Festus J. Wade, "that it is rather
mismanagement and selling of blue sky and water that has hurt the railroads, rather than state commissions?" "It is just such statements as you
have made that have hurt their credit," retorted the witness. The opponents of the increases wound up their case by demanding that rates be
adjusted to earnings, and that any such adjustments await the outcome
of the physical valuation study, a demand which was tantamount to deferring any increases for years.[32]

Through July and half of August the nation awaited the Commission's decision. Finally it came. Page after page noted the seriously
weakened condition of the western railroads: labor costs up from 37 per
cent of total operating revenues to 53 per cent; the operating ratio up to
79.5 per cent (it had been 68.6 per cent in 1901); recently invested capital showing a marginal return of seven-tenths of 1 per cent; the decline
in the market for railroad stocks pushing the carriers toward a higher

[29] *Ibid.*, 498; *NYT*, June 30, 1915, 10. This time La Follette did not insist that
the record of the hearings be printed.
[30] *NYT*, March 5, 1915, 11.   [31] 35 ICC 497, 507.   [32] *NYT*, March 6, 1914, 14.

and higher dependence upon bonds, admittedly a sign of poorer credit; an over-all return on investment, 1905 to 1914, of only 2 per cent. Due notice was taken of the fact that the railroads had tailored their applications along the lines of the Commission's suggestions in the eastern case. And then the blow fell. Of fourteen commodity categories in which the railroads requested increased rates, eight were denied altogether, including the broomcorn for which Clifford Thorne had been so solicitous. Of the remaining six categories, some were granted raises only in part.[33] The request for higher passenger fares? Excessive, said the Commission, now confessing that there *was* a relationship between intrastate and interstate fares after all. They might be raised to 2.6 cents, but not three.[34] This would not erase the passenger deficit which the Commission thought was such an imposition on shippers, but it was in line with rates in the East. Experts estimated that instead of the 2 per cent increase requested, the grant amounted to about three-tenths of 1 per cent and would yield increased operating revenues of barely $1.6 million.[35]

Five of the Commissioners signed the decision without dissent or comment. Their positions in the earlier cases had been based largely on the strict construction of the "reasonableness" clause, and they had been buttressed in this policy by Commissioner Harlan. Now they had remaining to them neither economic nor legal fig leaf, for that gentleman, to the surprise of nearly everybody, joined Daniels in declaring for the increases as proposed. The railroads, he said simply, had proved their case and they should get the increases. And he went on to suggest a number of reforms in regulatory legislation such as the power to set minumum rates and the elimination of conflict between intra- and inter-

[33] 35 ICC 497, *passim.*

[34] The passenger case was decided separately in 37 ICC 1. Note that the Commission ignored such a sophisticated concept as the much lower traffic density in the West, which alone would have justified considerably higher rates in the West than in the East. But the most remarkable feature of the passenger fare decision is its revelation that the Supreme Court, while it can open the door for a regulatory commission, cannot force it to walk through the door. A year earlier the Court, in the famous Shreveport case (234 U.S. 342), had ruled that where a state, by establishing unduly low *intrastate* rates, is effectively controlling *interstate* commerce (because both types of rates have an economic relationship), the federal agency could order the intrastate rates changed.

[35] *NYT,* Aug. 12, 1915, 8.

state regulation.[36] Daniels was disgusted. "It is not apparent how the carriers could have complied more fully," he wrote, referring to the criteria laid down by the Commission itself in the eastern case. But it was the pettiness of the Commission's insistence on muckraking which repelled him most of all. Withholding the increases because of chicanery (real or imagined) on the Frisco, the Rock Island, and the Alton was senseless. It penalized the just roads and the looted stockholders, while it did nothing to bring the malefactors to book. If he had come right out and said that his colleagues were refusing to discharge their public trust, he could not have made his stand much plainer. As it was, archaic Progressivism would be laying for him when his term expired eighteen months later.[37]

The press generally agreed that the decision amounted to a complete denial of the proposed increases, but midwestern papers saw the picture changing. "It takes no stretch of the imagination," said the Chicago *Tribune*, "to see Commissioners Daniels and Harlan accepted in the future." The St. Louis *Globe-Democrat* found itself in the same corner with the New York *Journal of Commerce* and the *Wall Street Journal* on the matter of punishing good roads along with bad ones. Many editors took up the western decision along with another big case the Commission had just decided. This was the anthracite decision, which required all of the railroads to give to all anthracite shippers the same low rates which those who owned mines gave their mining subsidiaries.[38] In that case the editors found the Commission's logic as faulty as in the western case. If the connection between carriers and coal companies was illegal, it should be prohibited, but it should not be considered a rate-making criterion. The New York *Times* noted that the ICC had punished *all* roads in the business of carrying anthracite, whether they owned mines or not. President Leonor F. Loree of the Delaware & Hudson Railroad said sadly that the cut might exceed the increases just awarded in the Five Per Cent Case. The Commission, he said, "gives it in drops and takes it back in bucketfuls." The *New Republic* demanded that the Commission stop its "futile attempts to regulate profits through

[36] 35 ICC 497, 680–81.

[37] *Ibid.*, 654–56, 660. Daniels' dissenting opinion ran to 26 pages and was obviously intended as a comprehensive minority report.

[38] 35 ICC 220.

rates." [39] Samuel O. Dunn pinpointed the situation for the readers of the *North American Review:* "The trouble is not with regulation in itself, and the remedy is not public ownership or a return to unregulated management . . . the trouble is with the particular policy of regulation that has been followed. . . . The remedy is a policy . . . predicated on the experience of the railways *since 1906 as well as before,* and which will be adaptable to any other tendencies or conditions that may develop." Enlarge and reorganize the ICC, Dunn demanded.[40] Railroad regulation in the tradition of archaic Progressivisim had touched bottom.[41]

IV

The President of the United States, standing at the rostrum of the House of Representatives, smiled up at the galleries, where six women had flung out a banner with the legend, "Mr. President, what will you do for woman suffrage?" Then he pressed on earnestly with the speech he was making to a joint session of the House and Senate. He had come to Capitol Hill that cold December day in 1916 to talk to the legislators about the nation's number-one domestic problem, and it was not votes for women but the railroad situation which had the President worried. As war came closer to the United States, it was becoming apparent to him, his advisers, and a growing band of concerned members of the Congress that the railroad problem had implications far beyond the domestic scene. Beginning with the most subtle remarks on the rate-increase issue in 1913, the President had become less and less deferential to the Interstate Commerce Commission as its incapacity to deal with

[39] "Double Railway Disappointment," *LD,* LI (Aug. 28, 1915), 393–94; *New Republic,* IV (Aug. 21, 1915), 58. Just what logic the carriers were following in this obvious policy of making their mining subsidiaries look good at the expense of their railroads is not clear, but it seems strange that the Commission should have thought the matter had anything to do with reasonableness of rates.

[40] Samuel O. Dunn, "What's the Matter with Railway Regulation?" *North American Review,* CCII (Nov., 1915), 736–45. Italics added.

[41] The historian of the ICC, himself an ardent supporter of the independent regulatory commission idea, finds the decision wanting in almost every respect; I. L. Sharfman, *The Interstate Commerce Commission: A Study in Administrative Law and Procedure* (4 vols. in 5, New York, 1931–37), IIIb, 72.

the problem became increasingly apparent. The shock of the 1915 western rate case; the growing insistence of the railroad labor unions on getting a bigger share of the carriers' productivity gains of the past decade (even if the railroads were not being allowed to collect them), heightened by rapidly rising wages in other sectors of the economy; and the fear, as winter approached, that the railroad system might falter under a volume of traffic greatly augmented by war goods destined for England and France and for America's own preparedness program—all of these factors had the President deeply worried. In the past year he had spent more hours of grinding, round-the-clock toil on railroad problems than on any other domestic issue. Perhaps he foresaw that very soon he would have no time at all for such matters. There was much that he wanted from Congress to heal the transportation sores of the nation, and he cleaved to the subject. In this speech, to the amazement of nearly everybody, he would mention neither submarines, nor Mexico, nor, in fact, foreign relations in any way.[42]

Both the President and much of the nation had come a long way, philosophically speaking, since the days when archaic Progressivism of the La Follette-Cummins variety and naïve New Freedomism of the Brandeisian stripe were riding high. Sometime during 1914, as the concept of a powerful federal agency to regulate industry was taking shape, Wilson had "seemed to lose all interest in the Clayton bill." When it came to selecting the men to run the vast, complicated, and totally untried Federal Reserve System, he had turned primarily to leading bankers and businessmen. Perhaps he knew that it was not doctrinaire idealists who would carry the nation's burdens. The mid-term elections that fall revealed a stampede back to the conservatism of the traditional Republican party which cut the Democratic majority in the House and strengthened the conservative Republican hand against the Progressives in the Senate. Shortly after, in a famous letter to William Gibbs Mc-

[42] *NYT*, Dec. 6, 1916, 1; *Messages and Papers of the Presidents*, ed. James D. Richardson *et al.* (20 vols., and supplements, Washington, 1898–1925), XVIII, 8183–87. The President received "the most enthusiastic greeting of any since he first addressed Congress." It was his first appearance since his reelection and the Democratic Congressmen were in a festive mood. As the applause at the President's appearance subsided, a Democratic member shouted, "Amen!" and a wave of laughter swept the chamber. William Jennings Bryan, exercising his floor privileges as a former member of Congress, beamed from a front-row seat.

Adoo, Secretary of the Treasury, the President indicated that he thought his program of domestic economic reform was complete. The trend in national politics was away from the heavy hand of reform, and in 1916 Wilson, with a strong "he-kept-us-out-of-war" campaign appeal and the support of numerous Progressives, would barely win a second term.[43] And out in Wisconsin there was growing evidence that reform at the municipal level (where, historically, it has been given its best rating) was also wearing out its welcome. The 1914 elections were hailed by some as a repudiation of La Follette's "Wisconsin Idea." Asked to explain the shift in sentiment, the head of the Home Rule and Taxpayers' League replied, "Nothing but the sting of outrageous taxation could have aroused the people to a proper sense of the dangerous tendencies into which they drifted—reform run wild, humanitarianism without common sense, education to the verge of bankruptcy, and an insolent interference with the liberties of the people." It had not gone unnoticed that the cost of local government had risen enormously in the preceding decade.[44]

The President's resolution to do something about railroad regulation hardened after the denial of relief to the western railroads in 1915. There is no doubt that his closest advisers were urging him to action. Perhaps the nearest Wilson came to having an economic adviser (not a recognized necessity in those days) was Winthrop M. Daniels. And if it is true that there is no fervor to match that of the convert, then the counsels of his Secretary of the Interior, Franklin K. Lane, must have been fervent indeed.[45] A thoroughgoing reform of the laws was desirable, but the President knew that such reform would take time and would have to originate at the very foundations of the legislative process. It was necessary to begin somewhere, however, so in December, 1915, as part of his message to Congress, the President asked for "a commission of inquiry to ascertain . . . whether our laws as at present

[43] These political transformations are admirably summarized in Arthur S. Link, *Woodrow Wilson and the Progressive Era* (New York, 1954), 72, 77, 78–79, and *passim*.

[44] "The Wisconsin Reaction," *New Republic,* II (April 17, 1915), 281.

[45] Lane had already concluded that government ownership would solve nothing. Franklin K. Lane, "Success of Federal Regulation: Is Government Ownership of Railroads Necessary?" New York *Journal of Commerce,* Annual Financial and Economic Section, Jan. 3, 1912, 4.

framed and administered are as serviceable as they might be in the solution of the problem." He praised commission regulation of railroads as originally conceived, although he pointedly refrained from heaping such sentiments on the way the Commission had carried out those concepts. "The question," he continued, "is not what should we undo? . . . What we are seeking now . . . is national efficiency and security." [46]

A few days later one of the staunchest supporters of the President's drive for a clearer national policy on regulation, Francis G. Newlands of Nevada, chairman of the Senate Committee on Interstate Commerce, introduced a resolution calling for a thorough investigation. It was to be conducted by a joint subcommittee of the House and Senate Committees on Interstate Commerce.[47] When the resolution seemed to make little progress in the House, the President wrote Representatives Claude Kitchin, of North Carolina, and William C. Adamson, of Georgia, chairman of the House Committee, requesting early action. "The railways of the country are becoming more and more the key to its successful industry," wrote Wilson, in a letter which was simultaneously released to the press. The investigation, he assured the Congressmen, was very much a part of his legislative program.[48] A precious year would slip by, however, before the special committee would begin its work. It was in the crucible of total war, not in the committee rooms of the Capitol, that the shortcomings of the regulatory system would be demonstrated.

If there remained any doubt about the importance which the President attached to the link between military and railroad preparedness, he dispelled it the following month. After a period of seeming indecision which had followed his marriage to Mrs. Edith Bolling, he had decided to speak out to the nation on his new belief in the need for greater military and industrial preparedness for war. The grand ballroom of the ornate old Waldorf-Astoria Hotel on January 27, 1916,

---

[46] *Messages and Papers of the Presidents,* XVIII, 8116–17; *NYT,* Dec. 8, 1915, 4.

[47] *NYT,* Dec. 18, 1915, 14. The role of the small states in the federal system, in achieving desirable reductions of state power in favor of national programs, is clearly revealed by this episode. Newlands was a strong advocate of federal charters for railroads, which could conceivably have removed them from any sort of state regulation, including taxation. His counterpart in the House, Adamson of Georgia, had strong reservations on this score.

[48] *Ibid.,* March 29, 1916, 2.

was the scene of the beginning of Wilson's preparedness program. "Prepare," adjured the President; "no man can be sure of the morrow." He confessed that he had changed his mind on the question. A country had to be ready to fight for its honor. More than a year had gone by since he had de-emphasized military readiness but, he declared, "I would be ashamed of myself if I had not learned something in these fourteen months." Then he spoke earnestly of the need for improved railroad transportation in his program. "The goods have got to be delivered," he said, and he added darkly, "I hope for my part that every man in public life gets just what is coming to him." His audience could not have been more sympathetic, for the President had chosen the annual dinner of the Railway Business Association to inaugurate his program.[49]

The year just beginning was to be filled with railroad headaches for the President. The eight-hour controversy, as we shall see, would tax his meager physical resources on the eve of a demanding campaign for reelection, the outcome of which was in gravest doubt. Early in September, while he was resting at Shadow Lawn, his summer place in Long Branch, New Jersey, Wilson was visited by the committee appointed by the Democratic convention to notify him officially of his nomination for a second term. Stepping out on the terrace to read his acceptance speech for the reporters, he showed his deep longing to be freed from the incubus of railroad confusion. "We must coordinate the railway systems of the country for national use," he said, "and must facilitate and promote their development with a view to that coordination and to their better adaptation as a whole to the life and trade and defense of the nation. The life and industry of the country can be free and unhampered only if these arteries are open, efficient, and complete." [50] Congress—and the ICC, if it chose to interpret its powers more broadly than it had theretofore—had been given the message loud and clear. The President wanted action.

Thus it was that when he went up to Capitol Hill the month after his reelection, to receive the suffragettes' message and to deliver his own, he had decided that whatever else Congress did, it should undertake a basic change in national regulatory policy. First he made it clear

[49] *Ibid.,* Jan. 28, 1916, 1; Link, *Woodrow Wilson and the Progressive Era,* 184–85.

[50] *Messages and Papers of the Presidents,* XVIII, 8159.

that he felt it unnecessary for Congress to direct the ICC to grant the railroads rate relief, remarking pointedly that the Commission had possessed that power all along. But there was work to be done. "Immediate provision for the enlargement and administrative reorganization of the ICC" was necessary, he declared, "in order that the Commission may be enabled to deal with the many great and various duties now devolving upon it with a promptness and thoroughness which are . . . [at present] impossible." [51]

It was not to be expected that the Insurgent Republicans who had molded national railroad policy since 1910 would acquiesce in this challenge to their power. In another four short years (perhaps even in two), Republicans had high hopes of being returned to power, and Senator Albert B. Cummins was already looking forward to resuming his position at the Commerce Committee's conference table. When the President submitted the name of Winthrop M. Daniels to the Senate for confirmation to a full seven-year term on the ICC, Cummins, enthusiastically backed by Senators La Follette, Norris, and Borah, went into action. [52] Once again the Senate was treated to the humid rhetoric of archaic Progressivism. The old charges of Wall Street conspiracies, the pose of neglected agrarianism, the fatal weakness for the most radical solutions, seemed archaic indeed as the Senator droned away most of January 3 and 6, 1917. He had dramatically demanded a secret session of the Senate, so that he might lay before it his grave charges of Daniels' "unfitness for the particular office which he has filled for the last two years and a half." He frankly admitted that his objection to Daniels had nothing to do with the man's intellect or integrity. The question at issue was one of philosophy, and Wilson's man did not pass the archaic Progressive's test:

I believe that we have reached the parting of the ways. I believe that our system of the control and regulation of common carriers is on final trial and that if the Commission is to be made up of men of Mr. Daniels' trend of mind the system must be abandoned. For one, I have no hesitation in declaring that if his views are to prevail I am for absolute and immediate government ownership and operation of our transportation facilities. If the

[51] *Ibid.*, 8183–87; *NYT*, Dec. 6, 1916, 1.

[52] K. Austin Kerr, *American Railroad Politics, 1914–1920* (Pittsburgh, 1968), 25. Mr. Kerr lucidly describes the resolution of diverse political forces which produced the Transportation Act of 1920.

charges for services rendered by our public carriers are to increase year
after year in the rapid ratio which the principles he advocates will . . . require, the burden, now heavy, will become insupportable.[53]

The Iowan claimed, no doubt to the Commission's surprise, that
"he [Daniels] has been the controlling influence on the Federal tribunal." Ever since his work on Wilson's New Jersey public utility commission, according to the Senator, the Princeton economist had
preached the evil doctrine of the value of intangible assets. It was just
such an evil doctrine which had led to the "ruin" of the Alton Railroad.
But to appreciate the invincible ignorance of the archaic Progressive *in
extremis,* we must again let Cummins speak for himself:

The speculators who ruined the Chicago and Alton Railroad had just the
same idea of public-utility economics [as Daniels] when they substantially
trebled the capitalization of the railroad company, adding but a few millions
to the actual property . . . and in a few months a road which had been
highly successful for more than a quarter of a century was absolutely insol-
vent.[54]

The defenders of historical rate levels would not continue to enjoy
in the future the victories they had won in the recent past. So much was
apparent to Cummins. The decision to raise rates in 1914, in the eyes
of the Senator, was not the outcome of an "investigation as to adequacy
of revenues" at all; it was the simple result of a victory of railroad
wealth spent in behalf of the continuing conspiracy of the money power.
These ideas Cummins shaped and reshaped during his two-day speech
until he produced this peroration:

Four great cases [the rate cases of 1910, 1913, 1914, and 1915], epochal in
their character, mark the . . . end of a successful effort on the part of the

[53] Albert B. Cummins, "Winthrop M. Daniels," Senate Document 673, 64th Cong.,
2d Sess., Jan. 3 and 6, 1917, 5. Cummins' speech is perhaps the most eloquent
confession of faith which these legatees of nineteenth-century populism have
left us on what they wanted to achieve in the regulation of railroads, and how
contented they were with their handiwork, even in the face of growing inadequacies in the system. How the Senator could have convinced himself that 1887
freight rates were a "heavy burden" on commodities fetching 1917 prices is beyond comprehension.

[54] *Ibid.,* 10–11. The Alton reorganization is one of the best examples of the
mythology of archaic Progressivism. The myth has remained beloved of historians long after the financial innovations which it involved have become common-
place. Cf. Harold U. Faulkner, *The Decline of Laissez Faire* (New York, 1951),
199–201. For the story of what really happened to the Alton, see Chapter III
above.

railway companies to overthrow the interstate commerce law, and to convert the commission into an instrument for the maintenance of the stock market of the country and of fictitious values upon worthless securities.[55]

An impatient Senate was in no mood to take Cummins seriously. On a motion of Senator William Hughes of Daniels' home state of New Jersey, the foolish secrecy motion was rescinded and Cummins' remarks made public. Then the chamber proceeded to confirm Daniels by the overwhelming vote of 42 to 13.[56] It was a heavy blow to the old notions into which Cummins had tried so hard to breathe new life. The future of railroad regulation lay, at least for the time being, with two key Democrats. Senator Newlands had already voiced his hearty approval of the President's policies in comments on the address of a month before. Representative Adamson, however, was still a question mark. After the President finished pleading for the rest of the legislative program he had requested at the time of the eight-hour crisis the previous summer, the Georgian had commented, "There is no prejudice against the roads. We will pass the balance of the program when we see the necessity for it." [57] Only a month before—nearly a year after Wilson had asked for it—had the special investigating committee begun its labors. Time had run out. By early 1917 the reality of America's involvement in the European war and the threat of labor strife on the nation's railroads had changed everything.

[55] Cummins, "Winthrop M. Daniels," 14, 21.   [56] *NYT,* Jan. 11, 1917, 24.
[57] *Ibid.,* Dec. 6, 1916, 3; Dec. 31, 1916, V, 1.

CHAPTER XI

SHOWDOWN

The Forgotten Man . . . is the only one for whom there is no provision in the great scramble and the big divide. . . . He works, he votes, generally he prays—but his chief business in life is to pay. . . . Who and where is the Forgotten Man in this case, who will have to pay for it all?
—WILLIAM GRAHAM SUMNER, *speech, 1883*

In times like this men go back to primal instincts. Now the public is the carcass and we are all perhaps the vultures. . . . The country will pay.
—A. B. GARRETSON, *chairman, Railway Brotherhood Conference Committee, 1916*

I

Government clerks strolling along Pennsylvania Avenue in front of the new Willard Hotel stared curiously at the middle-aged man, dressed in his Sunday best, who leaned out of the open-air sightseeing bus and waved at a dignified man seated in a big touring car. "Hello, Fred!" he hailed familiarly. "Hello, John!" shouted back Frederick D. Underwood, president of the Erie Railroad, as he returned the greeting of one of his engineers. Both men were out to see the sights of the nation's capital on that hot August Sunday afternoon in 1916. Both were in the city on the same business. Underwood was one of more than thirty railroad presidents and engineer John one of 600 railroad union chairmen who had been called to Washington by President Wilson in a frantic attempt to forestall a total shutdown of the country's railroads.[1] The workmen had chosen this juncture, when the heavy fall traffic of merchandise, food, and coal would shortly be added to a rapidly growing volume of war goods, for a showdown on their long-pending demands for institution of the eight-hour day. They had refused all offers

[1] *NYT*, Aug. 21, 1916, 1.

of arbitration and were determined to debate the issue on the basis of their staying power versus that of the railroads and the citizenry. The railroad managers were equally determined to see the issue submitted to binding arbitration, and had declared themselves prepared to fight for their point. Only the President, if anyone, now remained who could save the country from a strike which would mean, if not widespread starvation and death from exposure in the great northern and eastern cities, certainly untold hardship and misery.

The key to the threatened confrontation was the unions' position on arbitration. In 1912 the engineers had discovered that wage scales were so distorted that conductors were making nearly as much as they were (a situation which the elite of railroad labor could not tolerate) and had opened a nationwide drive for a raise. Mediation had been a total failure. Consenting to arbitration, the contestants had found themselves unable to agree on the selection of arbitrators, a decision which the Supreme Court had to make for them. The award was small, and the men of the four railroad brotherhoods concluded that in the future, joint, industry-wide bargaining on their part would have to replace their separate efforts.[2] The following year, however, engineers and firemen on the western railroads, heartened by the success of the Trainmen in achieving their goals under the recently adopted Newlands Act, launched a drive for higher wages. Total stalemate in mediation required the intervention of the President, who persuaded the railroads (the reluctant party this time) to accept arbitration. Again the award was a disappointment to the union. It was now crystal clear to the union leaders that the wielding of their ultimate power would serve them best in the future.[3] The general officers of the unions conferred on their eight-hour-day objectives at Chicago in December, 1915. Several, notably Warren Stone of the Engineers, counseled against going ahead with

[2] James William Kerley, "The Failure of Railway Labor Leadership: A Chapter in Railroad Labor Relations, 1900–1932" (unpublished doctoral dissertation, Columbia University, 1959), 56; George James Stevenson, "The Brotherhood of Locomotive Engineers and Its Leaders, 1863–1920" (unpublished doctoral dissertation, Vanderbilt University, 1954), 339.

[3] Kerley, "Failure of Railway Labor Leadership," 49; Stevenson, "Locomotive Engineers," 34–35. Charles F. Van Hise, chairman of the arbitration panel in the 1912 case, acknowledged that "the balance of power . . . has now passed to organized railway labor."

the movement in those critical times, but the consensus was that grass-roots feeling was too strong to buck. All railroad workers, it was agreed, would be "a unit" in the coming fight.[4]

In those days the only limitation on a day's work on the railroads was a 1907 federal law limiting a man to sixteen hours in a twenty-four-hour period.[5] Most railroaders worked a standard ten-hour day, with various arrangements for overtime beyond that. A few men, mostly in yard work, had the eight-hour day. In practice, as was never seriously denied by any of the parties to the dispute, a road man's workday, short of the sixteen-hour maximum, was determined by the run to which he was assigned. Some senior men on deluxe passenger runs completed their day's work in considerably less than eight hours. Others, especially those who worked local freights, spent as much time "in the hole" (side-tracked in favor of priority traffic) as they did in motion and were hard put to complete their terminal-to-terminal run in ten hours. An eight-hour-day requirement, therefore, even if it called for time-and-a-half for overtime beyond eight hours, would probably not give the men an eight-hour "trick," in the great majority of cases, but *would* result in a handsome increase in wages, inasmuch as the very heart of the eight-hour movement was the demand that wages for the shorter day be at least the same as for the old ten-hour stint.[6]

Railroad management never concealed its conviction that the unions were insincere in their eight-hour-day demands. What they really wanted, said the executives somewhat illogically, was a 40 per cent increase in wages. Such a boost would mean a drastic curtailment of improvement programs for even the most affluent lines and almost certain bankruptcy for some. Meeting in New York early in 1916, representatives of the eastern railroads voted to form a united front in opposition to the demands. Noting that the campaign for the eight-hour day was really no such thing, they added that even if they found a way to put all

---

[4] *NYT,* Jan. 7, 1916, 10; Stevenson, "Locomotive Engineers," 353. Only a substantial minority of total railroad workers were actually members of unions, but the key positions were well organized. It is doubtful that any one railroad in the country, left to its own resources, could have operated in the face of a strike of union men.

[5] 34 U.S. Statutes 1415, adopted March 4, 1907.

[6] Kerley, "Failure of Railway Labor Leadership," 66–67; Stevenson, "Locomotive Engineers," 358–59.

of their men on such a schedule, they would have to hire 87,000 men away from other industries in which, presumably, they were more badly needed than on the railroads.[7] When the unions announced that this time they would not entertain any suggestion of arbitration, the railroad men rushed to form a nationwide bargaining unit to match that which their men had already mounted. At the end of January they announced formation of the General Conference of Railway Managers, to be headed by the Pennsylvania's Elisha Lee, who already led the conference of eastern railroads. By early spring all of the union locals had voted authority for a strike if the railroads did not knuckle under. Only a supreme optimist could have doubted that a bruising strike was coming.[8]

By August of 1916 no progress whatsoever had been made in settling the dispute and the union general officers were walking around with full authority to call a strike at any time. Early in the month negotiations came to a head in New York, where the final round of talks was to begin on Tuesday, August 8, in the handsome new Engineering Societies building. The previous Sunday evening union leaders had gathered at the ovenlike New Amsterdam Opera House for a mass meeting. "If you are as hot as I am, you are ready for Tuesday morning right now," trumpeted W. G. Lee of the Trainmen, setting the radical tone of the meeting. "The public may be inconvenienced . . . but if we can break the arbitrary power from Wall Street that controls the railroads it will be time well spent," declaimed A. B. Garretson of the Conductors, who was the leader of the merged union forces. Belligerent Warren Stone, head of the elite Engineers, who could have passed for the dignified president of the most powerful bank in the city, brought the men to their feet in a roar of excitement. "They say it will cost them $100 million to give us what we are going to get," he bellowed. "It won't, but . . . if it did it would only be fifteen per cent of what has been paid for sons-in-laws with worthless titles by these same millionaires in the last ten years." [9] Who could remember when the unions had been on the same side with the railroads in the 1910 rate case? No one in the New

[7] *NYT,* Jan. 7, 1916, 10. This was no sterile deductive reasoning, as the labor shortage which marked America's war effort was already in evidence.
[8] *Ibid.,* Jan. 28, 1916, 12.   [9] *Ibid.,* Aug. 7, 1916, 1.

Amsterdam Opera House that night. Behind the oratorical façade one fact was clear. Union men had learned that railroads under archaic Progressive regulation were *losers,* and they were determined to move on to the winning side. In the coming months the unions would evolve a public stance which maintained that the railroads were perfectly able to grant their demands without any rate relief.

In the next week Judge Martin A. Knapp made one of his last appearances on the national railroad scene. As chairman of the board of mediation, he shuttled back and forth between the railroad managers' conference rooms at 70 East 45th Street, the unions' headquarters at the Woodstock Hotel, and his own board's rooms at the Manhattan Hotel near the elegant new Grand Central Station. The union men began to fret under mediation. Garretson, stalking through the lobby of his hotel after a fruitless session, waved eager reporters away. "I'm not talking," he growled; "I'm as calm as a Methodist preacher." On August 12 the mediators admitted defeat. The strike could begin immediately. A final vote, 94 per cent in favor of a walkout, had been announced a few days before.[10] But the union leaders hesitated, waiting to see what the President would do. Wilson's troubleshooter, Henry Morgenthau, Sr., held them at bay while he delivered a personal report to Washington. Realizing at last that he had no alternative but to undertake this most abrasive task, Wilson dispatched his confidential secretary, Joseph Tumulty, to New York on an afternoon train the following day with a summons to the contestants to come to Washington. Tumulty arrived in New York's other monumental new terminal, the Pennsylvania Station, at 9:00 P.M. and went directly to the headquarters of the union men and the railroad leaders. By 12:30 A.M. Tumulty was on the sleeper headed back to Washington. The railroad executives, making for the same train, scoffed at reporters' questions about the rumor that Wilson was ready to call out the army to avoid a strike. Noting that many of the roads had nonunion volunteers who were against the strike and who could run the trains if necessary, the executives denied that they had any intention of backing down. "This fight is to industry in America," they declared grimly, "what the war is to Europe."[11]

Woodrow Wilson had not wanted to get involved. His closest ad-

[10] *Ibid.,* Aug. 9, 1916, 1; Aug. 12, 1.   [11] *Ibid.,* Aug. 14, 1916, 1–2.

visers had warned him that settlement would require a major retreat by one of the parties from positions to which they were fundamentally committed. "The poker is hot at both ends," Josephus Daniels had told him; "let the railroad companies and their employees 'fight it out.' " [12] But no adviser could see the dilemma through a President's eyes, especially a President who in two short months would offer himself to the electorate for a second term. As Wilson would tell the railroad executives, he faced a condition, not a principle.[13] The President would later be criticized for choosing to side with labor in an election year, but it is hard to see how any other course could have succeeded. The eight-hour day, the President was convinced, was a good thing and had to come. To him, the entire system of railroad regulation was in need of a thorough revision. Whatever his rationalizations, he had made up his mind.

The union men walked through the great portals of yet another handsome new railroad terminal, Washington's Union Station, to be informed that the President wanted to see them at 10 A.M. From their hotel, the old National House, where they had had a hasty breakfast, Garretson walked them democratically to the White House, Warren Stone catching a reporter's eye by his "jaunty straw hat and suit of modish cut." Garretson spoke for two hours, explaining what the men wanted, as the President, seated under a portrait of Andrew Jackson in the Green Room, listened attentively. Then Wilson rose, thanked the men for coming so promptly, and told them that he did not seek to judge the issue, but only to prevent a strike. That afternoon, from the same seat, he listened briefly to Elisha Lee and then told the railroad executives what he wanted them to do. The burden of concessions, he said frankly, would be on the roads. They should grant the eight-hour day, without reduction in wages, and submit the demand for time-and-a-half to arbitration. As to higher rates, that was the province of the ICC and he could promise nothing. The railroad men then returned to the Willard where they conferred and adjourned for dinner at seven. Frederick Underwood, an old coal heaver to whom "Wall Street" was almost as hazy a geographical expression as it was to his men, was collared by reporters on his way to the dining room. If necessary, he

[12] Josephus Daniels, *The Life of Woodrow Wilson* (New York, 1924), 197.

[13] Arthur S. Link, *Wilson: Campaigns for Progressivism and Peace, 1916–1917* (Vol. V of a biography of Woodrow Wilson) (Princeton, 1965), 86.

snapped, he would "don overalls" and run a milk train before he would see the babies starve. It was a bitter cup that was being passed around in Washington that evening.[14]

By now the threatened strike was front-page news across the country. It was an election year and Democratic newspapers quickly fell into line behind the President, although there was evidence that Wilson's pro-labor policy made the choice difficult for some. The San Francisco *Chronicle* felt the men were bluffing and that the unions would not bring the country face to face with starvation. On the other side of the continent the New York *Call* declared that the threat was the "greatest attack on capital that has ever been maneuvered in all history." If the President thought that the railroad executives were going to buckle under the tremendous pressure he was putting on them, he might have reflected on the attitude of the *Railway Age Gazette,* which often supplied an articulateness that the companies themselves lacked. "Any railroad officer," snarled the paper, "who would suggest making any concession whatever, except after arbitration, ought to be branded as a coward, and as a traitor to the interests of the railways and the country." The *Commercial and Financial Chronicle* thought the managers had acted foolishly in deciding to bargain with the brotherhoods on a national basis rather than as separate railroads. The strategy of dramatizing the injustices of this $100-million assault on the railroads by making it a national issue would not work, said the *Chronicle*. By now the public was used to big figures and took them in stride. And, the editor might have added, the railroads had not had much success with appeals to the public conscience in the past.[15]

At sundown next day the President found himself in an intense state of frustration. He was "shocked" by the fact that although he had dropped all other business and parleyed with labor and management for two days, neither side would budge in the direction of the compromise he offered. Management wanted arbitration of everything while the men insisted on arbitration of nothing. Leaving the White House, the men had displayed a belligerence entirely out of keeping with the august character of their surroundings. Asked about the United States mails,

---

[14] *NYT,* Aug. 15, 1916, 1.
[15] "Facing Our Greatest Labor War," *LD,* LII (Aug. 19, 1916), 392–93.

Garretson had snapped at the reporter, "The railroads have the contract to carry the mails, and not the men." [16] Next day, in separate meetings with the unions and the railroad executives, the President laid it on the line. He wanted the eight-hour day adopted, and since neither side really seemed sure how it would work out or how much it would cost the railroads, he wanted a careful study made simultaneously by an impartial commission. The men were to drop their demand for time-and-a-half for overtime. He was ready to ask Congress to enact his program into law if labor and management would not put it into effect voluntarily. The union leaders, realizing they were on the brink of winning the greater part of what they had been after, indicated that they would accept the terms, subject, of course, to ratification by the more than 600 chairmen of the locals. The railroad executives returned to their hotel, took three unanimous ballots against the plan, and returned to the White House with their rejection. Gone was their taciturnity when they returned to the Willard that evening. The man who had called them to Washington was the President of the United States, but the man who had asked them to abandon their most basic principles was a politician facing an uphill fight for reelection. Wilson's plan, they declared without reserve, was a political move. They decried the mere possibility that the Democrats might win in November, and they were ready to leave Washington and "fight it out." "It will be a hot day," said one executive in the midst of the capital's oppressive summer climate, "when we ask Washington to help us out again." [17]

Meanwhile the railroads serving the capital had been scurrying about in search of additional Pullman cars to carry an unexpected increase in the already heavy vacation travel to Washington. The President, desiring to face the railroad executives with a *fait accompli,* had dramatically called all 600 of the local brotherhood chairmen to Washington. As soon as all but a few laggards had stowed their grips in the bulging National House, W. S. Carter of the Enginemen marched them to the White House. The President welcomed them to the capital, assured them of his concern for the nation's welfare, and asked their assent to his compromise plan. Then he said he would be glad to shake hands with them as they left. It was the first time the President had

[16] *NYT,* Aug. 16, 1916, 1.   [17] *Ibid.,* Aug. 17, 1916, 1.

matched grips with a large number of men who made their living handling shovels and locomotive throttles instead of pens and champagne
glasses. Carter, seeing the President wince at his men's enthusiastic
handclasps, warned them to take it easy. Then he marched them off to
the Bijou Theatre where he and the other union leaders spoke in favor
of the President's plan. Up sprang the usual firebrands who denounced
the weakness of their leaders and demanded total victory. The meeting
adjourned without a decision. Back at the White House, the President
tightened the screws. Out went telegrams to the presidents of thirty of
the largest railroads, summoning them to Washington. No longer would
he deal with delegates, but only with the principals.[18]

August 18 dawned hot and bright. By mid-morning the late-sum-
mer sun beat mercilessly against the walls of the White House as a
Negro attendant moved silently through the Green Room, drawing the
heavy draperies against the torrid sun. Up Pennsylvania Avenue from
the Bijou Theatre, where they had had a second and more successful
meeting, marched 600 railroad men, four abreast. Greeting them on the
White House lawn, the President heard their acceptance of his compromise, thanked them enthusiastically, and retreated to the relative cool-
ness of the old mansion. A few minutes later thirty railroad presidents
began to arrive by automobile at the front entrance, from which the
usher led them to the darkened Green Room. Fanning their perspiring
faces with their panamas and skimmers, they waited. Suddenly a portiere was drawn back at one end of the room to reveal the President,
immaculate in a white linen suit, standing in the brilliant sunlight.

No one was asked to sit. Hale Holden of the Burlington Railroad,
spokesman for the railroad men, stepped forward and quietly informed
the President that they could not do what he asked. Their position was
simply that the principle of arbitration could not be compromised if
they were to exercise any future role in the leadership of the nation's
railroads. Visibly seeking to control his emotions, the President thanked
the railroad men coldly for responding so quickly to his telegrams, and
for coming to Washington in such uncomfortable weather. He wanted,
he said, to tell them about an experience he had had while a teacher at
Princeton, because it would convey all he had to say to them. A student

[18] *Ibid.*, Aug. 18, 1916, 1.

who had failed his final examination came to him with the plea that he be given a passing mark. The shock of his failure, he said, would surely kill his invalid mother, thus making Professor Wilson responsible for her death. He had told the student, said the stern-voiced President, that the responsibility would rest squarely and exclusively upon the student for his failure to master the course. Now, as President, he was being faced with the responsibility of saving the nation's life. If the railroads would cooperate he was willing to do all he could to get the ICC to grant rate relief, provided that the eight-hour commission recommended it. Pointing his finger at the railroad presidents, he declared, "If a strike comes, the public will know where the responsibility rests. It will not be upon me." As abruptly as it had opened the portiere, the black hand drew it closed. The meeting had lasted barely twenty minutes. The thirty railroad presidents were left to find their way out of the room. "What in hell did the President mean?" said one. "I suppose he means it is up to us to settle the strike," said another.[19]

The President continued to invoke the sheer weight of numbers. Telegrams went out the next day to sixty-three more railroad presidents, after Wilson had considered and abandoned the idea of calling the members of their boards of directors. But management attitudes were hardening rapidly. In Chicago Edward P. Ripley angrily refused to come east. He was already represented there, he said. Another leader expressed a total lack of confidence in the President's ability to get anything out of the ICC; the Commission would merely resent any promises he might make, said the railroad man. The Pennsylvania announced that 35,000 employees had signed a petition in support of arbitration of the entire matter. By August 21, when the additional railroad chieftains had assembled, their ranks were more solid than ever. They released a statement in which they denounced the unions' demands as a cynical grab for a simple 20 per cent wage increase that would cost the railroads fifty million dollars a year. The President's demand that they settle without arbitration was "inconceivable in a democracy like ours," they fumed. Next day a delegation went to the White House and told the President that the price of their cooperation was at least partial arbitration—that is, of the time-and-a-half demand—and a guarantee

[19] Winthrop M. Daniels, *American Railroads: Four Phases of Their History* (Princeton, 1932), 84–86; Link, *Wilson,* V, 86; *NYT,* Aug. 19, 1961, 1.

of a rate increase, however the President chose to constitute the guarantee. All afternoon Wilson was closeted with Newlands and Adamson. At 8:30 that night the telephone rang in the railroad leaders' suite at the Willard. Would Messrs. Willard, Holden, and Lovett (of the Union Pacific) kindly come to the White House right away? There the President told them that he was considering a definite promise of a rate increase. Everyone was greatly relieved. Settlement was in sight.[20]

It was wishful thinking on everyone's part, however, to suppose that the President could guarantee rate relief, then or at any time in the future. Congress, for that matter, could guarantee nothing unless it was willing to disown its creature, the ICC, and archaic Progressivism was not that nearly dead. What the Congressional leaders told Wilson they *could* do was to press ahead with the recommendation to "reorganize" the ICC, which, stripped of the euphemism, meant to pack the panel with two new members who might swing it in the direction of Commissioners Daniels and Harlan. It would then be almost certain that one of the five hold-out members would come over, making a working majority of five to four. This was the President's "guarantee" to the railroad leaders. Next day a wave of excitement broke out in the lobby of the National House. A newspaperman had brought the news that the railroad presidents had found Wilson's guarantee wanting. "What if he isn't reelected?" one of them had asked. They had switched their tactics, offering to accept the eight-hour day but demanding arbitration of the rate of pay. This meant that labor, if it accepted, would lose the guarantee of ten hours' pay for eight hours of work. No one took the move seriously. The union chairmen, whose sessions at the Bijou Theatre had been growing more and more rebellious, prepared to leave Washington. On the 25th they gave the President a 72-hour ultimatum. They let it be known that they had fifteen million dollars in their strike fund. The following day Wilson's "guarantee" fell apart completely when Senator Newlands admitted that the Senate would debate the proposal to reorganize the ICC for at least a month. The union heads were furious at having had victory snatched from their grasp, but the railroad executives seemed strangely calm. Howard Elliott released a self-righteous statement which noted that whereas nations arbitrated, labor unions refused.

[20] *NYT*, Aug. 20, 1916, 1, 3; Aug. 22, 1; Aug. 23, 1; Aug. 24, 1.

On the 27th the 600 chairmen left Washington. It was a Sunday, but the
time for sightseeing was past.[21]

Next morning a sheepish group of brotherhood leaders stood before the President. Wilson had just heard a rumor that a strike order
had gone out for September 4. Was this true? Garretson and Stone admitted that it was. "Incredible," said the President. The solemn promise
had been made to him that no such unilateral action would be taken.
Rescind the order! Impossible, said the unhappy union men. The locals
had taken matters into their own hands. Newspapermen broke into the
dining room of the Willard, where the railroad presidents were at
breakfast. All a bluff, they said. From Altoona came big talk. "Let
them strike. We are ready with a capital R," said the superintendent of
the Pennsylvania's Middle Division, the most important stretch of railroad in the world. Perhaps they *were* ready. Word leaked out that the
conference of railroad presidents had chosen the Pennsylvania and the
Santa Fe to lead an all-out fight to break the strike. The executives announced that by reassignments of nonunion workers, calling back retired workers, and the use of supervisory personnel they expected to
keep one-fifth of the national railroad system in operation. Across the
nation the political flavor of the confrontation was heightened as newspapers divided along party lines. The President had tried to avoid going
to the Hill. Now he had to play his ace.[22]

The galleries of the House of Representatives wore a festive air
on the 29th as the spectators, all of them admitted on carefully doled
out passes, awaited the special message which President Wilson was
about to deliver, as he preferred, in person. They stared in astonishment
as a youthful-looking President, sportily dressed in an unusually well-
fitting navy blue jacket, white trousers, and white shoes, strode into the
chamber and up to the rostrum. Perhaps he smiled at Senator Cummins,
who had just delivered himself of the opinion that any law requiring the
eight-hour day would be unconstitutional. Rapidly the President summarized the situation. A nationwide railroad strike was out of the question. "The eight-hour day," he continued, "now undoubtedly has the
sanction of the judgment of society in its favor and should be adopted

[21] *Ibid.*, Aug. 25, 1916, 1; Aug. 26, 1; Aug. 27, I, 1; Aug. 28, 1.
[22] *Ibid.*, Aug. 29, 1916, 1.

as a basis for wages even where the actual work to be done cannot be completed within eight hours." Then he ticked off what he wanted. It boiled down to a law requiring the eight-hour day with undiminished pay; a commission to assess the workings and the financial impact of the law; and enlargement of the ICC by two members. Wilson had already been told by legislative leaders that he could not expect the Congress to approve more than the eight-hour law and the investigating commission in time to head off a strike. So be it. Head off the strike now, and leave the reform of railroad regulation to the proper bodies in their own good time was the President's policy at that critical moment.[23]

Two days later A. B. Garretson, chairman of the Railway Brotherhood Conference Committee, stood at the far end of the table from Senator Newlands in the committee room where a bill embodying the President's request was under consideration. The Senator demanded to know why his committee had to proceed under such pressure. Could not Garretson, the acknowledged leader of the railroad workers, call off the strike while Congress deliberated? Tears rolled down the railroad man's cheeks as he replied that if he did so he would be a "traitor." He recalled his days as a railroad man in Mexico, where the vultures would follow his train hoping that it would run over a cow, as it not infrequently did. "In times like this," he said, "men go back to primal instincts. . . . Now the public is the carcass. And we are all, perhaps, the vultures. . . . The country will pay." On September 2 Congress passed the Adamson Act, as the law was called, making eight hours the basic workday on the railroads after January 1, 1917, the details of the limitation to be worked out by a special commission of three to be appointed by the President. The Mexican motif was again noted during the brief debate in the Senate, one of whose members grumpily compared the proceedings to the national legislature of Mexico when the dictator's measures were before it. The unions rescinded the strike order, while the railroad executives set their lawyers to work to get the statute before the Supreme Court as quickly as possible.[24]

[23] "Arbitration and the Eight-Hour Day," *LD*, LIII (Sept. 2, 1916), 543–44; *NYT*, Aug. 30, 1916, 1, 3; *Messages and Papers of the Presidents*, ed. James D. Richardson *et al.* (20 vols., and supplements, Washington, 1898–1925), XVIII, 8144–49.

[24] *NYT*, Sept. 1, 1916, 1; Sept. 3, 1.

In Chicago Edward P. Ripley said that Wilson's plea for an eight-hour law proved that the President did not know what he was talking about, and it would not take long to demonstrate that Ripley had a point. Democratic newspapers across the country praised the advent of the eight-hour day but found little to crow about in the way it had been achieved. Papers which felt free to criticize the President did so unmercifully. "Let every American . . . remember . . . on November 7 that Woodrow Wilson, for political purposes, denied to the railways the square deal," said the New York *Sun.* "Blackmail," said the generally Democratic New York *Times.* Radical sheets were gleeful. "It proves," said the Socialist-Labor *Weekly People* in New York, "the great power of the working class when consolidated upon the field of industry. . . . Labor holds the whip hand if only it proceeds properly." [25] Cartoonists outdid themselves in chronicling this display of brute labor power. Bradley, in the Chicago *Daily News,* drew the President holding up a placard reading, "I am for arbitration as a principle but not in *this* case," while the crowned heads of Europe, peering over the ocean from a building labeled "The Hague," applauded, "Great! Fine! That's just what *we* always say!" Harding, in the Brooklyn *Eagle,* depicted labor as a thug standing over Uncle Sam with a club labeled "Strike," demanding that he sign the eight-hour bill. But the heartland of archaic Progressivism seemed, perversely, to favor this latest humbling of the railroads; the Grand Island, Nebraska, *Independent* (notwithstanding its name a Republican paper) and the Sioux City, Iowa, *Tribune* declared themselves in favor of the outcome.[26] Most of the 100 million Americans, however, merely breathed a sigh of relief that a strike had been avoided.

The railroads, on the other hand, regarded nothing as settled. It was clear that until the Supreme Court ruled on the constitutionality of this extraordinary invocation of the commerce clause, they recognized no obligation to implement the Adamson Act. Two months later implemen-

[25] "Paying for the Railroad Men's Victory," *LD,* LIII (Sept. 9, 1916), 591–92. The President could have done without Warren Stone's jubilant announcement that although a lifetime Republican, this time he was voting for Wilson; and without the Trainmen's establishment of "Wilson Clubs" among their membership. Stevenson, "Locomotive Engineers," 373–74.

[26] "Political Effects of the Labor Victory," *LD,* LIII (Sept. 16, 1916), 651; "The President's Hand in the Railway Crisis," *LD,* LIII (Aug. 26, 1916), 442.

tation was ostensibly bogged down by failure of labor and management to agree on an interpretation of the law. Elisha Lee said bluntly, "Nobody knows how to apply the law." In mid-November the unions announced that they would strike on January 1, 1917, if the law had not been put into effect by that date, regardless of what the Supreme Court might or might not do in the interim.[27] When the railroads threatened to apply for an injunction against the strike, however, and then agreed with a Department of Justice request to make benefits retroactive to January 1, 1917, if the court decision went against them, the brotherhoods let New Year's Day pass without a strike.[28]

And so the nation struggled through the worst winter weather in recent memory, its sadly overburdened railroad system tottering on the verge of a total shutdown. By mid-March it was obvious that America's entry into the war was imminent. On the 12th the brotherhoods announced that a strike would be called for the 17th. Only freight service would be affected, they promised, and defense goods would not be stopped. Panic now seemed to hit the well-oiled union machine. One of the brotherhoods released a statement explaining that they had to strike now, because once the country was at war they could not. On the 15th came the announcement that a five-day grace period was being allowed because it had been decided to strike passenger service, too. The President, in bed with a cold and already grieving at war developments, roused himself against his doctors' orders. Rounding up Secretaries of the Interior and Labor Lane and Wilson, Samuel Gompers, and Daniel Willard (all members of his Council of National Defense), he dispatched them to New York to stave off disaster.

As Lane and Willard drove together to the railroad station, both discussed the status of the Adamson Act in the Supreme Court. Lane knew how valuable an asset it would be in his approaching labors if he had some inkling of what the nine justices were going to do the following Monday morning, if anything. But, of course, that was out of the question. Or was it? Lane instructed the chauffeur to take them by

---

[27] At no time had labor admitted the necessity of legislation to gain their demands, which they intended to press regardless of the outcome of the Supreme Court decision. They had even announced that they were "passively" against a rate increase since it was their position that the railroads could afford the eight-hour day without one. *NYT*, Aug. 29, 1916, 1.

[28] *NYT*, Nov. 14, 1916, 1; Nov. 16, 1; Dec. 29, 1.

Chief Justice Edward White's residence. While Willard waited discreetly in the car, the aggressive Mr. Lane paid his respects to the Chief Justice. He emerged a few minutes later with a broad grin on his face and chattered amiably with Willard the rest of the way to the station. His manner telegraphed to the railroad man all that he needed to know when he went into conference with his colleagues that night. By midnight all four mediators were locked in conferences with the parties in New York which lasted until 3:45 A.M. and then resumed later on Saturday. Reluctantly, the brotherhoods agreed to a 48-hour postponement.[29]

Meanwhile, Willard was having no luck getting the railroad executives to read what was in his mind about the Supreme Court case. The following afternoon, Sunday, Lane was fighting his way through a crowd of reporters in his hotel lobby when he heard one of them shout that three American ships had been sunk by German submarines. The dreaded resumption of unrestricted submarine warfare had become a reality.[30]

Within minutes the Secretary was on the long-distance telephone with the President. There must be no strike, said the distracted man in the White House. Lane understood what he must do. Already the railroad leaders were preparing for the end. Before he could ask them, they were readying a statement. Briefly, without apparent bitterness and without reservation, they surrendered to the inevitable:

. . . therefore you are authorized to assure the nation that there will be no strike, and as a basis for such assurance we hereby authorize the Committee of the Council of National Defense to grant to employees who were about to strike whatever adjustment your Committee deems necessary to guarantee the uninterrupted and efficient operation of the railways as an indispensable arm of national defense.[31]

Now all that remained was to discover just what it would take to satisfy the workers. Late that night Lane called together the brotherhood leaders and the railroad representatives who had been so eager to

[29] Frederick Palmer, *Newton D. Baker: America at War* (2 vols., New York, 1931), I, 97–99; *NYT*, March 13, 1917, 1; March 15, 1; March 16, 1; March 17, 1; March 18, I, 1. Willard recalled the episode twenty years later, confirming the essential facts; Edward Hungerford, *Daniel Willard Rides the Line* (New York, 1938).

[30] *NYT*, March 19, 1917, 1.   [31] *Ibid.*

fight each other. In a one-hour speech which rang all the changes on the patriotism theme, the Secretary exhorted them to reach an agreement on a way to put the eight-hour day into effect. At dawn the next morning— Monday, decision day at the Supreme Court—they leaned back in their chairs exhausted, their work completed. W. S. Carter, of the Enginemen, went to the window of the hotel room. Pointing to a building "from which floated the American flag in the first light of dawn," he exclaimed, "Gentlemen, look there! It is the dawn of a new day." For whom, a sad, tired Dan Willard must have wondered; for whom? [32]

II

New York's usually busy harbor presented a strange sight in early February, 1917. "Cars, cars everywhere, and not a ship to load," reported an amazed observer. Along the Hudson River docks hundreds of car floats were tied up, loaded to capacity with railroad cars which, temporarily at least, had reached the end of their journey. Railroad yards abutting the piers were so packed with cars that hardly an unob-

---

[32] *Ibid.,* March 20, 1, 4. Lane described the scene for reporters. A few hours later the Supreme Court, in a split decision, ruled that the Adamson Act was constitutional (243 U.S. 332). The justices were divided five to four. Tipping the scales was Wilson's recent appointee, the newest man on the bench, Louis Dembitz Brandeis. *NYT,* March 20, 1917, 1. The decision was a closely reasoned rationalization that the commerce clause gave the Congress not only the power to fix conditions of employment, but "in an emergency arising from a nationwide dispute over wages" the power to fix wages as well, as long as the law was not confiscatory and extended for a reasonable time; 243 U.S. 332–33. "The contention that the act is unworkable is without merit," said the majority. The dissenters (Day, Pitney, McReynolds, and Van Devanter) argued that the law was not what it purported to be, that it was an act to raise wages, and would not limit hours of work. They also objected that the court was misinterpreting the historic doctrine of John Marshall that in interstate commerce the federal government was supreme, noting that Marshall had meant supreme over the state governments, but not supreme over individuals. McReynolds asserted that the decision cleared the way for maximum wage laws and compulsory arbitration.

Lane's biographer appears to overestimate the Secretary's powers of persuasion, inasmuch as he omits reference to the impact of the sinkings and the fact that the railroads had capitulated before the final meeting. Keith W. Olson, "Franklin K. Lane: A Biography" (unpublished doctoral dissertation, University of Wisconsin, 1964), 260–61. See also Kerley, "Failure of Railway Labor Leadership," 66–78; Franklin H. Martin, *Digest of the Proceedings of the Council of National Defense during the World War* (Washington, 1934), 103; and Samuel Gompers, *Seventy Years of Life and Labor* (2 vols., New York, 1925), II, 146.

structed track remained on which the switch engines could maneuver. For miles up the Palisades, loaded cars were strung out along the tracks of the New York Central's West Shore Division. Nowhere were the familiar sights of smoking funnels and white plumes of exhaust steam to be seen. In the Pennsylvania Railroad's Jersey City yards idlers stared incredulously as a giant wrecking crane stretched its powerful arm out over two adjoining tracks, grasped a boxcar, swung it clear of its fellows, and placed it down on the only unobstructed track in sight.[33]

America's railroads in the winter of 1916–17 fell further and further behind each day in their fight to keep up with the unprecedented demands on their facilities. They were reeling under a combination of circumstances which no one had ever thought possible—which might almost have been the work of a particularly evil genius. The trouble had begun when abnormally low temperatures and heavy snow had locked the entire East and Midwest in a winter grip that broke all records. At a time when railroad men were struggling to keep their lines open at all, the normal seasonal volume and pattern of freight shipments had failed to develop. Instead of declining once the cities' coalbins, grain elevators, and warehouses had been filled, traffic went right on climbing. To make matters infinitely worse, the traffic seemed perversely determined to move in one direction only: from the relatively free, open spaces of the heartland of America to the densely populated, congested maritime cities of the East. Traffic in the country as a whole was running 10 per cent ahead of January a year earlier—a substantial increase—but more significantly, exports (virtually all of which went through the ports of Boston, New York, Philadelphia, or Baltimore) had jumped 30 per cent.[34] Then terror had struck the East Coast, as Germany announced the resumption of unrestricted submarine warfare. Merchant ships loaded with vital cargoes for the Allies clung to their berths, afraid to put out to sea, while the arrival of empty bottoms into which the thousands of waiting railroad cars could be unloaded declined to a trickle and then stopped altogether.

America was headed toward a war for which she had barely begun to plan. So far the Allied procurement program and even the American

[33] *NYT,* Feb. 11, 1917, I, 1.

[34] U.S. Bureau of the Census, *Historical Statistics of the United States: Colonial Times to 1957* (Washington, 1960), 334, 339.

preparedness effort had been conducted on the basis of peacetime free enterprise. Freight cars were loaded with goods at the factories or interior grain elevators as fast as shippers could get their hands on them, the very rhythm of the plants being determined by the manufacturers' ability to push their finished goods through the doors. These cars were sent east without any promise of ocean shipping space. Boxcars loaded with goods of low priority and with no early prospect of ocean shipment blocked the piers, while high-priority goods for which ships were waiting in the harbor sat in the yards or were sidetracked miles from the coast. In extreme cases the railroads, in desperation, brought in cranes to sort out their cars the way a small boy impatiently lifts his toy train from its tracks. By midwinter the port of New York was approaching total shutdown. Everywhere, said an observer, there was "absolute stillness." [35]

Americans paid dearly in 1916 and 1917 for the neglect of their railroads. Not only were the lines short of virtually every kind of physical facility, notably locomotives, but the timid structure of the railroad business itself, based as it was on the old-fashioned philosophy of competition, turned out to be an intolerable incubus. The food and fuel situation in the eastern and northern cities showed the strain almost from the beginning. By November, 1916, coal dealers in New York spoke ominously of a price of twenty dollars a ton by the time winter was in full force. Burns Brothers, rationing their supplies and announcing that they would take no new customers, quoted $7.75 a ton in Manhattan and guaranteed the price for only twenty-four hours. Railroad officials openly accused a group of coal brokers in the Midwest of holding loaded cars in anticipation of higher prices in the East. The town of Conneaut, Ohio, went into the retail coal business. Employees of the Youngstown Sheet and Tube Company were allowed to buy coal from the dwindling piles which had also to feed the blast furnaces.[36] It occurred to a New York onion dealer that since he had no place to warehouse several carloads of his specialty, he might as well take his time about unloading them. When he finally did so he was pleasantly "surprised" to discover that the price had shot up from three dollars a bag to fourteen. Middlemen were not the only ones to profit. In Riverhead,

[35] *NYT*, Feb. 11, 1917, I, 1.   [36] *Ibid.*, Nov. 1, 1916, 1.

Long Island, potato farmers ordered 100 boxcars to be placed for loading. They loaded them, all right—and then fitted them with oil heaters to prevent freezing while they waited for prices to go up.[37]

Civil unrest threatened. In Chicago it was rumored that the city was about to run out of coke for its gasworks. In New York 5,000 people, apparently including virtually the entire socialist population of the city, demonstrated in Madison Square against high food prices. Word got out that the governor was at the St. Regis Hotel conferring with George Perkins about the city's food stocks. A delegation of "price agitators" invited themselves to join the conference, and the governor promised the capitalist and the socialists that he would support the city's takeover of food distribution facilities if necessary. A short while later a thousand of the demonstrators marched to the hotel, demanding to see the governor. They were told that he had left. Furious, the mob almost succeeded in pulling from his taxi a bewildered citizen who had just driven up. They remained in the area, blocking traffic and denouncing the rich, for another hour before police succeeded in making them move on. Meanwhile Perkins took some of the heat off by announcing that he was personally advancing over $100,000 to a group who were bringing in extra supplies of rice, a commodity which had been especially subject to profiteering.[38] Out in Chicago J. P. Griffin, president of the Board of Trade and an old railroad-baiter in the best tradition of archaic Progressivism, accused the railroads and the ICC, in a public telegram to the Commission, of favoring "industrials" over farmers in furnishing cars. Commissioner McChord hotly denied the charge. Indomitably vocal Frederick Underwood wired Griffin, "There is no danger of either riot or anarchy [Griffin had predicted both] if . . . men like you will stop talking about it. While you are sending stirring telegrams the Erie railroad is doing work." [39]

Throughout the winter the railroads tried various expedients in an effort to break up the congestion. In view of the limitations of the antitrust and interstate commerce laws (which prevented outright pooling), the continuing responsibility of each railroad to make a profit as a separate enterprise, and the insane demands of a completely uncoordinated

[37] Ibid., Nov. 18, 1916, I, 6; Feb. 24, 1917, 1.
[38] Ibid., Feb. 24, 1917, 1; Feb. 25, 1.   [39] Ibid., Feb. 22, 1917, 6.

government priority system, it is remarkable that any sort of muddling through was possible.[40] The chief weapon was the freight embargo. That fall the Pennsylvania had embargoed westbound freight out of Baltimore for the first time in its history. Railroad yards in Chicago, it appeared, were jammed with cars of grain headed east for export. By late winter that same grain was producing the same effects in East Coast yards. In mid-February one railroad had 49 car floats loaded with boxcars of export wheat, thus tying up both the floats and the cars. In December four eastern railroads were stopping all eastbound shipments, except perishable foodstuffs and government goods, at Pittsburgh, Buffalo, Detroit, and Marion, Ohio. By February it was estimated that in addition to all of the loaded cars sitting idly at the docks, there were 50,000 empties in the East while the West was short 60,000 cars. Out went the old custom of holding another road's car until there was a shipment available that would take it back to its home tracks. The railroads began to round up empties and send them west in solid trains, without regard to whose they were or whether the roads that owned them would earn the freight back. Thirty railroads formed a "gentlemen's agreement" to load and send east two fifty-car trainloads of grain each day from Minneapolis, in whatever cars and on whatever rails were available.[41]

Manufacturers, farmers, mining men, railroaders, all were agreed on one thing: no one wanted to go through another winter like the one just past. The need for extraordinary action was widely recognized. The cost of doing business, even when it could be done, had shot skyward as plants limped along without inbound or outbound transportation, then worked furiously to catch up when they could. Railroad executives faced a clouded future. They could not do the job as presently organized, but they were working out what promised to be a much more effective, yet still voluntary, coordination of their facilities. Meanwhile all looked eagerly for a reformation of government regulation to correct

[40] The railroads were still sorting things out a year after that memorable winter. Railroad men and shippers told many a wry story. ICC inspectors, it was said, had found cars of war materials sitting on sidings a year after they had been shipped. A religious congregation had finished building a new church and was eagerly awaiting arrival of the pews, but three months after they had left the factory no one knew where they were. *Ibid.*, Feb. 16, 1917, 1; Feb. 24, 1.

[41] *Ibid.*, Nov. 15, 1916, 8; Feb. 16, 1917, 1, 10; Feb. 18, I, 6; Feb. 24, 1.

the flaws which had now been so amply demonstrated. In January, 1917, A. H. Smith of the New York Central, whose own railroad was staggering under a load 40 per cent heavier than a year earlier, told a druggists' convention that the railroads wanted a "super-commission," with powers to end the insanities of forty-eight-state regulation. Daniel Willard and E. P. Ripley, on the same platform, applauded these sentiments heartily. In Washington the Newlands Committee had undertaken an investigation which promised to dwarf the studies that had led to the Acts of 1906 and 1910. Was there time to do things the "right way"?

III

There was reason to hope, if one were a railroad executive in the fall of 1916, that the Newlands Committee would elicit more sweet reasonableness and throw more light on the railroad situation than any body which had studied government regulation during the thirty years that it had been in effect. Even the ICC seemed to be turning toward reformation of the principles of rate-fixing. In its *Annual Report for 1916* it recommended that Congress "fix [existing] interstate rates, fares, etc. . . . as just and reasonable for the past," a move which would leave the Commission free to consider only the increases involved in rates proposed in the future.[42] Ever sensitive to the growing wave of criticism of its ineffectuality, the Commission was ponderously maneuvering itself into a position to accept general rate increases when they could not be staved off any longer. "It seems to us beyond question," the 1916 report stated, "that largely increased railroad facilities are necessary to handle adequately the commerce of the country, and that in some way those facilities must be provided." [43] Such a policy, of course, left the way wide open to government ownership in addition to (or, as many naïvely thought, instead of) higher rates.

Congress had not got around to authorizing the full-scale investigation of railroad regulation for which the President had asked in December, 1915, until the summer of the following year. And it was not until November, after the nation had sweltered through a summer of strike

[42] ICC, *Annual Report for 1916*, 92.   [43] *Ibid.*, 73.

threats, that hearings were begun. But it was a fully authoritative body which was to revise government regulation. The legislative struggles of 1905–6 and 1910 had shown that much time could be saved if the two houses of Congress could reach an early meeting of the minds on what was politically possible, rather than working separately at their own railroad bills. Consequently a joint subcommittee of the House and Senate interstate commerce committees was created. Newlands, chairman of the permanent committee in the Senate, became chairman of the joint body while his counterpart in the House, Adamson, became vice-chairman. Membership included Senator Cummins and Congressman Esch, the leading minority-party specialists in railroad regulation. From Newlands, at one end of the spectrum, therefore, to Cummins at the other, every color of regulatory philosophy was represented. As things turned out, the Newlands Committee had everything in its favor except time.[44]

The subcommittee's field of inquiry was as broad as its members' philosophies. It was not confined to railroad problems, but could consider all forms of transportation. It was charged first of all with the task of cleaning house at the ICC. Specifically, the committee was to find out whether the ICC was overloaded with work, and whether it would be wise to increase the Commission's membership and reorganize it. The committee, most significantly, was to determine whether the ICC should be limited explicitly to consideration of the reasonableness and fairness of individual rates. (As we have seen, nearly all of the Commissioners had started out with the belief that their jurisdiction was so limited, and a majority still professed to cling to that belief.) Blanket rate adjustments, presumably, would be passed on by some other body. The enabling resolution even directed that geographic decentralization of the ICC, along the lines of the federal courts, be investigated. Railroad finances were to be studied, with a view not to past irregularities but to present and future needs for capital. But the most important duty with which the committee was charged was that of recommending just what the federal government's basic responsibilities in the field of regulation should be. Should it regulate hours of work, for example, and wages as well as rates? Should it throw over the railroads the armor of federal incorporation? [45]

[44] Senate Joint Resolution 60, 64th Cong., 1st Sess., approved July 20, 1916.

[45] Public Joint Resolution 25, 64th Cong., 1st Sess.

Senator Newlands, busy with a backbreaking volume of other work, turned the gavel over to Senator Adamson shortly after hearings began on November 20, 1916. As usual, there was the question of procedure. Adamson had declared bluntly that he wanted to find out just what the nation's railroad leaders thought was wrong with regulation, and what they felt would make it right. But the railroad leaders were tired of being placed on the stand at the outset of such proceedings. They wanted to play neither the role of defendant, as in the past, nor the role of plaintiff now. They wanted, in short, to discourage the courtroom atmosphere in which they had fared so badly in the past. The first witness was Alfred P. Thom, an adroit lawyer and counsel for the Railroad Executives' Committee, which was trying to coordinate the railroad system for the job ahead. When Adamson directed him to proceed with the railroads' case, he balked. The committee, Thom said, had called several prominent economists, and others had come voluntarily. He could see some of them in the audience. Let them present the public picture first, then the railroads would be glad to say their piece. Noting that President Wilson had asked for an investigation in the public interest, and not in the interest of specific groups, he said earnestly, "We therefore seek to avoid . . . the reducing of this investigation to a plaintiff on the one side and defendants on the other. We do not desire to be placed in the position of plaintiffs in this investigation." [46]

This approach did not please Adamson at all. The witness has no reason to fear that the railroads' testimony will be prejudiced, he lectured Thom, just because he is a railroad lawyer. With the rudeness which often characterized exchanges between legislators and businessmen, he added, "Most of us would like to be [railroad lawyers] ourselves, and have your salary. . . . The people want to know what the troubles are . . . and the people are going to be willing to correct them." It was precisely because the President had been repeatedly told by railroad men that things were not being done right, Adamson reminded the witness, that the President had asked for the investigation.[47] So the railroad men bowed to the inevitable and began their presentation. It

[46] *Hearings before the Joint Committee on Interstate and Foreign Commerce,* 64th Cong., 1st and 2d Sess. (Washington, 1917), 28–29. Hereinafter referred to as Newlands Committee Hearings.

[47] *Ibid.,* 32.

quickly became apparent that the railroads wanted most of all to be freed from harassment by the states. The federal regulatory body was denying the railroads a chance to earn more money, it was true, but the states were costing them more and more of what money they still had available for badly needed improvements. Accordingly, Thom made a lengthy presentation built around a strong proposal for a system of federal incorporation. Such ideas brought representatives of the state commissions scurrying to Washington to sweep back the tide, and on December 7 William Jennings Bryan appeared and made a lengthy statement on the importance of retaining strong regulation of the railroads at the state level.[48]

But it was becoming increasingly difficult to keep such desultory proceedings moving in the hectic days of early 1917. The committee recessed on December 9, 1916, and was barely rescued from oblivion by a motion to renew early in 1917.[49] When hearings resumed in March, 1917, two new faces appeared to plead the railroads' cause. From the west came, first, R. S. Lovett, who had been piloting the Union Pacific through the major improvement program that had been less than half completed at Harriman's death in 1909. "Judge" Lovett called for "immediate nationalization of railroad control," waking up a corporal's guard of bored newspaper reporters as he did so. But Lovett was not using the word in its meaning of government ownership. What he wanted were the blessings of federal incorporation, which would have reduced the regulatory role of the states to a minimum, combined with the virtues of private ownership and operation.[50] He was followed by Julius Kruttschnitt, the plain-spoken, thick-skinned chairman of the Southern Pacific. The Californian cited the experience of the banks under the national banking system adopted during the Civil War. "It [the banking system] has been constructive. The regulations are fair . . . they have prospered and their shares are eagerly sought. [But] the regulation of railroads overthrows all principles of economical operation . . . and is a far more potent influence in affecting the credit of the carriers than the comparatively few cases of dishonest management."[51] Railroad men, furthermore, were finding their work harder and harder to accom-

[48] *Ibid.,* 457 and *passim.*   [49] *NYT,* Jan. 6, 1917, 5.

[50] Newlands Committee Hearings, 656–887; *NYT,* March 20, 1917, 4.

[51] Newlands Committee Hearings, 892.

plish because of the deteriorating loyalty and efficiency of labor. Representative Edward L. Hamilton, of Michigan, demanded to know just what Kruttschnitt was getting at, and the "Von Moltke of transportation" was glad to oblige. "Labor no longer looks to the carrier, to its employer, as being in charge of its wages and destiny, but looks elsewhere," declared Kruttschnitt grimly; "it looks to the state legislatures and to Washington." His answer was devastatingly frank. No authority, no responsibility; that was the warning which the railroad men were trying to convey to the nation's lawmakers.[52]

The westerner then showed the committee some charts which he had had prepared by a consulting economist. They proved to be some of the most sophisticated and most revealing analyses ever presented in such proceedings. He wanted to make just two points. The first—still highly abstract in 1917—was that freight charges in *real* terms (i.e, adjusted for changes in the purchasing power of the dollar) had consistently decreased since 1899. Since that year, he asserted, the nation's shippers had paid a grand total of nearly eight billion dollars less than they would have paid if freight rates had been permitted to rise no more than the general price level. How had the railroads been able to absorb such a reduction in real rates? By increased efficiency, almost all of which had been achieved through investment in improvement of the properties. But had not the railroads shared in the benefits of this increased efficiency? Indeed they had not. Holding up a chart of the trend in the number of tons which a single freight train was capable of pulling, Kruttschnitt noted as his second point that increased wages (dollar wages, that is) had closely kept pace with the increased output per train crew member.[53] Shippers and labor had reaped the benefits of the improvements, but little if any benefit was now going back into the railroads where the general welfare might have been served.

Senator Newlands had not appeared in the presiding officer's place since Lovett's testimony. Nor did he show up when W. M. Acworth, the British expert on railway regulation, appeared in May to present a lengthy report on government ownership of railways in Europe, which ended with an enthusiastic recommendation against such a policy for the United States. Newlands was in the chair, however, at the Palace

---

[52] *Ibid.*, 904.   [53] *Ibid.*, 907.

Hotel in San Francisco on November 1, 1917, to hear an impassioned
attack on federal incorporation from Max Thelen of the National Association of Railway Commissioners. Thelen's testimony was given in a
swiftly changing climate. Some of Newlands' work apart from the committee had recently borne fruit in the payment of another installment on
the "debt" which Congress still owed the President: the membership of
the ICC had been increased from seven to nine. Federal intervention in
behalf of the war effort was expected momentarily. When the lobbyist
was through, Adamson asked leave to address the committee. He announced that he was leaving the committee immediately, inasmuch as
further consideration of its subjects had been made impractical by the
war. A month later, back in Washington, Newlands adjourned the committee subject to the call of the chairman, a call which was never to
come.[54] Postwar American railroad policy would be worked out by Republican leaders whose philosophies of archaic Progressivism, and especially about government ownership, would be greatly chastened by the
events of 1917-20.[55]

IV

The burdens of war weighed more and more heavily on American
railroads after April, 1917. Railroad leaders found their two long-time
problems had reached the crisis stage. The coordination of their facilities for greater efficiency and the elimination of destructive competition
were now absolutely necessary. And the money for improvements once
desirable and now vital had to be found somewhere. Recognizing that

[54] *Ibid.*, Part 12, *passim;* Francis G. Newlands, *The Public Papers of Francis G. Newlands,* Edited and Placed in Historical Setting by Arthur B. Darling (2 vols., New York, 1932), II, 390, 400, 404.

[55] The political aspects of the formulation of postwar railroad policy are ably summarized in K. Austin Kerr, *American Railroad Politics, 1914–1920* (Pitts-burgh, 1968). Mr. Kerr concludes that the Transportation Act of 1920, sometimes called the Esch-Cummins Act, marked a return to Progressive regulation. Inas-much as the new law contained, with Cummins' blessing, provisions which he had stoutly opposed in the past (legalized pooling, amalgamation of systems, min-imum rates, and minimum fair return), it seems more accurate to conclude that the Act marked the death of archaic Progressivism as an influence on railroad regulation.

they were going to have to do everything possible short of illegally pooling their activities, they formed the Railroads' War Board in April. The board soon discovered, however, that a number of obstacles, all quite beyond its control, would make voluntary operation of the national railroad network as a fully unified system impossible. Especially frustrating was the priority system of the various government agencies shipping war materials. Each agency, quite naturally, considered its own traffic absolutely vital. No one will ever be able to calculate, for example, how much time was lost threading trains in and out of the miles of flatcars which for nearly a year blocked the main line of the Pennsylvania into Philadelphia, flatcars loaded with piling from Oregon and Washington, waiting for rail sidings to be laid at Hog Island shipyard, which would not even deliver its first ship until after the war was over.

Nearly as troublesome was the question of how to indemnify a railroad which voluntarily turned a shipment over to a competitor railroad better able, at a given moment, to handle it expeditiously. Traffic volume, now that the break-even point in railroad operations was so high, was more important than ever. A railroad like the Erie or the B. & O., less efficient in carrying New York–bound traffic, would slip into the deficit column with the loss of even a small percentage of its traffic. In a pooling arrangement, each railroad would simply have been "cut in" for a predetermined percentage of the total moneys received for hauling freight between two points, whether it ended up actually hauling somewhat more or somewhat less.[56] But pooling was a crime. And railroad executives were frank to admit, then and later, that getting freight agents to think as members of one big unified operation, when all of their training had been in the "root hog or die" tradition, and when their compensation still depended in many cases on the amount of business they solicited for their railroads, was hopeless. It has generally been overlooked that the Railroads' War Board never had any powers but the powers of persuasion, and as any military leader knows, it takes too much time to be tactful.[57]

[56] Julius Grodinsky, *The Iowa Pool* (Chicago, 1950), is a masterly treatment of this little-understood device as it actually worked in the nineteenth century.

[57] The efforts of the Railroads' War Board are summarized in Walker D. Hines, *War History of American Railroads* (New Haven, 1928), especially 13, 16, 18–20, 31. Less dependable because of prejudices which he developed in his first hectic months as Director General of the railroad industry during the war years

Most serious, however, was the financial problem. It is no accident that the railroads were most successful, in their voluntary unification efforts, in pooling the critically short supply of locomotives. Sheer necessity dictated success. Motive power had been the most worrisome feature of the railroad picture for several years. The unit cost of locomotives had risen to the point where many respectable lines had simply not kept up with requirements as dictated by traffic growth. Another sore spot, sure to cause trouble sooner or later, was the question of wages. Although the railroads were literally foundering on increased traffic, the eight-hour settlement meant financial pernicious anemia. Even so, the men who did the dangerous and exhausting work of moving the trains saw other men—some of them their erstwhile fellow workers—taking jobs in war industries at higher wages and under better working conditions. It became almost as much a problem of keeping the individual railroad man on the job at all, as of preventing a strike. "Railroad labor is grossly underpaid," Director General McAdoo's number-two man told him. The speaker was A. H. Smith, president of the New York Central, and he knew what he was talking about. "We're losing our skilled men daily; they are going into war industries where the pay is much higher." [58] Greatly increased wages were coming soon, so much was obvious. Suddenly nearly everybody began to see the light. Finally the "money power" had communicated the fact that what railroad financing was going on consisted of short-term refundings, while bank borrowings were nearing the one-billion-dollar mark. New issues were virtually impossible to float at any rate of interest. At the beginning of 1916 more railroads were in receivership (42,000 miles, including some of the largest lines, such as the Missouri Pacific and the Wabash) than at any time since the depression of the nineties. Former President Taft, in a Washington's Birthday address at Johns Hopkins University, confessed, "The inadequacy of our railroad system is startling. We have had many warnings from railroad men as to what would occur [and] . . . their warnings are now being vindicated." [59]

is William G. McAdoo, *Crowded Years* (New York, 1931), 448–49, 454, 456, 470, 477, 492. See also I. L. Sharfman, *The American Railroad Problem* (New York, 1921), 94.

[58] McAdoo, *Crowded Years*, 470.

[59] Quoted in William J. Cunningham, *American Railroads: Government Control and Reconstruction Policies* (New York, 1922), 11–13, 19–20, 21.

In the dying months of the Progressive era, therefore, the railroads decided to try once more to get a general rate increase approved under the old system. The entire episode is so similar to those that went before that it is hardly worth noting in detail. Everyone seemed to be in his place (except for Brandeis), playing his historically assigned role, right down to Clifford Thorne, who had added the oil jobbers to his list of clients by 1917. When the railroads asked for a 15 per cent increase in March, 1917, opposition by industrial shippers was almost nil. Those interests were so busy filling sheaves of orders at inflated prices that they could hardly have cared what happened to rates. Anything which promised an improvement in service had their approval. A month of hearings was held. It never occurred to anybody to publish the 6,000 pages of testimony.[60] The decision, rendered in June, was a masterpiece of shrinking from responsibility. The financial condition of the carriers was not good at the moment, admitted the Commissioners. It was true, too, that during the proceedings there had been a remarkably small number of protests from shippers. "But," said the men whose job it was to see that rates were reasonable, the small number of protests "are quite without significance as a basis for judging rates." The Commission seemed to be fatally fascinated with its impotence. Bad weather, congested tracks, the new wage levels—none of these factors could be considered in making rates. Everything that might justify immediately higher earnings, even the war itself, seemed to the Commission to be a temporary phenomenon, and "it would be unfair," said McChord, "to burden the public with a big rate increase" as a war measure. "The general operating results, looked at in the large through a series of years, show on the whole substantial improvement, general prosperity, and . . . ample financial resources . . . [but] we shall keep in closest touch." Denied was the entire application of the southern and western

[60] Kerr, *American Railroad Politics,* has dug these hearings out of the archives. He feels that Clifford Thorne's ability to get Rea of the Pennsylvania to admit that his road's credit was good was a decisive development. But nobody doubted the company's ability to pay its bills; Thorne was merely using the "have-you-stopped-beating-your-wife" technique. Thorne himself, realizing that the impasse in railroad regulation would soon be broken, turned to supporting government ownership in the naïve belief that rates would thereafter be permanently frozen at existing levels. As for the Pennsylvania, McAdoo soon found that Rea's warnings about that most strategically important railroad's growing inadequacies were all too true. McAdoo, *Crowded Years,* 477.

railroads. Denied also was the eastern application except for small increases on minerals and class rates.[61]

The nation would have been stunned, if such doings had not ceased to attract attention. Commissioner Daniels did not bother to comment, reasoning perhaps that he had nothing more to say. Harlan, by now completely disenchanted with the obscurantism of his colleagues, concurred only because he wanted to see "some affirmative results from this extended and laborious investigation." Commissioner Clements had died a week before, and if Harlan had not concurred with Daniels, Clark, and Hall, there would have been no increase at all, inasmuch as Meyer and McChord, the former state commissioners from Wisconsin and Kentucky, were dead set against any increase whatever. McChord, in one sense, was the most realistic of the group. He felt that because of the wartime emergency the entire problem should be dumped back in Congress' lap.

By the time the railroads applied for a rehearing in the fall, profit margins were disappearing rapidly. With nine months' operating results in, 1917 so far was disastrous. Volume for the eastern railroads had shot up $123 million, but net profit was down $57 million.[62] The trend could no longer be denied. By Christmas some of the oldest and proudest business institutions in the country, it seemed, would be wards of the state if something were not done. The ICC now actually did pass the buck to Congress. Opining that the railroads should be freed of the antipooling and antitrust laws, the Commissioners announced their refusal to reopen the case.[63] Had they done so, it is likely that the repressive policy of the preceding seven years would have been reversed, since the President was now in a position to appoint two additional members to the Commission. In November the Railroads' War Board announced a pooling arrangement east of Pittsburgh, followed immediately by an ur-

[61] 45 ICC 303, 303, 309, 310, 312–13, 316–17, 325, 326, 330, 335. Commissioner Meyer, now fully committed to the doctrines of archaic Progressivism, broke his customary silence and appended a dissent in which he objected to any increases whatever; 330. The historian of the ICC concluded that both the 1915 and 1917 cases "elicited a strikingly hesitant and meager response to the plea of financial need." I. L. Sharfman, *The Interstate Commerce Commission: A Study in Administrative Law and Procedure* (4 vols. in 5, New York, 1931–37), IIIb, 93.

[62] Hines, *War History of American Railroads*, 19.

[63] *Special Report of the Interstate Commerce Commission*, House Document 503, 65th Cong., 2d Sess., 1918, 1.

gent call from the Attorney General. As the members of the board seated themselves around his desk, the nation's chief law-enforcement officer informed them, with a perfectly straight face, that no one had repealed the Act of 1887 or the Sherman Antitrust Act, which, like all the other laws of the land, he was sworn to uphold to the letter.[64] The pooling plan was dropped. Frank A. Vanderlip, president of the National City Bank, now called for unification of the railroads under a single head for the duration of the war. Samuel Rea chimed in with a suggestion that the government lend the railroads a billion dollars at 4 per cent.[65]

Early next month another dying bellow was heard from archaic Progressivism. Representative Adolph J. Sabath of Illinois introduced a resolution in the House which would have placed that body on record as charging the railroads with deliberately holding up improvements in order to force the ICC's hand. The New York *Times*'s indignation boiled over:

> Someone should inform our servants at Washington what has happened in the country. They think that the railways have "broken down" and ought to be punished for their malicious failure to enjoy the blessings of regulation.
> They have not broken down. The history of railways affords no example of equal efficiency under such hindrances. What has broken down is the attempt to regulate business, all business, including railways. . . . The perfectionists thought that they could enact scientific management and moral precepts about how railways "ought" to be run. . . . The fact is that the policy of the Commission was doomed from the start, and can no more succeed in peace than in war, in the future than in the past.[66]

All year the burden of casting off the millstone of archaic Progressive regulation from the railroads, now the nation's number-two war industry, had shifted more and more to the shoulders of Senator Newlands. Members of the Railroads' War Board went to Washington to tell him flatly that they could go no further unless some way were found to suspend the antitrust and antipooling laws. In conference with the President, Newlands persuaded Wilson to come out publicly for a government loan of a billion dollars to the hard-pressed railroads, who were even then placing orders for locomotives which they could not afford.

---

[64] Hines, *War History of American Railroads*, 15, 19.

[65] *NYT*, Nov. 18, 1917, I, 7.   [66] *Ibid.*, Dec. 7, 1917, 12.

The subcommittee, in which the Senator had invested so much time and from which the nation had hoped for new and genuinely progressive legislation, was in limbo. Other, more expeditious legislation was needed now, and the chairman's lights burned later and later in the Senate Office Building. On Christmas Eve afternoon, hard at work, his heart rebelled and by late evening he was dead. An appreciative President and Mrs. Wilson were at the funeral service. "He was not showy," saluted the *Times,* "he was useful." [67] Two days after Christmas the President issued a proclamation assuming control of the railroads in behalf of the people of the United States. His grasp of the realities of the situation owed much to Newlands:

The Committee of railway executives . . . have done the utmost . . . but there were difficulties that they could neither escape nor neutralize. . . . The Committee was, of course, without power or authority to rearrange charges or effect proper compensations and adjustments of earnings. Several roads which were willingly and with admirable public spirit accepting the orders of the Committee have already suffered from these circumstances and should not be required to suffer further. In mere fairness to them the authority of the government must be substituted.[68]

Enterprise, thrice denied, gave way to public control, and the Railroad Age passed into history.

[67] *Ibid.,* 1; Dec. 11, 2; Dec. 25, 1; Dec. 26, 8; Dec. 28, 11.

[68] *Messages and Papers of the Presidents,* 8412. Kerr, *American Railroad Politics,* begins with a summary of the complex political developments which culminated in government assumption of control.

CHAPTER XII

POSTSCRIPT: WHAT DID IT ALL MEAN?

"Public Policy," said the English jurist, "is an unruly horse, and when once you get astride of it you never know where it will carry you." It is indeed unruly, for it lives in the feelings rather than logic, the field of values rather than mathematics. . . . Government officials . . . cannot escape valuing, consciously or unconsciously, the relative importance of the human interests at stake. Every transaction is weighed according to what is deemed a public purpose. . . . [But] the question always is, not, What *is a private purpose over against a public purpose? but, Is the private purpose* also *a public purpose, or* merely *a private purpose?*—JOHN R. COMMONS

I

Federalization of America's railroads has been advanced as proof, at one extreme, of the failure of an incompetent management to provide the nation with the transportation facilities it needed; and at the other extreme, as the culmination of a forty-year history of government intervention which, *post hoc, ergo propter hoc,* was a scheme to hold over the railroad companies an umbrella of profit which they could not provide for themselves.[1] It was neither.

Federalization was the moment of truth in which the failures of archaic Progressive regulation were stripped bare. The manner in which it was carried out and the policies which the Director General of the

[1] An excellent and popular college textbook, now in its third edition, offers the following reasons for federalization: "It is all too clear that the bankers sought primarily their own and their stockholders' gain, though this often meant charging exorbitant rates for poor service, bankrupting railroad properties, or debauching the politics of states. Indeed, the mismanagement of America's greatest single property interest from 1897 to 1914 reached such a point that only federal rehabilitation and operation of the railroads during the first World War saved the industry from virtual bankruptcy." Arthur S. Link and William B. Catton, *American Epoch: A History of the United States since the 1890's* (New York, 1967), 54. For the other, and even more remarkable, hypothesis, see Gabriel Kolko, *Railroads and Regulation* (Princeton, 1965). 212, 216, and *passim. Caveat lector.*

Railroad Administration adopted speak volumes about the oriental mess into which national railroad policy had wound itself. The government leased the railroads as a going concern, guaranteeing the owners a compensation not less than the average annual net profit which they had earned in a stipulated base period, and thereby became the sole provider of railroad transportation services to the nation's shippers, whether government agency or private firm. Like any private lessee, it was free to make changes or improvements in the leasehold so long as it returned the property to its owners at the end of the lease in at least as good condition as it found it. Key personnel of the railroads relinquished their positions with individual railroad companies and came to Washington to direct the various functions of the unified system. In the short period that the nation was actually at war, their successes were remarkable; so remarkable, in fact, that a brief period of enthusiasm for amalgamation of the roads into a limited number of systems ensued after the war.

The major change was that under federal control the railroads were subject to just so much regulation by the states as the national government was willing to recognize, and no more. Where existing state regulation posed no threat to efficient operation (as in the case of real estate taxes, Jim Crow laws, and other manifestations of the traditional taxing and police powers) there were few changes. In matters of rates (intrastate as well as interstate), crew laws, frequency and quality of service, local improvements, and the like, the state commissions were dead for the duration. Had it wanted to, the federal government could have operated the railroads in as complete ignorance of state governments as it operates the post office. (Small wonder, then, that grassroots enthusiasm for government ownership of the railroads died a sudden death during the war!) From the very beginning, therefore, federalization meant freedom from all of the artificial restrictions on full, rational exploitation of the physical properties, from the Act of 1887 down to the latest "atrocity" of a state railroad commission.

Federalization meant, much more significantly, that the palsied hand of the ICC was removed from the throttle in a manner which ensured that the impasse of the Progressive era would not be repeated—at least, not in the same form. Once the federal government and, therefore, the people were responsible for the financial performance of the roads —once, that is, that the railroads became without question a "public" concern—the cancer of repressive rate regulation was cut out without ceremony. One of the first acts of the Director General of the Railroad Administration was to put a small army of traffic experts to work on the rate question. Despairing of ever solving the problem on a rate-by-rate basis, the Director General decided, at the end of May, 1918, to adopt the only course which had seemed practicable to the railroad executives back in 1910: a flat, across-the-board increase tempered, of course, by exceptions in hardship cases. The amount of the increase? Add up the three raises which the railroads had sought in the discouraging years of Progressive regulation, and you will just about have it: 28 per cent. And before the government returned the railroads to private control, it raised rates yet another 32 per cent. These increases, in the words of the Director General, "being a war measure, were made without giving the shipping or traveling public any opportunity to be heard. There was not even any formal consultation with the ICC [or] the state commissions." [2]

Why did regulation of the railroads fail so abysmally during the bright years of Edwardian prosperity and Progressive enlightenment? In 1906 a new era had seemed to be dawning, in which the arbitrary actions of those who operated the public highways would be adjudicated by a fearless, impartial, and wise independent regulatory commission. In less than a decade the impotence of the ICC, like the unmistakable smell which rose from the body of the dead "saint" in *The Brothers Karamazov,* was a scandal which could be ignored only by a few diehards. And most of these diehards came around swiftly when the government showed what kind of proprietor it would make. Railroad regulation failed in this period for two principal reasons: first, because the philosophies and policies of archaic Progressivism were applicable to problems and conditions which no longer existed; and second, because the Commission simply did not constitute the fearless, impartial, and wise body which regulation presupposed. It was a boy on a man's errand.

The railroad problems of the Progressive era were not those of the Gilded Age, although many people, not surprisingly, continued to think and act as if they were. Rebating, long-haul–short-haul discrimination,

[2] The activities of the United States Railroad Administration are summarized in Walker D. Hines, *War History of American Railroads* (New Haven, 1928).

poor and unsafe service, daredevil financial gymnastics—all these were the symptoms of a railroad network built in a new country ahead of a consistently profitable volume of traffic. By 1897, when the greatest un-broken wave of prosperity the Western world has ever seen began, the problem became just the reverse. Staggering under a volume of traffic which their spindly nineteenth-century facilities could not carry, but re-joicing in a new-found stability which was the outcome of the "shake-out" of the nineties depression and the birth of the community of in-terests, the railroads set out to rebuild for what looked like an unlimited future. For this they would need gigantic sums of money. The gold was there. After all, the opportunity to make money in the legitimate pur-suit of the carrying trade was enormous. But the rate problem, which since the dawn of the railroad age had been one of the fairness and rea-sonableness of individual rates, had changed fundamentally. As the pur-chasing power of the dollar declined (which it was to do almost without interruption for twenty-five years following the depression), "real" rate levels declined, too. The fact that the matter was generally looked at the other way around—that is, that rates remained virtually fixed while costs increased—makes no difference. The fact is that regulation, if it was to be carried out with the needs of the railroads, and not just the shippers, in mind (or the "public," as the archaic Progressives insisted on dodging the issue), had to take cognizance of general rate levels. This was not done. The ICC insisted on seeing itself as a tribunal for adjudicating individual rates in respect to their reasonableness, one by weary one, right down to the collapse of prewar regulation. It is difficult to escape the conclusion that Americans were simply not playing fair with each other in this period, if, indeed, people anywhere have ever done so where matters of crucial importance are concerned. The Com-missioners had admitted that there was no objective criterion for deter-mining the reasonableness of rates. It follows, therefore, that the Com-mission *was* carrying out a judicial function, but was doing it in the guise of an administrative commission from whose orders there was no appeal.

The Commission lacked economic wisdom. Its members had seemed, at the beginning of the troubles, to be as well qualified for their task as anyone could expect. Nearly all of them were lawyers, and since when had anyone needed any other qualification to serve in government? Despite the warnings of a few far-seeing people like Theodore Roosevelt, nearly everybody looked upon the Commission as just another court. The Commission itself showed a pathetic yearning to judge rather than to research and to administer. While its members did not dress in robes, they willingly sat on their "bench" for photographers, fanning out on each side from the chairman in accordance with the strictest seniority. They dressed their orders up to look like judicial decisions headed, with the most elegant Anglo-Saxon reserve, "Lane, Commissioner," for example. They appear to have delighted in being referred to as "your honors" and do not seem ever to have corrected an attorney on this point. These, however, are petty observations and by themselves would mean nothing. The point is that in these years the nation needed a Commission which would apply, not accumulated judicial wisdom, but new and fresh concepts to the unprecedented problems before it. The Commissioners needed, in short, to rise above the legal and accounting approach which they so rigorously followed, and to apply the principles of economics which were beginning to make headway among academic and financial thinkers. The nation needed a body of men who understood the new financial techniques which Wall Street was using (even if money men themselves often did not quite understand them), not men who feared and hated them. It needed men who could think abstractly, in terms of intangible values and purchasing power dollars, not in the tired old shibboleths of watered stock, gold dollars, private gain versus public welfare, and fair return on physical value. Finally, it needed men who could take the reins of national transportation policy and set the best economic and business minds in the country to calculating comprehensively what the railroads' true capital needs were, and what was required in rate policy to attain them. What the nation got, unfortunately, was a physical valuation program which cost the government and the railroads many millions of dollars and proved to be of little real value in rate-making.

The nation also deserved an impartial Commission, and to a startling extent it did not get one. The 1910 hearings strongly suggest that the Commissioners' minds were made up before the first witness appeared. Lane's remarks during the proceedings, and his lengthy written decision, by the very multiplicity of reasons he cited against the proposed increases, revealed that he had meticulously checked every door to see that it was locked. Not a single railroad man, or even one who spoke favorably of the carriers in anything but the most fatuous generalities, sat on the Commission, except for Daniels, who arrived late; whereas two had been state railroad commissioners and one was a former railroad labor leader. And there is reason to doubt that the Commission was entirely fearless. Strict construction is a noble thing, especially when it leads to a decision which goes against one's emotional tendencies and material welfare. When it coincides with those factors it is often merely an easy way out. That, unfortunately, seems to have been the kind of strict constructionism in which the Commission dealt. Never did a group of men miss a more golden opportunity to take bad legislation and make good law of it. Congress, to whom the Commission was in reality a subcontractor in its legislative function, had left to these men the privilege of establishing what would constitute a test of reasonableness of rates. It had left to them the enormous power of deciding what would constitute proof in an application to change rates. And Congress had told the Supreme Court to keep hands off while they were doing so. Yet these men never offered the supplicants before them any guidance as to what would constitute reasonableness, and what they would have to do to prove it—except on one occasion, and they repudiated that six months later. Why?

Must we conclude that the Commissioners possessed so little confidence in their ability that they did not even attempt to solve these admittedly Herculean problems? Must we conclude that they feared to set up such criteria because of the possibility, however slight, that the railroads might satisfy them? We must, it seems, conclude all of that, but in the final analysis we must also conclude that the Commissioners were shrewd human beings with an instinct for survival, in a situation which placed a premium on such instincts. These men were not judges, appointed for life at an age and with such a background that they need take no thought for the morrow. They were professional civil servants, appointed (under all of the tyranny of the system of senatorial courtesy) for seven years—just long enough to make a damaging gap in their careers, but not long enough to take them to retirement. How else can one explain the failure of a B. H. Meyer to fulfill the promise of a youth which produced a fearless monograph denying any economic significance to the immensely popular Northern Securities decision? Neither

Meyer's scholarly works, all of which were written before he came to Washington, nor his work on the Wisconsin Railroad Commission prepares one for the federal Commissioner who would oppose every attempt to raise rates significantly. The fact is that Meyer liked being on the Commission, where he stayed for twenty-one years. What had he had to fear in 1911, 1914, 1915, and 1917? The answer is that he was from Wisconsin, and so was "Fighting Bob" La Follette. Cummins' bitter fight against Daniels' reappointment was a lesson that could not be missed. If Daniels had been from Iowa or Wisconsin he would not have had a chance. But it is not fair to suggest that the Commissioners were the only ones whose behavior was affected by the white-hot political character of the railroad question. Every man who had to deal with the problem, from the Rough Rider to the New Jersey Schoolmaster, had to reckon with the unpopularity of higher railroad rates. Once it was clear that the government's hand was on the throttle—that is, once the Act of 1906 was on the books—it was inevitable that anyone who attempted to open the valve was bound to get scalded.[3]

Regulation, as practiced under archaic Progressivism, sought to ignore two of the most fundamental principles of social organization. The first—that responsibility for a given task implies the authority to command the necessary resources—is so self-evident that if it were not for the fact that it is constantly contravened, it would hardly be worth mentioning. The other principle, which William Graham Sumner elucidated so well at the peak of the Progressive era, is that reform measures which ignore the deep-grained mores of a society are bound to

---

[3] Students of this never-solved problem have spoken with candor. Robert E. Cushman, *The Independent Regulatory Commissions* (New York, 1941), 115, noted that "the Act of 1920 embodied our first constructive railroad policy." E. Pendleton Herring, *Public Administration and the Public Interest* (New York, 1936), 157, asserted: "He [the Commissioner] cannot make his way against adverse economic and social pressures, unless his administrative purpose is clear and his authority is commensurate with his goal. Establishing these conditions is a duty of political leadership which, if neglected, leaves the administrator as the residuary legatee of those political pressures to which the legislator is the rightful heir." In his *Federal Commissioners: A Study of Their Careers and Qualifications* (Cambridge, Mass., 1936), 9, Herring wrote: "Tenure of office is important in securing independence of action. . . . The completion of each term means that the Commissioner is that much further removed from the practice of his vocation." In a report which then President-elect John F. Kennedy asked him to prepare, the late James M. Landis recommended permanent chairmen for commissions. *Report on Regulatory Agencies to the President-Elect* (Washington, 1960), 37.

fail. Railroad regulation in the Progressive era was loudly touted as a triumph of "public" over "private" interests, but in practice it turned out to be a revision of the relative strengths of a group of interests who continued to prosecute their own self-interest in that tradition of true liberalism which Adam Smith had enunciated so well, and under conditions of state favoritism which Smith had condemned in such rolling periods. Even government officials were more generally motivated by these instincts than we have recognized. Thus the Postmaster General in 1913 held the railroads rigidly to an unfair and inequitable contract, as if the matter were a business deal between two private parties, counting his ability to drive a hard bargain as a great public service. When the railroads were deprived of the freedom to follow *their* own self-interest in a society in which all others retained that right, the ultimate failure of regulation was assured.[4]

Most of these problems and dilemmas appear to plague our commissions and bureaus today as they struggle, Laocoön-like, to get free of the toils of contradictory legislation. Old-fashioned competition and self-interest are as flourishing in the Federal Triangle as they ever were in Wall Street. Thus we are treated to the spectacle of the Antitrust Division and the Interstate Commerce Commission arguing as the parties at interest before the Supreme Court of the United States, the one against and the other in favor of the amalgamation of railroads into a limited number of systems. Contemporary Quixotes charge through the halls of government in a whirlwind of television appearances and a cloud of paperback books and, having made it into the television limelight at a committee hearing, let us all down hard with an archaic Progressive demand that General Motors be broken up into "competing" companies.

The greatest responsibility for the failure of railroad regulation in the two decades before World War I must be shouldered by those who had the most to do with it. The archaic Progressives, as I have chosen to call them, never were so numerous or so strong politically as to explain their overweening influence in the drafting, the passage, and the

---

[4] In an interview in April, 1969, with the late I. L. Sharfman, historian of the ICC, I realized how little faith the men who came of age in the Progressive era had in the self-interest principles of economic liberalism. Reminded of the failures of the prewar Commission, Dr. Sharfman remarked in despair, "How else are you going to regulate the railroads?"

uncompromising enforcement of the Act of 1910, that unworkable piece of legislation which caused most of the trouble. It was their intense concentration on this one issue which must account for their success—that, and the vigor of youth which they possessed. The frustrations, the hostilities, the fears and hatreds of the lean years of the eighties and nineties had crippled the personalities of the people of the Great Plains and the Midwest. Like the secessionists of 1860, they had little in their favor except the fantastic energy which came from the blind, passionate feeling in their guts that they had been conspired against and robbed. Insurgent passion on the railroad problem and other reform issues was to the Republican party of the early twentieth century what Populist and Bryanesque free silver was to the Democratic party in the nineties. The shibboleths of both periods were nourished by a desire to apply old interpretations to a greatly changed world, and reveal the fascinating phenomenon that the "young" are often more conservative and backward than the "old." [5] Both sets of beliefs provided an external cause, a scapegoat, for the disappointments of life on the plains, where millions "missed that broken skyline that I know." The stubborn backwardness, the continuing inferiority complex of the archaic Progressives, in the first decade and a half of the incredibly prosperous new century, proves only that cultural lag is greater than most people realize. Like Alexandra's brothers in Willa Cather's *O Pioneers!*, they could not believe that a new era had dawned. The more events proved their railroad policies wrong, the more stubbornly they insisted upon them, until it almost seemed that they wanted regulation by commission to fail.

II

It is relatively easy to demonstrate statistically that some other, higher trendline of investment in the railroad facilities of the United

[5] I have used the lines of Vachel Lindsay ("Defeat of the alfalfa and the Mariposa lily . . . Defeat of the young by the old and silly") at the beginning of Chapter X to evoke the tragedy which I believe the denial of rate relief to western railroads was to the people of the West. The lines are actually from his poem "Bryan, Bryan, Bryan, Bryan." But historians might do well to ask themselves who *were* the young, the old, and the silly in the Progressive era, at least where railroad problems were concerned?

States would have ruled if an enlightened, rather than a repressive, policy of rate regulation had been followed. It has been estimated that $5.6 billion of capital that might have gone into a continuation of the remarkable technological transformation of the railroads that marked the decade from 1897 to 1907 went elsewhere. But the great tragedy of this failure of human beings intelligently to order their economic environment lies in the long-term effects on the railroad system as an enterprise. American railroads, quite literally, never got over the shock which archaic Progressivism's cruel repudiation of their leadership produced. It was not just that the country had lost a few billions of dollars in railroad investment, which could eventually be made up. What was lost was something much more precious. What was lost was the spirit of enterprise which had produced such remarkable results from 1897 to 1907, and which had seemed then to stand on the threshold of even greater accomplishments.

Enterprise is the ability and the willingness to innovate, to take a chance, to "take the road less traveled by," and it can exist only in a social climate which recognizes the need and provides the freedom for innovation. This restless quest for the "better way" which, without question so far as the entrepreneur is concerned, *does* exist—this innovation in a product or a service, or in the process by which they are produced is the *sine qua non* of economic growth. It is enterprise which produces innovation, and as Keynes said, profit is the engine of enterprise. But "profit" was a dirty word to the archaic Progressives, and to many another American then and now, it must be confessed. Profit was something which the seller took out of what you paid him and which was not reflected in what you got. Without profit, the price would be lower. Therefore, to make a profit larger than a fair amount (whatever *that* might be) was to fatten one's purse at the expense of another. If the goods or services involved were not essential, then the seller was an immoralist and the buyer a fool. But if essential goods or services were involved, then the seller was a knave indeed. Large profits meant that someone was getting something he did not deserve. Harriman was condemned for amassing a fortune far greater than he could ever spend, even living in baronial splendor in the Ramapos. And, ironically, just because the archaic Progressives believed so passionately in the institution of private property, yet had so little of it themselves, they were unable to distinguish between personal property and private property. The former, which is the capitalized value of that portion of the rich man's income that he and his family consume, we know today to be a small fraction of the capitalist's total fortune. Private property, however, is the body of resources over which he exercises authority in respect to its prudent investment and for which he shoulders the responsibility. Its proper size is entirely relative to the results which the rich man is able to produce. A million dollars may be too much for one man, as witness the great popularity of lifetime trust funds. A billion may not tax the powers of a Harriman, standing at the apex of a well-run organization. In our day of giant corporations, when power has been separated from property, as Adolf Berle has put it, this distinction is obvious. In 1910 few people sensed the distinction, and fewer still could articulate it. Today men in giant corporations in the United States exercise the privileges of private property, just as do the economic commissars of Soviet Russia; and both groups hold office only so long as they get results— always making allowances for the fact that politics exists in business as elsewhere.

But even if the railroad leaders could not articulate the economic role of profit, they were smart enough to sense that if they were not going to be permitted to make all they could, plowing most of it back into the innovative process which produced it, then the American people were not willing to pay the price for innovation on the railroads. The laborer is not merely worthy of his hire. He will get his worth, if not in one field then in another. And in 1919 there were many other fields which beckoned more brightly than railroading. Automobiles, electrical appliances, radio, the exciting game of Wall Street, building and real estate, the glamorous new field of advertising with its opportunity to inhabit the publishing and show business worlds simultaneously, even that sickly infant, aviation, all upstaged the tired old steam locomotive. Industrially no less than politically, nations get the kinds of leaders they deserve. After 1921 what the railroads wanted was someone who could play the game according to externally defined rules. In the autumnal warmth of the 1920s it must have seemed that "spring came on forever." There was little demand for the bright young man who saw in every dusty corner of the roundhouse, in every freight solicitor's expense account, in every damaged, delayed, or lost piece of freight, a better way to do things. The amalgamation clause of the Transportation Act of 1920 lay unused: why commit corporate hara-kiri on oneself by merging with other railroads? Developments like the diesel locomotive were delayed twenty years even though the steam locomotive had passed its peak by 1914. Routes that should have been double-tracked, like the western portions of the Pennsylvania and the B. & O. into the important gateway of St. Louis, remained single-track lines. Block signaling expanded with agonizing slowness. Air conditioning of passenger trains lagged behind the introduction of the comfort in practically every other form of public accommodation. The "first-class" surcharge for sleeping and parlor car accommodations, introduced during the war, was retained, and as a result this type of travel went into a decline from which it never recovered. Electrification, a promising development in the prewar decade, languished. The great industries which supplied the railroads withered or diversified into other fields. The diesel locomotive, when it finally arrived, was primarily the work of automotive and electrical equipment concerns which had barely been born in 1897. And when railroad executives finally woke up to the fabulous opportunity to integrate their operations with motor freight lines, it was too late.

The Republican leaders of Congress who took over responsibility for returning the railroads to a peacetime footing, although they were led by Albert B. Cummins, left no stone unturned to correct the flaws in prewar legislation.[6] The Transportation Act of 1920 repealed the antipooling feature of the Act of 1887; recognized the duty of the ICC to consider rates from the standpoint of their effects on the financial condition of the carriers; provided for the ultimate amalgamation of the railroads into a limited number of systems, if they chose to take the step; and sought to even out profits by a "recapture clause" which took from the rich (those making more than a certain rate of profit) and gave to the poor. But the railroads soon found themselves again the victims, rather than the beneficiaries, of regulation. At the very moment that the ICC had been given the power to set *minimum* rates, new and powerful

[6] Realization that government ownership was no guarantee against rate increases was sufficient reason for Cummins to change his position. He had already begun to court the conservatives of his party, however, during his 1916 bid for the presidential nomination. James Holt, *Congressional Insurgents and the Party System, 1909–1916* (Cambridge, Mass., 1967), 155–59.

competition had begun to emerge in the form of the motor truck. The trucks, essentially a high-cost form of transportation, found that they could compete effectively with the railroads for high-class freight (mainly manufactured goods) at the minimum rates in effect at their advent; could, in fact, take the business away almost entirely where pickup and delivery and speed were factors. Too late, the railroads found that they had been deprived of the expedient of price competition at the low end of the scale as well as at the high. And since flexibility and the freedom to adapt to changing conditions are significant factors in the success of all forms of business enterprise, commission regulation has continued to be the nemesis it so dramatically proved to be after 1910.[7]

III

What, then, did it all mean? What lesson does history have for those who must wrestle with the chaotic national transportation situation in the dangerous days ahead? The most important lesson is that simplistic history is the worst possible guide for transportation policy. Over and over again legislative leaders have attempted to reform policy in the light of past problems, and each time new laws have been passed which mired the nation ever deeper in the bad habits of hidden subsidies and misallocation of national resources. Today the cry is against regulation by commission, on the basis of a growing belief that it has proved an utter failure. Such might appear to be the conclusion of this book. Indeed, it is easy to agree with a recent candid and highly perceptive evaluation of the past sixty years of regulation: "In terms of economic efficiency alone, a policy that ended all rate regulation and common carrier obligations would create benefits far in excess of costs." [8]

[7] By 1970, after two decades of greatly revitalized management and massive improvement of physical plant, the railroads were again in deep trouble. But the tough, realistic men who headed them seemed determined to break the bonds of regulation which had prevented them from building integrated, multimedia transportation systems. That ICC policy since the advent of motor freight regulation has encouraged wastage of national transportation resources on a gigantic scale is illustrated in scholarly, if shy, fashion, in Ernest W. Williams, Jr., *The Regulation of Rail-Motor Rate Competition* (New York, 1958), especially pp. 209–17.

[8] Ann F. Friedlander, *The Dilemma of Freight Transport Regulation* (Washington, 1969), Summary.

It would be a mistake, however, to conclude that because the ICC failed to do something which it was functionally incapable of doing, and which the Congress never foresaw it even attempting, the Commission should be abolished. There remains today, even more emphatically than in 1906, the need for an ombudsman agency to rule on the reasonableness of individual rates; to prevent discrimination between persons and between places, whether due to ignorance, arrogance, bureaucratic callousness, or just plain dishonesty; and to eliminate rates which are patently too high in relation to the value of the service. Such regulation by the Commission, or some similar body, can and should continue, even if we should be so courageous and intelligent as to remove the fetters of minimum rates and the hobble of advance approval of rate changes.

There is another lesson to be learned from this story: that the old "private versus public interest" dodge is, as Mr. Justice Holmes said, little more than a phrase. When some member of a specific interest group begins to condemn some other group for acting in its own private interest and against the public welfare, we should anxiously pat our wallets. The public interest, in fact, is nothing more than the algebraic sum of all of the private interests. To maintain otherwise is to throw sand in the eyes of the citizens or, what is worse if one is advancing himself as an "expert," to commit the sin of not being logical. There has been some evidence in recent years that these home truths were being recognized, but the conspiracy interpretation continues to hold a fatal fascination for on-the-make reformers and prize-winning journalists who "expose" the Interstate Commerce Commission as the servant of the regulated interests, railroads included, against the interests of the public.

Today the mills of archaic Progressivism continue inexorably to grind salt into the wounds of the railroad men, while the railroads' share of total freight carried continues to sink to new low levels.[9] But the problems of the future are not likely to be those of the past—not even the recent past. By any statistical extrapolation we should expect

[9] K. Austin Kerr, *American Railroad Politics, 1914–1920* (Pittsburgh, 1968), sees the struggle which resulted in the Transportation Act of 1920 as taking place between a number of private-interest groups, including the railroads, rather than between the "public" and the railroads. Louis M. Kohlmeier, *The Regulators: Watchdog Agencies and the Public Interest* (New York, 1969), is a recent statement of the popular but wrongheaded view of transportation regulation.

the railroads' share of total freight transportation to continue to decline until the last caboose disappears into the tunnel, never to reemerge. The admirably articulate representatives of the trucking industry declare, indeed, that the present age is the "highway age." But, "on the other hand, not so fast," as Mr. Dooley said. It is true that the public outcry against ever-larger and ever more numerous trailer trucks to batter our proud new superhighways, against pollution of our cities, and against the ever-increasing noise and danger over our jet airports will have to get a great deal louder before mere indignation cramps the style of truck and air freight transportation. But that is not the point. The fact is that the trucks are in deep, serious trouble. Herded along by one of the strongest and most determined labor unions in the country, and pitifully limited in their ability to counter higher wages with higher productivity (as contrasted with the railroads throughout most of their history), the trucking companies are beginning to find revenues inadequate even at the artificially high rates afforded by the minimum-rate legislation that slipped into the picture in 1920. Higher rates for shippers are inevitable, especially now that the grimmer factor of crime has entered the picture.[10] What does this mean to the legislator? It means that the true dollars-and-cents cost of the cowardly transportation policy of the past sixty years can no longer be swept under the rug. Not only are freight rates beginning to rise just as uncontrollably as most other prices were rising at the beginning of the 1970s, but the inability of the railroads forever to counter higher costs and a declining share of business with greater efficiency has at last caught up with us. Throughout the frustrating course of the era of strict regulation of railroads, many a close observer must have asked himself, How much longer can this sort of thing go on? Finally, it seems, the answer is at hand. *No* longer. Americans must choose, and very soon, between a return to competition on the basis of natural advantage, and the payment of massive subsidies which will inevitably jeopardize, as much as Viet Nam ever did, the social-

---

[10] Losses to shippers and their insurance companies as a result of truck highjackings and other forms of cargo theft totaled $702 million in 1969. The problem is almost as serious for air freight, but considerably less for rail freight. Alan Bible, Chairman, U.S. Senate Committee on Small Business, "The Businessman and the Cargo Crime Crisis," Address before the Commerce and Industry Association of New York, April 29, 1970.

improvement projects on which so many fond young hopes are being lavished.

Railroad men themselves have learned one lesson very well. Ever since the rate controversies of the Progressive era, they have been painfully aware of how few friends they had. One reason, it was apparent, was that industries which have the bad fortune to deal directly with the public—especially where the public's total physical and mental welfare are one's responsibility for periods of from an hour to three or four days at a stretch—will always be fair game for public abuse. Perhaps a realization of this fact, as much as operating losses, accounts for the roads' eagerness to quit the passenger business completely, once and for all. Certain it was that in the days when a person took the train or didn't go, the general public managed to accumulate a monumental hostility toward the faithful retainer. We were willing to pay any price, even emasculation itself in Herbert Croly's metaphor, to cut this haughty servant down to size. We got, it seems, what we paid for.

APPENDIX

Estimates of Net New Investment Required by American Railroads in Relation to Demands on the System, 1898–1915

I. PURPOSES OF THE DATA

These data are intended to accomplish the following objectives, which are fundamental to the principal hypothesis of this book:

1. To demonstrate that the relationship between the trendlines of railroad transportation output (i.e., demands on the system) and net annual new investment (i.e., the absolute volume of national resources going to increase the capacity and efficiency of the system) is "rational" in the 1898–1906 period, and "irrational" thereafter.

2. To generate a figure representative of the annual and cumulative deficiency of the flow of investment funds into the railroad system.

II. THE METHOD

The principal assumption on which these computations are based may be briefly stated as follows:

The consistent and steep rise in demands on the American railroad system which characterized the Progressive era called for a consistent and equally steep increase in net new investment in the system such that, after the advent of government regulation of rates in 1906, investment would at least keep pace with the rise in demand; that is, that the relationship between demand and investment which the system had attained by 1905–7 should have been maintained in the critical years prior to World War I.

A simple historical defense is offered for this assumption. There was a dramatic rise in net new investment *in relation to demands on the system* from the end of the depression of the nineties to the panic year of 1907; and an equally dramatic decline thereafter, not only *relative* to the upward trend in demand, but in absolute dollar volume as well. (See Chart p. 131.) This trend expressed the constant broadening of vision and the ever-increasing realization of the high rate of growth in the American economy, which characterized American railroad executives throughout the years from 1898 to late 1907. It revealed the hesitation which investment flow into the railroad system experienced in the uncertain years from 1906 to 1911, when the Interstate Commerce Commission's policy in regard to general rate adjustments under the laws of 1906 and 1910 was emerging; and the dire effects of the collapse of the profitability of railroad operations after 1911. It would be historiographically meaningless, and nothing less than crude "present-mindedness," to condemn those who were responsible for making public railroad policy in the years from 1906 to 1914 on the basis of the backbreaking demands on the system which occurred during and following World War I. These data avoid such a pitfall, for they reveal that abundant evidence in support of a liberal policy toward the railroads existed throughout the period when the Commission was groping for any policy at all.

The technique by which "required" investment flow has been projected for the years under consideration is a simple one, and may be explained briefly.

I have converted the total annual output of transportation services (freight and passenger) to index numbers. I have done the same for annual net new investment in the railroad system. As a base period, I have used the average for the central years 1905–7. Adverting to my basic assumption, I have computed, year by year for the period 1898–1915, what the annual net new investment would have been if it had been of the same magnitude in relation to the base period as was transportation output. It is therefore necessary to defend (1) the selection of the base period and (2) the historical meaningfulness of this procedure.

I support the choice of the base period, first of all, by reference to formal index number theory.[1] The period chosen, furthermore, is at the

---

[1] Irving Fisher, in his classic and exhaustive study, *The Making of Index Numbers* (Boston and New York, 1927), virtually ignored the question of selection of a base period. The only reference, on page 19, is a simple definition of the base period. Bruce D. Mudgett, *Index Numbers* (New York, 1952), 17, declares that "the tool [index numbers] that measures them [price and quantity variation],

mid-point of the over-all period: there are seven years from 1898 through 1904, and eight from 1908 through 1915. I have used, moreover, not a single year but the average for three, and these years constitute an exceptionally good year, a good year, and one that was only fair. The three years are not the most favorable investment period, inasmuch as 1906–8 was better. The base period is computed, furthermore, on the approximate median values of the independent variable, transportation demand. And finally, my base period is one which marks a distinct shift in the behavior of the data over the total period: in the early period, the trend is distinctly upward, while in the later period the trend is just as distinctly downward.

It remains to be shown what historical meaningfulness there may be in such an apparently gratuitous procedure. By way of introduction, I wish to emphasize that I do not believe that there is any history other than what actually happened. The actual volume of national resources which went into expanding and improving the American railroads in the crucial years of the Progressive era is forever a matter of record. There is no other figure which has any *unique* claim to represent the "ideal" investment flow which could or ought to have taken place in these years. Whether, in fact, more money could or should have been spent on the railroad system is a hypothesis which must be supported by the historical narrative of this book if it is to be supported at all. I do not adhere, in short, to the "counterfactual" school of historical interpretation.[2] I believe that this school errs in "accepting" certain histori-

---

therefore, should be fashioned to deal with the historical material, and its ultimate efficiency as an instrument of measurement should be judged by reference to the actual record of prices, quantities, and values with which men have been faced." He also notes "the greater accuracy of comparisons of adjacent periods and the tendency for accuracy to decline with increase in distance or time" (p. 80). Finally, he mildly ridicules textbooks which insist that base periods must be "normal," tracing this idea to business cycle theorists, who have to have a normal period for reference; and to W. S. Mitchell's classic, *The Making and Use of Index Numbers* (Bull. 284 of the U.S. Department of Labor). "Which index shall be calculated [i.e., as between two base-periods], is a matter of the interest of the index number maker, and his decision has no necessary relationship to the normality of either period" (pp. 65–66).

[2] Unless, of course, this term is confined to mean only a freewheeling discussion of "what might have happened," in which case I suggest that there is nothing new to the method, and that we should avoid the addition of yet another bit of useless jargon by using the perfectly good term "speculative" instead of "counterfactual."

cal factors while "rejecting" (for "experimental" purposes) some other factor, inasmuch as the relationship between all factors is one of total interdependence. The counterfactual school might say that my analysis leads to the conclusion that *if* the railroads had been granted the rate increases they sought, investment *would* have been at the level I have projected. It is not my intention to say anything like this. For one thing, the requested increases were probably smaller than the rise in the price level alone would justify, and were decided upon by the railroad leaders merely because they thought the increases were the most they could get. My projections, on the contrary, are for the sole purpose of demonstrating quantitatively that some higher investment volume than actually took place was plausible, that is, under different circumstances it might have happened; and to suggest what that higher volume might have been. To be sure, any contemporary evidence which appears to support the conclusion enhances its historical meaningfulness. Therefore, I might point out (as I did at the end of Chapter II) that in 1907 James J. Hill was talking about a five-billion-dollar deficiency in investment in American railroads. Doubtless Mr. Hill had no detailed industry-wide capital budget to propose at that time, but he knew a great deal about his subject and it is nice to have him on one's side.

Second, I wish to emphasize that I do not suggest that my projection procedure is one which can be carried out indefinitely in either direction from the base period. The more distant a given year is from the base period, the less reasonable becomes the projected investment figure computed for it. The outer limits of the period thus treated should be finite, and amenable to acceptable rules of historical periodization. I believe that they are in this case. In 1898, the nation had finally emerged from the most disastrous economic depression in its history. The railroad system had been put through the wringer of financial reorganization and the old regime of multitudinous corporations in ruinous competition with each other had been fundamentally altered, if not destroyed. In that year demands on the nation's transportation system began an upward trend which was to be virtually uninterrupted for the next thirty-two years. Annual net new investment in railroad plant climbed consistently through the record year of 1907, and then turned almost as consistently downward after the climate of doubt and repression set in with government regulation in 1906. By 1914 the railroad

system was showing unmistakable signs of distress owing to capital undernourishment, and the ICC had had finally to recede, in principle,
from its policy of granting no general rate increases. Within two years
the badly repressed system would almost collapse under the weight of
wartime demands, and the government would have to assume in form
the proprietary responsibility for the nation's railroads which it had so
desultorily assumed in fact after 1906.

It remains to explain in detail how the projected data were arrived
at. The various steps are shown in the accompanying table. The following is an explanation of the arithmetic operations performed on the
original data, all of which are taken from the annual statistical reports
of the ICC, except for the index of wholesale prices, which is the Bureau of Labor Statistics series adjusted to the 1905–7 base. Data from
the Commission are for the twelve months ended June 30 of the years
indicated.

Column (1). The index of ton-miles of freight hauled is based on
1905–7 equals 100, as are all other indexes presented herein.

Column (2). Passenger-miles are indexed in the same manner as
ton-miles.

Column (3). Computation of an over-all output figure (whether in
"transportation units" or in the form of an index) necessitates weighting
freight ton-miles and passenger-miles to reflect, in some degree, the difference in the physical volume of service represented by the two magni-
tudes. In computing transportation units, one may weight the two series
by the average gross revenue received for each.[3] This has the effect of
weighting freight and passenger services in the ratio of three to one on
an index-number basis. In the present instance I have not needed a
transportation unit figure and have accordingly faced only the problem
of weighting the two indexes to get a combined index. I have been
struck by the fact that although by the end of our period freight revenues in total were running nearly three times the level of passenger revenues, *train-miles* performed for the two services were much more
nearly equal, and in fact were converging toward the end of the period.
This reflects the fact, pointed out in Chapter III, that productivity in
freight service rose more rapidly than in passenger service. Accord-

[3] This is the procedure used in Thor Hultgren, *American Transportation in Prosperity and Depression* (New York, 1948), 233.

A Projection of Net New Investment Required by American

Year	Index of ton-miles	Index of passenger-miles	Weighted output index	Net increase from previous year in		Retained earnings
				Stock	Funded debt	
	(1)	(2)	(3)	(4)	(5)	(6)
1898	54	52	53	$ 16*	$138*	$ 78*
1899	58	57	58	87	76	93
1900	66	63	65	27	109	143
1901	69	68	69	(27)	204	150
1902	74	77	75	49	197	173
1903	81	82	81	91	288	191
1904	82	86	84	127	370	144
1905	88	93	90	147	325	185
1906	101	98	100	171	445	243
1907	111	108	110	380	826	152
1908	103	114	108	11	577	101
1909	103	114	108	215	351	177
1910	120	126	123	247	363	177
1911	119	129	123	317	352	88
1912	124	129	126	(78)	158	53
1913	142	135	139	44	198	178
1914	135	138	136	201	198	(53)
1915	130	127	129	115	464	29

* Millions of dollars.

( ) = Deficit.

ingly, in view of the fact that the railroads appear to have been devoting a much more nearly equal portion of their resources to the furnishing of passenger transportation than would appear from revenue figures, I have been reluctant to weight the ton-mile index over the passenger-mile index in any greater ratio than 6 to 4. Having performed this theoretically necessary step, I would point out that while over the entire history of railroad operations such weighting procedures are absolutely necessary, they are uniquely unimportant, if not unnecessary, in the period under study. For, while freight transportation was rising rapidly relative to passenger service in the decades preceding the start of our period, the phenomenal growth of travel in the Progressive era produced a remarkably stable relationship between ton- and passenger-miles, as a glance at the two indexes (Columns 1 and 2) will reveal.

Columns (4) and (5). For American railroads in total, I have

Railroads in Relation to Demands on the System, 1898–1915

Year	Available investment funds	Index of available investment funds	Required investment funds	Adjusted required investment funds	Deficiency in net new investment
	(7)	(8)	(9)	(10)	(11)
1898	$ 232*	23	$ 525*	$ 408*	$ 176*
1899	256	26	575	481	225
1900	279	28	644	579	300
1901	327	33	684	606	279
1902	419	42	743	701	282
1903	570	58	803	767	197
1904	641	65	832	796	155
1905	657	66	892	859	202
1906	859	87	991	981	122
1907	1458	147	1090	1139	(319)
1908	689	70	1070	1079	390
1909	743	75	1070	1159	416
1910	787	79	1219	1375	588
1911	757	76	1249	1268	511
1912	133	13	1249	1383	1250
1913	420	42	1377	1541	1121
1914	346	35	1348	1471	1125
1915	608	61	1278	1424	816

found no more satisfactory practical method of estimating net annual investment in the form of equity capital (4) and debt capital (5) than simply to subtract the previous year amounts reported in the consolidated balance sheets published by the ICC. These amounts represent *net* securities held by the reporting corporations: that is, the securities of subsidiary roads owned by parent corporations have been eliminated because these values are pyramided in the securities of the parent. After 1909 this computation was performed by the Commission. For the years before 1909 I have seized the simple expedient of netting out duplicate values by applying the average relationship between gross and net securities implicit in the Commission's figures after 1909. It is recognized that no procedure for estimating annual investment in American railroads would have been more roundly condemned than this during the Progressive era. But the accusation of "watered stock," however accurate it may have been in respect to specific railroads (or to railroads in general during the Gilded Age), was laid to rest in 1920 when the Commission's report on its massive physical evaluation project placed the value of the properties *at prewar prices* at 95 per cent of book value. (See Chapter IV.) My procedure, furthermore, is more conservative than it may seem at first. I was struck by the fact that very strong roads like the Pennsylvania, which were able to sell their stock considerably above par in the first decade of our period, conservatively entered it on the books at par, and wrote off the excess as current-period net profit.

Following the enactment of the Hepburn Act in 1906 the Commission began requiring the railroads to capitalize certain expenditures which the roads had previously charged off as expense because of their "nonproductive" character. The greater part of these expenditures appear to have stemmed from state and local laws which made certain demands on the roads, but did not occasion greater efficiency of operation. But the railroads were often very conservative about the capitalization of their voluntary investment, as well. I have not made any attempt either to eliminate these sums in the data after 1906, or to add them into the pre-1906 data. This has the effect of moderately overstating investment in the post-1906 period, and is therefore a conservative bias.

Column (6). Retained earnings invested in the railroads is simply reported net income, after debt service, minus the amount paid out in dividends.

Column (7). The sum of columns 4, 5, and 6.

Column (8). An index of column 7, included here because it is shown on the Chart.

Column (9). This is my unadjusted projection of required investment funds. It is computed by multiplying the actual average amount invested annually in the base period by the index of transportation output for the year for which required investment is being computed. For example, actual investment in 1898 was $232 million, which is equal to 23 per cent of the base period. But the demand for transportation services in 1898 was at 48 per cent of the base-period level; if investment had been "at par," it would have totaled $525 million in that year before adjustment for price changes.

Column (10). My basic definition of the "required" investment level for a given year is an amount which bears the same relationship to investment in the base period as transportation demand bears to demand in the base period, in terms of purchasing power. In view of the fact that this was a period of rapidly rising price levels, whatever contemporary price series one examines, it is only fair that my projections should be deflated in the years before the base period, and inflated in the years following. There was considerable publicity about the rise in prices of everything the railroads bought in this period, and at least one attempt was made to compute a "cost of living index" for the railroads,[4] but I feel that my purposes are fairly served by applying the index of the general level of wholesale prices of the Bureau of Labor Statistics. Labor, of course, was a major input to the railroads and must be accounted for; but as I have noted in Chapter IV, the increase in wage rates of railroad workers in these years just about kept pace with the rise in the cost of living.

Column (11). The deficiency in net new investment is the adjusted required investment (Column 10) minus actual investment (Column 7).

III. COMPARISON WITH OTHER ESTIMATES OF
NET INVESTMENT

Earlier efforts to compute the flow of long-term resources into the American railroad system have been made by Ulmer[5] and Neal.[6] Strictly speaking, their estimates are not comparable to mine, because they sought to estimate capital formation, while I am interested in the total net commitment of resources to the railroad system. The principal difference implied thereby is that they have included only "reproducible" capital, which means that real estate purchases are excluded. Such purchases by American railroads were very large in these years of passenger and freight terminal rebuilding and expansion, and the transfer

[4] J. C. Hooker, "A Cost of Living Index for Steam Railroads," *Journal of Accountancy* (July, 1924), 22–30. Only wages, however, are included in the index.

[5] M. J. Ulmer, *Capital in Transportation, Communications, and Public Utilities* (Princeton, 1960), 256–57.

[6] Larry Neal, "Investment Behavior by American Railroads: 1897–1914," *Review of Economics and Statistics,* LI (May, 1969), 126–35.

of real estate from one form of economic employment to another, while it may not represent capital formation in the broadest sense, is indeed germane to my estimates. I do not say that the differences between my estimates and those of Ulmer and Neal are to be accounted for entirely by my inclusion of real estate. Indeed, we shall probably never know what the companies spent for land in these years, inasmuch as the railroads were no less close-mouthed about what they paid for acreage than any other type of purchaser. But the amounts were unquestionably very large. The exclusion of net accumulation of working capital also resulted in lower estimates for Ulmer and Neal.

Both Ulmer and Neal projected their estimates from samples. Ulmer interpolated data from state commissions for most of the years before 1914, and is understandably hesitant about drawing any conclusions from these data. Neal studied the reports of twenty-one large railroad corporations and projected their investment flow to the total industry on the basis of their share of total route mileage. This procedure would appear to have at least two serious biases. The twenty-one large corporations probably accounted for a much larger share of total transportation in their areas than their share of route mileage would indicate —that is, their traffic density was probably higher than average—and their per-mile need for funds was probably correspondingly larger. This would constitute an upward bias. Also, there was probably a difference in the rapidity with which railroad companies reacted to the collapse of profitability of operations after 1910. The big, prosperous roads naturally carried through their ambitious improvement programs to a considerable degree, but lesser roads, especially in the hard-hit Midwest, retrenched drastically out of sheer necessity. This would account for the fact that Neal's data do not drop off as precipitately as mine after 1911.

No estimates of actual investment or capital formation, net or gross, can produce figures which are "pure" in and of themselves. Only a massive study of corporate records in this period could theoretically produce such a figure, and even then differences in accounting methods and questions of interpretation would intervene. All of the estimates, however—Ulmer's, Neal's, and my own—confirm the one salient point: the flow of resources into American railroads rose consistently until about 1907, hesitated, and then sagged dramatically:

(Millions of dollars)

Year	Neal	Ulmer	Martin
1898	128	65	232
1899	172	129	256
1900	314	190	279
1901	287	196	327
1902	400	193	419
1903	497	209	570
1904	475	234	641
1905	406	290	657
1906	672	402	859
1907	824	522	1458
1908	601	573	689
1909	360	601	743
1910	672	670	787
1911	602	653	757
1912	439	645	133
1913	693	659	420
1914	604	574	346
1915	291	373	608

A significant contribution by Neal is his acknowledgment that specific historical events must take precedence over the fitting of a stock "curve" (growth, maturity, or whatever), to a series of data in order to draw conclusions about the trend: "But this result [the better fit which his equation seems to have to the data] does not reconstitute the life cycle hypothesis so much as it indicates the value of paying attention to the major features of an industry's economic history when attempting to explain its investment behavior. Such attention to economic history might also mitigate against facile acceptance of faulty data and the misleading results they may produce." [7] Neal addressed himself to the financial events (interest rates and securities prices fluctuations) which influenced railroad investment in this period, and found that they did indeed explain more about railroad investment data than any stock curve could. It is striking that he did not address himself to the repressive effects of archaic Progressive regulation after 1906, which I believe to be the most dominant historical influence in this period. Perhaps it will now be possible to include this factor in future studies of capital formation in the American railroad industry.

[7] Neal, "Investment Behavior," 135.

BIBLIOGRAPHY

I. MANUSCRIPTS, PAPERS, AND LETTERS

Brown, William C. *Freight Rates and Railway Conditions: Addresses and Correspondence, 1908–1909.* New York, 1909.

Bureau of Railway Economics. *First Report of the Director.* Washington, 1911. Also related files.

Depew, Chauncey M. "A Retrospect of Twenty-five Years with the New York Central Railroad and Its Allied Lines, 1866–1891." New York, 1892.

Finley, William Wilson. *Addresses and Letters.* Compilation of the Bureau of Railway Economics, Association of American Railroads. 2 vols. 1907–10 and 1911–13.

Haines, Henry S., American Railway Management. *Addresses Delivered before the American Railway Association.* New York, 1897.

Interstate Commerce Commission. Addresses, Papers, etc., by the Commissioners and Secretary [compilation of the library of the ICC]. 3 vols. 1885–1903; 1903–8; 1908–9.

Lane, Franklin Knight. *The Letters of Franklin K. Lane.* Boston and New York, 1923.

Messages and Papers of the Presidents. Ed. by James D. Richardson *et al.* 20 vols. and supplements. Washington, 1898–1925.

Newlands, Francis G. *The Public Papers of Francis G. Newland.* Edited and Placed in Historical Setting by Arthur B. Darling. 2 vols. New York, 1932.

Perkins, George Walbridge. Papers. MSS in the Library of Columbia University.

Roosevelt, Theodore. *The Letters of Theodore Roosevelt.* Ed. by Elting E. Morison. 8 vols. Cambridge, Mass., 1951–54.

II. OFFICIAL GOVERNMENT DOCUMENTS

Adams, Henry Carter. *Digest of Hearings on Railway Rates. Testimony before Senate Committee on Interstate Commerce.* Senate Document 244 [Vol. 21], 59th Cong., 1st Sess. Washington, 1905.

"Concerning Advances in Railway Rates," *Report of Senate Committee on Interstate Commerce to Accompany S. 423*. Senate Report 933, 60th Cong., 2d Sess., Feb. 8, 1909. [Elkins Report.]

Evidence Taken by the Interstate Commerce Commission in the Matter of Proposed Advances in Freight Rates by Carriers. Senate Document 725, 61st Cong., 3d Sess. 10 vols. Washington, 1911. [1910 Hearings.]

Hearings before the Committee on Interstate and Foreign Commerce of the House of Representatives on H.R. 10431 . . . [10 other House bills] *to Amend the Interstate Commerce Law*. Washington, 1905.

Hearings before the ICC in the "Five Per Cent Case." Senate Document 466, 63d Cong., 2d Sess. 14 vols. Washington, 1914.

Hearings before the Joint Committee on Interstate and Foreign Commerce Pursuant to Public Joint Res. 25. 2 vols. Washington, 1916, 1917. [Newlands Committee Hearings.]

Interstate Commerce Commission. *First Annual Report of the Block Signal and Train Control Board to the ICC.* Washington, 1909.

——*Interstate Commerce Commission Activities, 1887–1937*. Washington, 1937.

——*Minutes of Conference* [Official record of decisions of the Commission]. Vol. X, Oct. 9, 1909, to Aug. 29, 1910; Vol. XI, Aug. 30, 1910, to Aug. 24, 1911.

——*Reports.*

Knapp, Martin A. *Report of the ICC on Block-Signal Systems and Appliances for the Automatic Control of Railway Trains*. Senate Document 342, 59th Cong., 2d Sess.

Opinions of the United States Commerce Court. Cases Adjudged in the United States Commerce Court During Its Existence, February, 1911, to December, 1913.

Regulation of Railway Rates. Hearings before the Committee on Interstate Commerce, Senate of the United States, December 16, 1904, to May 23, 1905, on Bills to Amend the Interstate Commerce Act. Senate Document 243, 59th Cong., 1st Sess. 5 vols. Washington, 1905. [1905 Senate Hearings.]

Report of the Board of Arbitration on the Matter of the Controversy between the Eastern Railroads and the Brotherhood of Locomotive Engineers. Washington, 1912.

Report of the Industrial Commission. 19 vols. Washington, 1900–2.

Report of the Railroad Securities Commission to the President. House Document 256, 62d Cong., 2d Sess. Washington, 1911. [Hadley Commission Report.]

Reports of the Immigration Commission. 42 vols. Washington, 1911.

Rossiter, William S. *Increase of Population in the United States, 1910–20*. Bureau of the Census Monograph I. Washington, 1922.

Safety on the Railroads. Hearings before a Subcommittee of the Committee on

Interstate and Foreign Commerce, 63d Cong., 2d Sess., House of Representatives. Washington, 1913.

Special Report of the Interstate Commerce Commission. House Document 503, 65th Cong., 2d Sess., 1918.

U.S. Bureau of the Census. *Historical Statistics of the United States: Colonial Times to 1957.* Washington, 1960.

U.S. Department of Agriculture. *Farmers in a Changing World* [Yearbook]. Washington, 1940.

III. BOOKS, PAMPHLETS, AND DOCTORAL DISSERTATIONS

Acworth, W. M. "American and English Railways Compared." Reprinted from the London *Times.* Chicago, 1898.

Adams, Braman B. *The Block System of Signaling on American Railroads.* New York, 1901.

Adams, Charles Francis, Jr. *Railroads: Their Origins and Problems.* Rev. ed. New York, 1893.

Alexander, Edwin P. *The Pennsylvania Railroad: A Pictorial History.* New York, 1947.

American Association of General Passenger and Ticket Agents. *Proceedings.* 1879–1902.

American Association of Local Freight Agents. *Compilation of Convention Topics.* N.p., 1909.

American Association of Passenger Traffic Officers. *Proceedings.* 1916.

American Railway Association. *Car Builders' Cyclopedia of American Practice.* New York, 1905–

———*Proceedings.* 1899–1909.

American Railway Engineering Association. *Manual.* Chicago, 1929.

Amory, Cleveland. *The Last Resorts.* New York, 1952.

Association of American Railroads. *Public Relations of the Railroad Industry in the United States: A Bibliography, 1808–1955.* Washington, 1956.

Bailey, James Montgomery. *History of Danbury, Connecticut, 1684–1896.* Ed. by Susan Benedict Hill. New York, 1896.

Baltimore & Ohio Railroad. *Catalogue of the Centenary Exhibition of the B. & O. R.R., 1827–1927.* Baltimore, 1927.

Barger, Harold. *The Transportation Industries, 1889–1946.* New York, 1951.

Barger, Harold, and Hans Landsberg. *American Agriculture, 1899–1939.* New York, 1942.

Barger, Harold, and Sam H. Schurr. *The Mining Industries, 1899–1939: A Study of Output, Employment and Productivity.* New York, 1944.

Berg, Walter Gilman. *American Railway Shop Systems.* New York, 1904.

——*Buildings and Structures of American Railroads.* New York, 1900.

Bernstein, Marver H. *Regulating Business by Independent Commissions.* Princeton, 1955.

Bishop, David Wendell. *Railroad Decisions of the Interstate Commerce Commission: Their Guiding Principles.* Washington, 1961.

Bonbright, James C. *Railroad Capitalization: A Study of the Principles of Regulation of Railroad Securities.* New York, 1920.

Bragdon, Henry W. *Woodrow Wilson, the Academic Years.* Cambridge, Mass., 1967.

Brandeis, Louis D. *Business—a Profession.* Boston, 1914.

——*Other People's Money.* New York, 1914.

Brown, Harry Gunnison. *Transportation Rates and Their Regulation.* New York, 1916.

Bruce, Alfred W. *The Steam Locomotive: Its Development in the Twentieth Century.* New York, 1952.

Bryce, James. *The American Commonwealth.* 2 vols. London, 1889.

Bureau of Railway Economics. *Comment on the Decision in the Western Advanced Rate Case No. 3500.* Washington, 1911.

——*Railway Economics: A Collective Catalogue of Books in Fourteen American Libraries.* Chicago, 1912.

Caine, Stanley P. *The Myth of a Progressive Reform.* Madison, 1970.

Cameron, Jenks. *The National Park Service: Its History, Activities, and Organization.* New York, 1922.

Campbell, Edward G. *The Reorganization of the American Railroad System, 1893–1900.* New York, 1938.

Chandler, Alfred D. *The Railroads: The Nation's First Big Business.* New York, 1965.

Chandler, Allison. *Trolley Through the Countryside.* Denver, 1963.

Cherington, Paul. Address to the Travel Research Association. *Proceedings of Third Annual Travel Conference.* Boston, 1965.

Clark, Victor. *History of Manufactures.* 3 vols. New York, 1929.

Corliss, Carlton J. *Main Line of Mid-America.* New York, 1950.

Crandall, Charles L., and Fred A. Barnes. *Railroad Construction.* New York, 1913.

Creamer, Daniel. *Is Industry Decentralizing?* Philadelphia, 1935.

Croly, Herbert D. *Progressive Democracy.* New York, 1914.

——*The Promise of American Life.* New York, 1909.

Cunningham, William J. *American Railroads: Government Control and Reconstruction Policies.* New York, 1922.

Cushman, Robert E. *The Independent Regulatory Commissions.* New York, 1941.

Daggett, Stuart. *Chapters on the History of the Southern Pacific.* New York, 1922.

Daniels, Winthrop More. *American Railroads: Four Phases of Their History.* Princeton, 1932.

Day, Edmund E., and Woodlief Thomas. *The Growth of Manufactures, 1899–1923.* Census Monograph VIII. Washington, 1928.

Dearing, Charles L. *American Highway Policy.* Washington, 1942.

DeHaven, George. *Passenger Fares and the Law and Practice in the Several States.* Grand Rapids, 1898.

Dewey, Ralph L. *The Long and Short Haul Principle of Rate Regulation.* Columbus, 1935.

Dixon, Frank H. *Railroads and Government: Their Relations in the United States, 1910–1921.* New York, 1922.

Dorfman, Joseph. *The Economic Mind in American Civilization.* 5 vols. New York, 1949–59.

Douglas, Paul H. *Real Wages in the United States, 1890–1926.* Boston, 1930.

Douglass, Michael C. "A History of the Association of American Railroads." Unpublished B.S. thesis, Wharton School of Finance and Commerce of the University of Pennsylvania, 1962.

Droege, John A. *Freight Terminals and Trains.* New York, 1912?; rev. ed., 1925.

——*Passenger Terminals and Trains.* New York, 1916.

Eckenrode, H. J., and Pocahontas Edmunds. *E. H. Harriman, the Little Giant of Wall Street.* New York, 1933.

Fabricant, Solomon. *The Output of Manufacturing Industries.* New York, 1940.

Faulkner, Harold U. *The Decline of Laissez Faire.* New York, 1951.

Ferguson, Maxwell. *State Regulation of Railroads in the South.* New York, 1916.

Fisher, Irving. *The Making of Index Numbers.* Boston and New York, 1927.

Fishlow, Albert. "Productivity and Technological Change in the Railroad Sector," in *Output, Employment, and Productivity in the United States After 1800.* Vol. 30 of "Studies in Income and Wealth." New York, 1966.

Flory, Raymond L. "The Political Career of Chester I. Long." Unpublished doctoral dissertation, University of Kansas, 1955.

Fogel, Robert W. *Railroads and American Economic Growth.* Baltimore, 1964.

Forcey, Charles. *The Crossroads of Liberalism: Croly, Weyl, Lippmann, and the Progressive Era, 1900–1925.* New York, 1961.

Friedman, Milton, and Anna J. Schwartz. *A Monetary History of the United States, 1867–1960*. Princeton, 1963.

Garraty, John A. *Right-Hand Man*. New York, 1960.

Garvy, George, and Martin R. Blyn. *The Velocity of Money*. New York, 1969.

General Railway Signal Co. *Electric Interlocking Handbook*. Rochester, 1913.

Gilbert, G. H., *et al. Subways and Tunnels of New York*. New York, 1912.

Ginger, Ray. *The Bending Cross: A Biography of Eugene Victor Debs*. New Brunswick, 1949.

Gompers, Samuel. *Seventy Years of Life and Labor*. 2 vols. New York, 1925.

Greenleaf, William. *Monopoly on Wheels*. Detroit, 1961.

Grodinsky, Julius. *The Iowa Pool*. Chicago, 1950.

———*Jay Gould: His Business Career*. Philadelphia, 1955.

Guedalla, Philip. *The Hundred Years*. London, 1936.

Haber, Samuel. *Efficiency and Uplift: Scientific Management in the Progressive Era, 1890–1920*. Chicago, 1964.

Harriman, E. H. "Testimony before the ICC, February 1907." New York, 1907.

Hays, Samuel P. *The Response to Industrialization, 1885–1914*. Chicago, 1957.

Healy, Kent T. *Electrification in Steam Railroads*. New York, 1929.

Hechler, Kenneth W. *Insurgency*. New York, 1940.

Hendrick, Burton. *Life of Andrew Carnegie*. 2 vols. Garden City, N.Y., 1932.

Hennes, Robert G., and Martin Ekse. *Fundamentals of Transportation Engineering*. New York, 1955.

Herring, E. Pendleton. *Federal Commissioners: A Study of Their Careers and Qualifications*. Cambridge, Mass., 1936.

———*Public Administration and the Public Interest*. New York, 1936.

Hill, James J. *Highways of Progress*. New York, 1910.

Hilton, George W., and John F. Due. *The Electric Interurban Railways in America*. Stanford, 1960.

Hine, Charles D. *Letters from an Old Railway Official to His Son, a Division Superintendent*. Chicago, 1904.

———*Modern Organization: An Exposition of the Unit System*. New York, 1912.

Hines, Walker D. *War History of American Railroads*. New Haven, 1928.

Hoff, W. [Superior Privy Councilor of the German Empire], and F. Schwabach [Privy Councilor]. *North American Railroads: Their Administration and Economic Policy*] "Special expert private translation" of the official report of representatives of the Prussian State Railways]. New York, 1906.

Hofstadter, Richard. *The Age of Reform*. New York, 1955.

Holt, James. *Congressional Insurgents and the Party System, 1909–1916.* Cambridge, Mass., 1967.

Hultgren, Thor. *American Transportation in Prosperity and Depression.* New York, 1948.

——"Railroad Travel and the State of Business." National Bureau of Economic Research Occasional Paper No. 13. New York, 1943.

Hungerford, Edward. *Daniel Willard Rides the Line.* New York, 1938.

——*Modern Railroads.* New York, 1911.

——*The Story of the Baltimore & Ohio Railroad, 1827–1927.* 2 vols. New York, 1928.

Hutchinson, Robert. *Mr. Dooley on Ivrything and Ivrybody by Finley Peter Dunne.* New York, 1963.

Jarman, Rufus. *A Bed for the Night.* New York, 1952.

Jenks, Jeremiah W., and W. Jett Lauck. *The Immigration Problem.* New York, 1911; rev. ed., 1926.

Jerome, Harry. *Mechanization in Industry.* New York, 1934.

Jessup, Philip C. *Elihu Root.* 2 vols. New York, 1938.

Johnson, Emory R. *American Railway Transportation.* New York, 1903; rev. ed., 1912.

——*Railroad Traffic and Rates.* New York, 1911.

Johnson, Emory R., and Thurman W. VanMetre. *Principles of Railroad Transportation.* New York, 1916.

Johnson, Ralph P. *The Steam Locomotive.* New York, 1942.

Kahn, Otto. *Our Economic and Other Problems: A Financier's Point of View.* New York, 1920.

Kendrick, John W. *Productivity Trends in the United States.* New York, 1956.

Kennan, George. *The Chicago and Alton Case: A Misunderstood Transaction.* New York, 1916.

——*E. H. Harriman: A Biography.* 2 vols. Boston, 1922.

Kennedy, Edward E. *The Automobile Industry.* New York, 1941.

Kennedy, Miles C., and George H. Burgess. *Centennial History of the Pennsylvania Railroad, 1846–1946.* Philadelphia, 1949.

Kerley, James Wiliiam. "The Failure of Railway Labor Leadership: A Chapter in Railroad Labor Relations, 1900–1932." Unpublished doctoral dissertation, Columbia University, 1959.

Kerr, K. Austin. *American Railroad Politics, 1914–1920.* Pittsburgh, 1968.

Keynes, John Maynard. *A Treatise on Money.* London, 1930.

Kiefer, Paul W. *A Practical Evaluation of Railroad Motive Power.* New York, 1947.

King, Edward Everett. *Railway Signaling*. New York, 1921.

King, Wilford I. *The National Income and Its Purchasing Power*. New York, 1930.

Kohlmeier, Louis M. *The Regulators: Watchdog Agencies and the Public Interest*. New York, 1969.

Kolko, Gabriel. *Railroads and Regulation*. Princeton, 1965.

Kouwenhoven, John A. *The Columbia Historical Portrait of New York*. New York, 1953.

Kranzberg, Melvin, and Carroll W. Pursell, Jr. *Technology in Western Civilization*. 2 vols. New York, 1967.

Kurtz, Charles M. *Track and Turnout Engineering*. New York, 1927. Revision of 1910 ed.

Kuznets, Simon, *et al. Population Redistribution and Economic Growth, United States, 1870–1950*. 3 vols. Philadelphia, 1957–60.

La Follette, Belle C., and Fola La Follette. *Robert M. La Follette*. 2 vols. New York, 1953.

Lake, Isaac Beverly. *Discrimination by Railroads and Other Public Utilities*. Raleigh, 1947.

Lambert, Oscar Doane. *Stephen B. Elkins*. Pittsburgh, 1955.

Landes, David S. *The Unbound Prometheus: Technological Change and Industrial Development in Western Europe from 1750 to the Present*. Cambridge, 1969.

Landis, James M. *Report on Regulatory Agencies to the President-Elect*. Washington, 1960.

Latimer, James Brandt. *Railway Signaling in Theory and Practice*. Chicago, 1909.

Lee, Ivy. *Human Nature and the Railroads*. Philadelphia, 1915.

Leopold, Richard William. *Elihu Root and the Conservative Tradition*. Boston, 1954.

Lescohier, Don D., and Elizabeth Brandeis. *History of Labor in the United States, 1896–1932*. New York, 1935.

Leuchtenburg, William E. *Theodore Roosevelt: The New Nationalism*. New York, 1961.

—— *Woodrow Wilson: The New Freedom*. New York, 1961.

Levy, David W. "The Life and Thought of Herbert Croly, 1869–1914." Unpublished doctoral dissertation, University of Wisconsin, 1966.

Link, Arthur S. *Wilson: Campaigns for Progressivism and Peace, 1916–1917*. Vol. V of a biography of Woodrow Wilson. Princeton, 1965.

—— *Wilson: The New Freedom*. Vol. II of a biography of Woodrow Wilson. Princeton, 1956.

——*Woodrow Wilson and the Progressive Era*. New York, 1954.

Link, Arthur S., and William B. Catton. *American Epoch: A History of the United States since the 1890's*. New York, 1967.

Lippmann, Walter. *Drift and Mastery: An Attempt to Diagnose the Current Unrest*. New York, 1914.

Lorwin, Lewis L., and John M. Blair. *Technology in Our Economy*. Temporary National Economic Committee Monograph No. 22. Washington, 1941.

Lovett, Robert S. "Statement before the Railroad Securities [Hadley] Commission, December 21, 1910." New York, 1911.

Lucas, Walter Arndt, ed. *One Hundred Years of Railroad Cars*. New York, 1958.

McAdoo, William Gibbs. *Crowded Years*. New York, 1931.

MacAvoy, Paul W. *The Economic Effects of Regulation: The Trunk-Line Railroad Cartels and the Interstate Commerce Commission before 1900*. Cambridge, Mass., 1965.

McCarty, Harold H. *The Geographic Basis of American Economic Life*. New York, 1940.

McCready, Harold. *Alternating Current Signaling*. Swissvale, Pa., 1915.

McFall, Robert James. *Railway Monopoly and Rate Regulation*. New York, 1916.

McPherson, Logan G. *Four Railroad Speeches*. Washington, 1911.

Marshall, James. *Santa Fe: The Railroad That Built an Empire*. New York, 1945.

Martin, Franklin H. *Digest of the Proceedings of the Council of National Defense during the World War*. Washington, 1934.

Mason, Alpheus T. *Brandeis: A Free Man's Life*. New York, 1946.

May, Henry F. *The End of American Innocence*. New York, 1959.

Mayer, Grace M. *Once Upon a City*. New York, 1958.

Meeks, Carroll L. V. *The Railroad Station: An Architectural History*. New Haven, 1956.

Mencken, August. *The Railroad Passenger Car*. Baltimore, 1957.

Merritt, Albert N. *Federal Regulation of Railway Rates*. Boston and New York, 1907.

Meyer, Balthasar H. "The Administration of Prussian Railroads," *Annals of the American Academy of Political and Social Science*, X, No. 3 (Publication No. 215) (Philadelphia, 1897), 389–423.

——*A History of the Northern Securities Case*. Madison, 1906.

——*Railway Legislation in the United States*. New York, 1903.

Meyer, Hugo Richard. *Government Regulation of Railway Rates*. New York, 1905.

Middleton, P. Harvey. *Railways and Public Opinion: Eleven Decades.* Chicago, 1941.

Miller, C. A. "The Lives of the Interstate Commerce Commissioners and the Commissioners' Secretaries," *ICC Practitioners Journal,* Vol. XII (June, 1946.)

Mills, Frederick C. *Economic Tendencies in the United States.* New York, 1932.

Miller, John A. *Fares, Please!* New York, 1941.

Morgenthau, Henry. *All in a Lifetime.* Garden City, N.Y., 1922.

Mowry, George E. *The Era of Theodore Roosevelt and the Birth of Modern America, 1900–1912.* New York, 1958.

——*Theodore Roosevelt and the Progressive Movement.* Madison, 1947.

Mudgett, Bruce D. *Index Numbers.* New York, 1952.

New York Central. "Freight Rate Primer." Chicago, 1908.

Noble, David. *The Paradox of Progressive Thought.* Minneapolis, 1958.

Noble, H. G. S. *The New York Stock Exchange in the Crisis of 1914.* New York, 1915.

Nye, Russell B. *Midwestern Progressive Politics: A Historical Study of Its Origins and Developments, 1870–1950.* East Lansing, 1951.

Olson, Keith Waldemar. "Franklin K. Lane: A Biography." Unpublished doctoral dissertation, University of Wisconsin, 1964.

Orrock, John Wilson. *Railroad Structures and Estimates.* New York, 1909.

Palmer, Frederick. *Newton D. Baker: America at War.* 2 vols. New York, 1931.

Parsons, Frank. *The Heart of the Railroad Problem.* Boston, 1906.

Peterson, Robert Louis. "State Regulation of Railroads in Texas, 1836–1920." Unpublished doctoral dissertation, University of Texas, 1960.

Pringle, Henry F. *The Life and Times of William Howard Taft.* 2 vols. New York, 1939.

——*Theodore Roosevelt: A Biography.* New York, 1939.

Railway Age Gazette, ed. *The Car Builders' Dictionary.* New York, 1909.

Railway Signal Association. *Digest of Proceedings of the Railway Signal Association, 1895–1905.* 2 vols. N.p.

Railway World. "Depreciated Currency and Diminished Railway Rates." Philadelphia, 1909.

Raucher, Alan R. *Public Relations and Business, 1900–1929.* Baltimore, 1968.

Raymond, William Galt. *Elements of Railroad Engineering.* 6th ed. New York, 1947.

Rees, Albert. *Real Wages in Manufacturing.* Princeton, 1961.

Ripley, William Z. *Railroads: Finance and Organization.* New York, 1915.

——*Railroads: Rates and Regulation.* New York, 1912.

Ripley, William Z., ed. *Railway Problems.* 2d ed. New York, 1913.

Robbins, Edwin Clyde. *The Order of Railway Conductors.* New York, 1914.

Ross, Thomas Richard. *Jonathan Prentiss Dolliver: A Study in Political Integrity and Independence.* Iowa City, 1958.

Rostow, Walt W. *The Stages of Economic Growth.* Cambridge, 1960.

Sageser, A. Bower. *Joseph L. Bristow: Kansas Progressive.* Lawrence, 1968.

Sayre, Ralph Mills. "Albert Baird Cummins and the Progressive Movement in Iowa." Unpublished doctoral dissertation, Columbia University, 1958.

Schurr, Sam H. *The Mining Industry.* New York, 1944.

Scott, Ralph. *Automatic Block Signals and Signal Circuits.* New York, 1908.

Scully, Francis J. *Hot Springs, Arkansas, and Hot Springs National Park.* Little Rock, 1966.

Sharfman, I. L. *The American Railroad Problem.* New York, 1921.

——*The Interstate Commerce Commission: A Study in Administrative Law and Procedure.* 4 vols in 5. New York, 1931–37.

——*Railway Regulation.* Chicago, 1915.

Sinclair, Angus. *Development of the Locomotive Engine.* New York, 1907.

Solvick, Stanley D. "William Howard Taft and the Progressive Movement." Unpublished doctoral dissertation, University of Michigan, 1963.

Spearman, Frank H. *The Strategy of Great Railroads.* New York, 1904.

Stephenson, Nathaniel W. *Nelson W. Aldrich: A Leader in American Politics.* New York, 1930.

Stevenson, George James. "The Brotherhood of Locomotive Engineers and Its Leaders, 1863–1920." Unpublished doctoral dissertation, Vanderbilt University, 1954.

Stockett, J. Noble. *Arbitrational Determination of Railway Wages.* Boston, 1918.

Talbot, Fred A. *Cassell's Railways of the World.* 2 vols. London (?), 19?

Tennant, Richard B. *The American Cigarette Industry.* New Haven, 1950.

Thompson, Slason. *A Short History of American Railways.* Chicago, 1925.

Thompson, Slason, ed. *The Railway Library and Statistics.* Chicago, 1909–15.

Thorne, Clifford. "Principle versus Precedent." Unpublished doctoral dissertation, Yale University, 1901.

Thornthwaite, C. Warren, and Helen I. Slentz. *Internal Migration in the United States.* Philadelphia, 1934.

Ulmer, M. J. *Capital in Transportation, Communications, and Public Utilities.* Princeton, 1960.

Union Switch & Signal Co. *Electro-Pneumatic Interlocking.* Swissvale, Pa., 1914.

Urofsky, Melvin Irving. "Big Steel and the Wilson Administration: A Study in Business-Government Relations." Unpublished doctoral dissertation, Columbia University, 1968.

Walworth, Arthur. *Woodrow Wilson.* 2 vols. New York, 1958; rev. ed., 1965.

Warner, Paul T. *Locomotives of the Pennsylvania Railroad, 1834–1924.* Chicago, 1959.

Webb, Walter Loring. *Railroad Construction, Theory and Practice.* 9th ed. New York, 1932.

Westinghouse, George. *The Electrification of Railways, and the Imperative Need for the Selection of a System for Universal Use.* New York, 1910.

Weyl, Walter E. *The New Democracy.* New York, 1912.

White, William Allen. *The Old Order Changeth: A View of American Democracy.* New York, 1910.

Wiebe, Robert H. *Businessmen and Reform.* Cambridge, Mass., 1962.

Willard, William Clyde. *Maintenance of Way and Structures.* New York, 1915.

Williams, Ernest W., Jr. *The Regulation of Rail-Motor Rate Competition.* New York, 1958.

Williamson, Harold F., *et al. The American Petroleum Industry.* Vol. II: *The Age of Energy, 1899–1959.* Evanston, 1963.

Williamson, Jefferson. *The American Hotel: An Anecdotal History.* New York, 1930.

Willis, H. Parker, and John M. Chapman. *The Economics of Inflation.* New York, 1935.

Wood, Arthur Julius. *Principles of Locomotive Operation.* 2d ed. New York, 1925.

INDEX